Interest Rates, Exchange Rates and World Monetary Policy

John E. Floyd

Interest Rates, Exchange Rates and World Monetary Policy

Springer

Prof. John E. Floyd
Department of Economics
University of Toronto
150 St. George Street
Toronto, ON M5S 3G7
Canada
floyd@chass.utoronto.ca

ISBN 978-3-642-10279-0 e-ISBN 978-3-642-10280-6
DOI 10.1007/978-3-642-10280-6
Springer Heidelberg Dordrecht London New York

Library of Congress Control Number: 2009941852

Cover design: WMXDesign GmbH, Heidelberg, Germany

Printed on acid-free paper

Springer is part of Springer Science+Business Media (www.springer.com)

To Juney with Love

Preface

This book is the result of many years of thinking about international monetary economics. I must thank my long-time colleague Allan Hynes for ongoing discussions of the issues analysed here as well as for important comments on the organization and presentation of the material. I also want to thank Kit Pasula for reading through the manuscript and finding many typos and points needing clarification. Colleagues Gordon Anderson and John Maheu must be gratefully acknowledged for helping me learn about and deal with the econometric issues involved. Angelo Melino deserves similar gratitude with regard to both economics and econometrics, as does Alex Maynard for our many discussions about the forward premium puzzle and for helping me obtain data. Special thanks go to Alice Blanck and Niels Peter Thomas of Springer-Verlag in Heidelberg, Germany for their editorial assistance and encouragement. Finally, this book could not have been completed were it not for my wife, June, putting up with my almost constant preoccupation with thinking about economics.

University of Toronto,
June 2009

John Floyd
Professor of Economics

Contents

1 Introduction

This monograph presents an analysis of the workings of monetary policy in a world-wide setting where technological change and capital expansion results in substantial movements of real exchange rates and countries have to choose whether to adopt flexible or fixed exchange rates or currency union with their trading partners. It divides this task into three parts. First, it rigorously develops an appropriate theoretical framework that establishes the theoretical principles that underlie the analysis that follows. Readers will find this framework interesting in and of itself because it extends and modernizes the traditional IS-LM framework to incorporate real exchange rate movements and make it consistent with the basics of intertemporal maximization. This, it turns out, yields an approach to monetary policy consistent with standard Fleming-Mundell perfect capital mobility analysis under circumstances where capital is less than perfectly internationally mobile. The economic consequences of fiscal policy, on the other hand, turn out to be critically dependent on the specific nature of each individual policy action, and the standard Keynesian multiplier results disappear. Second, this book presents a statistical analysis of the behaviour of real exchange rates in response to a range of real and monetary shocks and investigates the role of these shocks in determining international interest rate differentials. The results suggest implications for the nature of international monetary policy which, in connection with analysis that subsequently follows, essentially resolves the exchange rate disconnect puzzle. And the analysis of exchange rate determination, where it focuses on forward and spot rates, also resolves to a large degree the forward premium puzzle. Finally, the implications of these exchange rate results are combined with the basics of the theoretical framework to analyse how monetary policy is and should be conducted in a multi-

J.E. Floyd, *Interest Rates, Exchange Rates and World Monetary Policy*,
DOI 10.1007/978-3-642-10280-6_1, © Springer-Verlag Berlin Heidelberg 2010

country world economy. The theoretical results, together with the empirical evidence, yield the conclusion that, apart from core inflation rate differences, the monetary authorities of the countries examined have tended to continually produce domestically the same monetary conditions as exist in the United States. These results also prompt some analysis of the potential success of monetary unions like that in Europe.

While this work will be of interest to academic researchers as well as practitioners in the business community and government, the technical exposition is pitched at a level understandable to readers who have MA level training in economics and a decent mathematical and econometric background. Indeed the material developed here constitutes a rather complete presentation of what all MA and PhD students in international monetary economics should learn before proceeding to work in the financial district or advancing to the complex mathematical analysis of macroeconomic models on which contemporary PhD courses focus.

The book consists of this introductory chapter followed by three parts, each containing several chapters, and then a final concluding chapter that also contains suggestions for further work. In Part I, the basic theoretical framework is rigorously developed and its reliability established with reference to widely accepted empirical evidence. It is expected that this framework, particularly the parts used in subsequent empirical and policy analysis, will be acceptable to any well-trained international monetary economist. The exposition is intuitive and diagrammatic where possible with some very basic mathematics used, as necessary, to verify the logic. A thorough and careful exposition of all theoretical arguments that will be used in the subsequent two parts of the book is presented. A conclusion from this theoretical analysis combined with open international capital markets is that, apart from large countries like the United States that are big enough to affect world interest rates, monetary policy operates through its effects on nominal and real exchange rates and their effects, in turn, on domestic output, employment and prices. Domestic interest rates relevant for current real investment are determined primarily by conditions in world markets rather than by the domestic central bank. Although this conclusion has a long history, going back to the Nobel-Prize-winning work of R. A. Mundell [79] in the early 1960s,[1] it is still inconsistent with the public statements of most business-sector economists that specialize in macroeconomics. This is probably due

[1] And also the equivalent path-breaking analysis of Marcus Fleming [39].

to the fact that economists in small-open-economies think primarily in terms of the closed-economy models that overwhelmingly dominate university macroeconomics courses.

Readers who understand and are willing to accept the following five basic theoretical principles can by-pass the theoretical development in Part I and proceed directly to Parts II and III, returning to Part I later to perhaps broaden their overall conceptual framework.

1. Utility maximization involves the smoothing of consumption through time so that the level of current consumption is largely independent of deviations of real income around its full-employment level, with these deviations being channelled into temporary accumulations and decumulations of capital.

2. Increases in investment lead to adjustment costs of adapting the new capital to existing stocks that increase with the level of investment in relation to the capital stock, causing the cost of capital to increase and the real interest rate to decline.

3. Increases and decreases of a country's real exchange rate, at given levels of technology, lead to reductions and expansions of world demand for its output as the price of that output thereby rises and falls relative to the prices of output in the rest of the world. Correspondingly, an expansion of a country's output at a given level of technology will cause its real exchange rate to fall.

4. The quantity of money demanded in every country is negatively related to the domestic nominal interest rate and positively related to domestic output, as is standard in the conventional literature.

5. A shift of the demand or supply of money in a country, given flexible nominal exchange rates, will cause that country's nominal exchange rate to overshoot its new long-run equilibrium level in the very short run.

The empirical work in Part II is based on econometric analysis within a theoretical framework that is adequately covered in the first chapter in that part of the book. And the theoretical model that forms the basis for the analysis in Part III is carefully developed in its first chapter, although to proceed directly to Part III the reader must be willing to accept the basic empirical results of Part II.

Part II presents empirical evidence on the behaviour of real exchange rates and interest rates in Canada, Japan, the United Kingdom, France and Germany (prior to the adoption of the Euro in the case of the latter two countries) relative to the United States.[2] The theoretical issues involved in the analysis are carefully exposited, making this part of the book self-contained for readers who do not feel the need for the more detailed development of the overall conceptual theoretical framework in Part I. The empirical relationships between forward exchange rates and future spot rates and forward premiums and future rates of change of nominal exchange rates are examined and interpreted and an explanation of the forward premium puzzle is advanced. The main conclusion of Part II is that real exchange rates have moved very substantially in response to number of plausible real forces such as changes in countries' real net capital inflows as fractions of their outputs, changes in world oil and commodity prices, and changes in countries' terms of trade, and that few substantive effects of monetary shocks on real exchange rates can be found in the data. Another conclusion is that interest rate changes, to the extent that they are correlated with real exchange rate changes, can be viewed as responses to those real exchange rate changes rather than as causes of them, a result attributable to the fact that real exchange rates tend to be correlated with factors determining expected inflation. And the virtual absence of effects of observed unanticipated money supply shocks on real exchange rates suggests that occasionally identified negative empirical relationships between interest rates and unanticipated money supply shocks must represent responses of the monetary authorities to world and corresponding domestic interest rate changes rather than effects of monetary policy on interest rates. The basis for this monetary response is the avoidance of overshooting movements of exchange rates, well-known in the literature and carefully explained in the final chapter of Part I, that would result if monetary policy were not accommodating in the face of domestic and world money demand shocks, including those resulting from world interest rate changes. The fact that no overshooting exchange rate changes in response to monetary forces can be observed in the data suggests that any surviving excess money supply or demand shocks that would lead to overshooting were of infinitesimal magnitude.

Part III develops the rationale for monetary policy of a sort consistent with the empirical evidence presented in Part II. It shows that the most sensible policies central banks in modern industrial countries other than the United States can follow will be to allow the domestic exchange rates to float and create at home the same monetary conditions that exist abroad, subject to any desired difference between the

[2] The analysis with respect to the Canadian case extends results obtained by John Johnston [62] using a very similar approach.

underlying politically acceptable 'core' rate of domestic inflation and corresponding 'core' inflation rates abroad. This 'even keel' type of policy avoids the disorderly overshooting exchange rate movements that would result from money supply changes necessarily associated with attempts to pursue domestic monetary independence. To the extent that different domestic policies need to be followed, the appropriate procedure would be to adjust base money so as to press upon the exchange rate in the appropriate direction while maintaining an apparent orderly market. Historical evidence that business cycle movements in output and inflation rates are highly correlated across countries and that policy makers act in a fashion predicted by the theory is then presented. And the viability of the alternative of adopting common currencies, with particular reference to Canada, the United States and the European Union, is also analyzed. In developing the arguments in this part of the book, the essential features of the basic theoretical framework set out in Part I are again restated in simple form as needed, and the above-mentioned conclusions carefully derived from them. This means that readers who are willing to accept the empirical evidence presented in Part II and can understand the basic theoretical framework will be able to move directly from this introductory chapter to Part III.

In addition to the above conclusions, the analysis also provides a simple, systematic and thorough basic framework within which students and practitioners can understand the basics of international monetary economics. For students, this framework will provide a foundation for subsequent exploration of more specific mathematically rigorous models of dynamic adjustment that can suggest and evaluate more innovative policy measures for adoption by governments and central banks.

Finally, all the empirical work here is programmed using the freely available statistics and econometrics programs, Gretl and XLispStat, in a few instances R, and in one case the commercial program Rats. The author's web-site provides the necessary econometric functions for XLispStat, along with a big manual that in many ways doubles as an appropriate econometrics tutorial and a short manual for day-to-day work, as well as links to manuals for Gretl and R. It also makes the data used here available in forms appropriate for these programs as well as in Excel worksheet files, allowing readers to check and extend the results.[3] Programming operations are performed in both XLispStat and R while, with a few exceptions, the statistical analysis is done using

[3] To obtain all data and statistical input and output files referred to in what follows, go to `www.economics.utoronto.ca/floyd` and click on the link to the new book.

both Gretl and XLispStat. Two programs are used for each operation as a check against mechanical errors.

Part I

A Theoretical Framework

The goal here is to develop a general equilibrium framework for analyzing the effects of domestic and rest-of-world real and monetary shocks on interest rates, real and nominal exchange rates, output, income and prices in individual countries comprising a world economy, with a focus on short-term rather than long-term steady state effects. Readers will recognize this framework as similar in structure to the standard *IS-LM* model which has a long history and is still used in intermediate textbooks and business forecasting. Although that model could be used in a standard way to analyse the issues of concern here, it suffers from the fact that it is neither conceptually based on nor rigorously derived from intertemporal utility maximization, with the result that applications of it are sometimes misleading. The framework developed here is derived from better theoretical foundations to avoid the problems with crude *IS-LM* analysis while addressing broad issues that are beyond the scope of conventional narrowly focused mathematical models because of the complexities that would have to be introduced into those models.

2

Specifications and Assumptions

The analysis in this book will focus primarily on deviations of output and employment from their full-employment levels, where the latter are interpreted as the natural levels around which employment and output can deviate in both directions. The full-employment levels will be those levels that would occur if wages and output prices were instantaneously flexible in response to excess aggregate demand and supply. The underlying model will be an aggregative one in which it will be assumed either that prices are rigid and do not change in response to aggregate demand and supply shocks or that prices are flexible and immediately adjust. Equilibrium will be at or between these extremes and no attempt will be made to specify dynamics of adjustment, although it will be assumed that adjustment to full-employment levels will eventually occur. The conclusions will thus be limited to those that are consistent with a wide variety of possible theories of the nature and speed of price adjustment.

A growth path of each country's output under full employment will be assumed, with output representing the return off the nation's capital stock, broadly defined to include human capital, knowledge and technology. The full-employment level of output, which represents the marginal product of the aggregate capital stock, will depend upon how efficiently total capital is allocated between its various forms, and will vary through time as a result of new investment in ideas and technology and random shocks to productivity. The precise nature of this growth path will be inconsequential with respect to conclusions reached in this monograph – any specification that generates a time-path of full-employment output could be used. The formulation here is chosen for its comprehensiveness, generality, and intellectual appeal, not for its

J.E. Floyd, *Interest Rates, Exchange Rates and World Monetary Policy*,
DOI 10.1007/978-3-642-10280-6_2, © Springer-Verlag Berlin Heidelberg 2010

ability to generate empirically testable hypotheses about the growth process.

Individuals will be assumed to choose consumption paths that maximize intertemporal utility functions, resulting in a smoothing of consumption over time. Shocks to output around its full-employment level will thus involve equivalent increases or decreases in saving and investment with little effect on consumption.

Investment goods in each country are assumed to be produced at constant cost in terms of consumer goods but the marginal costs of adapting new investment goods to the existing stocks of human and physical capital are assumed to increase with increases in the level of investment as a fraction of the capital stock. These adjustment costs drive a wedge between the rate of interest and the marginal productivity of capital that increases as the level of investment increases relative to the capital stock with the result that the interest rate will fall relative to the income stream from the capital stock as the level of investment increases.

In general, countries will export a portion of their output and import, consume and invest portions of the outputs of other countries. Every country's output will be assumed to contain traded and nontraded components. A country's real exchange rate with respect to a trading partner will be defined as the relative price of its output in terms of the trading partner's output. Since output has both traded and nontraded components, an increase in the real exchange rate can represent an increase in the world prices of domestic traded components relative to the prices of foreign traded components, or an increase in the domestic relative to the foreign prices of nontraded components of output. It will be assumed that full-employment equilibrium real exchange rates will evolve through time as the world economy grows in ways that will be determined by the nature of underlying technology growth and the world distribution of those natural resources that will be used by different technologies. One can thus expect growth of full-employment output in the various countries to be accompanied by corresponding changes of real exchange rates in either direction, depending upon the circumstances. And this growth will also typically be accompanied by capital inflows and outflows as world investment is reallocated among countries according to the locations of the natural resources favored by newly developed technologies or in the direction of countries that improve their efficiency of resource allocation and thereby generate larger outputs from their employed capital stocks.

An important assumption running through all the analysis will be that an increase in a country's output relative to that of other countries at given levels of the countries' capital stocks, broadly defined to include human capital and technology, will cause the world relative price of its output – that is, its real exchange rate – to fall. By the same token, a fall in a country's real exchange rate at given domestic and foreign capital stocks will cause world demand to shift to its output from that of other countries.

The quantity demanded of each country's money will be assumed to depend negatively on the real interest rate and the expected rate of inflation in that country – that is, on the cost of holding money – and positively on the volume of transactions, represented by the level of the country's output. Conceptually, one can think in terms of an underlying stock of liquidity where cash and demand deposits are completely liquid, time deposits are highly liquid, and other assets possess degrees of liquidity that depend on the ease with which they can be exchanged for cash at prices known in advance. Alternative money stock measures thus represent different measures of the stock of liquidity in the economy.

Because asset holders must hold all of their wealth in the form of either monetary or non-monetary assets, a situation where the existing stock of monetary assets is willingly held will imply zero excess demand for or supply of the aggregate stock of non-monetary assets. But simultaneous money market equilibrium in all countries does not imply that the market for any individual non-monetary asset will be in equilibrium. For that to occur, the desired mix of the various assets held by world residents must be the same as the actual mix of these assets in existence. The prices of the income streams yielded by the various assets will be bid up or down, and the implied interest rates on these assets will correspondingly be bid down or up, until the existing mix of assets in the world is willingly held. This will apply both to direct claims on the outputs from the various types of capital stock and to intermediate assets which are claims to consolidated earnings from collections of those types of capital. Since it will be assumed that the residents of each country are free to purchase a wide range of primary and intermediate assets issued in the rest of the world, the interest rate on each asset in each country will be a consequence of world, not just domestic, demand for it. It will be concluded that the underlying real interest rate at which a country's aggregate capital stock is evaluated and to which its investment responds, will be determined primarily in the world as a whole, since all countries' residents are free to purchase and hold the great majority of these assets. The big exception will of course be human capital in a world where slavery is extinct. Foreign ownership of certain types of assets may also be prohibited in some countries.

Population growth, which will not figure in the analysis directly, will be assumed to occur in conjunction with intergenerational capital accumulation as a consequence of each generation's choice as to the number of children, the amount of current income to consume per person and the amount to pass on to the next generation as income-yielding capital.

Three types of shocks to the system will be considered. First, there will be monetary shocks that take the form of shifts of the demand function for liquidity or the supply of assets that yield liquidity. Second, there will be real shocks that take the form of permanent shifts of the full-employment level of output and the associated full-employment real interest rate, and permanent shifts of the full-employment real exchange rate that may or may not be accompanied by shocks to the full-employment output and interest rate levels. Third, there will be real shocks that take the form of temporary shifts of the full-employment equilibrium real interest rate and/or real exchange rate at unchanged full-employment levels of income. Of course, real shocks that lead to changes in real interest rates will indirectly also represent monetary shocks in that they change the quantity of liquidity demanded in the face of an unchanged demand-for-liquidity function. And world general equilibrium will require real exchange rate, real income and other adjustments necessary to continually maintain equilibrium relationships between the various countries' real interest rates.

The effects of these shocks will be analyzed with respect to three situations:

1. An open economy that is so large that nothing happening abroad will significantly affect any variables of interest.
2. An open economy that is so small that domestic forces have no significant effects on world commodity and asset prices and interest rates.
3. A world consisting of two economies, each of sufficient size to affect world commodity and asset prices and interest rates.

Extensions of these three cases to one or two big countries and many small ones will then be addressed within this analytical framework.

3

Underlying Equilibrium Growth Paths

A required foundation for all the analysis that follows is an understanding of the underlying full-employment growth paths around which relevant variables can deviate in the short run. The purpose of this chapter is to develop and present the theory relating to how these growth paths are determined.

3.1 Aggregate Production and Income

The first step in the formulation is to recognize that the entire output of every economy is the result of the services rendered by that economy's capital stock, which is composed of many parts. The obvious part is the myriad of structures, machinery, and inventories of goods in hand. A less obvious part is the human skills embodied in the people resident in the economy, the services of which enable the production, in conjunction with the just-mentioned physical capital stock, of the economy's output of goods and services. An even less obvious part of the nation's capital stock is the set of designs of alternative forms of human and physical capital and the underlying procedures available for coordinating their use – what could be referred to as the stock of technology. This portion of the capital stock consists of the characteristics of the human and physical capital available to the economy for embodiment in physical structures and humans and the alternative ways in which those resources can be combined. The final, much less precisely observed, form of capital is the basic knowledge available for use in producing additional technological capital. There is also, of course, the set of institutions – the markets, customs, legal structure and political processes through which everything in the economy is organized. These

J.E. Floyd, *Interest Rates, Exchange Rates and World Monetary Policy*,
DOI 10.1007/978-3-642-10280-6_3, © Springer-Verlag Berlin Heidelberg 2010

will be instrumental in determining the flow of output the above-noted forms of capital actually produce.

Let K denote the aggregate capital stock, where each of its components can be produced at constant cost in terms of each other and in terms of consumer goods. Then the flow of income produced with this aggregate capital stock can be written

$$Y = (m - \delta) K \tag{3.1}$$

where m is the marginal product of the aggregate capital stock and δ is the rate at which that capital stock depreciates. It is assumed that m and δ, though they may change from time to time as a result of changes in the institutions generated by the political process, exhibit no long term trends. This assumption is consistent with the fact that underlying real interest rates, which represent flows of output as a percentages of capital stock, have exhibited no identifiable trends over the past couple of centuries in countries experiencing stable institutional conditions.[1]

A crucial issue is the efficiency with which the capital stock is allocated among its alternative forms. For example, the failure to produce additional technological capital will result in diminishing returns to growth of the remaining capital stock. Assuming that the marginal products of all forms and types of capital diminish with increases in their quantity relative to that of other kinds of capital, the condition for optimization will be

$$\frac{\partial Y}{\partial K_i} = \frac{\partial Y}{\partial K_j} \tag{3.2}$$

for all capital-types i and j. If the marginal product of capital-type i exceeds that of capital-type j, output can be increased by increasing the stock of type i relative to that of type j. A useful conceptualization is presented in Fig. 3.1 where the optimal ratio of type 1 capital to the total is 0.3. The quantitative magnitudes should not be taken seriously, of course, because the figure is purely illustrative – all that is necessary is that the marginal product curves of the two types of capital decline as their quantities increase. The derivation of the figure is presented in detail in Appendix A.

In general, the capital stock in an economy will not be optimally allocated among its alternative forms. Let γ represent the proportional

[1] This type of formulation is known in the literature as an AK model. For a general discussion of AK models and criticisms of them in the literature see McGrattan [75].

loss of real output as a result of this misallocation of capital. Then equation (3.1) can be rewritten as

$$Y = [\hat{m}\,(1-\gamma) - \delta]\,K \tag{3.3}$$

where $\hat{m}$ is the maximum achievable marginal product of the aggregate capital stock when that capital stock is perfectly allocated among its alternative forms, and $m = \hat{m}\,(1-\gamma)$ is the marginal product of the aggregate capital stock that actually occurs. Resource misallocations in production reduce the economy's output flow by increasing γ.

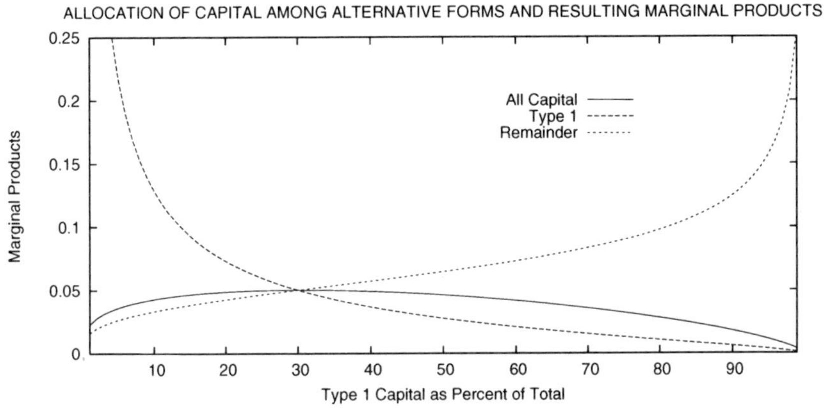

Fig. 3.1. The marginal product of capital under different allocations among alternative forms in the special case where $Y = .0921\,K_1^{.3}(K - K_1)^{.7}$.

3.2 Intertemporal Optimization: The Equilibrium Growth Rate

The utility of the economy's residents depends on their entire time-paths of consumption. A convenient representation of the utility function of consumers in the aggregate is the intertemporally additive form

$$U = U(C_t) + \left(\frac{1}{1+\varpi}\right) U(C_{t+1}) + \left(\frac{1}{1+\varpi}\right)^2 U(C_{t+2}) + \left(\frac{1}{1+\varpi}\right)^3 U(C_{t+3}) + \left(\frac{1}{1+\varpi}\right)^4 U(C_{t+4}) \ldots\ldots\ldots \tag{3.4}$$

where ϖ is the rate of time preference, and the time-horizon is infinite.[2] This utility function is maximized subject to a budget constraint for each period.

Assuming for the moment an absence of international trade, each period's output can be absorbed into consumption or into an addition to the economy's capital stock. While it is assumed that consumption goods can be transformed into all forms of capital goods at constant cost, putting new capital into productive form by adapting it to the existing capital stock involves additional resource costs – commonly called adjustment costs. These are assumed to increase in proportion to the square of the relative change in the aggregate capital stock. This yields the current-period budget constraint

$$\begin{aligned} C_t &= [\hat{m}(1-\gamma) - \delta]\, K_t - (K_{t+1} - K_t) - \alpha\, K_t \left(\frac{K_{t+1} - K_t}{K_t}\right)^2 \\ &= [\hat{m}(1-\gamma) - \delta - g_{kt} - \alpha\, g_{kt}^2]\, K_t \end{aligned} \tag{3.5}$$

where

$$g_{kt} = \frac{K_{t+1} - K_t}{K_t}$$

is the growth rate of the capital stock – that is, the ratio of investment to the stock of capital. The term $\alpha\, g_{kt}^2$ expresses the adjustment costs of putting new capital into productive form as a constant fraction α of the capital stock multiplied by the square of its current-period growth rate. While this form of the adjustment cost function is convenient for the general framework being developed here, one might want to modify it in a more detailed analysis. It is assumed that a permanent reduction of the capital stock requires the same adjustment costs as does a permanent addition.

Since two variables, C_t and K_{t+1}, are subject to choice in each period, optimization requires that, together with the intertemporal budget constraint, two conditions hold. First, it should be impossible to increase utility by shifting a unit of consumption between any two periods. This requires that the marginal utility of a unit of consumption in any period be equal to the present-value in utility terms of the number of units of consumption that can be obtained in the next period by currently foregoing that unit of consumption.

$$U'(C_t)\, dC_t = \frac{1}{1+\varpi}\, U'(C_{t+1})\, (1 + r_t)\, dC_t \tag{3.6}$$

[2] For a discussion of the reasons why this form of the intertemporal utility function is a useful choice, see Obstfeld and Rogoff [82], pages 12–14.

where r_t is the real interest rate in period t and $(1 + r_t)\,dC_t$ represents the amount of consumption obtained in period $t + 1$ as a result of the sacrifice of dC_t units of consumption in period t, $U'(C_{t+1})$ is the utility of that additional consumption, and $1/(1 + \varpi)$ discounts that next-period utility back to the current period, with the rate of time preference ϖ being the discount rate. This expression can be reorganized to yield

$$\frac{U'(C_t)}{U'(C_{t+1})} = \frac{1 + r_t}{1 + \varpi}. \tag{3.7}$$

Under the expositionally convenient assumption that the function $U(C)$ is of the form $log(C)$, $U'(C) = 1/C$ and the above expression becomes

$$\frac{1 + r_t}{1 + \varpi} = \frac{C_{t+1}}{C_t} = \frac{C_t + \Delta C_t}{C_t} = 1 + \frac{\Delta C_t}{C_t} = 1 + g_{ct} \tag{3.8}$$

where g_{ct} is the growth rate of consumption. At this point resource misallocation that takes the form of interference with the rate of consumption growth can be introduced as an implicit tax τ on savings. The condition then becomes

$$1 + g_{ct} = \frac{(1 + r_t)(1 - \tau)}{1 + \varpi}. \tag{3.9}$$

This equation has a simple interpretation. If there is no allocative distortion of the savings rate so that $\tau = 0$, consumption growth will be positive if the real rate of interest exceeds the rate of time preference. The real interest rate is the increase in future consumption that can be obtained by the sacrifice of a unit of current consumption. The rate of time preference is the increase in future consumption required to induce the consumer to forego a unit of current consumption. If the sacrifice of current consumption produces a greater increase in future consumption than required, consumption growth will occur. When r_t equals ϖ consumption growth will be zero and when it is less than ϖ consumers will eat up capital stock and consumption growth will be negative. A positive value of τ, which is equivalent to a tax on saving, will reduce the amount of future consumption that can be obtained by sacrificing a unit of current consumption, making the consumption-growth rate lower.

The second condition of optimization requires that the present value of an additional unit of capital added to the capital stock and brought into production in any period be equal to its marginal cost. With an appropriate choice of units, the marginal cost equals unity – the one unit of consumption that must be sacrificed to produce a unit of capital – plus the marginal adjustment cost which is the absolute value of the derivative of

$$\alpha K_t \left(\frac{K_{t+1} - K_t}{K_t}\right)^2$$

with respect to K_{t+1},

$$2\alpha \left(\frac{|K_{t+1} - K_t|}{K_t}\right) = 2\alpha \, |g_{kt}|.$$

The marginal cost is the same whether a given growth rate is positive or negative. Where the currently observed values of $\hat{m}$, γ and δ are expected to remain constant in all future periods, the present value of a unit of capital will be

$$\frac{\hat{m}(1-\gamma) - \delta}{r_t}.$$

The second condition of optimization is thus

$$1 + 2\alpha \, |g_{kt}| = \frac{\hat{m}(1-\gamma) - \delta}{r_t} \tag{3.10}$$

which says that the marginal cost of a unit of capital, measured in output units, must equal the present value of that unit of capital, given by the perpetual per-period return to it divided by the interest rate. As noted above, the marginal cost consists of two parts. The first is the integer unity which, by appropriate choice of units, is the cost in terms of consumer goods of producing an additional unit of capital. The second is the cost of adapting that unit of capital to the already existing mix of capital-types. This second component of marginal cost increases with the magnitude of the current change in the stock of capital as a proportion of the pre-existing capital stock. The period-t interest rate can thus be expressed

$$r_t = \frac{\hat{m}(1-\gamma) - \delta}{1 + 2\alpha \, |g_{kt}|} \tag{3.11}$$

When investment is zero, the real rate of interest will equal the realized marginal product of capital. As the level of investment expands, that interest rate will fall relative to capital's marginal product, increasing the present value of capital to match the increase in the marginal cost of producing it and putting it in place.[3] Since consumption is growing at a constant rate in equilibrium, output and the capital stock must be growing at the same rate. Were consumption to grow faster than the capital stock, the latter would eventually become zero, implying zero consumption and utility beyond that point. A slower rate of growth of consumption than that of the capital stock would reduce the flow of utility by resulting in a lower level of consumption in the current and all future periods than could otherwise be achieved. Accordingly,

$$g = g_{ct} = g_{kt}$$

is the economy's steady-state growth rate.

The equilibrium levels of g and r are determined by the two conditions of optimization, which can be rewritten as

$$g = \frac{(1+r)(1-\tau)}{1+\varpi} - 1 \tag{3.12}$$

and

$$r = \frac{\hat{m}(1-\gamma) - \delta}{1 + 2\alpha\,|g|}. \tag{3.13}$$

The first of these can be rearranged as

$$r = \frac{1+\varpi}{1-\tau}(1+g) - 1 \tag{3.14}$$

which upon substitution into the second yields

$$\frac{\hat{m}(1-\gamma) - \delta}{1 + 2\alpha\,|g|} = \frac{1+\varpi}{1-\tau}(1+g) - 1. \tag{3.15}$$

This last equation can be solved numerically for the equilibrium steady state growth rate arising from any given set of parameters m, γ, δ, α, ϖ and τ. That growth rate can then be substituted into either (3.13) or (3.14) to obtain the equilibrium level of r. For example, the values $\hat{m} = .16$, $\delta = .05$, $\varpi = .015$, $\alpha = 20.00$, $\gamma = .20$ and $\tau = .015$ yield a growth rate of 1.63% and a real interest rate of 4.7%. As can be seen from equation (3.13) an upward shift of $\hat{m}(1-\gamma)$ will result in an increase in the interest rate which will cause the growth rate to increase in equation (3.14). These increases in g and r will be moderated by the

[3] The ratio of the present value of capital to its marginal cost of production, net of adjustment costs, is known in the literature as Tobin's q. See Tobin [103] and pages 105–114 of Obstfeld and Rogoff [82] for details.

effect of g on r in equation (3.13). If γ is reduced to .1, for example, the steady-state growth rate rises to 2.05% and the real interest rate rises to 5.16%. A reduction of τ to .01 will further increase the growth rate to 2.3% but it reduces the real interest rate to 4.9% because the associated increase in steady-state investment increases the adjustment costs of putting capital in place, raising the present value of capital relative to its unitary production cost in terms of consumer goods. At the opposite extreme, with resource misallocation running rampant, increasing γ to .4 and τ to .03, with the other parameters unchanged, will reduce the equilibrium growth rate to zero.[4]

3.3 A Digression on Population Growth

Obviously, per-capita income growth will depend on the rate of growth of the population in addition to the principles outlined above. Since the concern in this book is with deviations of income and other variables around their underlying full-employment growth rates, nothing is lost by assuming that population growth is constant, or even zero. Nevertheless, it is useful to discuss briefly the economic forces that determine population growth in order to complete the underlying conceptual framework.

Since the intertemporal utility function is maximized over an infinite horizon, it is implicitly assumed that the current generation cares about future generations' utility – it is extended families' utility that is intertemporally maximized. As well as choosing aggregate consumption, the extended family must decide how many people will share that aggregate – the higher the population, the lower will be per-capita consumption. Because it is human capital, and not the mere presence of labour, that combines with other forms of capital to produce output, new capital has to be embodied in all individuals to make them productive. This is part of the allocation of capital among its alternative forms discussed above. Because the population must grow or decline on a continuous basis according to birth and death rates, so that one-shot increases and decreases are here ruled out, the embodiment of the appropriate types of human capital in new additions to that population will take place automatically as new investment occurs throughout the economy. No diminishing returns to labour will be present in the aggregate. Per-capita income will depend directly on the per-capita capital

[4] The above calculations are performed in XLispStat and R using appropriately modified versions of the batch or script files `ssgrth.lsp` and `ssgrth.R`.

stock and will thus be determined entirely by the growth of that capital stock relative to the growth of population.

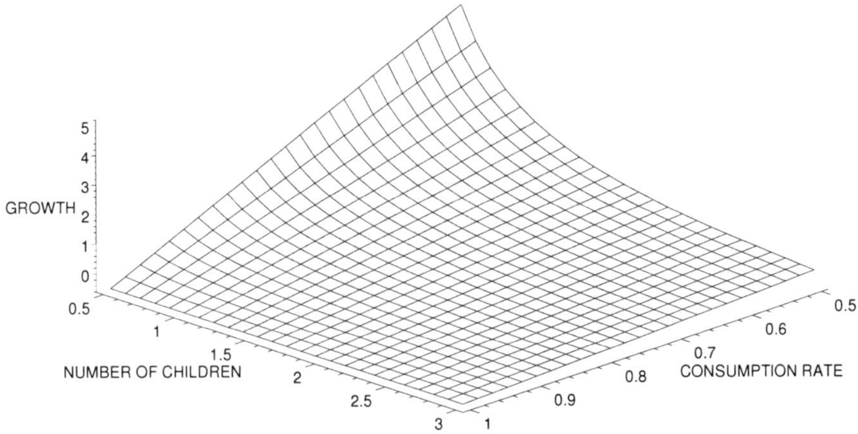

Fig. 3.2. The current generation's tradeoff between the fraction of income consumed, the number of children per adult and the per-capita income growth rate.

The current generation can choose two of three variables – the fraction of current output it will consume, the number of children it will produce per adult member of the population and, as a result of these two choices, the growth rate of per-capita income. The underlying constraint is illustrated by the three-dimensional surface plotted in Fig. 3.2 – utility maximization involves choosing a point on that surface. The position of the point with respect to the right-most scale will determine the fraction of income consumed and, hence, the rate of growth of the capital stock and aggregate output, denoted by g in the previous section. The position of the point with respect to the scale on the left at the bottom will determine the rate of population growth. As a result of the community's choice with respect to these two variables, a level of per capita income growth, measured on the vertical scale, will be determined.

The concern in this monograph is with aggregate output and income and not particularly with income per capita. To include the latter, the function $U(C)$ in equation (3.4) would have to be written as $U(C, N)$ where N is the population. Maximization at each point in time t would require that the present values of the sequence of partial derivatives $\partial U(C_{t+i}, N_{t+i})/\partial N_{t+i}$, where $dN_{t+i} = dN_t$ for i ranging from 0 to ∞, must equal zero under the assumption that any change in population is regarded as permanent. This maximum will occur when the adverse effect on the present value of total utility of the future decline in per-capita consumption resulting from a one-unit increase in population is exactly equal to the direct gain in the present value of total utility from having bigger extended families.

3.4 Money and Output

In the absence of money, a significant fraction of the economy's resources will be used up in the process of making transactions, reducing the output available for consumption and investment. These transactions costs, and the role of money in reducing them, must now be incorporated into the analytical framework.

Suppose that there exists a government that can eject liquidity into the economy by issuing a monetary asset from which other monetary assets will be derived. It is useful to think of the stock of liquidity in the economy as different from the stock of any particular monetary asset because there are many types of monetary assets – cash, demand deposits and different types of time deposits – as well as some non-monetary assets that also possess various degrees of liquidity. Denote the level of real liquidity by L. Assume for the moment that the government engineers the creation of a stock of liquidity that will maximize the output that the economy can produce, thereby achieving the Friedman rule.[5] If the optimum amount of liquidity is thereby present at all times, the formulation of the previous two sections can go through without modification. The entire flow of output from the capital stock as previously defined can simply be assumed to represent final output.

The consequence of insufficient liquidity is a reduction of the income associated with any given capital stock. Equation (3.3) can be modified to impose a loss from insufficient liquidity by multiplying the output flow by a term, here conveniently specified as

$$\left[1 - \frac{1}{3\lambda}\left(\varphi - \lambda\frac{L}{K}\right)^3\right],$$

where $\varphi > 0$ and $\lambda > 0$, that reduces that output flow by a fraction which declines as the real stock of liquidity increases. The flow of income from the capital stock now becomes

[5] See Friedman [40], pages 1–50.

$$Y = [\hat{m}(1-\gamma)-\delta]\left[1-\frac{1}{3\lambda}\left(\varphi-\lambda\frac{L}{K}\right)^3\right]K \qquad (3.16)$$

where

$$\frac{L}{K} \leq \frac{\varphi}{\lambda}.$$

In the case where the above condition holds with equality, (3.16) reduces to (3.3). Any excess of

$$\frac{L}{K} \quad \text{over} \quad \frac{\varphi}{\lambda}$$

is simply assumed to leave output unaffected. When there is no liquidity in the system (3.16) reduces to

$$\frac{Y}{K} = [\hat{m}(1-\gamma)-\delta]\,\Upsilon \qquad (3.17)$$

where Υ,

$$0 < \Upsilon = \left[1-\frac{\varphi^3}{3\lambda}\right] < 1,$$

is the fraction of output remaining when there is no government-arranged liquidity in the economy.

The real interest rate equation, previously (3.13), now becomes

$$r = \frac{\hat{m}(1-\gamma)-\delta}{1+2\alpha\,|g_{kt}|}\left[1-\frac{1}{3\lambda}\left(\varphi-\lambda\frac{L}{K}\right)^3\right] \qquad (3.18)$$

with the growth-rate equation, represented by (3.14), remaining unchanged. Combining these two equations yields the following new version of equation (3.15)

$$\frac{\hat{m}(1-\gamma)-\delta}{1+2\alpha\,|g|}\left[1-\frac{1}{3\lambda}\left(\varphi-\lambda\frac{L}{K}\right)^3\right] = \frac{1+\varpi}{1-\tau}(1+g)-1 \quad (3.19)$$

from which the equilibrium growth rate can be extracted. Substitution of that growth rate into (3.18) yields the equilibrium real interest rate.

The demand function for real liquidity can be obtained by setting the derivative of (3.16) with respect to L equal to the opportunity cost of holding an additional unit of liquidity. This opportunity cost can be represented by the real interest rate r plus additional institutional factors, including the expected rate of inflation, that are denoted by o.

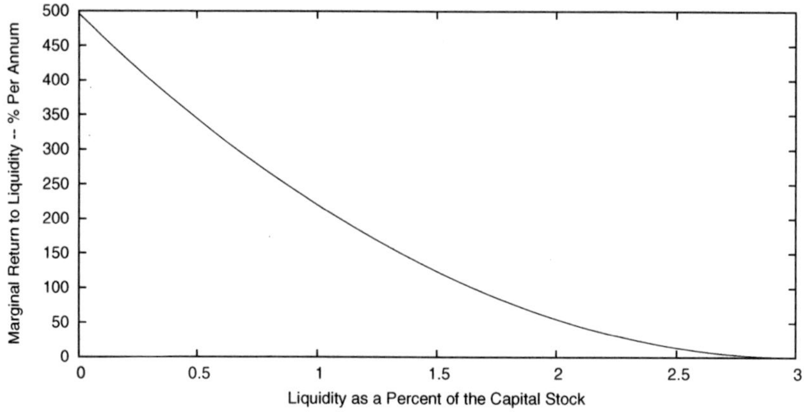

Fig. 3.3. Marginal return to the liquidity enabled by government as a function of the stock of that liquidity as a percentage of the capital stock where $\hat{m} = .14$, $\delta = .05$, $\gamma = .20$, $\varphi = 8.94$ and $\lambda = 298.14$

$$r + o = [\hat{m}(1-\gamma) - \delta] \left(\varphi - \lambda\frac{L}{K}\right)^2 \tag{3.20}$$

As shown in Fig. 3.3, this demand function is a parabola that crosses the vertical axis at $[\hat{m}(1-\gamma)-\delta]\,\varphi^2$ and becomes tangent and equal to the horizontal (L/K) axis at a liquidity/capital ratio of $L/K = \varphi/\lambda$. The calculations are based on the underlying assumption that output would be reduced by 80 percent if no effort is made by the government to provide liquidity, and the optimum level of liquidity government could enable is set at 3 percent of the capital stock.[6] These assumptions are purely illustrative although they seem to make sense. The maximum loss of output resulting from a complete absence of liquidity and the return to the first unit of liquidity are enormous, as might be expected from the fact that the public would be forced to use cigarettes, other local commodities, precious metals or private debt instruments in order to make exchange. Given that income would be in the order of 6 percent of the capital stock at the optimum ratio of liquidity to that capital stock, the implied ratio of liquidity to income also seems rather high. It must be kept in mind, however, that liquidity is a broader concept than any of the conventional money stock measures, the latter being merely indicators of the quantity of liquidity in the economy. A wide range of non-monetary assets will posses varying degrees of liquidity

[6] These calculations are made in the XLispStat batch file `rettoliq.lsp` and also in the R script file `rettoliq.R`. The results are in the respective output files `rettoliq.lou` and `rettoliq.Rot`.

when government monetary assets are available to facilitate exchange. And the ratios of the M1 aggregates to income are as high as .28 for France and .36 for Japan and the ratios of the M2 aggregates to income are as high as .60 for Germany, 2.26 for the U.K. and 1.64 for Japan.[7]

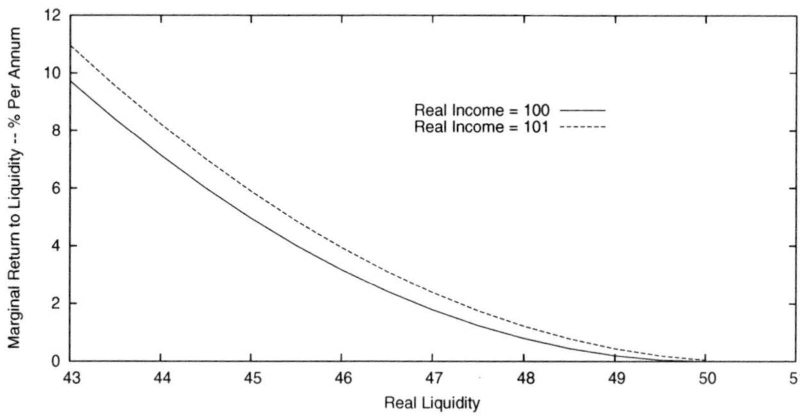

Fig. 3.4. Marginal return to government enabled liquidity as a function of the stock of that liquidity as a percentage of income where $\hat{m} = .14$, $\delta = .05$, $\gamma = .20$, $\varphi = 8.94$ and $\lambda = 298.14$

A more appropriate representation of the demand function for liquidity would be based on the quantity of liquidity as a fraction of income rather than the capital stock. This is accomplished in Fig. 3.4 by assuming that income is 6 percent of the capital stock. The horizontal scale is also limited to include only those levels of liquidity that would be within a range likely to be found in practice when the government provides instruments that enable a not-necessarily optimal level of liquidity. An inaccuracy arises when the level of income is assumed to be a constant underlying the curve because the level of total income produced by a given stock of capital will be affected by the amount of liquidity. It turns out, however, that having a level of real liquidity equal to 43 percent of income rather than the optimum of 50 percent

[7] Averages for base money, M1 and M2 for Canada, the United Kingdom, Japan, France and Germany are calculated in the XLispStat batch file `rmongdp.lsp`, and the Gretl script file `rmongdp.inp` and the results are contained in the respective output files `rmongdp.lou`, and `rmongdp.got`. The data range used was 1964:Q1 through 2007:Q4, for the U.S., Canada and Japan, 1964:Q1 through 2006:Q1 for the U.K. and 1965:Q1 through 1998:Q4 for France and Germany. The data are in the files `jfdataqt.gdt`, `jfdataqt.lsp`, and `jfdataqt.xls`. They are described in the text file `jfdataqt.cat` as well as in the gretl data file.

will reduce the level of income produced by a given capital stock by little more than two-tenths of one percent, making the bias in the slope of the curve of trivial magnitude.[8] The effect of a 1 percent increase in real income on the demand for liquidity is also portrayed on the graph.

For practical analysis, the conceptual definition of liquidity above is of little use, being too imprecise to permit measurement. For this reason, liquidity is conventionally measured by monetary aggregates such as total currency, M1 (currency plus demand deposits), M2 (currency plus both demand and time deposits) and M3 (currency plus all deposits), or variations thereof. And underlying these aggregates is the stock of base money (currency plus commercial bank reserves), which is the aggregate that the government directly controls.

Suppose that a particular aggregate, such as M1 or M2, is used as an appropriate liquidity measure. An increase in this aggregate, in real terms, engineered by institutional changes that reduce the cost of holding it, will increase the stock liquidity in the economy at any given level of income and thereby reduce its marginal return. An increase in income will generate an increase in the demand for this aggregate, along with the demand for liquidity in general, as the volume of transactions increases. This will cause the marginal value of the monetary aggregate to rise at each quantity. Following the convention of treating the marginal cost of holding the aggregate as directly related to the nominal interest rate, a standard demand-for-money function portrayed in Fig. 3.5 can be used. The curve will shift to the right with an increase in output. The horizontal scale must start at a quantity well in excess of zero and the intersection or tangency of the function with that axis at the socially optimal quantity can be ignored because none of the analysis in this book addresses issues relating to the optimal quantity of money. All that is necessary for what follows is a negative slope with a rightward shift in response to an increase in output.

Equations (3.16), (3.18), (3.19) and (3.20) determine the steady-state growth path and the full-employment equilibrium levels of the variables on that path. The last three of these equations determine the steady state levels of g, r and the liquidity/capital ratio L/K. The remaining equation gives the full-employment level of Y associated with any level of K – that is, the Y/K ratio – on that steady-state growth path. The exogenous variables, which are really parameters that can change through time, are $\hat{m}$, γ, τ, α and o.

---

[8] The fractional losses of output due to non-optimality of the stock of liquidity are shown in the XLispStat and R output files `rettoliq.lou` and `rettoliq.Rot`, which were generated from the batch or script files `rettoliq.lsp` and `rettoliq.R`.

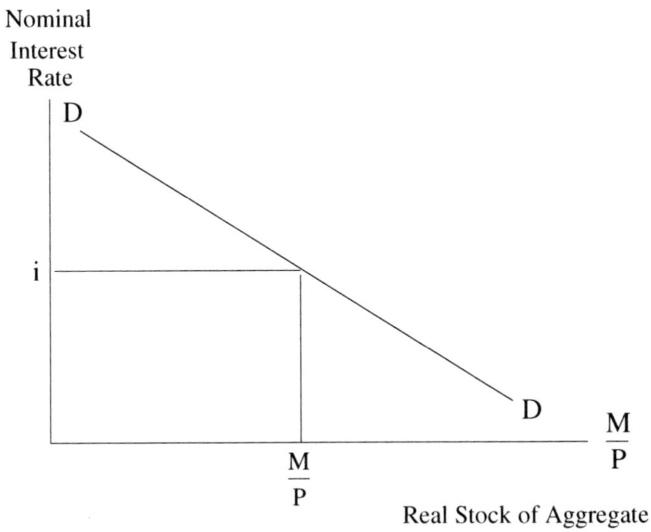

Fig. 3.5. Demand function for the monetary aggregate M

The introduction of money has no significant effects on the comparative statics results presented earlier – increases in $\hat{m}$ and reductions in the capital allocation inefficiency parameter γ will raise both r and g and reduce very slightly the liquidity/capital ratio by increasing the cost of liquidity as a consequence of the increase in r. A rise in the implicit intertemporal consumption allocation tax τ will reduce g and increase r, again reducing the liquidity/capital ratio slightly. And a rise in investment adjustment cost parameter α in a growing economy will reduce the rate of growth and lower r. The one new result is that a rise in the cost of holding money parameter o will have a downward effect on the liquidity/capital ratio and on the level of r although, at the values of the parameters chosen in the above empirical calculations, these effects will be tiny. All adjustments in the liquidity/capital ratio will arise through changes in the nominal price of output that will take place in the background.

3.5 Two Countries

Now visualize two countries, domestic and foreign, with the latter's variables denoted by a * superscript. It is useful to begin with the preposterous assumption, which will be relaxed later, that the outputs of the two countries represent the same good. Domestic and foreign versions of equation (3.12),

$$g_c = \frac{(1+r)(1-\tau)}{1+\varpi} - 1 \tag{3.21}$$

and

$$g_c^* = \frac{(1+r)(1-\tau^*)}{1+\varpi^*} - 1, \tag{3.22}$$

combine to yield the world steady-state consumption growth rate

$$g_w = \frac{s\,(1+r)(1-\tau)}{1+\varpi} + \frac{(1-s)(1+r)(1-\tau^*)}{1+\varpi^*} - 1 \tag{3.23}$$

where s is the share of the domestic capital stock in the world capital stock.[9] And domestic and foreign versions of equation (3.18) can be manipulated to yield the domestic and foreign growth rates of home-employed capital stock

$$g_k = \frac{\hat{m}(1-\gamma)-\delta}{2\,\alpha\,r}\left[1 - \frac{1}{3\lambda}\left(\varphi - \lambda\frac{L}{K}\right)^3\right] - \frac{1}{2\alpha} \tag{3.24}$$

and

$$g_k^* = \frac{\hat{m}^*(1-\gamma^*)-\delta^*}{2\,\alpha^*\,r}\left[1 - \frac{1}{3\lambda^*}\left(\varphi^* - \lambda\frac{L^*}{K^*}\right)^3\right] - \frac{1}{2\alpha^*} \tag{3.25}$$

which can be combined in an expression for world steady-state capital stock growth

$$\begin{aligned} g_w = s\,\frac{\hat{m}(1-\gamma)-\delta}{2\,\alpha\,r}\left[1 - \frac{1}{3\lambda}\left(\varphi - \lambda\frac{L}{K}\right)^3\right] - \left[\frac{s}{2\,\alpha} + \frac{1-s}{2\,\alpha^*}\right] \\ + (1-s)\,\frac{\hat{m}^*(1-\gamma^*)-\delta^*}{2\,\alpha^*\,r}\left[1 - \frac{1}{3\lambda^*}\left(\varphi^* - \lambda^*\frac{L}{K}\right)^3\right] \end{aligned} \tag{3.26}$$

---

[9] This will also equal the share of domestic consumption in world consumption in an initial situation where all the parameters are the same in both countries and, as a result, consumption and capital stock growth are the same.

where, in equilibrium, the world steady-state growth rates of consumption and the capital stock are equal and denoted by g_w. Equating the right-hand-sides of (3.23) and (3.26) yields

$$\begin{aligned} r\,(1+r)\left[s\,\frac{1-\tau}{1+\varpi}+(1-s)\,\frac{1-\tau^*}{1+\varpi^*}\right] = \\ \frac{s\,[\hat{m}(1-\gamma)-\delta]}{2\,\alpha}\,\Gamma + \frac{(1-s)\,[\hat{m}^*(1-\gamma^*)-\delta^*]}{2\,\alpha^*}\,\Gamma^* \\ + r\left[1-\frac{s}{2\,\alpha}-\frac{1-s}{2\,\alpha^*}\right] \end{aligned} \tag{3.27}$$

where

$$\Gamma = 1-\frac{1}{3\lambda}\left(\varphi-\lambda\frac{L}{K}\right)^3 \quad \text{and} \quad \Gamma^* = 1-\frac{1}{3\lambda^*}\left(\varphi^*-\lambda^*\frac{L}{K}\right)^3.$$

Expressions for

$$\varphi-\lambda\frac{L}{K} \quad \text{and} \quad \varphi^*-\lambda^*\frac{L}{K}$$

and corresponding expressions for Γ and Γ^* can be obtained from the demand for liquidity equation (3.20). Taking the square root of a simple rearrangement of (3.20) yields

$$\varphi-\lambda\frac{L}{K} = \sqrt{\frac{r+o}{\hat{m}(1-\gamma)-\delta}} \tag{3.28}$$

$$\varphi^*-\lambda^*\frac{L^*}{K^*} = \sqrt{\frac{r+o^*}{\hat{m}^*(1-\gamma^*)-\delta^*}} \tag{3.29}$$

where λ, φ, λ^* and φ^* must be such that both expressions are non-negative. Expressions for Γ and Γ^* follow directly

$$\Gamma = 1-\frac{1}{3\lambda}\left(\sqrt{\frac{r+o}{\hat{m}(1-\gamma)-\delta}}\right)^3 \tag{3.30}$$

$$\Gamma^* = 1-\frac{1}{3\lambda^*}\left(\sqrt{\frac{r+o^*}{\hat{m}^*(1-\gamma^*)-\delta^*}}\right)^3 \tag{3.31}$$

and substitute into (3.27) to yield

$$0 = r\left[(1+r)\left(s\,\frac{1-\tau}{1+\varpi}+(1-s)\,\frac{1-\tau^*}{1+\varpi^*}\right)-\left(1-\frac{s}{2\,\alpha}-\frac{1-s}{2\,\alpha^*}\right)\right]$$
$$-\frac{s\,[\hat{m}(1-\gamma)-\delta]}{2\,\alpha}\left[1-\frac{1}{3\lambda}\left(\sqrt{\frac{r+o}{\hat{m}(1-\gamma)-\delta}}\right)^3\right]$$
$$-\frac{(1-s)\,[\hat{m}^*(1-\gamma^*)-\delta^*]}{2\,\alpha^*}\left[1-\frac{1}{3\lambda^*}\left(\sqrt{\frac{r+o^*}{\hat{m}^*(1-\gamma^*)-\delta^*}}\right)^3\right] \quad (3.32)$$

from which world real interest rate can be solved for numerically. The resulting equilibrium value of r can then be substituted into (3.21), (3.22) and (3.23) to obtain the respective domestic, foreign and world steady-state consumption growth rates and into (3.24), (3.25) and (3.26) to obtain the respective domestic, foreign and world steady-state capital stock growth rates.

Table 3.1 presents calculations of the effects on the domestic and foreign steady-state growth rates and the world real interest rate of shocks to the domestic resource allocation parameters γ, τ and o, and adjustment costs of investment parameter α for various alternative sizes s of the domestic economy as a fraction of the world economy.[10]

In the top section of the table the consumption growth rates, real interest rate and capital stock growth rates are given for initial base values of the parameters, identical for both countries, shown in the note at the bottom of the table.

[10] These calculations are performed using the XLispStat batch file `ssgrthtc.lsp` and the R script `ssgrthtc.R`. To simplify the calculations, components of (3.32) are collected into the following composite variables:

$$\text{tpterm} = s\,\frac{1-\tau}{1+\varpi}+(1-s)\,\frac{1-\tau^*}{1+\varpi^*}$$
$$\text{aacterm} = 1-\frac{s}{2\,\alpha}-\frac{1-s}{2\,\alpha^*}$$
$$\text{dmaterm} = \frac{s\,[\hat{m}(1-\gamma)-\delta]}{2\,\alpha}$$
$$\text{fmaterm} = \frac{(1-s)\,[\hat{m}^*(1-\gamma^*)-\delta^*]}{2\,\alpha^*}$$
$$\text{dsrterm} = 1-\frac{1}{3\lambda}\left(\sqrt{\frac{r+o}{\hat{m}(1-\gamma)-\delta}}\right)^3$$
$$\text{fsrterm} = 1-\frac{1}{3\lambda^*}\left(\sqrt{\frac{r+o^*}{\hat{m}^*(1-\gamma^*)-\delta^*}}\right)^3$$

The entire collection of XLispStat results are presented in the file `ssrgthtc.txt`.

Table 3.1. Effects of changes in domestic allocative efficiency and adjustment costs of new investment on the domestic and foreign growth rates

s		.99	.75	.50	.25	.01
	g_c	.0214	.0214	.0214	.0214	.0214
	g_c^*	.0214	.0214	.0214	.0214	.0214
	g_{cw}	.0214	.0214	.0214	.0214	.0214
Base values	r	.0420	.0420	.0420	.0420	.0420
	g_k	.0214	.0214	.0214	.0214	.0214
	g_k^*	.0214	.0214	.0214	.0214	.0214
	g_{kw}	.0214	.0214	.0214	.0214	.0214
	g_c	.0256	.0246	.0236	.0225	.0214
	g_c^*	.0256	.0246	.0236	.0225	.0214
	g_{cw}	.0256	.0246	.0236	.0225	.0214
$\gamma = .1$	r	.0483	.0453	.0442	.0431	.0421
	g_k	.0257	.0268	.0281	.0294	.0308
	g_k^*	.0171	.0180	.0190	.0202	.0214
	g_{kw}	.0256	.0246	.0236	.0225	.0214
	g_c	.0161	.0148	.0135	.0123	.0111
	g_c^*	.0265	.0252	.0239	.0226	.0214
	g_{cw}	.0162	.0174	.0187	.0200	.0213
$\tau = .02$	r	.0472	.0459	.0446	.0433	.0421
	g_k	.0162	.0174	.0187	.0200	.0213
	g_k^*	.0162	.0174	.0187	.0200	.0213
	g_{kw}	.0162	.0174	.0187	.0200	.0213
	g_c	.0243	.0237	.0230	.0222	.0214
	g_c^*	.0243	.0237	.0230	.0222	.0214
	g_{cw}	.0243	.0237	.0230	.0222	.0214
$\alpha = 15$	r	.0450	.0444	.0436	.0428	.0420
	g_k	.0243	.0252	.0262	.0273	.0285
	g_k^*	.0183	.0189	.0197	.0205	.0214
	g_{kw}	.0243	.0237	.0230	.0222	.0214
	g_c	.0214	.0214	.0214	.0214	.0214
	g_c^*	.0214	.0214	.0214	.0214	.0214
	g_{cw}	.0214	.0214	.0214	.0214	.0214
$o = .05$	r	.0420	.0420	.0420	.0240	.0420
	g_k	.0214	.0214	.0213	.0213	.0213
	g_k^*	.0214	.0214	.0214	.0214	.0214
	g_{kw}	.0214	.0214	.0214	.0214	.0214

Note: The base values of the parameters in both countries are $\hat{m} = \hat{m}^* = .16$, $\delta = \delta^* = .05$, $\varpi = \varpi^* = .01$, $\alpha = \alpha^* = 20$, $\gamma = \gamma^* = .2$, $\tau = \tau^* = .01$, $o = o^* = 0$, $\varphi = \varphi^* = 8.94$ and $\lambda = \lambda^* = 298.14$.

The second section from the top shows the magnitudes of these variables when γ is reduced from 0.2 to 0.1 as a result of a substantial improvement of the efficiency of allocation of the domestic-employed capital stock among its various forms. When the domestic economy comprises .99 of the world economy, the real interest rate rises from .0420 to .0483 and the rate of growth of the domestic-employed capital stock increases from .0214 to .0257. This occurs because the output flow from the domestic capital stock is now substantially higher. The steady-state rate of growth of the foreign capital stock declines from .0214 to .0171 as foreign savings are channelled into investment in the domestic as opposed to the foreign economy. The steady-state consumption growth rate increases by the same amount in both countries, to .0256 from .0214, because the world interest rate is now higher relative to the two countries' common rate of time preference. As the domestic economy becomes an increasingly smaller fraction of the world economy, the real interest rate increase gets smaller and smaller, and is only .0001 above its base level when s is .01. The smaller the relative size of the domestic economy, the smaller the effect of the fall in γ on the flow of output from the world capital stock and the smaller the resulting rise in the world real interest rate. The growth of world consumption also gets smaller and smaller as s declines and the increase in the world interest rate relative to the equal rates of time preference in the two countries becomes smaller. The increase in the steady-state growth rate of the domestic-employed capital stock gets increasingly larger, to .0308, and the steady-state growth rate of the foreign capital stock also rises as s declines, reaching a level only slightly below the base level of .0214, when s equals .01. As the increase in the real interest rate gets smaller, the downward pressure on the market value of foreign-employed capital declines accordingly. The rate of growth of the domestic-employed capital stock remains much higher, at .0308, than the base growth rate of .0214 because, with s equal to .01, the country is so small that expansion of its investment now results from a rise in the present value of domestically employed capital that is no longer being moderated by a significant increase in the world real interest rate.

An increase in τ, the implicit tax on domestic savings, from .01 to .02 results in a reduction of the growth rate of domestic consumption and an increase in the growth rate of consumption in the rest of the world when the domestic economy is a fraction .99 of the world economy. As the flow of domestic and foreign investment declines correspondingly, the adjustment costs of new investment are reduced and the real interest rate rises. It is this rise in the world interest rate relative to the rate of time preference that causes the foreign rate of consumption growth to increase. Steady-state world capital stock growth declines by an amount equivalent to the decline in world consumption growth. The downward effect on domestic steady-state consumption growth gets larger as the domestic economy becomes a smaller fraction of the world economy. When the domestic economy is only 1% of the world, the steady-state growth rate of domestic consumption is only .0111 as compared to .0214 in the base case, while real interest rates and foreign consumption growth return, along with domestic and world capital stock growth, almost to their pre-shock levels. When s is .01, virtually the entire effect of the implicit tax on domestic savings is borne domestically in the form of a lower rate of steady-state domestic consumption growth – the domestic economy is too small to significantly affect the world real interest rate and thereby the steady-state growth of the world capital stock.

Now consider the effects of reducing the domestic adjustment cost of investment parameter α from 20 to 15, shown in the second section from the bottom of the table. When s equals .99, the world real interest rate rises as the adjustment costs decline for each level of domestic investment – this can be seen from equation (3.18), taking into account the fact that the domestic economy represents almost the whole world. Given unchanged rates of time preference, this increases the steady-state consumption growth rates in both countries by the same amount. The steady-state growth rate of the domestic capital stock increases as a result of the reduced adjustment costs while capital stock growth in the foreign economy declines because of the higher world interest rate in the face of unchanged foreign adjustment costs, as can again be seen by looking at equation (3.18) and applying it to the foreign economy. All these effects, other than that on the steady-state rate of growth of the domestic capital stock, gradually disappear as s becomes smaller. When the domestic economy represents only 1% of the world economy, the only significant effect that remains is a higher rate of steady-state domestic capital stock growth resulting from the fact that domestic adjustment costs are lower but the world real interest rate is virtually the same – the remaining effects on the other steady-state growth rates are but a few thousands of a percentage point.

The bottom section of Table 3.1 shows the effects of a 5% increase in the domestic inflation rate. This reduces domestic output by reducing the stock of liquidity held, resulting in a decline in the steady-state growth rate of the domestic capital stock and, when the domestic economy is a large fraction of the world, a decline in the world interest rate and increase in the growth rate of capital in the foreign country, which does not suffer from an increase in transactions costs of making exchange. But the magnitudes of the effects are trivial, never exceeding .0001, and disappear as the domestic economy becomes smaller. This is consistent with the calculations of the wealth effects of changes in the stock of liquidity made earlier. While one could undoubtedly find functional forms and parameter values for which these liquidity effects would become larger, it is not clear that such a calibration would be consistent with available evidence on the nature of countries' demand functions for money.

3.5.1 The Real Exchange Rate

The assumption that the same good is produced in the domestic and foreign economies must now be relaxed. Let domestic consumption, C_t, be characterized as a constant-elasticity-of-substitution (CES) function of the quantities of the domestic and rest-of-world outputs consumed

$$C_t = \left[\xi^{\frac{1}{\sigma}} (C_{Dt})^{\frac{\sigma-1}{\sigma}} + (1-\xi)^{\frac{1}{\sigma}} (\tilde{C}_{Dt})^{\frac{\sigma-1}{\sigma}}\right]^{\frac{\sigma}{\sigma-1}} \tag{3.33}$$

where C_{Dt} is domestic consumption of domestic output and $\tilde{C}_{Dt}$ is domestic consumption of rest-of-world output, ξ is the share of domestic consumption consisting of domestic output, and σ is the elasticity of substitution between the two outputs in domestic consumption. To keep the analysis simple, domestic investment, $I_t = K_{t+1} - K_t$, is assumed to be the same CES function of domestic and rest-of-world outputs

$$I_t = \left[\xi^{\frac{1}{\sigma}} (I_{Dt})^{\frac{\sigma-1}{\sigma}} + (1-\xi)^{\frac{1}{\sigma}} (\tilde{I}_{Dt})^{\frac{\sigma-1}{\sigma}}\right]^{\frac{\sigma}{\sigma-1}} \tag{3.34}$$

where I_{Dt} is domestic investment of domestic output and $\tilde{I}_{Dt}$ is domestic investment of rest-of-world output. Similarly, rest-of-world consumption and investment, C_t^* and I_t^* $(= K_{t+1}^* - K_t^*)$, are assumed to be identical CES functions of domestic and rest-of-world outputs

$$C_t^* = \left[\tilde{\xi}^{\frac{1}{\sigma}} (C_{Ft})^{\frac{\sigma-1}{\sigma}} + (1-\tilde{\xi})^{\frac{1}{\sigma}} (\tilde{C}_{Ft})^{\frac{\sigma-1}{\sigma}}\right]^{\frac{\sigma}{\sigma-1}} \tag{3.35}$$

$$I_t^* = \left[\tilde{\xi}^{\frac{1}{\sigma}} (I_{Ft})^{\frac{\sigma-1}{\sigma}} + (1-\tilde{\xi})^{\frac{1}{\sigma}} (\tilde{I}_{Ft})^{\frac{\sigma-1}{\sigma}}\right]^{\frac{\sigma}{\sigma-1}} \tag{3.36}$$

where C_{Ft} and I_{Ft} are rest-of-world consumption and investment of domestic output and $\tilde{C}_{Ft}$ and $\tilde{I}_{Ft}$ are rest-of-world consumption and investment of its own output, $\tilde{\xi}$ is the share of rest-of-world consumption and investment comprised of domestic output, and the elasticity of substitution is the same as in the domestic economy.[11]

The relative price of domestic output in terms of rest-of-world output is the domestic real exchange rate, hereafter denoted by Q. This relative price must equate the marginal returns to domestic and rest-of-world output in generating domestic and rest-of-world consumption and investment, and will therefore equal the ratios of the relevant marginal products:

$$\begin{aligned} Q_t = \left(\frac{\xi}{1-\xi}\right)^{\frac{1}{\sigma}} \left(\frac{\tilde{C}_{Dt}}{C_{Dt}}\right)^{\frac{1}{\sigma}} &= \left(\frac{\xi}{1-\xi}\right)^{\frac{1}{\sigma}} \left(\frac{\tilde{I}_{Dt}}{I_{Dt}}\right)^{\frac{1}{\sigma}} \\ = \left(\frac{\tilde{\xi}}{1-\tilde{\xi}}\right)^{\frac{1}{\sigma}} \left(\frac{\tilde{C}_{Ft}}{C_{Ft}}\right)^{\frac{1}{\sigma}} &= \left(\frac{\tilde{\xi}}{1-\tilde{\xi}}\right)^{\frac{1}{\sigma}} \left(\frac{\tilde{I}_{Ft}}{I_{Ft}}\right)^{\frac{1}{\sigma}} \end{aligned} \qquad (3.37)$$

It is easily shown that the elasticities of C_{Dt}, I_{Dt}, C_{Ft}, and I_{Ft} with respect to Q are equal to $-\sigma$ and the elasticities of $\tilde{C}_{Dt}$, $\tilde{I}_{Dt}$, $\tilde{C}_{Ft}$, and $\tilde{I}_{Ft}$ with respect to Q are equal to σ. This, along with derivation of the real exchange rate is shown in Appendix B.

Even if the two countries are of the same size, ξ and $\tilde{\xi}$ will almost certainly differ in magnitude – for them to be equal, the countries would each have to absorb through consumption and investment exactly half of their own output and half of the other country's output. If the domestic economy is tiny, the fraction of foreign consumption and investment produced from domestic output, $\tilde{\xi}$, will necessarily also be tiny while the fraction of domestic consumption and investment produced from domestic output, ξ, will be substantial. It might appear obvious from (3.37) above that an increase in domestic output relative to world output at a given world interest rate will necessarily result in a decline in the domestic real exchange rate – after all, C_{Dt} and I_{Dt} must increase relative to $\tilde{I}_{Dt}$ and $\tilde{I}_{Dt}$ by equal amounts. In a short-run environment where consumption does not deviate from its long-run steady-state path this would certainly be true, a result that will be expanded upon and exploited in the next chapter. But the question here is whether an increase in the steady-state equilibrium growth rate of domestic relative to foreign output, at a given world real interest

[11] To avoid notational confusion, the reader should keep in mind that the presence or absence of a ˜ superscript denotes the country, foreign or domestic, whose good is being used to create consumption and investment and the $_D$ and $_F$ subscripts denote the country whose residents are purchasing the goods for that purpose.

rate and given rates of steady-state domestic and foreign consumption growth, will cause the growth rate of Q to decline.

If the domestic economy is growing faster, the world will be investing a larger fraction of its savings in the domestic economy and a smaller fraction in the foreign economy than was the case before the increase in the rate of domestic relative to foreign output growth. But in this environment, where the capital stock employed in the domestic economy is growing faster, along with domestic output, relative to the capital stock and output abroad, the underlying technology will be changing in the domestic relative to the foreign economy at a faster rate. As Balassa [2] and Samuelson [95] have argued, the type of economic growth envisioned here leads to an increase in the relative prices of the service components of output as real wage rates rise. This will necessarily increase the price of the non-traded component of output relative to the traded component. Accordingly, a greater rate of steady-state output growth in the domestic economy than abroad will increase through time the price of the domestic relative to the foreign non-traded component of output. Given the equality of the domestic and foreign prices of the traded output-components, it follows that the relative price of domestic output and therefore the real exchange rate must be growing at a faster rate, or declining at a slower rate, than before. In terms of (3.37), this means that ξ and $\tilde{\xi}$ cannot be constant through time and will be growing or declining in response to differential rates of growth of domestic and foreign technological capital. Their growth will be such as to produce a more rapid rate of growth, or smaller rate of decline, of Q as the domestic capital stock grows relative to the foreign capital stock.

The situation is further complicated by the fact that as the capital stocks grow in the domestic and foreign economies, even at the same rates, the growth of technology may at times favour one or other of the two economies, depending upon the location of the underlying natural resource capital that particular increments to technological capital in each country will work with. It would therefore be reasonable to expect that the real exchange rate will tend to increase and decrease through time as the on-going steady-state world growth process evolves. The exact pattern of variation could only be identified in a detailed model of technological expansion in the growth process. Were such a model to be constructed here, the quantitative results would depend entirely on the assumptions made about the nature of technological change, with little basis for choosing one set of assumptions rather than another. The purpose here is satisfied by simple recognition that there will be a full-employment level of the real exchange rate that may well move up and down as the full-employment levels of output grow through time.

The results in Table 3.1 are those that will arise if $\sigma \rightarrow \infty$. In the more general case, where σ can take more realistic values, it is not clear how the magnitudes of the results would change, but it would seem reasonable to argue that if the shocks to the pattern of output growth change the rate of growth of Q, this different rate of real exchange rate change would be unlikely to reverse the direction of the effects of the shocks on the steady-state growth rates that caused it to occur. Yet it is conceivable that changes in technology associated with a greater rate of output growth in one of the countries, while unaffected by the direction of change in Q, could nevertheless cause opposite directional changes in that variable resulting from the types of natural resource capital used by the new technology as opposed to the old. Thus, in the case where σ is finite the results in Table 3.1 must be interpreted as valid only in situations where the associated changes in Q are not of major magnitude.

Since the emphasis in the research presented here is strictly on the effects of monetary and real shocks on the deviation of outputs, real interest rates and real exchange rates from their full-employment levels, the detailed determinants of the underlying time-paths of those variables need not be of concern. The purpose of this chapter was to develop a conceptual understanding of the full-employment growth process. The development of a rigorous model of deviations from this full-employment path can now be pursued.

4

Variations in Employment

Standard real business cycle theory postulates variations in the level of output resulting from the effects of ongoing investment in the technological portion of the aggregate capital stock, which should be thought of as consisting of many types of capital rather than merely the two types postulated in the equation illustrated in Fig. 3.1. These variations would usually be accompanied by changes in labour-leisure choice by those in whom the human capital portion of the aggregate capital stock is embodied. The focus here, however, is on more traditional changes in the level of employment that involve involuntary changes in the degree of utilization of the human and non-human portions of the aggregate capital stock.

Since such employment and output changes are temporary, they can be viewed as changes in the level of income Y independent of changes in the level of the broadly defined capital stock K with the income changes coming from changes in the fraction of K utilized. These changes in income, being temporary, will have no effects on the expected future income flow from capital or on current consumption, which will depend on the average future level of income, conventionally called permanent income. Variations in current income around its permanent full-employment level will thus be channeled into temporary increases and decreases in the stock of capital K – increases in the capital stock when utilization is high will subsequently be drawn down to maintain the constant flow of consumption when utilization is low.[1]

[1] When individuals are credit constrained, they may find it useful to make temporary adjustments in consumption – it may be more useful to defer consumption of luxury items than pay high interest on a loan or allow the existing stock of durables such as automobiles or houses to deteriorate. Such issues are ignored in

J.E. Floyd, *Interest Rates, Exchange Rates and World Monetary Policy*,
DOI 10.1007/978-3-642-10280-6_4, © Springer-Verlag Berlin Heidelberg 2010

It is useful to first examine the short-run equilibrium conditions for a closed economy or, what is the same thing, for the rest of the world from the point of view of a small open economy. The principles can then be extended to deal with the situation in the small open economy itself and then to the case of two big open economies.

4.1 Equilibrium in Asset and Output-Flow Markets: Closed Economy

Asset equilibrium holds in a closed economy whenever the real quantity of liquidity is at its equilibrium level – otherwise, there would be excess demand or supply of liquid monetary assets and corresponding excess supply or demand for the other assets. The market for the flow of output is in equilibrium when the quantity of output produced equals the quantity the public wants to absorb through private and public consumption and investment.

Equations (3.18), (3.19) and (3.20) can be viewed as the conditions of short-term equilibrium when K is replaced with the quantity of capital actually utilized. The capital stock will be over-utilized or under-utilized to the extent that income is above or below its full-employment level. Letting ΔY represent the excess of the current level of income over its full-employment level, the quantity of capital utilized can be expressed as

$$K_U = \frac{Y_f + \Delta Y}{Y_f} K. \tag{4.1}$$

Then K_U can be substituted for K in (3.18) and (3.20) to obtain

$$r = \frac{\hat{m}(1-\gamma) - \delta}{1 + 2\alpha\,(g + \Delta Y/K)} \left[1 - \frac{1}{3\lambda}\left(\varphi - \lambda \frac{L}{Y_f + \Delta Y}\frac{Y_f}{K}\right)^3\right] \tag{4.2}$$

and

$$r + o = [\hat{m}(1-\gamma) - \delta]\left[\varphi - \lambda \frac{L}{Y_f + \Delta Y}\frac{Y_f}{K}\right]^2 \tag{4.3}$$

where Y_f is the full-employment level of income, $g + \Delta Y/K$ is the level of investment as a fraction of the capital stock and g is the

the formal analytical framework because they make little difference with respect to the fundamental results.

full-employment-equilibrium growth rate, which is assumed to be positive. Note that all of the temporary deviation of output from its full-employment level represents a change in the level of investment, with consumption remaining on its long-run equilibrium growth path.

Equation (4.2) gives the combinations of the real interest rate r and the current level of output $Y_f + \Delta Y$, associated with any given level of the stock of liquidity L and the stock of capital K, for which the market for the current output flow is in equilibrium. An increase in ΔY at given levels of Y_f, L and K will result in a decline in r for two reasons. First, the denominator of the left-most term to the right of the equal sign will increase – this gives the positive effect of the higher level of investment on the adjustment costs of putting capital in place and, hence, on the cost of capital relative to its present value. Second, the increase in current output relative to the stock of liquidity in the right-most term in the square brackets increases the resources required to cover the transaction costs of making exchange, reducing the output flow from the capital stock. As demonstrated in the previous chapter, this latter effect will be very small under reasonable assumptions.

These combinations of r and $Y_f + \Delta Y$ for which the market for the current output flow is in equilibrium can be portrayed as the negatively sloped curve GG in Fig. 4.1. This curve is a rigorously-derived counterpart to the traditional IS curve although, as will be shown, the basis for shifts in it are more subtle than in the case of IS.

Equation (4.3) gives the combinations of r and $Y_f + \Delta Y$, again at given levels of L, Y_f and K, for which there is zero excess demand for liquidity. When the economy is closed to international trade, this will imply that all asset markets are in equilibrium. An increase in ΔY raises the level of transactions, increases the quantity of resources used up making them and thereby increasing the marginal return to additional liquidity, requiring an increase in r to reduce desired liquidity to its original level. The full-employment real interest rate is represented by the level of r when ΔY is zero. These combinations of r and $Y_f + \Delta Y$ appear as the positively sloped curve AA in Fig. 4.1 which, apart from its more rigorous derivation, is identical to the traditional LM curve. It shifts to the right when the supply of liquidity increases or the demand for it falls, as indicated by $A'A'$ in the figure. The equilibrium real interest rate in the economy and the current equilibrium level of output will be determined by the intersection of AA and GG. The vertical line Y_f denotes the full-employment level of output. These curves and the equilibrium they represent are derived and drawn mathematically in Appendix C.

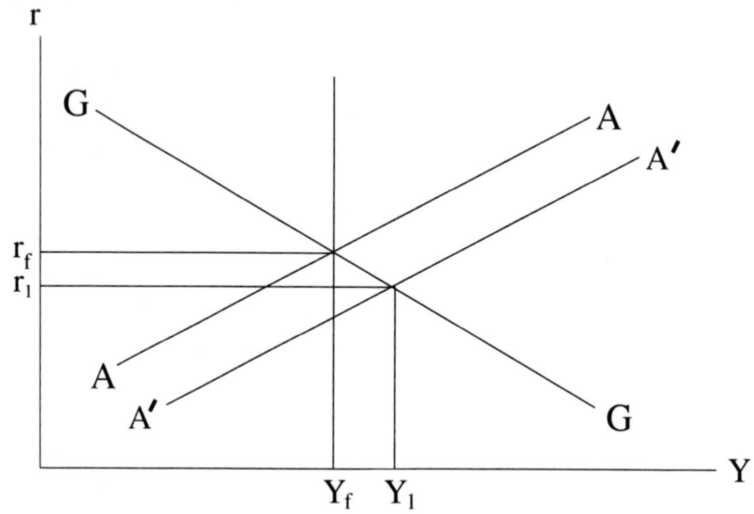

Fig. 4.1. Effect of positive monetary shock in a closed or dominant rest-of-world economy.

Along the steady-state equilibrium growth path the stock of capital and the resulting full-employment level of output will increase at a constant rate. Given the constant steady-state real interest rate, the GG curve and the vertical Y_f line will shift to the right by the same amount as shown in Fig. 4.2. Continuous full-employment will require that the AA curve also shift to the right by the same amount. In the face of short-run price-level rigidity, the authorities will have to expand base money continuously by an appropriate amount. Failure to do this will result in a gradual increase in the unemployment rate until the price level begins to fall – full-employment will be achieved when the price level is continuously falling at a rate sufficient to shift AA to the right in step with the ongoing rightward shift of GG.

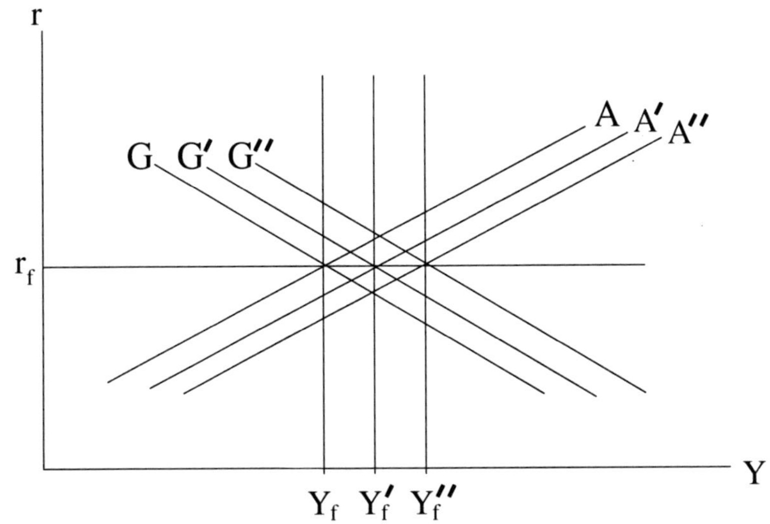

Fig. 4.2. Adjustments along the steady-state growth path.

4.1.1 Monetary and Real Shocks

The effects of monetary real shocks are derived rigorously in Appendix C. Monetary shocks can be understood intuitively from Fig. 4.1. An increase in the stock of liquidity or a reduction in the demand for it results in a shift of AA to the right. The public, faced with excess money holdings, tries to purchase non-monetary assets to restore portfolio equilibrium. Asset prices rise and interest rates fall, leading to an increase in investment which drives output above its full-employment level in the short run when prices are rigid. In the long run with flexible prices, the price level rises in proportion to the initial excess supply of liquidity, shifting AA back to its original level.

The output and employment effects of real shocks are much more complex. Consider first the case of an improvement of resource allocation that lowers γ and permanently increases the full-employment level of output. The full-employment level of income increases in approximate proportion to the increase in $\hat{m}(1-\gamma)-\delta$ and the full-employment real interest rate increases upward by roughly the same proportion.[2] This new full-employment equilibrium is given by the intersection of the curve $G'G'$ with the vertical Y_f' line in Fig. 4.3. To maintain output

[2] The shifts in Y_f and r_f are not exactly proportional because the level of investment, and corresponding adjustment costs, will increase with the level of full-employment income.

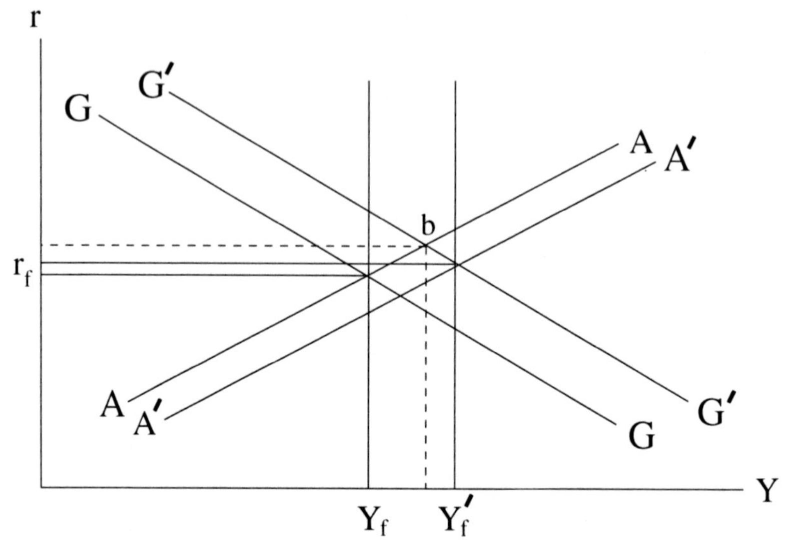

Fig. 4.3. The short- and long-term effects of productivity shocks to the full-employment output level in a closed or large world-dominant economy.

at its full-employment level in the short run, the authorities will have to increase the stock of base money sufficiently to shift the AA curve to $A'A'$. Barring this, output and the real interest rate will increase in the short run only to the levels indicated by the intersection of AA and $G'G'$ at point b in the diagram, with the result being an increase in the unemployment rate – as income rises the increase in the demand for money causes asset prices to fall and interest rates to rise, leading to a reduction of investment and moderation of the output growth. The conclusion that the unemployment rate increases depends critically on the steepness of the AA curve – the rise in the interest rate required to reduce the quantity of liquidity demanded by the same percentage as it is increased by the rise in the full-employment level of output must be more than proportional to the increase in the full-employment interest rate, which will be roughly proportional to the increase in the full-employment output level. It turns out that this requirement is likely to hold in practice since estimates of the interest elasticity of demand for liquidity tend to be much smaller than estimates of the income elasticity of demand for liquidity – the latter tend to be above unity, while the former are far below unity.[3]

The above analysis applies only to real productivity shocks that are permanent and widely known to be so. As the capital stock increases through time the underlying output flow denoted by $\hat{m}$ should not be expected to be constant – the output effects of improvements of continuous technological growth will typically be larger or smaller than average over short periods, as implied by real business-cycle models. Since consumption will be based on the permanent rather than the current level of full-employment income, these income variations will flow primarily to investment rather than consumption when the temporary nature of these shocks is recognized.[4] As a result, in response to associated changes in the adjustment costs of investment, the equilibrium full-employment real interest rate, associated with the full-employment level of output, will tend to rise and fall through time – that is, the GG curve will tend to shift upward and downward relative to its average level as the economy grows. At the same time, however, the full-employment level of output will also rise and fall shifting the vertical full-employment line to the right and left. The effects can again be seen with reference to Fig. 4.3 except that one can no longer rule out

[3] See Laidler [67] for a summary of the empirical evidence. A simple representation of the demand for real liquidity function

$$L = L(r, Y)$$

can be differentiated totally, holding the stock of liquidity constant, to yield

$$dL = \frac{\partial L}{\partial r} dr + \frac{\partial L}{\partial Y} dY = 0$$

which can be manipulated to represent the elasticity of the AA curve with respect to the r axis as equal to minus the ratio of the income elasticity of demand for liquidity to the interest elasticity of demand for liquidity,

$$\frac{dY}{dr}\frac{r}{Y} = -\frac{\partial L}{\partial Y}\frac{Y}{L} \div \frac{\partial L}{\partial r}\frac{r}{L}.$$

[4] The extreme assumption in the mathematical model that the actual and expected future flow of output from the capital stock is a constant must be informally modified. As long as time preference is positive, a temporary change in income will have some effect in the same direction on consumption because consumption in the near future yields, at the margin, more utility than that in the distant future. Nevertheless, the conclusions here still hold because this effect on consumption will be much smaller than the effect of an equivalent increase or decrease in income in every future period – most of a temporary shock to income will flow to investment.

the possibility that GG will shift upward sufficiently to drive income above its full-employment level in the short-run – virtually all of the increase in income represents an expansion of investment, whereas only a small fraction flows to investment in the case where the shock is permanent. The GG curve will shift upward by a larger amount when the income shock represents investment expansion because a larger increase in the real interest rate would be required to completely choke off the expansion. Thus, while the effect on the level of income is unambiguous, the unemployment rate could change in either direction.

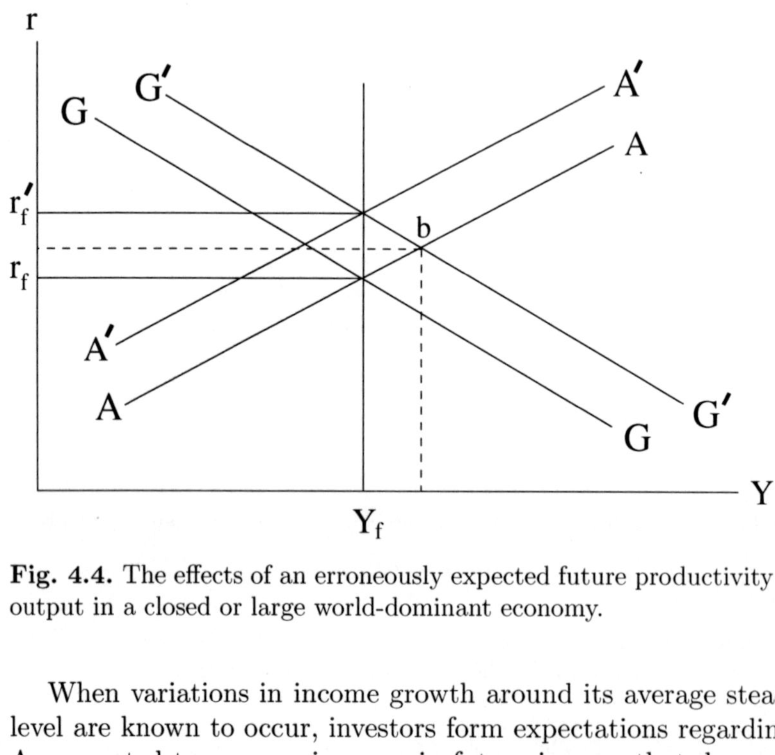

Fig. 4.4. The effects of an erroneously expected future productivity shock to output in a closed or large world-dominant economy.

When variations in income growth around its average steady-state level are known to occur, investors form expectations regarding them. An expected temporary increase in future income that does not actually occur will have the same short-term effect on investment as one for which the expectations are realized. But the increase in the full-employment income level will only occur in the latter case. The short-term income and employment effect will be unambiguous, as can be seen with reference to Fig. 4.4. An expected temporary future expansion of income will result in a short-run increase in income and employment as indicated by point b in the figure. To choke off this increase in income and employment, the quantity of money would have to decline sufficiently to shift AA to the left to $A'A'$. Long-run effects on prices will not occur, in the absence of permanent monetary adjustments, given the temporary nature of the real shock.

Finally, there are real shocks such as changes weather or other unpredictable random events that take the form of stochastic variations in $\hat{m}$. The consequences can be seen in Fig. 4.5. If prices are perfectly flexible, the real interest rate will fall as a result of the increase in income being channeled entirely into investment. In the short-run, when prices cannot adjust, income will remain unchanged. The expected future level of $\hat{m}(1-\gamma)-\delta$, which determines the profitability of investment will remain unchanged. Given the constant level of liquidity implied by an unchanged AA curve, income will be prevented from increasing above its initial level. The decline in the real interest rate and the resulting rise in the present value of additions to the capital stock required to stimulate investment by the amount of the random increase in income cannot occur. The upward shock to full-employment income will be completely offset by an equivalent rise in unemployment.

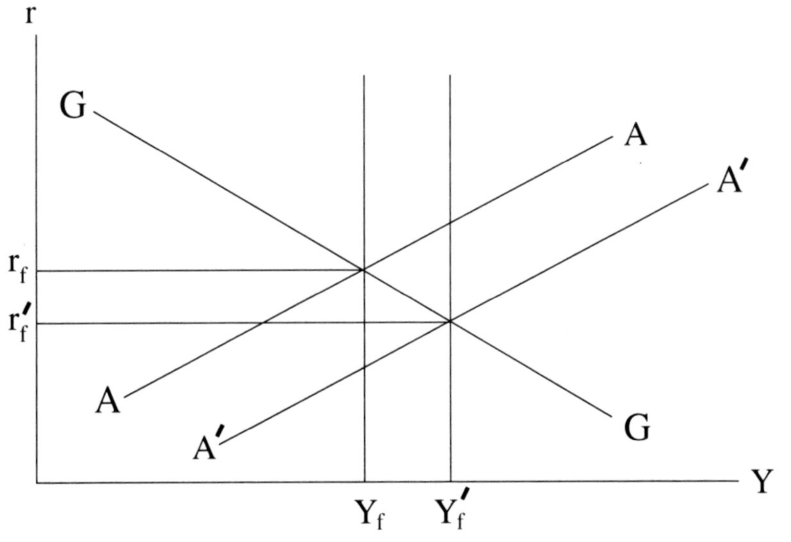

Fig. 4.5. The effects of unanticipated temporary random shocks to the full-employment output level in a closed or large world-dominant economy.

This last situation, as the model portrays it, strains one's view of reality. Is one to believe that a good crop in a given year will result in an equivalent reduction of output somewhere else in the economy? The problem is that the downward adjustment of employment can occur only when those individuals whose income has increased get around to increasing appropriately their holdings of money and thereby prevent the interest rate from falling below its original full-employment level and, correspondingly, prevent the temporary increase in the level of investment required by the fact that the levels of current and permanent consumption are unaffected. It would seem reasonable to expect that, in the short-run, output would increase with little if any reduction in employment. To correctly analyse this situation in the short-run it would be necessary to incorporate assumptions about how fast people learn and react, dragging into the analysis the same problems that arise with attempts to deal with the issue of how fast the price level will adjust to a difference between current output and its full-employment level. Accordingly, no attempt will be made here to analyse the effects of temporary random shocks to full-employment output that are unanticipated. And, while it is clear that shifts in expectations about the future level of output that will be produced by the current capital stock will, as shown in Fig. 4.4, necessarily result in a positive effect on income and employment in a length of run that is long enough for effects to occur but short enough for the error in expectations to remain, no attempt will be made here to attach empirical magnitudes to such effects. In addition, it is obvious that in any real-world situation the division of observed movements in income into the portions that have arisen from different types of real shock will be a difficult empirical task.

4.1.2 Monetary and Fiscal Policy

As noted above, the effects of monetary policy are straight-forward and in the direction desired. For fiscal policy, the situation is complex. Basic improvements in resource allocation will clearly have a positive effect on consumption and welfare although the unemployment rate need not decline in the short-run. And, of course, a detailed analysis of any proposed policy needs to be undertaken to ensure that it actually improves the allocation of resources. With respect to short-run counter-cyclical policy, two types of approach are standard in the literature – a tax cut financed by increased government debt, and an increase in government expenditure financed by taxes or by increased government debt.[5]

It is now well known that a tax cut financed by floating government debt will have but a minor effect on private wealth. The buyers of the newly issued debt in effect give a loan to the rest of the community that

[5] A tax cut financed by monetary expansion is viewed here as a monetary policy.

has to be paid back with interest at the government bond rate, with the present value of the resulting increase in future taxes being equal to the current tax cut. Individuals who do not care about their heirs, or do not have any, will experience a wealth gain from a current tax cut because others in the society will end up paying back the debt. The rest of the community, to the extent that it understands this, may well reduce their current consumption expenditure in order to transfer resources to their heirs in compensation.[6] In addition, even though the present value of the tax cut financed by public debt issue is zero at the current interest rate on government bonds, private wealth will increase because that interest rate is much lower than the rate that would have to be charged on a private loan from those who purchase the government bonds to those who do not because the government, through its taxing power, guarantees repayment of the loan. This kind of guarantee is not possible in private markets. Clearly, the optimum steady-state stock of public debt is not zero and temporary increases in it in bad times will reduce the cyclical fluctuations in private sector wealth. But, contrary to the traditional Keynesian view, such short-term increases in wealth that do occur will have a minor effect on consumption because they will be much smaller than the associated tax cuts. Of course, some short-run increases in consumption expenditure will arise and these will be augmented to the extent that people feel wealthier as a result of lack of understanding of the long-run implications of the policy and mistakenly view their increased current income as permanent.

The intertemporal framework developed here suggests a different focus on the way in which temporary tax cuts can increase aggregate income and expenditure. Individuals smooth consumption by buying debt in good times and selling it when times are bad, or alternatively, by borrowing to maintain consumption in bad times and paying back the loans in good times. Those facing credit constraints, typically people at the lower end of the income distribution, may simply allow their consumer durables – clothes, automobiles, household appliances, etc. – to depreciate during bad times and repair or replace them in good times.[7] A tax cut during bad times, therefore, represents a loan which can be used to replace investment in durables while a tax increase in good times represents a repayment of the loan. The individuals who purchase and sell the associated increments to the public debt, however,

---

[6] See Barro [3] and, for a broader discussion, [4].

[7] One also cannot rule out the possibility that an individual might choose to postpone consumption of a luxury item in order to avoid having to draw down a valuable element of household capital.

will smooth their consumption by increasing and drawing down other assets. For the aggregate effect of a tax cut to be positive, investment must not be reduced elsewhere in the economy by the full amount of additional government debt purchased.

All things considered, it is probably reasonable to expect that tax cuts in bad times will lead to some increase in expenditure, shifting *GG* to the right, and tax increases in boom years will shift it to the left. But the magnitudes of these shifts are not easy to determine and are quite likely small relative to the magnitudes of the tax changes that produce them.

An increase in government expenditure financed by floating public debt is equivalent to one financed by a tax increase plus a tax cut financed by issuing debt, the effects of which are discussed above. It is therefore sufficient to focus on the effect of an increase in government expenditure financed by taxes. Everything will depend upon what type of expenditure the government undertakes. At the one extreme, where the government simply imposes a lump-sum tax on part of the population and gives a lump-sum subsidy to another, the effect will depend on the consumption propensities of the two groups. Distortions of production and consumption will arise, of course, if the taxes and subsidies are not lump-sum.

Suppose alternatively that the government taxes the community and uses the funds to hire unemployed resources to produce a consumption good which it makes available free to the community. If the good produced by the government has close substitutes in the private sector, private production will simply decline by an amount roughly equivalent to the additional consumption provided freely by the government and the *GG* curve will be unaffected. The government will have, in effect, charged the public for producing a freely available good that the private sector would otherwise have produced and sold to them. And even if the government consumption good is a poor substitute for privately produced goods the public, in its desire to maintain a smooth steady-state consumption path, will reduce consumption elsewhere although, to the extent that wealth has temporarily increased, this reduction in private sector consumption will be matched by an increase in investment which, given unchanged aggregate consumption, will shift *GG* somewhat to the right.

Another alternative is for the government to tax the community and use the funds to hire unemployed resources to produce a capital good. Again, if this capital good is a perfect substitute for privately produced capital goods the effect will be nil. Private investment will decline by the amount that public investment increases and no increase in income and employment will occur. To the extent that the government-produced capital good is productive and has no privately-produced counterpart, wealth will temporarily increase. An increase in income and employment, represented by a rightward shift of the GG curve, will result from this greater investment with consumption remaining at its steady-state level. As in the case of government production of consumption goods, the average or permanent level of government investment, and its distribution among alternative commodities should ideally be such as to minimize the resource misallocation parameter γ.

Finally, suppose that the changes in government investment or consumption goods production involve worthless busy-work that is of no value to the community – unemployed resources are being activated to produce nothing. It is as though the authorities were to tax one segment of the community and give the funds to the unemployed in return for jumping through hoops – the result will depend simply on the propensities to consume of the two groups and, obviously, the long-run steady state level of wealth will be increased by entirely eliminating this type of government expenditure.

It is reasonable to conclude that changes in the stock of base money will clearly cause real income and employment to change in the desired direction. Government tax and expenditure policies, on the other hand, will have effects that can only be identified though careful study of the nature and effects of each individual policy.[8]

4.2 Small Open Economy Equilibrium

When the economy in the model is a small one in which a wide range of goods and capital assets can be purchased and sold abroad, some major additions must be made to the above analytical framework. First, the domestic real interest rate becomes

$$r = \tilde{r} + \rho - E_Q \tag{4.4}$$

where $\tilde{r}$ is the interest rate in the rest of the world, ρ is the risk premium on domestic assets and E_Q is the expected rate of change in the domestic real exchange rate with respect to the rest of the world. The latter

[8] An old-style Keynesian would draw attention to the fact that the effectiveness of monetary policy hinges on the assumption that the AA curve is positively sloped – that is, the demand for money is not perfectly elastic with respect to the rate of interest so as to result in a liquidity trap. Monetary policy will have the effect here postulated as long as monetary and non-monetary assets are not perfect substitutes for each other in portfolios.

is a determinant of the domestic real interest rate because an expected increase in Q implies that domestic output, and hence the return from domestically employed capital, is expected to become more valuable in terms of world output. This expected capital gain will make world asset holders willing to hold domestic assets at a lower market interest rate than otherwise, resulting in a decline in the domestic relative to the rest-of-world real interest rate.

Second, as noted in the previous chapter, the full-employment growth rate of the domestic employed capital stock no longer equals the growth rate of domestic consumption. The growth rate of capital employed in the domestic economy, denoted by g_k, will be determined by the full-employment version of equation (4.2) which becomes

$$\tilde{r} + \rho - E_Q = \frac{\hat{m}(1-\gamma) - \delta}{1 + 2\,\alpha\,g_k}\left[1 - \frac{1}{3\lambda}\left(\varphi - \lambda\frac{L}{K}\right)^3\right] \tag{4.5}$$

with the domestic price level adjusting in the background to maintain the equilibrium real stock of liquidity L. The growth rate of domestic consumption will be determined by a modified version of equation (3.21),

$$g_c = \frac{(1+\tilde{r})(1-\tau)}{1+\varpi} - 1, \tag{4.6}$$

where domestic consumers are indifferent between r and $\tilde{r}$ once compensation in the form of $\rho - E_Q$ is provided.

The third modification is that the deviation of the real exchange rate from its full-employment level, denoted by ΔQ, will be negatively related to the deviation of domestic output from its full-employment level – when domestic output becomes cheaper in world markets, more of it will be bought.[9] The deviation of domestic income from its full-employment level now consists of two parts – the deviation resulting from short-run movements of the domestic real interest rate plus the deviation resulting from short-term movements of Q in relation to Q_f. The former can be obtained by substituting equation (4.4) into equation (4.2) and rearranging the latter to move ΔY to the left side of the equality. The result will be an equation of the form

$$(\Delta Y)_1 = G(r, \Phi_d, L) \tag{4.7}$$

where $\partial(\Delta Y_1)/\partial r$ is negative and equal to the reciprocal of the slope of the GG curve and $\partial(\Delta Y_1)/\partial \Phi_d$, which is positive, gives the effect

[9] See the set of equations (3.37) for a formal derivation.

of domestic real shocks, represented by changes in Φ_d, of the form previously discussed that shift GG. On the basis of what was shown in the previous chapter, $\partial(\Delta Y)_1/\partial L$, while positive, will likely be of trivial magnitude. The effect of changes in the difference of the real exchange rate from its full-employment level on the difference between Y and its full-employment level can be expressed in the form

$$(\Delta Y)_2 = F(\Delta Q, \Phi_w) \tag{4.8}$$

where $\partial(\Delta Y)_2/\partial\Delta Q$ is negative and $\partial(\Delta Y)_2/\partial\Phi_w$, which is positive, encorporates the effects of short-run world shocks to domestic output, represented by changes in Φ_w, that are independent of the existing short-run level of Q. While the above two equations are very general as to the magnitudes of the effects, all that is necessary for the arguments that follow is that the underlying effects be monotonic within the ranges considered. The deviation of income from its full-employment level can thus be expressed as

$$\begin{aligned} \Delta Y &= (\Delta Y)_1 + (\Delta Y)_2 \\ &= G(r, \Phi_d, L) + F(\Delta Q, \Phi_w) \end{aligned} \tag{4.9}$$

This equation describes the GG curve in Fig. 4.6 below. The effect on ΔY of changes in r represents a movement along the curve, while the effects on ΔY of the other variables represent a shift of the curve.

Short-term equilibrium of the small open economy will be determined by the two equations (4.4) and (4.9) together with a third equation yielding the AA curve in Fig. 4.6. This equation is (4.3), which can be more conveniently expressed here in the general form

$$r = A(\Delta Y, L, \Phi_m) \tag{4.10}$$

where $\partial r/\partial\Delta Y > 0$, $\partial r/\partial L < 0$ and $\partial r/\partial\Phi_m > 0$ with changes in Φ_m representing shocks to the demand for real liquidity.

The three equations, (4.4), (4.9) and (4.10) solve for the three variables r, ΔY and ΔQ when the exchange rate is flexible and r, ΔY and L when the small country adopts a fixed exchange rate. The real stock of liquidity L becomes exogenous, along with Φ_d, Φ_w and Φ_m when the exchange rate is flexible and ΔQ becomes exogenous when the exchange rate is fixed. In the short-run, a fixed nominal exchange rate implies a fixed real exchange rate because the domestic price level is fixed and the rest-of-world price level is determined exogenously by conditions abroad.

In terms of Fig. 4.6, the horizontal line $\tilde{r}\tilde{r}$, representing equation (4.4), determines the domestic real interest rate. When the exchange

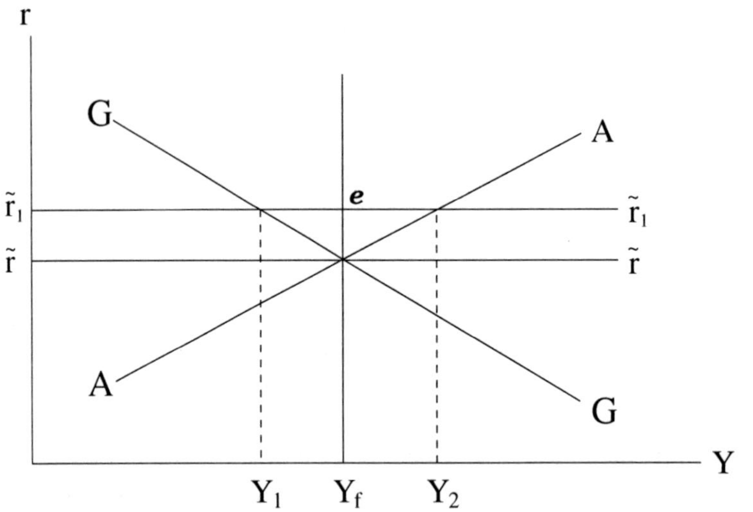

Fig. 4.6. Equilibrium output and employment in a small open economy.

rate is flexible, this real interest rate substitutes into equation (4.10) to determine the short-run level of income, given by the intersection of AA and $\tilde{r}\tilde{r}$. A short-term adjustment of Q relative to its full-employment level – that is, an equilibrating movement of the nominal and real exchange rates – occurs automatically, shifting the GG curve to pass through the intersection of AA and $\tilde{r}\tilde{r}$. When the exchange rate is fixed, the internationally determined real interest rate substitutes into equation (4.9) to determine the short-run equilibrium level of output, given by the intersection of GG and $\tilde{r}\tilde{r}$. Recall that the partial derivative of the function $G(r, \Phi_d, L)$ with respect to L is of trivial magnitude so that the GG curve can be treated as unaffected by changes in the real stock of liquidity. To maintain the fixed exchange rate parity the authorities are forced to adjust the stock of liquidity by purchasing or selling either foreign exchange reserves or domestic assets in return for base money until equation (4.10) is satisfied – this shifts the AA curve to pass through the intersection of GG and $\tilde{r}\tilde{r}$. Under full-employment conditions with exchange rate flexibility, the domestic price level will adjust to ensure that the real stock of liquidity will be such as to shift the AA curve to where it passes through the intersection of $\tilde{r}\tilde{r}$ and the vertical Y_f line. And the nominal exchange rate will adjust, driving the real exchange rate to the point where the GG curve passes through this same intersection. With full-employment and a domestically imposed fixed exchange rate, the domestic price level will be bid up or down adjusting the real exchange rate to shift the GG curve to pass through the intersection of $\tilde{r}\tilde{r}$ and the vertical Y_f line. Then, to maintain the fixed exchange rate parity, the authorities will be forced to adjust the stock of liquidity until the AA curve passes through that same intersection.

The key implication of the above is the fact that the small country's authorities have the option of controlling either the stock of liquidity or the nominal exchange rate – monetary policy is impotent when the exchange rate is fixed. And any effects of fiscal policy or other real shocks under a flexible exchange will be offset by movements of the nominal and real exchange rates required to ensure that the GG curve pass through the intersection of the $\tilde{r}\tilde{r}$ line and the AA curve determined by monetary policy. This is the well-known Fleming-Mundell result.[10]

The effect on the small open economy of shocks in the rest of the world can be seen from the rise in the real interest rate to $\hat{r}_1\hat{r}_1$ in Fig. 4.6 which, one could suppose for the sake of argument, resulted from tight rest-of-world monetary policy. Under a fixed exchange rate, domestic income falls to Y_1 and the domestic authorities are required to reduce the stock of liquidity until the AA curve has shifted sufficiently to the left to cross the GG curve at that income level. Under a flexible exchange rate, domestic income will rise to Y_2, moving in the opposite direction to rest-of-world income, with the domestic nominal and real exchange rates devaluating to shift GG to the right to cross the AA curve at that income level. The rise in the interest rate reduces the quantity of domestic real liquidity demanded by increasing its cost. Domestic residents attempt to dispose of their excess liquidity by purchasing assets abroad. The resulting incipient balance of payments deficit is corrected by a devaluation of the domestic currency which shifts world demand onto domestic goods increasing output and income until the demand for liquidity has returned to equality with the existing unchanged supply. To maintain the domestic economy at full-employment in the face of the rise in the world interest rate, the domestic authorities have to reduce the stock of liquidity just sufficiently to shift the AA curve to the left to pass through point e. This will limit the devaluation to keep the GG curve from shifting to the right beyond the point at which it too passes through point e.

[10] See Fleming [39] and Mundell [79].

4.3 World Equilibrium With Two Big Countries

In the case where the world consists of two large countries, domestic and foreign, the world GG curve will be the horizontal sum of the GG curves of the two countries which, based on equation (4.9), are

$$\Delta Y = G(r, \Phi_d, L) + F(\Delta Q, \Delta\tilde{Y}, \Phi_b) \tag{4.11}$$
$$\Delta\tilde{Y} = \tilde{G}(\tilde{r}, \tilde{\Phi}_d, \tilde{L}) + \tilde{F}(\Delta Q, \Delta Y, \Phi_b) \tag{4.12}$$

where the shock Φ_w has been broken down into separate components, one resulting directly from a change in the deviation of rest-of-world income from its full-employment level and the other consisting of joint international shocks affecting the domestic relative to the foreign economy. The latter is denoted by Φ_b which affects the two economies in opposite directions. The deviation of world income from its full-employment level is the sum of the domestic and foreign deviations, $\Delta Y + \Delta\tilde{Y}$.

The world AA curve is the horizontal sum of the two individual countries' AA curves, which can be conveniently expressed in nominal demand-for-liquidity form

$$m\,H = P\,L \;=\; P\,L(r, \Delta Y, \Phi_m) \tag{4.13}$$
$$\tilde{m}\,\tilde{H} = \tilde{P}\,\tilde{L} \;=\; \tilde{P}\,\tilde{L}(\tilde{r}, \Delta\tilde{Y}, \tilde{\Phi}_m) \tag{4.14}$$

where H and $\tilde{H}$ are the domestic and foreign nominal stocks of base money and m and $\tilde{m}$ are the respective liquidity multipliers – the ratios of the stocks of liquidity to the respective stocks of base money. World asset equilibrium is determined by these two equations plus equation (4.4) which is reproduced here for convenience.

$$r = \tilde{r} + \rho - E_Q \tag{4.4}$$

The five equations (4.11), (4.12), (4.13), (4.14) and (4.4) solve for the five variables ΔY, $\Delta\tilde{Y}$, r, $\tilde{r}$ and ΔQ when the exchange rate is flexible. If one of the countries fixes the exchange rate, that country's stock of base money becomes endogenous and ΔQ becomes exogenous. In this latter case, with the domestic exchange rate being fixed, the domestic stock of base money can be divided into two source components – the component that has resulted from the accumulation of foreign exchange reserves by the domestic authorities, denoted by R, and the component that was created by the purchase of domestic securities from either the private sector or from a branch of government, denoted by D.[11]

$$H = R + D \tag{4.15}$$

Substitution of this expression into equation (4.13) yields

$$R = \frac{1}{m} P\,L(r, \Delta Y, \Phi_m) - D \tag{4.16}$$

Differentiation of this equation with respect to time yields the balance of payments condition

$$\frac{dR}{dt} = \frac{1}{m} \frac{d[P\,L(r, \Delta Y, \Phi_m)]}{dt} - \frac{dD}{dt} \tag{4.17}$$

which holds regardless of the size of the domestic economy in relation to the rest of the world. This equation reiterates the proposition that by fixing its exchange rate a country loses control over its money supply. Any stock of foreign exchange reserves desired can be obtained costlessly, in terms of effects on output and the price level, by simply adjusting the domestic source component of the money supply D. The optimal stock, or inventory, of reserves is the one that minimizes the day-to-day costs of maintaining the fixed exchange rate, given that changing D to produce a given level of R is more costly than buying and selling foreign exchange reserves directly while, at the same time, foreign exchange reserves are likely to yield a minimal interest-rate return.

In this fixed exchange rate case, the liquidity demand function of the country whose currency is being fixed to – conventionally referred to as the key-currency country – must also be modified to the extent that some of its currency is being taken out of circulation as reserves held by the authorities of the country that is fixing the exchange rate. The key currency country's nominal stock of base money now becomes

$$\tilde{H} - \varrho R$$

where $\tilde{H}$ is the quantity of base money created by the country's authorities and ϱ is the fraction of the other country's stock of foreign exchange reserves held in cash or other liquid form. Equation (4.14) must be rewritten as

---

[11] When the central bank purchases securities from another branch of government, which spends the funds so obtained, the government is financing its activities strictly by printing money. When it borrows from the private sector, it is financing its activities by issuing money in return for a reduction in the public debt.

$$\tilde{m}\,\tilde{H} - \varrho R = \tilde{P}\,\tilde{L}(\tilde{r}, \tilde{\Delta Y}, \tilde{\Phi}_m) \tag{4.18}$$

which allows for the possibility that the country fixing the exchange rate may have some effect on the key-currency country's money supply and thereby on world output, employment and prices. This effect is not likely to be of significant magnitude unless the key-currency country is very small in relation to the rest of the world since countries hold most of their foreign exchange reserves in treasury bills and other short-term securities.

It is easily seen that in the fixed exchange rate case, the key-currency country runs world monetary policy. When ϱ approaches zero, the four equations (4.4),(4.11), (4.12) and (4.18) determine the four variables ΔY, $\Delta\tilde{Y}$, r and $\tilde{r}$, with equation (4.16) determining R for any choice of D by the authorities of the country fixing the exchange rate. That country's real stock of liquidity and hence base money is determined endogenously – its authorities only get to choose the the division of that base money stock between its domestic and foreign source components. This result holds regardless of the size of the key currency country, as long as ϱ is sufficiently small, and regardless of whether the rest of the world is a single country as postulated here or an aggregate of small peripheral countries that fix their currencies to that of the key-currency country. Indeed, nothing changes if there are two or more key-currency countries, each surrounded by its own group of peripheral countries, with flexible exchange rates between the key currencies. Each key-currency country runs the monetary policies of itself and the peripheral countries whose currencies are pegged to its currency. Joint determination of monetary policy could only result in the case of a tiny key-currency country surrounded by large peripheral countries whose authorities hold substantial foreign exchange reserves in the key-currency and whose foreign exchange reserve adjustments therefore affect the stock of liquidity in the key-currency country and its associated peripheral countries.

Under conditions of price flexibility and full employment, a country loses control over its price level by fixing its exchange rate. This can be most easily seen from the definition of the real exchange rate

$$Q_f = \frac{\bar{\Pi} P}{\tilde{P}} \tag{4.19}$$

where the real exchange rate is replaced by its full-employment level and the nominal exchange rate is fixed at $\bar{\Pi}$. The domestic price level will move up an down through time in proportion to changes in $\tilde{P}$, which is determined in the key-currency country, and in proportion to movements of the full-employment-equilibrium real exchange rate that arise as the world economy grows.

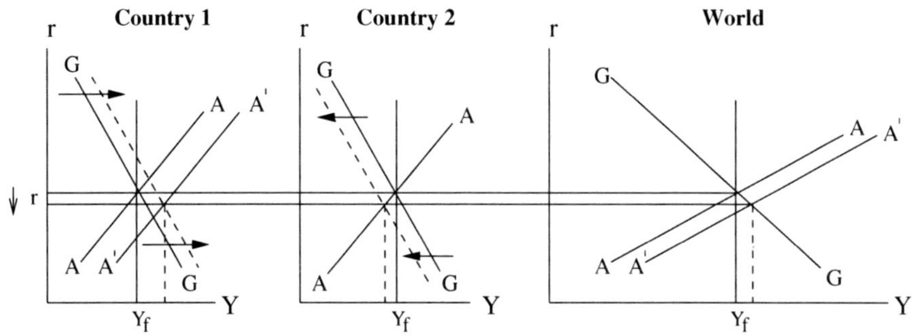

Fig. 4.7. World response to a monetary shock in country 1 with two countries of similar size and with a flexible exchange rate

These principles can be illustrated with reference to Figures 4.7 and 4.8 which portray a world consisting of two countries of roughly equal size. The horizontal distance of each curve from the vertical axis in the right-most panels, representing the entire world, is the sum of the corresponding distances for the panels representing the respective countries. To visualize why this is the case, note first that the sum of the two countries' full-employment incomes must equal the world full-employment income. Then start with a given full-employment world real interest rate and imagine that interest rate increasing and decreasing relative to its full-employment position. World income will always be the sum of the two countries' incomes. Now imagine that the stock of liquidity in each country is consistent with full-employment at the world full-employment interest rate. The world income consistent with that level of world liquidity will be the sum of the two countries' full-employment incomes. And as the world interest rate varies around its full-employment level, the level of world income consistent with asset equilibrium will be the sum of the incomes consistent with asset equilibrium in the two countries.

Suppose that there is a positive monetary shock in Country 1 that shifts its AA curve to the right to $A'A'$ in the two figures. This will cause the world AA curve to shift to the right by the same amount, as indicated by $A'A'$ in the third panel on the right in Fig. 4.7. Country 1 residents try to purchase real capital assets with their excess holdings of the monetary asset. When the exchange rate is flexible, the resulting excess supply of Country 1's currency in the foreign exchange market will cause it to devalue, shifting world demand to domestic output from the output of Country 2. Country 1's GG curve shifts to the right and Country 2's GG curve shifts to the left. In the short run, income rises in Country 1 at the expense of income in Country 2. At the same time, since Country 1 is large its excess supply of liquidity represents significant excess supply of liquidity in the world as a whole with the result that the world real interest rate falls. In the short-run, therefore, Country 1 gains income both as a result of the fall in the world interest rate and as a result of the shift of world demand to its output from that of Country 2 caused by the decline in the real exchange rate as the nominal exchange rate falls with price levels fixed in the two countries. Expansionary monetary policy in one country causes its income to increase and the income of the other country to fall – the two countries' incomes move in opposite directions. In the long-run, assuming complete price level flexibility, Country 1's price level will rise, returning its AA curve and the world AA curve to their original levels. Real incomes in both countries will return to their full-employment levels. Country 1's nominal exchange rate with respect to Country 2 will ultimately remain sufficiently devalued to offset the rise in its price level with the real exchange rate returning to its initial level. Country 2's price level will remain unchanged.

Clearly, the magnitude of the fall in the world interest rate as a result of a positive monetary shock in Country 1 will be bigger the larger is Country 1 in relation to the rest of the world.[12]

Now suppose that, in the face of the above monetary shock, Country 2 fixes its nominal exchange rate with respect to Country 1. The excess supply of liquidity in Country 1, and the corresponding excess demand for real assets by the residents of Country 2 induced by a decline in the world interest rate, now leads to a surplus in Country 2's

---

[12] This can be seen by adding the two equations (4.13) and (4.14) to obtain

$$H_w = m\,H + \tilde{m}\,\tilde{H} \;=\; P\,L(r, \Delta Y, \Phi_m) + \tilde{P}\,\tilde{L}(\tilde{r}, \Delta\tilde{Y}, \tilde{\Phi}_m)$$

which can be differentiated totally, letting $r = \tilde{r}$ and holding the income levels constant, with the result translated into relative changes and manipulated to yield

$$dr = (s/[s\,\eta + (1-s)\,\tilde{\eta}])\,(dH/H \;-\; d\Phi_m/\Phi_m)$$
$$+\,((1-s)/[s\,\eta + (1-s)\,\tilde{\eta}])\,(d\tilde{H}/\tilde{H} \;-\; d\tilde{\Phi}_m/\tilde{\Phi}_m)$$

where η and $\tilde{\eta}$ are the two countries' negative interest semi-elasticities of demand for liquidity and s is the share of Country 1 in the world real stock of liquidity. It is obvious that as s becomes smaller the effect of Country 1 money shocks on the world interest rate also gets smaller.

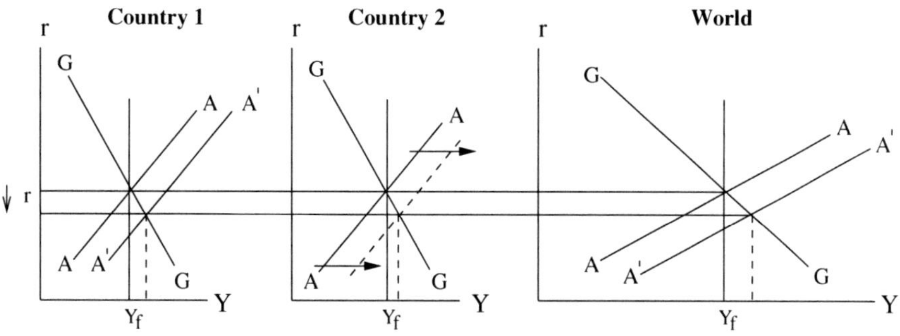

Fig. 4.8. World response to monetary shock in country 1 with two countries of similar size where country 2 fixes the exchange rate

balance of payments which its authorities have to finance by accumulating foreign assets representing foreign exchange reserves. Where the two countries are identical, the ultimate result is an increase in the supply of the monetary asset in Country 2 in proportion to the increased supply of the monetary asset in Country 1. Country 2's government then owns additional reserves of foreign-employed capital equal in value to the increase in the quantity of the domestic monetary asset, and Country 2 residents' private holdings of domestically-employed capital, some of which they sold to their government in return for increased money holdings, are less by the same amount. The residents of Country 2 are not worse off, of course, because the future returns from the government held foreign-employed capital will eventually accrue to them. The conclusion is that any increase in the excess supply of liquidity in Country 1 must necessarily be matched by an increase in the supply of liquidity in Country 2 of equal proportion – otherwise, Country 2's nominal exchange rate with respect to Country 1 would appreciate. Country 2's AA curve thus shifts to the right by the same amount as Country 1's in Fig. 4.8, with the world AA curve shifting to the right by the sum of these two amounts. The world real interest rate falls and income rises in both countries in the short-run. In the long run when prices are flexible, they rise in the same proportion in both countries with the nominal and real exchange rates remaining unchanged.

It is clear that, when the Country 2's authorities fix the exchange rate, Country 1's authorities run world monetary policy. And Country 2's authorities, to maintain the nominal exchange rate fixed, must continually supply whatever stock of liquidity its residents demand. Moreover, the effects on the world real interest rate and the world price level of monetary shocks in Country 1 are completely independent of the size of Country 1 in relation to the rest of the world. All the above conclusions also hold when Country 2 is an aggregate of small countries rather than a single country.

As noted earlier, this conclusion that even a small key-currency country runs world monetary policy depends critically on the assumption that the peripheral countries hold their foreign exchange reserves in ownership claims to capital employed in the key-currency country and not in key-currency-country currency or bank deposits. Otherwise, a large peripheral country could change the supply of liquidity in the key-currency country, and thereby shift that country's *AA* curve, by moving foreign exchange reserves between claims on real capital and money holdings. Peripheral-country holdings of the key-currency country's monetary asset will not be part of the latter country's money supply because they cannot be used by its residents for making transactions.

It turns out that one country (say Country 1) can be, in essence, a key-currency country and thereby run world monetary policy even under a system of flexible exchange rates if the other countries' authorities routinely adjust their home money supplies to maintain their exchange rates with respect to the key-currency country more or less constant, even though no official exchange rate parities have been declared.

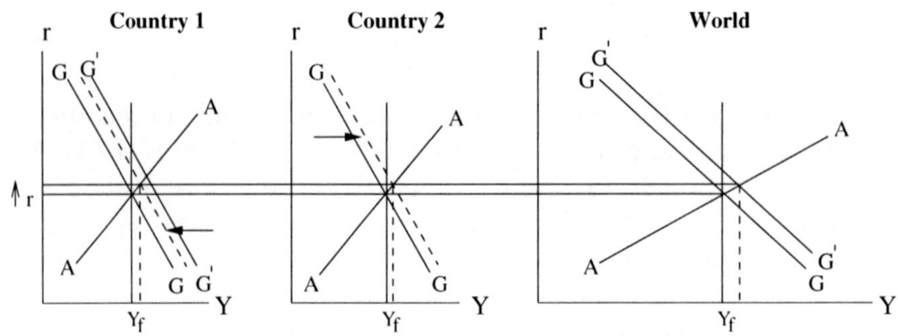

Fig. 4.9. World response to real shock in country 1 with two countries of similar size with a flexible exchange rate

The effects of a real shock in Country 1 that shifts its *GG* curve to the right, leaving the full-employment level of output unchanged can be seen with respect to Figures 4.9 and 4.10. A positive real shock in Country 1 shifts its *GG* curve and the world *GG* curve to the right by the same amount. The effects on the two countries when the exchange rate is flexible are shown in Fig. 4.9. The immediate effect is to create an excess demand for liquidity in Country 1 and an excess supply of liquidity in Country 2, causing former country's residents to try to sell non-monetary assets to the residents of the latter country. The result is an appreciation of Country 1's nominal and real exchange rates which moderates the rightward shift of its GG curve and shifts the GG curve of Country 2 to the right. Income and employment increase in both countries in the short-run. Unlike monetary shocks, real shocks in one country cause income to move in both countries in the same direction when the exchange rate is flexible. In the long-run, the world real interest rate will rise to the intersection of $G'G'$ with the vertical world full-employment income line in the right-most panel with both countries' price levels rising in about the same proportion. Country 1's real exchange rate will end up higher than initially, as a consequence of an appreciation of its equilibrium nominal exchange rate.

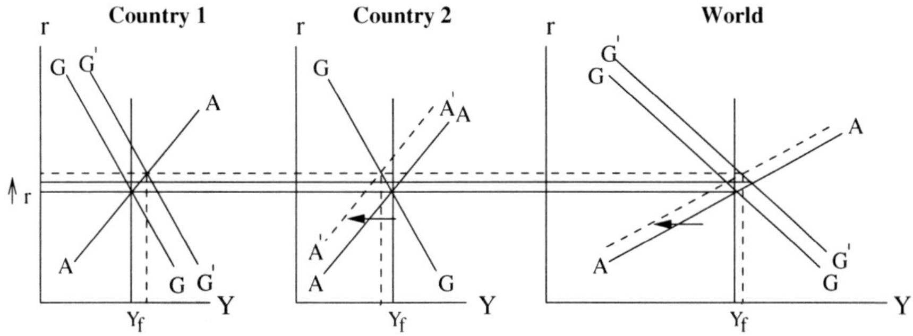

Fig. 4.10. World response to real shock in country 1 with two countries of similar size where country 2 fixes the exchange rate

The results when Country 2's authorities fix its exchange rate are shown in Fig. 4.10. Since a devaluation of that country's currency cannot be allowed to happen its authorities are forced to contract its stock of liquidity, shifting its AA curve to the left. This reduces the world money supply, further raising the world real interest rate. In fact, Country 2's stock of liquidity has to fall until the world interest rate has risen to pass through the intersection of Country 1's post-shock GG curve, $G'G'$, and its original AA curve. At that point, Country 2's income and employment will have fallen in the face of a rise in income and employment in Country 1. Under fixed exchange rates, a real shock in the key-currency country affects foreign output and employment in the opposite direction to domestic output and employment – the opposite to what happens in the case of a key-currency monetary shock. In the long run with price-level flexibility, the world real interest rate and real exchange rate will be the same as occurred when the exchange rate was flexible, with the price level in Country 1 rising relative to that in Country 2 by an amount sufficient to produce the required increase in the former country's real exchange rate. The actual direction of movement of Country 2's price level cannot be determined graphically because its real exchange rate moves in the opposite direction to the other country's price level – detailed information about the underlying functions in the model is required.

Finally, consider the effects of the above real shock when Country 1, where the shock initiates, fixes the exchange rate. As can be seen from Fig. 4.11, nothing happens in Country 2 in the short-run. Given fixed price levels in the two countries and a commitment of the country experiencing the shock to fix the exchange rate, the authorities of the latter country are forced to create whatever stock of liquidity is required to maintain an unchanged level of Q. And with fixed price levels and no change in the real exchange rate, nothing can happen to output and employment in Country 2. In the long-run with price level flexibility, the result will be identical to that in the case where Country 2 fixed the exchange rate. All movements of real variables are the same, as will be the movements in the two countries' price levels – it matters not which country fixed the exchange rate. Again, the direction of movement of Country 2's price level will be impossible to determine without knowledge of the underlying functions.

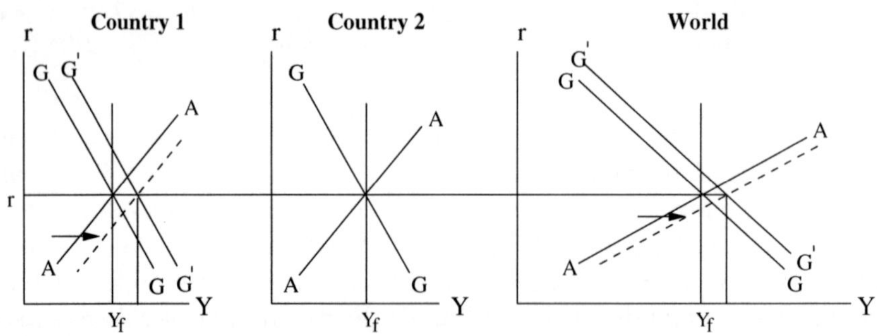

Fig. 4.11. World response to real shock in country 1 with two countries of similar size where country 1 fixes the exchange rate

The above analysis of the effects of real shocks deals with the simplest possible shock in which neither country's full-employment income level is affected and there is no direct pass-through of the shock from the initiating country to the other country via shifts in the real trade balance or real capital accumulation. In those more general cases the effects of shocks will be even more difficult to determine in a world where the initiating country is large than it was in the closed economy case examined earlier. This re-enforces the earlier conclusion that little can be said about the nature and effects of real shocks within the broad framework developed here – a careful and rigorous analysis of each individual shock is required.

4.4 Equilibrium in Common Currency Areas

The classic common currency area is, of course, the individual country with many states or provinces. And the most recent multi-country common currency area is the European Union. But the focus of analysis of common currency situations has been the classical gold standard.

All that needs to be added to the material presented above is a recognition of the nature of the process of adjustment to shocks that occur in one country or part of a region with a common currency. In common currency areas like Canada and the United States, a shock to the demand for money in one region will immediately result in an exchange of monetary and non-monetary assets with the rest of the country – this will occur with minimal frictions. Income and employment in all parts of the country will be simultaneously affected, and in the long run the price level will rise in proportion in all regions. Real shocks in a segment of the country will have much more complicated effects and, as was the case in previous sections, little can be said without a careful analysis of each individual shock.

Historical analysis of monetary shocks under gold, or commodity, standards has focused on the well-known price-specie-flow mechanism, the origins of which go back at least to the work of David Hume in 1752 [56].[13] According to this theory, an increase in the stock of gold in one country will cause prices to be bid up in that country, leading to a reduction of exports and an increase in imports. The associated balance of payments deficit leads to an outflow of gold which lowers the domestic price level and increases the price level abroad until all countries' prices are higher in proportion to the increase in the world stock of gold. While this analysis is correct when there is no international capital mobility, it breaks down when assets can be bought and sold abroad. Then, when the residents of a country are confronted with excess gold holdings, they

[13] For a more modern classical presentation, see Viner [106].

simply purchase non-monetary assets from abroad with the excess gold. The gold spreads evenly throughout the gold standard area and price levels rise simultaneously everywhere. The empirical validity of this interpretation has been established with reference to Canada by the present author in collaboration with Trevor Dick [20] [21] [23] and for Australia in collaboration with Trevor Dick and David Pope [22]. It has also been shown to hold for the United States in the Jacksonian Period in in the early 19th century in a working paper with Trevor Dick [24]. The gold standard evidence is thus fully consistent with the analytical framework developed here. Short-run balance of payments equilibrium can be expressed, as in any fixed exchange rate system, by a version of equation (4.17) – in this case

$$\frac{dG}{dt} = \frac{1}{m} \frac{d[P\,L(\tilde{r}, \Delta Y, \Phi_m)]}{dt} \tag{4.20}$$

where G is the domestic stock of gold. An increase in the world gold stock will cause a fall in the world real interest rate in the short-run and thereby lead to a corresponding increase in the equilibrium domestic stock. The parameter m will increase in response to any expansion of liquid assets by the domestic authorities – a practice which, if carried far enough, will eventually undermine the gold standard. It will be shown below that under any fixed exchange rate system, including a gold standard, there is no direct causal relationship between the balance of trade and the balance of payments surplus or deficit.

4.5 More on the Determination of Risk Premiums

The above discussion has sidestepped important issues regarding the pricing of risk, an issue that will subsequently be important. The basics can now be exposited – for a rigorous treatment the reader is directed to Appendix D. Risk is the variance of one's portfolio return, and the contribution of any asset to that risk is its contribution to the variance of the return to the portfolio. The only variance of an asset's return that matters is the variance that cannot be diversified away by holding the asset in conjunction with other assets – this is called systematic or non-diversifiable risk. A large group of assets whose returns are uncorrelated will have a nearly constant average return. A risk-free asset is an asset or aggregate of assets whose return is constant – this constant return equals the risk-free interest rate.

The risk premium on each risky asset is inversely related to the covariance of the return on that asset with the marginal utility of consumption and, hence, positively related to the covariance of the return on the asset with the level of consumption. When consumption is low and the marginal utility of consumption is therefore high, the gain from a positive increment to income and consumption is larger than would be the case when consumption is high and the marginal utility of consumption is low. Hence, a variable asset return that is highly inversely correlated with the marginal utility of consumption – that is, tends to be high when the marginal utility of consumption is low and low when the marginal utility of consumption is high – will be less valuable than one that is less inversely correlated, or positively correlated, with the marginal utility of consumption. The positive shock to income will tend to occur when consumption is already high and the negative shock will tend to occur when consumption is already low. As a result, that asset will have to yield a higher expected return to get people to hold it – it will have a higher risk premium. A negative risk premium will require that the positive shocks to the asset return occur more frequently when consumption is low and the marginal utility of consumption is high and negative shocks occur more frequently when consumption is high and the marginal utility of consumption is low – in this case investors will be willing to hold the asset at an expected return lower than the risk-free rate of interest.

Imagine now a composite asset whose return is perfectly positively correlated with consumption and hence perfectly negatively correlated with the marginal utility of consumption. This asset can be thought of as a market portfolio consisting of every asset in the economy weighted in proportion to its share of the country's wealth – its return is the return to capital in the economy as a whole. The i-th asset will be more risky than the market portfolio when its return is positively correlated with the return to the market portfolio and its covariance with the return to the market portfolio exceeds the variance of the return to that portfolio – that is, when its return varies directly with and more widely than the return to capital in the economy as a whole. Wealth owners will require an expected return above the expected return on the market portfolio to make it worth their while to hold this asset and will thereby bid the price of the asset down appropriately relative to its flow of earnings. Assets whose returns are positively correlated with the return to the market portfolio but fluctuate less than it will be less risky than the market portfolio. Asset holders will be willing to hold these assets at an expected return below the expected return on the market portfolio, bidding their prices up relative to their flows of earnings. If the variations in the return to an asset are uncorrelated with variations in the return to the market portfolio no risk premium will be required to get people to hold the asset – its effect on the variance of the overall portfolio can be completely diversified away. Finally, if the return to an asset covaries negatively with the return to capital in the economy as a whole it provides a hedge against the risk of the market portfolio and wealthowners will be willing to hold it at an expected rate of return lower than the riskless rate.

The above analysis suggests that the risk premium on domestic assets in world markets should depend on how the earnings on those assets covary with the return to capital in the world economy, and hence, how much of the variance in those earnings that world asset holders can diversify away. The problem with applying this principle, of course, is the fact that many assets that individuals hold – especially human capital – may not be tradeable. And the relevant market portfolio is therefore likely to be different for each individual, making the market portfolio relevant for the pricing of any particular asset difficult to determine.[14] And comparisons of the covariance of the returns to particular assets with the marginal utility of consumption require that allowance be made for the fact that variations in consumption may reflect changes in savings rather than changes in the income flow from the capital stock.

[14] Imagine, for example, an asset whose return is highly negatively correlated with the return on human capital and less highly negatively correlated with the return on marketable capital assets.

5

Some Important Implications

A number of issues that were previously modeled correctly but remained in the background must now be addressed. A careful examination of these reveals implications of the above theoretical framework that are important for understanding contemporary policy issues. The first deals with the relationship between the net international capital flow, the real exchange rate and current account adjustment. A second notes the absence of any causal relationship between changes in the current account and changes in any balance of payments surplus or deficit under a fixed exchange rate. The third reexamines contemporary views on the effects of countries' monetary policy on domestic interest rates.

5.1 The Real Exchange Rate and the Current and Capital Accounts

It was noted that if consumption in the small open economy is growing faster in the steady state than the domestically employed capital stock, domestic residents will be continually investing some fraction of domestic savings in capital employed in the rest of the world, and continually earning a fraction domestic income from that foreign-employed capital. Domestic income is equal to domestic output plus net earnings from domestically owned capital employed abroad minus earnings from domestically employed capital owned by foreigners. That is,

$$\hat{Y}_t = Y_t + DSB_t \tag{5.1}$$

where $\hat{Y}_t$ and Y_t are respectively GNP and GDP, as conventionally defined, and DSB_t is the debt service balance, defined as earnings from domestically owned foreign capital minus earnings from foreign owned

J.E. Floyd, *Interest Rates, Exchange Rates and World Monetary Policy*,
DOI 10.1007/978-3-642-10280-6_5, © Springer-Verlag Berlin Heidelberg 2010

domestic capital. Along the steady-state growth path, consumption and income will be growing at the same constant rate and domestic output and the domestically employed capital stock will also be growing at the same constant rate, although their growth rates may differ from the growth rate of consumption and income in an open economy. If income is growing faster than output in the steady-state, the difference between them – that is, the debt service balance – must be growing constantly through time. This in turn implies that in every period a portion of domestic savings must be flowing to investment in foreign employed capital – that is, domestic savings must exceed domestic investment. From the fact that domestic output, net of depreciation, is the sum of domestic consumption, domestic net investment, and net sales of output to foreigners,

$$Y_t = C_t + I_t + B_{Tt}, \tag{5.2}$$

where B_{Tt} is the balance of trade, equation (5.1) can be expressed[1]

$$\hat{Y}_t = C_t + I_t + B_{Tt} + DSB_t. \tag{5.3}$$

Subtraction of $C_t + I_t$ from both sides of this equation yields

$$\hat{Y}_t - C_t - I_t = B_{Tt} + DSB_t \tag{5.4}$$

or

$$NCO = S_t - I_t = B_{Tt} + DSB_t = CAB \tag{5.5}$$

where $S_t = \hat{Y}_t - C_t$ is savings, NCO is the net capital outflow and CAB is the current account balance. All these magnitudes are measured in real terms.

This relationship between domestic saving and investment, the real exchange rate and the current account balance in the long run can be analyzed with reference to Fig. 5.1. The real exchange rate is on the vertical axis and the real current account balance is on the horizontal

[1] All these magnitudes include transactions on both private and public account with the result that taxes and government expenditures do not appear separately as in traditional Keynesian models. Also, output could be equivalently written as

$$Y_t = C'_t + I'_t + E'_t$$

where C'_t, I'_t and E'_t are the outputs of consumption, net investment and exported goods. To obtain (5.2) one simply adds and subtracts imports and defines C_t and I_t and B_{Tt} as consumption, net investment and net exports of both domestic and imported output.

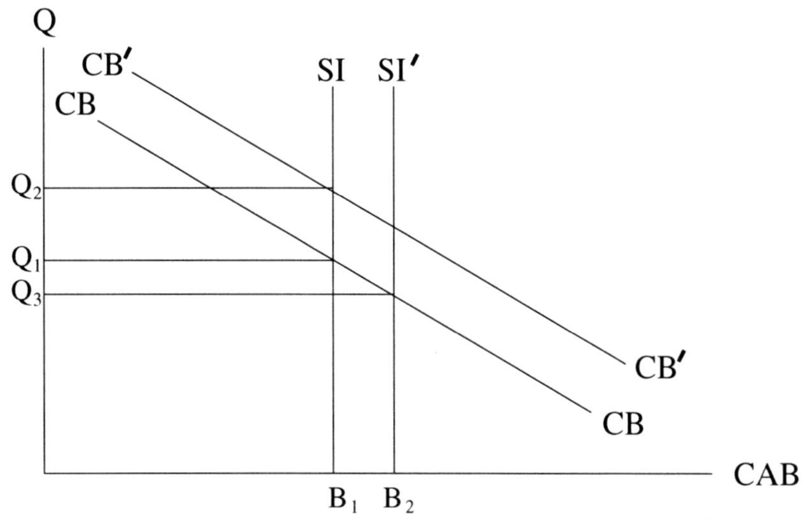

Fig. 5.1. The real exchange rate and current account balance in a small open economy in the long run.

one. The vertical SI line imposes the condition that real exchange rate changes do not lead directly to changes in real savings and investment – they simply involve changes in the relative price of domestic output in terms of foreign output. Such real exchange rate changes reflect changes in the price of the non-traded component of domestic output relative to the price of the non-traded component of foreign output, where prices are measured in one country's currency. In addition, while traded components of output will have the same prices all over the world, the relative prices of different traded components can change through time as the world economy grows, and the particular traded components may not all be produced in all countries. These relative prices will also be reflected in real exchange rate changes, in which case terms of trade changes and real exchange rate changes may be positively related.

One therefore cannot rule out the possibility that a decline in the real exchange rate may lead to a reduction in domestic real income via an effect on the terms of trade and thereby affect savings. In the long-run, this would appear as a slight change in the steady-state growth rate of income and consumption. At the same time, however, this reduction in the terms of trade would reduce slightly the profitability of investment in the domestic economy, since output of traded components is less valuable than before. This would be reflected in a slight decline in the productivity of the aggregate domestic capital stock and hence a slight reduction in its growth rate. The effect of these forces on the slope of SI would be ambiguous in that the savings and investment will be affected in the same direction. The assumption that the SI line is vertical in the long-run steady state would therefore seem to be reasonable as a rough approximation.

The negatively sloped CB curve states simply that a fall in the real exchange rate will lead to an increase in net purchases of consumption and investment goods abroad. The real exchange rate will adjust to bring the equilibrium current account balance into line with the net capital flow. In the long run, the current account balance will thus be determined primarily by domestic residents' choices regarding real savings and investment – that is, it represents net intertemporal lending.[2]

Contrary to what often is claimed in the popular press, the imposition of a tariff on imports or a subsidy on exports that has no impact on saving and investment will not increase the current account balance in the long-run – the real exchange rate will simply adjust to maintain its equality with the unchanged real net capital flow. It is also the case that an increase in rest-of-world demand for a country's exports will not lead to an increase in the current account balance unless domestic savings and investment are also affected. As indicated by the rightward shift of the CB curve to CB', the effect will be a rise in the real exchange rate with no change in the current account balance.

Another common fallacy is the argument that an observed increase in, or so-called 'improvement' of, the current account balance implies that the country is better off because it now has a better market for its goods abroad. As can be seen in Fig. 5.1, an increase in the current account surplus results from a rightward shift of the SI line. Assuming that wealth, and therefore the steady-state growth path of income and consumption, has not changed, domestic investment must have declined relative to domestic saving—that is, the domestic economy has become a poorer place in which to invest. Indeed, unless the demand for the country's exports increases along with the decline in domestic investment, the 'improvement' of the current account balance will have resulted from the fall in the real exchange rate required to create an increase in the current account surplus equal to the increase in the net capital outflow.

A tariff on imports or subsidy of exports will nevertheless have a positive effect on the current account balance in the short run when the

---

[2] For a rigorous presentation of this argument, see Chapter 1 of the book by Obstfeld and Rogoff [82].

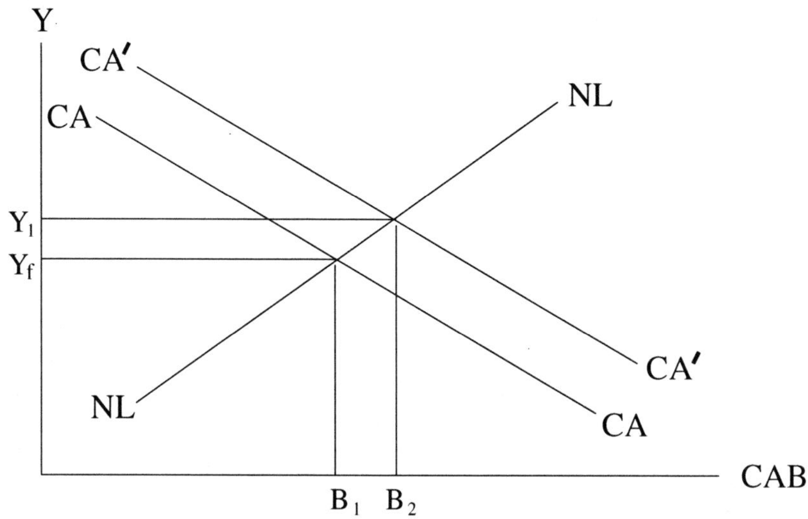

Fig. 5.2. The real exchange rate, real income and the current account balance in a small open economy in the short run.

utilization of the current human and physical capital stock can change. This can be seen from Fig. 5.2, where the current account balance is on the horizontal axis and the vertical axis now gives the level of income and employment. The positive slope of the *NL* curve indicates that as income temporarily rises relative to its full-employment level Y_f, saving increases because individuals will intertemporally smooth consumption. The desired net capital outflow thereby increases. The negative slope of the *CA* curve indicates that as income increases relative to its full-employment level, holding the real exchange rate constant, imports will increase relative to exports, reducing the current account balance. Given a constant real exchange rate, the levels of domestic employment, output and income must adjust to maintain equality between the current account balance and the net capital inflow. If the nominal exchange rate is flexible, both the real exchange rate and output and income can adjust simultaneously in the short-run, making the causal forces bringing about particular observed current account and real exchange rate adjustments difficult to determine.

5.2 Balance of Payments Disequilibria and the Current Account

The standard Fleming-Mundell result regarding the short-run effects of real and monetary shocks on output and income in a small open economy has been fully verified in the analysis of the previous sections and can be reviewed with reference to Fig. 5.3. When the nominal exchange rate is flexible, equilibrium output and income in the small open economy is established by monetary factors at the intersection of the AA curve and the rest-of-world determined interest rate line rZ. The real exchange rate will then adjust until the GG curve crosses rZ at that same intersection point. Unless they somehow affect asset equilibrium, real shocks will simply lead to equilibrium real exchange rate adjustments without affecting output and employment. When the nominal exchange rate is fixed, equilibrium output and income is established by real factors at the intersection of the GG curve and the rZ line. To the extent that the AA curve does not pass through that intersection there will be an excess demand or supply of liquidity resulting in attempts to reestablish portfolio equilibrium by buying or selling the monetary asset in return for claims on real capital. To maintain the fixed exchange rate, the authorities are forced to provide the stock of liquidity the public wishes to hold at the fixed interest rate and equilibrium level of output and income. The AA curve will thereby adjust until it passes through the GG-rZ intersection.

These adjustments of the AA curve under fixed exchange rates are directly related to the process by which balance of payments equilibrium is maintained. The stock of liquidity in the economy can be altered in two ways by the actions of the authorities – by purchasing or selling foreign exchange reserves in return for the domestic monetary asset, or by purchasing real capital from domestic residents in exchange for the monetary asset and holding ownership of that capital on public account. Simply printing nominal units of the monetary asset and handing them out would be equivalent to the latter alternative. The foreign exchange reserves are, of course, claims on foreign employed capital held on public account. This relationship between the domestic and foreign source components of the stock of base money was set out in equation (4.15) and the change in the stock of foreign exchange reserves between two points in time – that is, the balance of payments surplus – took the form

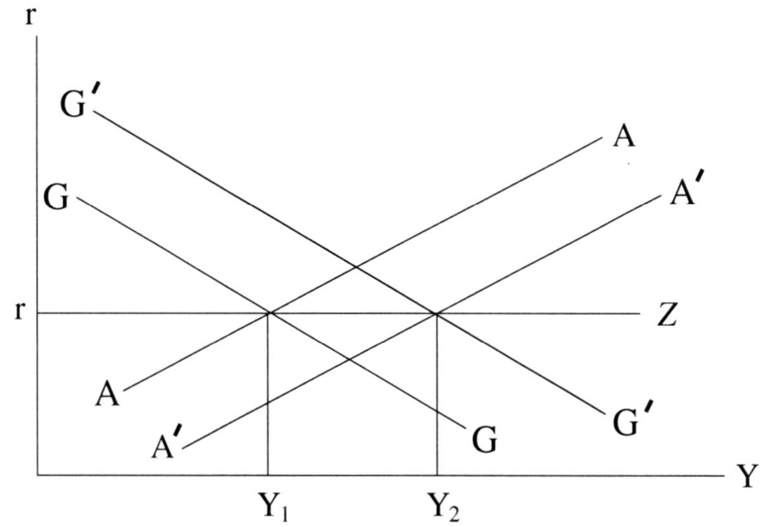

Fig. 5.3. Response of a small open economy to short-term monetary and real shocks.

$$R_t - R_{t-1} = \frac{1}{m}[P_t\, L(r_t, Y_t, \Phi_{mt}) - P_{t-1}\, L(r_{t-1}, Y_{t-1}, \Phi_{m(t-1)})] \\ - [D_t - D_{t-1}] \qquad (5.6)$$

where R_t is the stock of foreign exchange reserves and D_t is the quantity of base money that has been created without the purchase of foreign exchange reserves, m is the ratio of the stock of liquidity to the stock of base money and Y is the level of income which, in the analysis here, could change as a result of a change in the deviation of output from its full-employment level or a change in that full-employment level. Assuming that $r_t = r_{t-1}$ because of constancy of the risk premium and a zero expected rate of change in the real exchange rate, the shift in the GG curve in Fig. 5.3 is represented by $Y_t - Y_{t-1}$ and the remaining terms represent shifts in the AA curve. A change in Y will lead to a change in R in the same direction unless the authorities compensate with an equivalent change in D. A change in the demand for liquidity via a change in Φ_m will require the authorities to change D by an identical amount to maintain the AA curve in an initial equilibrium position if the stock of foreign exchange reserves is to be unaffected. And an exogenous increase in D by the authorities will result in an equivalent reduction in R with no change in the stock of liquidity –

the authorities have no monetary control once they fix the nominal exchange rate.

The important thing to notice here is that there is no relationship between the current account balance and the balance of payments. The current account balance is determined by the real forces outlined in Figures 5.1 and 5.2. Those same real forces establish the equilibrium levels of income and the real exchange rate in the short- and long-runs. A balance of payments disequilibrium is consistent with any level of the real current account balance and the associated level of real capital outflow – it arises simply because the authorities are expanding D at a slower or faster rate than the demand for liquidity is growing.

It is traditional to define balance of payments equilibrium as a situation where autonomous receipts from the sale of goods and capital abroad equal the autonomous payments for goods and capital abroad or, what is the same thing, a situation where net induced payments are zero. Induced receipts and payments are defined as transactions conducted by the authorities to maintain a pre-determined level of the nominal exchange rate, or to influence the level of the exchange rate under a floating rate system. In the above analysis, induced transactions are represented by changes in the level of the stock of foreign exchange reserves held by the authorities. While these induced transactions are strictly monetary, one can also think of induced transactions designed to alter the real and nominal exchange rates by subsidizing exports or taxing imports – as noted, however, unless these restrictions affect savings or investment differentially, they will have no effect on the current account balance.

The balance of payments surplus is traditionally defined as

$$R_t - R_{t-1} = CAB_t - ANCO_t \tag{5.7}$$

where CAB_t and $ANCO_t$ are, respectively, the current account balance and the autonomous net capital outflow. The actual observed level of the current account balance will be equal to the autonomous level unless the domestic authorities are imposing restrictions on trade for the purpose of affecting the balance of payments. As a matter of arithmetic then, the total capital outflow, NCO_t, must equal the autonomous net capital outflow plus the induced capital outflow which is simply the purchase of foreign exchange reserves by the authorities. That is,

$$NCO_t = ANCO_t + (R_t - R_{t-1}) = CAB_t \tag{5.8}$$

which implies that the balance of payments surplus must be equal to the difference between the total and autonomous net capital outflows,

$$R_t - R_{t-1} = NCO_t - ANCO_t. \tag{5.9}$$

Observed balance of payments disequilibria are exclusively asset phenomena. Because the authorities want to maintain a particular level of the exchange rate, they are forced to accumulate or decumulate foreign exchange reserves to make up any difference between the existing stock of non-monetary assets and the amount the private sector wishes to hold. Any difference between the existing stock of non-monetary assets and the desired stock – that is the excess supply of non-monetary assets – is always equal to the excess demand for the monetary asset. An increase in the current account balance, holding the autonomous net capital outflow constant, will be matched an increase in the balance of payments surplus because it represents an equivalent increase in the total net capital outflow – this relationship, however, is arithmetic rather than causal since a behind-the-scene change in the demand for money must also be occurring to induce the increase in reserves.

As noted in the earlier sections, whenever the nominal exchange rate is fixed, a balance of payment disequilibrium can always be corrected simply by changing the rate of growth of the supply of the monetary asset through manipulation of the variable D. No short-term changes in income and employment and other real variables, or in the level of prices in the long run, will result. And the size of the domestic stock of foreign exchange reserves is irrelevant as long as it is sufficient to cover normal day-to-day variations in the demand for liquidity – any surplus or deficiency of the level of the stock of reserves can be immediately corrected by an appropriate change in the level of D.

5.3 Monetary Policy and Interest Rates

The previously noted conclusion that monetary policy leads to a change in the domestic real interest rate only to the extent that the country makes up a sufficient fraction of the world economy for world interest rates to be affected is inconsistent with what one reads in the financial press and in reports from central banks – it is widely believed that central banks in all countries, large and small, conduct monetary policy by controlling domestic interest rates. This traditional view that monetary policy operates even in small open economies through its effects on interest rates is based on the notion that international capital flows are a function of, and not perfectly responsive to, domestic/foreign interest rate differentials. Under the conventional assumption of less-than-perfect international capital mobility, the attempt to purchase capital by domestic residents as a consequence of domestic monetary expansion causes the price of domestic assets to rise and the domestic interest rate to fall, making foreign assets more profitable to hold than domestic ones and leading to a net capital outflow. This fall in domestic relative to foreign interest rates, which will occur unless domestic and foreign assets are perfect substitutes in portfolios, stimulates domestic investment leading to a temporary increase in income and employment.

This tendency to treat international capital outflows as an increasing function of the foreign/domestic interest rate differential appeared in the gold standard literature as well as in conventional, path-breaking macroeconomic research up until the late 1960s and is still occasionally present in textbooks. Common sense strongly suggests that individuals, with unchanged attitudes toward and perception of risk, will shift some of their portfolios in the direction of assets on which interest rates have increased. Unfortunately, however, generalizing this conclusion to describe aggregate behaviour involves a fallacy of composition – the fact that it pays each individual, acting alone, to do something does not mean that it will pay all individuals together to do it. Should the interest rate happen to fall in one country, the attempt of residents of all countries to shift their part of their portfolios out of that country's assets will cause its asset prices to fall, and the interest rates on them to rise, until the existing stock is again willingly held. Equilibrium will hold when the relative interest rates on all assets reflect the willingness of asset holders in the aggregate to hold them – the interest rate on an asset can decrease only if the willingness of asset holders in the aggregate to hold that asset has increased. If new information about the return to an asset becomes simultaneously available to every asset holder, the interest rate on that asset will change without a single transaction taking place. In practice, of course, trades will always occur with those who are optimistic about the future return to an asset purchasing a quantity from those who are pessimistic. The situation with respect to the assets of individual countries is fully described by equation (4.4) which is here reproduced and re-numbered for convenience.

$$r = \tilde{r} + \rho - E_Q \tag{5.10}$$

For monetary expansion in a small country to reduce its domestic interest rate, at given exchange rate expectations, it must somehow reduce the risk premium world residents attach to domestic assets. The mere statement that domestic and foreign assets are imperfect substitutes in portfolios is, by itself, insufficient to permit one to postulate that the desired *flow* of capital between two countries at given levels of output, employment and technology will depend on domestic/foreign real interest rate differential. On the contrary, the levels of domestic and foreign output, employment and technology and the resulting valuation of domestic and foreign assets, will simultaneously determine both the interest rate differential and the underlying steady-state real net capital flow. The interest rate differential is a condition of stock, not flow, equilibrium – it arises as a result of world residents' willingness to hold the existing stocks of domestic and foreign assets and not as a result of the relative rates of change in those stocks through time.[3]

Is there any basis for concluding, based on conditions of stock equilibrium, that an expansionary monetary policy will cause the risk premium on domestic assets to fall? Under a flexible exchange rate system the answer is technically yes, because changes in flows cause the stocks to change, but the empirical magnitude of the effect would likely be of trivial magnitude. When domestic residents attempt to re-balance their portfolios in the face of a positive monetary shock by purchasing domestic and foreign assets from foreigners, the exchange rate must instantaneously adjust to prevent any net purchase from actually taking place. The resulting elimination of the excess supply of domestic currency on the foreign exchange market automatically removes the excess demand for assets. With time, of course, the associated fall in the real exchange rate will shift world demand onto domestic output, causing domestic income and employment to increase. World output will remain unchanged, however, as foreign output will fall by the same amount as domestic output increases. Since the domestic and foreign output changes are temporary, the corresponding changes in current domestic and foreign incomes will result in equal and offsetting changes in capital accumulation by domestic and foreign residents. Although the world capital stock, like world output, will be unaffected, domestic residents will seek to purchase a greater ratio of domestic to foreign assets than foreign residents will want to sell, given the well-known fact that asset holders tend to hold greater fractions of their wealth in home-country assets. Technically, this implies an excess demand for domestic assets with the result that domestic asset prices should rise relative to foreign asset prices. The shock to the demand for foreign assets will obviously be so small that foreign asset prices and interest

[3] The present author realized the problem with the then-conventional view in the late 1960s [41] [42] but nevertheless failed to get the conditions of flow in relation to stock equilibrium exactly correct. He thanks his colleague Allan Hynes for pointing out the required correction in the mid-1970s, ensuring correct presentations in subsequent work. See [43] for an earlier, and correct, presentation of some of the analysis here.

rates will be essentially unaffected. The question is whether the excess demand for domestic assets will have an observable downward effect on the domestic interest rate.

Suppose for the sake of argument that the increase in domestic income is 1 percent and that domestic residents hold 90 percent of the capital employed in the domestic economy, with rest-of-world residents holding the remaining 10 percent. Since all of the increase in domestic income will be used to purchase assets, this will create an increase in the demand for the domestic capital stock of 0.9 percent of domestic income. Assuming a real interest rate no higher than 5%, and that domestic income is therefore about 5% of the domestic capital stock, this will imply an increase in the demand for domestic capital of $0.05 \times .9 = .045$ of a percentage point. If the domestic economy is 1% of the world economy, this will require that domestic residents have to persuade rest-of-world residents to sell them an amount of domestic capital equal to $0.01 \times .045 = .00045$ percent of foreign residents' wealth. It is difficult to imagine how a shift of the mix of foreigners' wealth holdings of this magnitude could require a reduction in their evaluation of the risk of holding domestic assets by any observable amount.

Suppose, alternatively, that the domestic authorities are holding the exchange rate fixed. In this event, domestic residents will be successful in disposing of excess liquidity by purchasing assets from foreigners, with the authorities being required to supply the necessary foreign exchange in order to prevent a devaluation of the domestic currency. As equation (4.15) states, $H = R + D$, and any change in the domestic source component of base money will result in an equal and opposite change in the stock of reserves since the quantity of base money demanded and the stock of liquidity in the economy will be unchanged. This was shown formally in equation (5.6).

Constancy of the interest rate requires that the risk premium on domestic capital be unaffected by a change in foreign exchange reserves resulting from a change in D. When the authorities increase the stock of base money by purchasing assets from domestic residents, those asset holders simply replace their asset holdings by purchasing assets from foreigners. And the authorities, to prevent devaluation of the currency, have to reduce their foreign asset holdings by the same amount as private asset holdings have increased. If official foreign exchange reserves are held in foreign assets that are typically also held by private residents, there will be no change in the mix of assets held on combined private and public account by domestic asset holders, who will simply buy and sell particular assets in the world market to reproduce their original portfolios. If the initial increase in base money resulted from a retirement of government debt by the authorities, an equivalent quantity of future tax liabilities would also be eliminated with the result that the net wealth effect would be zero. To the extent that the authorities hold the country's foreign exchange reserves in non-interest-bearing foreign monetary assets, however, domestic wealth will increase because domestic residents as they re-balance their portfolios will be exchanging non-interest bearing assets held on public account for interest bearing assets held on private account. The question is whether this increase in wealth will reduce the risk premium on domestic assets. Technically, the answer must be yes because domestic residents will want to purchase a higher ratio of domestic to foreign assets than foreign residents will be willing to sell at existing asset prices. But the magnitude of such an effect would surely be trivial.

The means of the quarterly absolute changes in nominal base money as percentages of income for the past few decades for Canada, Japan, the United Kingdom, the United States, France and Germany are as follows:[4]

Canada	1974–2007	0.067
Japan	1974–2007	0.395
United Kingdom	1974–2005	0.291
United States	1974–2007	0.091
France	1974–1998	0.223
Germany	1974–1998	0.206

Taking 0.3 percentage points of real income as the magnitude of a typical base money shock and assuming that the real interest rate is no more than 5%, this base money shock in relation to domestic wealth will be no more than $.05 \times .3 = .015$ percentage points. If the domestic capital stock is, say, 1% of the rest-of-world capital stock, the required asset adjustment will be .00015 percent of rest-of-world wealth. It is difficult to imagine how an adjustment of this relative magnitude could result in a noticeable change in the risk premium on domestic assets in the world market.

It is also important to consider the situation where there are substantial though not binding government controls on international capital movements, as was the case in most countries prior to the early

[4] These estimates are calculated in the XLispStat batch file `pcmongdp.lsp` and written in the corresponding output file `pcmongdp.lou`. The same calculations are made in Gretl script file `pcmongdp.inp` with results written in the output file `pcmongdp.got`.

1970s, and is still true in many less-developed small countries. When the small country's residents attempt to re-balance their portfolios in response to a positive monetary shock, they will bid the prices of domestic assets up and interest rates on those assets down. This will create profit opportunities for individuals who can work around the rules. One option is, of course, to bribe public officials where possible. A legal alternative is for domestic firms who have been extending trade credit on exports to foreigners to increase that credit by allowing longer payment periods, financing themselves by selling assets to domestic residents. This results in foreign firms being able to reduce their borrowings from foreign residents by purchasing foreign assets. The net effect is to shift world asset holdings from foreign to domestic residents. Similarly, domestic firms importing goods and services from abroad can make their payments earlier than required, financing themselves by selling assets to domestic residents, with the corresponding foreign firms purchasing assets from residents of their countries with the working balances no longer required. Researchers who have studied the British balance of payments during the Bretton-Woods period have noted that even comprehensive foreign exchange controls were unable to prevent large international capital movements from occurring through this avenue.[5]

Although nominal interest rates on many domestic securities will clearly decline in response to positive monetary shocks when there are capital controls, reflecting asset market distortions, it is less clear whether there will be much effect on those real interest rates that are relevant for capital expansion. The real risk premium the market attaches to the country's capital stock would have to fall. Suppose for the sake of argument that the underlying real interest rate changes by some constant κ times the change in the real stock of reserves.

$$dr = \kappa \frac{dR}{P} \tag{5.11}$$

[5] See Cairncross and Eichengreen, [11].

The total differential of equation (4.16) after replacing ΔY with Y, yields

$$
\begin{aligned}
dR &= \frac{P}{m}\left(\frac{\partial L}{\partial r}\,dr + \frac{\partial L}{\partial Y}\,dY + \frac{\partial L}{\partial \Phi_m}\,d\Phi_m\right) \\
&\qquad + L\left(\frac{m\,dP - P\,dm}{m^2}\right) - dD \\
&= \frac{P\,L}{m}\left(\frac{1}{L}\frac{\partial L}{\partial r}\,dr + \frac{Y}{L}\frac{\partial L}{\partial Y}\frac{dY}{Y} + \frac{\Phi_m}{L}\frac{\partial L}{\partial \Phi_m}\frac{d\Phi_m}{\Phi_m}\right) \\
&\qquad + \frac{P\,L}{m}\left(\frac{dP}{P} - \frac{dm}{m}\right) - dD \\
\frac{dR}{P} &= h\,\eta\,dr + h\,\epsilon\,\frac{dY}{Y} + h\,\frac{d\Phi}{\Phi} + h\,\frac{dP}{P} - h\,\frac{dm}{m} - \frac{dD}{P} \qquad (5.12)
\end{aligned}
$$

where η (< 0) is the interest semi-elasticity of demand for liquidity, ϵ (> 0) is the income elasticity of demand for liquidity,

$$h = \frac{H}{P} = \frac{L}{m} \quad \text{and} \quad \frac{\Phi_m}{L}\frac{\partial L}{\partial \Phi_m} = 1.$$

Substitution of equation (5.11) into this expression yields

$$
\begin{aligned}
\frac{dR}{P} &= h\,\eta\,\kappa\,\frac{dR}{P} + h\,\epsilon\,\frac{dY}{Y} + h\,\frac{d\Phi}{\Phi} + h\,\frac{dP}{P} + h\,\frac{dm}{m} - \frac{dD}{P} \\
&= \frac{h\,\epsilon}{1 - h\,\eta\,\kappa}\frac{dY}{Y} + \frac{h}{1 - h\,\eta\,\kappa}\frac{d\Phi}{\Phi} + \frac{h}{1 - h\,\eta\,\kappa}\frac{dP}{P} \\
&\qquad + \frac{h}{1 - h\,\eta\,\kappa}\frac{dm}{m} - \frac{1}{1 - h\,\eta\,\kappa}\frac{dD}{P} \qquad (5.13)
\end{aligned}
$$

with the coefficient of dD/P, commonly called the offset coefficient, being greater than -1 to the extent that $\kappa > 0$. A positive shock to the domestic source component will thus lead to a less-than-equal decline in the stock of reserves and therefore some increase in the money supply and decline in the real interest rate.

Nevertheless, recent empirical evidence regarding the magnitude of the offset coefficient, in two papers by Kit Pasula, indicates that it was not significantly different from -1 in the cases of Canada, the Netherlands, West Germany, Italy, and even the United Kingdom in the Bretton-Woods period.[6] This implies that κ was not significantly different from zero.

[6] The first four countries are covered in [86] while the British case is covered in [87]. The data are quarterly for the periods 1962:Q3 through 1970:Q1 for Canada, 1957:Q1 through 1971:Q1 for West Germany and the Netherlands, 1958:Q1 through 1971:Q2 for Italy and 1957:Q4 through 1971:Q2 for the United Kingdom.

Alternatively, the belief that expansionary monetary policy in small open economies operates in part through a decline in interest rates is now frequently rationalized by the argument that the associated fall in the real exchange rate, being temporary, will be expected to reverse in the future. The resulting rise in E_Q in equation (5.10) will lower the domestic real interest rate, leading to an expansion of investment. The problem with this argument is that it ignores the fact, first established by Meese and Rogoff [76], that it is virtually impossible to forecast future exchange rates. As will be shown below in Part II, real exchange rates over relatively short time-horizons can be appropriately described as near random walks.

6

Exchange Rate Overshooting

Thus far it has been assumed that the price of a country's output, or the domestic price level, does not change in the short-run but will fully adjust in the long-run to its new equilibrium level. Whether this failure to adjust in the short-run is due to lack of information of producers about current changes in demand, or to costs of continually making immediate price adjustments in response to frequent and often temporary changes in demand, is of little concern – all that is necessary for validity of the analysis is that prices do not change immediately but do change eventually. Moreover, since the speed at which the relevant individuals learn about economic changes that have occurred will almost certainly vary from instance to instance, and the cost of making price changes will vary in accordance with the institutional setting and the particular industries involved, any model of dynamic adjustment paths will be dependent upon assumptions that are specific to the time and place.

6.1 The Basis for Overshooting

There is, however, a further type of rigidity to which the analysis must be extended. These are the rigidities in trade balance adjustment that lead to exchange rate overshooting taking the form of a short-term response of the nominal exchange rate to a monetary shock that exceeds its ultimate long-term response. Under a flexible exchange rate the process of adjustment to excess liquidity involves an attempted purchase of assets abroad that leads to a devaluation of the real and nominal exchange rates and an increase in the level of output and income sufficient to induce domestic residents to willingly hold this greater liquidity. It

J.E. Floyd, *Interest Rates, Exchange Rates and World Monetary Policy*,
DOI 10.1007/978-3-642-10280-6_6, © Springer-Verlag Berlin Heidelberg 2010

is inevitable that the process of adjustment of the current account balance and output in response to a devaluation will take time. In the very short run – say, a day or week – very little adjustment, if any, can occur.

The nature of these issues can be seen from log linear representations of the equation of the AA curve, in its demand for liquidity form, and equation (4.4)

$$l_t = \phi_t + p_t + \epsilon\, y_t + \eta\, r_t + \eta\,(E\{p_{t+1}\} - p_t) \tag{6.1}$$
$$r_t = \tilde{r}_t + \rho - (E\{q_{t+1}\} - q_t) \tag{6.2}$$

where y_t is the logarithm of domestic income,[1] ρ is the risk premium on domestic assets, q_t is the logarithm of the real exchange rate, l_t is the logarithm of the nominal stock of liquidity and p_t is the logarithm of the domestic price level – that is, $l_t - p_t$ is the logarithm of L – and ϵ (> 0) and η (< 0) are, respectively, the income elasticity and the interest semi-elasticity of demand for liquidity. Note that r_t and $\tilde{r}_t$ are the levels, not the logarithms, of small-country and rest-of-world interest rates and that changes in ϕ_t represent logarithmic shocks to the demand for liquidity. Assuming that the price level in the rest of the world is normalized at unity, the logarithm of the real exchange rate can be expressed

$$q_t = p_t + \pi_t \tag{6.3}$$

where π_t is the logarithm of the nominal exchange rate $\mathit{\Pi}$, defined as the price of the small country's currency in rest-of-world currency. It can be easily seen that if price level adjustment is instantaneous, a positive monetary shock – that is, a one-time increase in l_t or a decline in ϕ_t – will result in an immediate increase in p_t and fall in π_t in the same proportion as the monetary shock. Since the shock is a one-off occurrence, the expected inflation rate and rate of change of the real exchange rate will be unaffected. The real interest rate will remain unchanged and price level flexibility will guarantee that y_t stays constant at its full employment level. As a result, from equations (6.1) and (6.3),

$$\Delta p_t = -\Delta \pi_t = \Delta(l_t - \phi_t)$$

and

$$\Delta q_t = 0.$$

[1] This formulation is equivalent to normalizing the full-employment levels of Y in ΔY and Q_f in ΔQ at unity.

where Δ here simply denotes a change in the logarithm of the level of the variable.

Now suppose a length of run sufficiently short for changes in q_t to have no effect on y_t as well as for p_t and $E\{p_{t+1}\}$ to remain unchanged. Assume also that the risk premium on domestic assets does not change and that everyone regards the real exchange rate as a random walk, implying that $E\{q_{t+1}\} = q_t$. This will imply an unchanged level of r_t in (6.2) and the left side of equation (6.1) will exceed the right side. Because of the attempt of domestic residents to dispose of their excess liquidity by purchasing claims on real capital from abroad, π_t and q_t will fall, both in the same proportion. Since neither r_t or y_t are affected, there is no mechanism to bring the right and left sides of equation (6.1) together and the small country's currency will devalue without limit. There will be no short-run equilibrium!

6.2 Two Avenues to Equilibrium

It turns out that there are two ways in which a stable equilibrium can occur. The first involves the fact that domestic and foreign outputs can be divided into tradeable and non-tradeable components. In the previous chapters it was assumed that each country's consumption and investment is divided between both countries' outputs, with the relative price of the two outputs denoted by the real exchange rate Q. One can visualize a part of each country's output, the non-tradeable component, as available only for home consumption and investment, and the remaining part, the tradeable component, as available for consumption and investment in both countries. The tradeable components can be thought of as having the same price, measured in either currency, in both countries while the output components restricted to consumption and investment in the country in which they are produced will, of course, have different prices. One need not equate traded and non-traded output components with traded and non-traded goods, as every good will have embedded in it both traded and non-traded components.[2]

[2] For example, the classic non-traded good, haircuts, will typically contain a traded component because the hair-stylist will use hair cream, scissors, chairs and other materials that may be traded across the international border. Of course, these imported items will themselves contain non-traded as well as traded components because domestic labour will be used in the process of importing, warehousing and distributing them.

The small country's price level can therefore be expressed as a weighted average of the domestic-currency prices of the traded and non-traded components of output.

$$p_t = \theta\, p_t^n - (1 - \theta)\, \pi_t \tag{6.4}$$

where θ is the share of output that is non-traded, p_t^n is the domestic-currency price of the non-traded output component, and the price of the traded output component in rest-of-world currency units is normalized at unity.[3] It is obvious from this equation that a devaluation of the small country's currency will increase its price level even if the home-currency price of domestic non-traded component of output and price of the traded component in rest-of-world currency are fixed. It follows from (6.1) that the short-term equilibrium change in the logarithm of the nominal exchange rate will be

$$\Delta\pi_t = -\frac{1}{1-\theta}\,\Delta(l_t - \phi_t) = -\frac{1}{1-\theta}\,\Delta p_t. \tag{6.5}$$

Since none of the other variables in (6.1) are affected, the increase in the price level will be proportional to the increase in the stock of liquidity, while the nominal exchange rate will decrease by some multiple of the increase in liquidity – the exchange rate overshoots its long-run equilibrium value, which will be below its initial value by an amount proportional to the increase in the money stock. The short-run change in the real exchange rate will be

$$\begin{aligned}\Delta q_t &= \Delta p_t + \Delta\pi_t \\ &= \left[1 - \frac{1}{1-\theta}\right]\,\Delta(l_t - \phi_t) \\ &= -\frac{\theta}{1-\theta}\,\Delta(l_t - \phi_t).\end{aligned} \tag{6.6}$$

and will be negative as long as the nominal exchange rate overshoots its final equilibrium value, which will happen whenever the non-traded component of output is positive—that is, $\theta > 0$.

It has recently been argued that even traded goods prices may not respond to exchange rate movements because of local-currency-pricing

[3] Since Π_t is the price of domestic currency in terms of foreign currency, - π_t is the logarithm of the domestic currency price of foreign currency, which the rest-of-world price of the traded output component must be multiplied by to express it in units of domestic currency.

by firms that have monopsony power in international markets.[4] Letting υ represent the fraction of the small country's traded component of output that is *not* priced in local currency independently of the nominal exchange rate, the change in p_t in response to a change in π_t becomes, from (6.4),

$$\Delta p_t = -\upsilon\,(1-\theta)\,\Delta\pi_t. \tag{6.7}$$

and equation (6.5) becomes

$$\Delta\pi_t = \frac{-1}{\upsilon\,(1-\theta)}\,\Delta(l_t - \phi_t). \tag{6.8}$$

If the price of the traded component is set entirely in the small country's currency and does not respond to movements in the exchange rate, $\upsilon = 0$ and Δp_t will therefore also be zero. The nominal and real exchange rates will fall without limit in response to a positive monetary shock even if the traded component represents a substantial fraction of output.

It has thus-far assumed that the expected future rate of change in the real exchange rate is unaffected by this short-run overshooting movement in the nominal exchange rate. This would be reasonable if there is a lot of noise in the nominal and real exchange rates and everyone acts as though the real exchange rate is a random walk. Suppose, however, that people know when the real exchange rate has fallen below its long-run equilibrium level and expect it to rise back to that level.[5] The term $(E\{q_{t+1}\} - q_t)$ in equation (6.2) will become positive, causing the domestic interest rate to fall. The quantity of liquidity demanded will thus increase in equation (6.1), offsetting some of the shock to the excess supply of money and moderating, and possibly even eliminating, the overshooting of the nominal exchange rate. This will be the case whenever the real exchange rate falls in response to a monetary shock as long as people understand that the fall is temporary.[6]

Suppose that investors currently expect future capital gains, as a result of subsequent reversal of the decline in the real exchange rate,

---

4 For recent literature on this issue, see Devereux [18], Betts and Devereux [6] and Devereux and Engel [19].

5 If this is the case, it can no longer be assumed that the prices of non-traded output components are fixed on account of agents' unawareness that a shock of aggregate demand has occurred. The only basis for price level rigidity becomes menu and other costs of initiating price change. Colleague Allan Hynes must be thanked for noting this point.

6 This idea originated with Rudiger Dornbusch [27].

yielding a current-period return of ϱ times the real exchange rate decline. Equation (6.2) now yields

$$\begin{aligned} \Delta r_t &= -\Delta(E\{q_{t+1}\} - q_t) \\ &= \varrho\,\Delta q_t \\ &= \varrho\,(\Delta p_t + \Delta \pi_t) \\ &= \varrho\,[1 - \upsilon\,(1-\theta)]\,\Delta \pi_i \end{aligned} \tag{6.9}$$

which, along with equations (6.1) and (6.7), produces

$$\begin{aligned} \Delta(l_t - \phi_t) &= -\,\upsilon\,(1-\theta)\,\Delta\pi_t + \eta\,\varrho\,[1 - \upsilon\,(1-\theta)]\,\Delta\pi_t \\ &= -[\upsilon\,(1-\theta)(1+\eta\,\varrho) - \eta\,\varrho]\,\Delta\pi_t \end{aligned}$$

or

$$\Delta\pi_t = \frac{-1}{\upsilon\,(1-\theta)(1+\eta\varrho) - \eta\,\varrho}\,\Delta(l_t - \phi_t). \tag{6.10}$$

A stable equilibrium will occur unless one of υ and $(1-\theta)$ and one of η and ϱ are zero. If either υ or $(1-\theta)$ are zero, the above expression becomes

$$\Delta\pi_t = \frac{1}{\eta\,\varrho}\,\Delta(l_t - \phi_t) \tag{6.11}$$

and the nominal exchange rate will overshoot its long-run equilibrium level whenever $\eta\,\varrho > -1$. If either η or ϱ are zero, the expression reduces to

$$\Delta\pi_t = -\,\frac{1}{\upsilon\,(1-\theta)}\,\Delta(l_t - \phi_t) \tag{6.12}$$

and overshooting will occur unless $\upsilon = 1$ and $\theta = 0$. Assuming that the demand for liquidity is negatively sloped with respect to the interest rate and some component of output is tradeable, an equilibrium will exist if not all domestic output is priced in local currency without regard to exchange rate movements or if the current change in the real exchange rate is expected to be temporary.

6.3 Will Overshooting in Fact Occur?

For reasonable values of the parameters it would seem likely that monetary shocks will lead to very substantial temporary movements in nominal and real exchange rates. Based on evidence summarized by David Laidler [67], -0.2 would represent a reasonable upper bound on the short-run elasticity of demand for money. Setting the interest cost of holding money at 5%, the resulting interest semi-elasticity of demand for money will be -4.0. Although real exchange rates are not random walks, the degree of mean reversion is extremely small in that, based on the work of Rogoff [91], 50% of the full adjustment to temporary shocks will take from 3 to 5 years. If the reversion of the real exchange rate to its equilibrium value is expected to be evenly spread out over future months, ϱ will be less than .015 when the unit of time is one month.[7] If one sets the share of non-traded output components in total output equal to 0.6 and assumes that the domestic price of the entire traded component adjusts to incorporate nominal exchange rate changes, a 1% excess supply of liquidity will cause the exchange rate to devalue by over 2%. If by the end of one month only half of the domestic price of traded output components has adjusted to reflect the change in the nominal exchange rate the exchange rate will devalue by 4%. And it would be reasonable to expect that in the first week or two following a money supply shock the overshooting will be much greater. Once the exchange rate begins to change in response to the portfolio-adjustment effect of the liquidity change, it is unlikely that much corresponding adjustment of the domestic prices of the traded components of output will occur during the following week. If, say, $\vartheta = .1$ over this interval, the exchange rate adjustment will be 25 times the liquidity shock unless asset holders come to expect the real exchange rate adjustment to reverse itself within a week or two. If, alternatively, they act speculatively in the belief the exchange rate will continue to change in the same direction, the overshooting will be even more extreme.

Of course, once sufficient time has elapsed for domestic output to respond to declines in the real exchange rate the overshooting will dissipate. Overshooting will also be smaller if market participants can determine which exchange rate movements are due to short-term monetary shocks and which are not. In this respect, however, it must be kept in mind that no forecasting approach has been able to consistently

[7] Letting n be the number of months until 50% of the adjustment to a real exchange rate shock is achieved, $n\varrho = .5$ so that $\varrho = .0139$ when $n = 36$.

outperform the simple prediction that tomorrow's real exchange rate will, on average, equal today's.[8]

[8] This was first noticed by Richard Meese and Kenneth Rogoff [76].

Part II

Exchange Rate Determination

This part of the monograph presents the relevant empirical evidence on the nature and causes of observed movements of the nominal and real exchange rates of a number of countries – Canada, the United Kingdom, Japan, France and Germany – with respect to the United States. As a prelude, the first chapter that follows draws together the relevant theoretical issues with regard to the determinants of nominal and real exchange rates. The basis for this is the theoretical framework developed in Part I although there are two extensions relevant specifically to this part of the book. The first is a standard presentation of the nature of and relationship between forward and spot exchange rates and domestic/foreign interest rate differentials, conventionally known as covered and uncovered interest parity. This leads to a review of essential features of the literature on efficient markets as it applies to foreign exchange rates. The second is an examination of the question of whether exchange rates should be viewed exclusively as asset prices, as is sometimes done in the literature.

Empirical work is presented in the remaining five chapters of Part II. The first of these investigates the time-series properties of observed movements in real exchange rates. The conclusions of Rogoff [91] are shown to be correct over a longer period than he examined and, although most real exchange rate series will appear as random-walk variables if examined over relatively short periods, one must conclude that they are most surely stationary. The next chapter investigates the evidence on covered and uncovered interest parity and puts forward the conclusion that for the major industrial countries examined the best predictor of next period's exchange rate is this period's rate although in appropriate situations it will be useful to impose an adjustment for any substantial differences between domestic and foreign core inflation rates. Moreover, there is no forward premium puzzle of the sort conventionally claimed although there remain related issues of minor economic significance that need to be more fully investigated in future research.

The last three chapters of this part of the book provide clear empirical evidence that real exchange rate movements are almost entirely the result of real forces related to international reallocations of investment between countries and changes in oil and other commodity prices and in the terms of trade as the world stock of human, physical and technological capital grows. The first of these chapters investigates the just-mentioned real shocks, and the second adds unanticipated money supply shocks to the set of explanatory variables. It is clearly the case that money supply shocks have been of little consequence – no significant observed effects on the real exchange rates examined can be found.

The role of real and monetary shocks in determining domestic/foreign interest rate differentials is also investigated and it cannot be concluded that money supply shocks in any of the countries examined, other than the United States, have had the conventionally presumed effects on domestic interest rates or the domestic minus U.S. interest rate differentials.

The final chapter of Part II examines the possibility that money demand shocks might be important by conducting a Blanchard-Quah VAR analysis of nominal and real exchange rates. Some evidence of money shocks is found but, except in the case of Germany, these shocks explain a trivial part of observed real exchange rate movements. No significant exchange rate overshooting can be detected.

7

Issues Regarding Exchange Rate Determination

The first task in this part of the book is to present a simple, clear theoretical analysis of the basics of exchange rate determination, pulling together and extending the arguments introduced in Part I and outlining specifically the issues that will arise in the five chapters that follow.[1]

A country's real exchange rate is the relative price of its output in terms of foreign output. This suggests that the focus of analysis should be on the factors that determine these relative prices in a world undergoing capital accumulation and associated technological change. The exposition begins by focusing on an economy that is continually at full-employment.

7.1 General Equilibrium Issues

The real exchange rate is defined as

$$Q = \frac{\Pi P}{\tilde{P}} \tag{7.1}$$

[1] There is an extensive literature here. Much of the early work arose from attempts to test purchasing power parity – see Balassa [2], Samuelson [95], Officer [84], Korteweg [63] and Kravis and Lipsey [64]. Subsequently the emphasis shifted toward representative agent models – see Stockman [99] [100], Stockman and Svensson [101], Helpman [52], Helpman and Razin [53] and Edwards [30]. Most recently, the focus has been on 'new open-economy' models, starting with Obstfeld and Rogoff [81] with empirical work by Engel [34] and Engel and Rogers [36]. For the most recent contributions, see Johnston [62], Devereux [18], Betts and Devereux [6], Engel [35], Devereux and Engel [19], Chari, Kehoe and McGrattan [14] and Duarte [29].

J.E. Floyd, *Interest Rates, Exchange Rates and World Monetary Policy*,
DOI 10.1007/978-3-642-10280-6_7,

where Q is the real exchange rate, Π the nominal exchange rate defined as the foreign currency price of domestic currency, P the domestic price level and $\tilde{P}$ the foreign price level. Although the price levels are viewed conceptually as indices of the respective countries' output prices, it will be convenient in subsequent empirical analysis to use consumer price indices.

While it has been traditional to separate the goods produced in each country into traded and non-traded goods, one must be careful because there is substantial evidence that traded goods typically sell for different prices, measured in the same currency, in different countries – that is, that the law of one price does not hold.[2] A more sensible procedure is to divide the output of each good, and hence the output of each country, into traded and non-traded components.

While the actual division of the range of goods produced in a country into their traded and non-traded components is an empirical nightmare, all that will be necessary here is to assume that the non-traded component of aggregate domestic output is substantially positive. On this basis the domestic and foreign price levels can be expressed as the geometric indices

$$P = P_N^{\theta} P_T^{1-\theta} \tag{7.2}$$

and

$$\tilde{P} = \tilde{P}_N^{\tilde{\theta}} \tilde{P}_T^{1-\tilde{\theta}} \tag{7.3}$$

where $\theta > 0$ and $\tilde{\theta} > 0$ are the fractions of domestic and foreign output represented by non-traded components. Although the traded components of domestic and foreign output typically will not involve the same goods because the countries may trade with different third countries as well as with each other, one can nevertheless express the domestic traded component in the foreign country's currency by replacing P_T with $\tilde{P}_{T_D}/\Pi$ where $\tilde{P}_{T_D}$ is the foreign currency price of the domestic traded component of output. Equation (7.1) can then be rewritten as

$$\begin{aligned} Q = \frac{\Pi\, P_N^{\theta} P_T^{1-\theta}}{\tilde{P}_N^{\tilde{\theta}} \tilde{P}_T^{1-\tilde{\theta}}} &= \frac{\Pi\, P_N^{\theta} (\tilde{P}_{T_D}/\Pi)^{1-\theta}}{\tilde{P}_N^{\tilde{\theta}} \tilde{P}_T^{1-\tilde{\theta}}} \\ = \frac{(\Pi/\Pi^{1-\theta})\, P_N^{\theta} \tilde{P}_{T_D}^{1-\theta}}{\tilde{P}_N^{\tilde{\theta}} \tilde{P}_T^{1-\tilde{\theta}}} &= \left[\frac{(\Pi P_N)^{\theta}}{\tilde{P}_N^{\tilde{\theta}}}\right] \left[\frac{\tilde{P}_{T_D}^{1-\theta}}{\tilde{P}_T^{1-\tilde{\theta}}}\right] . \end{aligned} \tag{7.4}$$

[2] See, for example, the papers by Engel [34] and Engel and Rogers [36].

As can be seen from the above equation, the long-run equilibrium effects of world technological change and capital accumulation on a country's real exchange rate with respect to some other country will depend on the effects of these forces on the price of domestic relative to foreign traded output-components and the price of domestic relative to foreign non-traded output-components, where all prices are measured in a single currency.

Consider first the effects of real income growth and the associated rise in labour productivity in the two economies. Since the non-traded components of output are primarily labour services and are less amenable to increases in labour productivity than the traded-components, the relative price of the non-traded components should tend to rise as real income expands leading us to expect that the real exchange rate of the more rapidly growing country will tend to rise through time. That is, other things equal, the real exchange rate should be positively related to the level of domestic relative to foreign real income holding everything else constant. This is the well-known Balassa-Samuelson hypothesis.[3]

A second force leading to real exchange rate movements is changes in the allocation of world investment among countries. As technology advances, the resources of different countries become favored for development and world investment shifts to those locations. The implications can be usefully analyzed from the perspective of the standard textbook relation between income and expenditure

$$Y = C + I + B_T + DSB \tag{7.5}$$

where Y is total income earned by domestic residents, or GNP, C and I are aggregate consumption and investment of both public and private goods, B_T is the balance of trade and DSB is the debt service balance. All of these magnitudes are measured in real terms. Subtraction of $C+I$ from both sides of the above equation yields

$$Y - C - I = S - I = NCO = B_T + DSB \tag{7.6}$$

where S is gross real domestic savings, $S - I = NCO$ is the domestic real net capital outflow and $B_T + DSB$ is the domestic current account balance. Domestic savings and investment will depend on the domestic real interest rate, denoted by r, domestic real income and exogenous shift factors which are aggregated into the shift-variable Ψ_{S-I}. The domestic balance of trade will depend upon domestic and foreign incomes

[3] See Balassa [2] and Samuelson [95].

and on the domestic real exchange rate with respect to the rest of the world, here represented as Q, and an exogenous shift variable Ψ_{B_T}. The debt service balance is determined by past domestic savings and investment and is therefore unaffected by the current-period levels of other variables. Equation (7.6) thus becomes

$$N(Y, r, \Psi_{S-I}) = B_T(Y, \tilde{Y}, Q, \Psi_{B_T}) + DSB \tag{7.7}$$

where $N()$ is the function determining the net capital outflow and $B_T()$ is the function determining the balance of trade. When the variables are expressed as desired magnitudes, equation (7.7) (and, equivalently, equations (7.5) and (7.6)) can be viewed as the condition of equilibrium in the domestic real output market – the condition that the aggregate supply of domestic output must equal the aggregate demand for it.

Domestic and rest-of-world nominal interest rates, i and $\tilde{i}$, are related according to the interest parity condition

$$i - \tilde{i} = -\Phi + \rho_c \tag{7.8}$$

where Φ is the forward premium on domestic currency on the foreign exchange market and ρ_c is the country-specific risk premium on domestic assets. Were this condition to not hold, individuals could make a sure profit by shifting asset holdings between the two countries while simultaneously hedging themselves by purchasing or selling their currency forward. Suppose, for example, that the domestic interest rate exceeds the foreign rate by less than the sum of the risk premium required on the domestic asset and the forward discount – or negative forward premium – on the domestic currency for a given transaction period. One could sell domestic bonds and purchase foreign ones of equivalent value, while at the same time buying an equivalent amount of domestic currency forward at the current forward rate, and make a profit. Of course, this profit will depend on the possibility of making the three transactions at prices that do not change while those transactions are in the process of being made.

Foreign exchange market efficiency – that is, rational behaviour of market participants – implies that the forward premium on the domestic currency equal the expected future change in the exchange rate over the relevant forward contract period plus an adjustment to cover risk. Suppose, for example, that the domestic currency is expected to appreciate over some future period by more than the forward premium and that one is risk neutral. An expected gain can be had by selling foreign currency forward at the current forward rate and purchasing that currency spot when the contract becomes due at a price lower than that agreed to in the forward contract. This is not a sure profit, of course, because one's expectations as to the future spot price of the domestic currency may be wrong. To compensate for the possibility of having wrongly estimated the future spot rate, a risk premium will be deducted. This implies that, in equilibrium, the forward premium will equal

$$\Phi = E_{\Pi} - \rho_x \tag{7.9}$$

where E_{Π} is here the expected relative change in the value of the domestic currency in terms of the foreign currency and ρ_x is the foreign-exchange risk premium required in the market by individuals taking uncovered positions. The market will thus bid the forward premium to the point where it equals the expected future increase in the price of domestic currency in terms of foreign currency minus an amount to compensate for risk. Those individuals who anticipate that the currency will appreciate by more than indicated in equation (7.9), and are willing to take an uncovered position, will sell foreign currency forward to other willing risk-takers who anticipate that the domestic currency will appreciate by less than implied by that equation.

Substitution of (7.9) into (7.8) yields

$$i = \tilde{i} - E_{\Pi} + \rho_x + \rho_c \quad = \quad \tilde{i} - E_{\Pi} + \rho \tag{7.10}$$

were $\rho = \rho_c + \rho_x$ is the combined risk premium. Here ρ_c is commonly called the country risk premium because it measures the risk of holding domestic instead of foreign assets in a situation where the exchange rate cannot change – as would be the case, for example, in a currency union – while ρ_x is called foreign exchange risk because it compensates for the risk of taking an uncovered foreign exchange position.

A corresponding relationship between domestic and foreign real interest rates can be obtained by substituting for each nominal interest rate the respective real interest rate plus the expected home inflation rate, thereby obtaining

$$\begin{aligned} r &= \tilde{r} - E_P - E_{\Pi} + E_{\tilde{P}} + \rho \\ &= \tilde{r} - E_Q + \rho \end{aligned} \tag{7.11}$$

where E_P and $E_{\tilde{P}}$ are the expected rates of inflation in the domestic and foreign economies and E_Q is the expected rate of change in the domestic real exchange rate with respect to the foreign economy. Note that a rise in the domestic real exchange rate increases the real value of domestically employed capital relative to foreign employed capital, creating a capital gain to world residents from holding domestic as compared to foreign capital. The expectation of such a rise will mean that the price of domestically employed capital will be bid up relative to that of foreign employed capital, lowering the net-of-capital-gains real interest rate differential. Expressions equivalent in structure to equations (7.8) through (7.11) can be written for the domestic economy with respect to any foreign country or combination of countries – one simply needs to appropriately modify the scope of the relevant variables.

As is clear from equation (7.11), the domestic real interest rate in equation (7.7) will be determined by conditions in the rest of the world and by the risk of holding domestic as compared to foreign assets together with expectations about the future course of the real exchange rate of the two economies' outputs. Under the assumption of price flexibility and full employment, domestic and foreign real incomes at any point in time will depend on past savings and associated technology growth and real interest rates will be determined by risk conditions in the domestic and foreign economies at the full-employment levels of output and investment. The only variable that can respond to a disequilibrium between aggregate supply and aggregate demand is Q, taken as the relative price of domestic output in the world (including domestic) market. Given a reallocation of world investment toward the domestic economy, Ψ_{S-I} will fall, reducing the left side of (7.7) and expanding aggregate demand, assuming that no offsetting change in Ψ_{B_T} occurs.[4] The real exchange rate Q must rise, either through an increase in the domestic price level or a rise in the nominal exchange rate, to expand imports relative to exports and reduce equivalently the right side of (7.7), bringing aggregate demand for domestic output back into line with aggregate supply. A technology induced shift of world investment into the domestic economy increases aggregate demand for domestic output which, if unaccompanied by a corresponding inflow of capital goods, will cause the relative price of domestic output to rise. The fact that investment spending in the domestic economy has increased with not all of it being spent on traded output components means that the price of domestic non-traded output components will rise relative to the price of non-traded components in the rest of the world. In analyzing the effects of shifts of world investment on the real exchange rate of one country with respect to another one should therefore look at the real net capital inflow (or the negative of the current account balance) of the recipient country as a fraction of its

[4] This abstracts from any changes in risk and the productivities of capital in the domestic and foreign economies associated with the shift of Ψ_{S-I}.

output in comparison with the real net capital inflow of the trading partner as a fraction of that country's output. Other things equal, one would expect the real exchange rate of the country experiencing the largest real net capital inflow (or smallest real net capital outflow) as a percentage of output to be higher.

Another potential cause of real exchange rate changes is shifts of residents' preferences among goods having different traded and non-traded output components. Although private preferences are impossible to model in this context, it would seem that shifts in government output as a fraction of domestic real income might well lead to real exchange rate changes in that governments tend to be biased toward the purchase of domestic goods rather than goods imported from abroad. As a consequence one might expect that the bigger the fraction of output consisting of government expenditure in the domestic relative to the foreign economy, the higher will be the demand for domestic relative to foreign non-traded output components and the higher will be the domestic real exchange rate.

Then there are a whole range of factors that might be expected to change the domestic relative to the foreign prices of traded components of output. An obvious example relevant to the Canadian economy is the trends in world commodity prices, Canada having been historically a producer of base metals, coal, grains and other such commodities. To the extent that commodities are a bigger fraction of domestic output than that of a trading partner one would expect that a fall in world commodity prices would reduce the domestic real exchange rate with respect to that partner. Of course, there are a myriad of goods with high traded components and on-going technological change would be expected to bring about changes in the relative prices of these components, causing the real exchanges rates of producing countries to change in ways that will be very difficult to predict. Assuming that countries' export components of output constitute higher fractions of output than import components of output, it would seem reasonable to expect that a rise in the terms of trade of a country with respect to all other countries relative to the terms of trade of another country with respect to all other countries would result in an increase in its real exchange rate with respect to that other country. And clearly, a rise in the terms of trade of a country with respect to a particular trading partner should result in an increase in its real exchange rate with respect to that partner.

The above analysis has ignored market imperfections which are an important focus of the modern literature.[5] These distortions should not be of importance in the broad framework outlined above. The long-run equilibrium real exchange rate would be expected to depend on real net capital inflows, real income growth, and the time paths of world prices of particular traded components of output even in the face of the usual distortions in the relative price structure. Market imperfections become important, as emphasized in the modern literature, with respect to short-term variations in real exchange rates around their long-run equilibrium levels.

The forces determining nominal exchange rates under full employment conditions should now be obvious. An appropriate rearrangement of equation (7.1) yields

$$\Pi = \frac{Q\tilde{P}}{P} \tag{7.12}$$

from which it is clear that the nominal exchange rate will move proportionally with movements in the full-employment level of the real exchange rate and will rise and fall in proportion to the ratio of the foreign to domestic price levels which, of course, will be determined by the foreign and domestic monetary policies in the face of the demands for liquidity in the two economies.

7.2 Exchange Rate Determination under Less-Than-Full-Employment Conditions

In a short-run situation where the price levels cannot change, the real and nominal exchange rates will move in proportion. This is obvious from equation (7.12) above. Movements of the real exchange rate in response to real forces of the kind noted in the previous section will be brought to fruition by adjustments of the nominal exchange rate. Now, however, situations will arise where movements of the nominal exchange rate brought about by attempts of the public to maintain portfolio equilibrium will drag the real exchange rate along with it.

The classic case of short-run portfolio adjustment effects on the exchange rate is the impact of a shock to the demand or supply of liquidity. Confronted with excess money holdings, people will attempt to re-balance their portfolios by exchanging this excess money

[5] For a clear discussion of the role of market imperfections in real exchange rate determination, see Devereux [18].

for non-monetary assets. The result, which can easily be seen from a re-statement of the demand function for liquidity

$$L = P\,L(\tilde{r} + \rho - E_Q + E_P, Y, \Phi_m) \tag{7.13}$$

where L is real liquidity, P is the domestic price level, $\tilde{r}$ is the foreign real interest rate, ρ is the risk premium on domestic assets, E_Q and E_P are the expected rates of change in the real exchange rate and domestic price level, Y is real income, and Φ_m is a demand-for-liquidity shift variable. The Fleming-Mundell result is that an increase in L or decline in Φ_m causes the nominal and real exchange rates to devalue, shifting world demand from foreign to domestic goods and thereby raising Y until the equality in (7.13) is re-established.

Exchange rate overshooting, which was the subject of the previous chapter, arises because the current account balance, and hence income, will only increase in response to a change in the real exchange rate after some time has elapsed. When the domestic price level is fixed, and E_Q is zero, there will be no mechanism to bring about equilibrium in the very short run and the real and nominal exchange rates will fall without limit. As noted in Chapter 6, there are two possible avenues through which an equilibrium can occur. One arises because the price level can be appropriately defined as a geometrically weighted index of the prices of the non-traded and traded components of output

$$P = P_N^{\theta} P_T^{1-\theta}.$$

where the subscripts N and T refer to the non-traded and traded output components and θ is the share of the non-traded component in total output. If one can assume that the domestic price of the traded component of output P_T will adjust upward in response to a devaluation of the exchange rate, the overall price level will also adjust. Since the price level must increase in proportion to the increase in the excess demand for money, the price of the traded component and hence the exchange rate must increase in greater proportion as long as $\theta > 0$ – the exchange rate will overshoot. If one believes that pricing-to-market will occur – that is domestic traded-component prices will be set independently of the level of the nominal exchange rate – this avenue of adjustment will be closed off.

A second possible avenue to equilibrium in the very short run arises if people realize that the nominal exchange rate is overshooting. While in the long run the nominal exchange rate must depreciate in proportion to the increase in the price level, the real exchange rate will always return to its previous equilibrium level. If this is expected to happen, E_Q will become increasingly positive as Q falls, driving down the domestic interest rate and reducing the cost of holding money and bringing equation (7.13) back into equality. The problem with this view is that it conflicts with the well-known fact that future exchange rate movements are virtually impossible to predict – the best forecast is that the exchange rate is equally likely to fall as rise between any two adjacent periods.

In conclusion, as noted in the previous chapter, it is highly likely that substantial overshooting movements of the exchange rate will occur in response to monetary shocks.

7.3 Exchange Rates as Asset Prices

During the past three decades traditional foreign exchange market analysis has viewed the exchange rate as an asset price. Deviations of the exchange rate from some constant purchasing power parity level were seen as consequences of the evolution of asset prices in the face of policy shocks and other news affecting asset returns, with the focus directed toward issues regarding asset market efficiency.[6]

The analysis in the last section of Chapter 4 suggests that the risk premium on an uncovered forward position in foreign exchange should depend on how the return on that forward position covaries with the return to capital in the economy as a whole, and hence, how much of the variance in that return the asset holder can diversify away. This is a useful insight as to how to think about foreign exchange risk, but it is as yet impossible to implement in practice. To obtain direct estimates of foreign exchange risk using these principles one needs a measure of the return to capital in the economy as a whole – that is, to the market portfolio. The relevant market portfolio here is presumably one containing every asset owned in the country, including the human capital of the entire population. How can the return on that portfolio be calculated?

One possibility is to use aggregate real consumption but consumption is an endogenous variable that is affected by people's savings decisions, so variations in it may reflect wealth owners choices and not the earnings flow on their wealth.[7] Also, it must be recognized that a sizable fraction of the world capital stock is non-tradeable human capital

[6] Robert Hodrick [54] makes a comprehensive presentation of the issues. See also Mussa [80] and Levich [68].

[7] Lucas [71] explores the implications of truly exogenous consumption for asset pricing by modeling an economy in which output in each period is an exogenous and

embodied in the person of its owners – these human capital assets have no market price. No attempt will be made to grapple with these issues in this book – it is simply assumed that some aggregate 'portfolio' lies behind the scenes and that there will exist risk premiums related to the covariance structure of asset returns with this unobservable aggregate.

Although foreign currency holdings are obviously assets whose value is represented by the exchange rate, exchange rates have a much less direct role in pricing bonds, equities and other assets whose earnings are denominated in a currency foreign to their owner. As in the case of pure forward positions in foreign currency, changes in the exchange rate may signify capital gains and losses. But, unlike that case, exchange rate changes may also reflect rather than cause changes in capital values. Imagine the situation faced by a New York resident who owns capital in California. Gains and losses of the value of that capital will occur in the ordinary course of business. If one were then to imagine that California is given its own currency, in which all assets in the State are then denominated, what difference would it make to the New York resident? Presumably none once allowance is made for price flexibility because the value of the California dollar in terms of the U.S. dollar will adjust until everything in California is worth the same in U.S. dollars as if the latter were the medium of exchange in California – money is a veil. A change in the California dollar price of the U.S. dollar can occur without there being any change in the real value of the New Yorker's holdings of a particular California asset if the exchange rate and the asset price in California dollars move in unison. The real value of a New Yorker's holdings of California assets may or may not be correlated with movements of the exchange rate.

Suppose that the real exchange rate happens to be constant. Then movements in the nominal exchange rate simply reflect differences in the movements of the domestic and foreign price levels. If there is unexpected inflation abroad, capital losses will be experienced on assets whose nominal earnings are fixed in foreign currency. This will be reflected in a devaluation of the foreign currency but the exchange rate movement is simply a reflection of the foreign inflation. Assets whose earnings are fixed in real terms abroad will experience no capital loss, measured in units of either foreign or domestic output. Their nominal prices will rise with the rise in the price level abroad but this will be exactly compensated for by the decline in the domestic currency value of foreign currency. If there is anticipated inflation abroad then an in-

perishable endowment, with consumption is equal to output because no saving is possible.

flation premium will be added to interest rates in the foreign economy to compensate lenders. This rise in the foreign nominal interest rate relative to the domestic nominal interest rate will be exactly matched by a rise in the forward premium on domestic currency in equation (7.8). Again, the exchange rate movements reflect the anticipated inflationary conditions in the foreign economy – they play no independent role. Since the real exchange rate is constant in the above discussion, E_Q will equal zero and the foreign inflation will have no effect on the domestic/foreign real interest rate differential – $E_{\hat{P}}$ and E_{Π} both rise by the same amount in equation (7.11).

Now suppose that both countries experience zero inflation and that the real exchange rate changes. An increase in the real exchange rate represents a rise in the price of domestic output in units of foreign output. This implies that domestically employed capital, whose service flow is measured in units of domestic output, is now more valuable in units of foreign output. The owners of capital employed in the domestic economy receive a capital gain. When P and P^* are constant the domestic currency must appreciate – Π must rise. But the capital gain is fundamentally unrelated to the nominal exchange rate movement in the sense that had the nominal exchange rate been fixed (or had the two countries had a common currency) the real exchange rate would still have changed and the capital gain on domestically employed capital would still have been received. The domestic price level would have then risen relative to the foreign price level by the increase in the relative value of domestic goods in terms of foreign goods. The nominal exchange rate is playing a passive role.

If an increase in the real exchange rate is anticipated (by the residents of both countries) one can see from (7.11) that the domestic real interest rate will decline relative to the foreign real interest rate. This happens because the owners of domestically employed capital anticipate a future capital gain and are willing to hold that capital at a lower (net of capital gain) real interest rate than previously. This interest rate effect would also occur independently of whether the nominal exchange rate is fixed or flexible – the capital gain has to do with technological or other real-sector developments in the domestic relative to the foreign economy and is independent of the currency system.

A fundamental issue of concern in the chapters that follow is the relationship between exchange rates and the risk premiums on countries' assets. The issues involved are exceedingly complex. Assume for the moment that the real exchange rate is constant and that in the absence of international capital mobility the return to the underlying unobservable market portfolio in the domestic economy varies more widely than but is highly correlated with the return to the underlying unobservable market portfolio abroad. Domestic residents will be living with greater risk than residents abroad and, assuming that domestic and foreign residents have the same risk aversion, the premium of market interest rates over the risk-free rate will be greater in the domestic economy than abroad. When international trade in securities is then allowed, one can imagine this risk differential persisting, although to the extent that domestic and foreign asset returns are not perfectly correlated with each other there will be a gain to portfolio diversification that will induce each countries' residents to hold a fraction of their portfolio in ownership claims to capital employed in the other country. This international pooling of asset holdings will increase if domestic and foreign residents have different aversions to risk. The relevant market portfolio will now be the world market portfolio and interest rates on domestic equities will be above the rate of return on this portfolio and interest rates on foreign equities will be below it. The domestic/foreign interest rate differential will depend on the amplitude of the variation of the return to domestic equities relative to the amplitude of variation of the return to foreign equities as compared to the variation of the return on the underlying unobservable international market portfolio.

Things change when the possibility of variations in the real exchange rate is introduced. Suppose for the moment that countries' real exchange rate movements with respect to the rest of the world are completely uncorrelated with movements in the returns to the separate domestic and foreign portfolios that would exist in the absence of international trade in assets. A rise (fall) in the real exchange rate will create a capital gain (loss) on foreign residents' holdings of domestic assets and a capital loss (gain) on domestic residents' holdings of foreign assets, assuming that the residents of every country measure their wealth in units of home-country output. These variations in wealth can only be diversified away by holding very small fractions of total portfolios in rest-of-world assets. Even if a country's asset holders diversified their foreign holdings across assets in all other countries, the resulting diversified asset should not have a weight in excess of that of any of the individual home country assets in the overall portfolio because the return to any bundle of foreign assets varies directly with the real exchange rate with respect to the rest of the world and is uncorrelated with the return to a composite of domestic assets.[8] The introduction

[8] Only if the domestic real exchange rates with respect to each individual foreign country were variable with the real exchange rate with respect to the aggregate

of real exchange rate variability, uncorrelated with the returns to capital in the domestic and foreign economies measured in units of home output would thus cause asset holders to hold high fractions of their wealth in their own country's assets. This is a potential explanation of the well-known 'home bias portfolio puzzle'.[9]

A positive covariance of these real exchange rate shocks with the returns on domestic assets, on the other hand, will act as a hedge against variations in domestic asset returns, moderating both the increases and decreases in wealth over the course of the business cycle and leading domestic asset holders to hold more foreign assets in their portfolios than they otherwise would. It would have the reverse effect, however, on the desired portfolio holdings of domestic assets by foreign asset holders.

The exact nature of these wealth effects of real exchange rate variability becomes less clear when we allow for the fact that residents of each country consume and domestically invest goods obtained abroad. Capital gains and losses should then be measured in terms of a weighted average of domestic and foreign output units with the weight depending on the fractions of consumption and investment utilizing goods produced outside the country.

It is clear from the above analysis that while uncovered forward positions in the exchange market are clearly assets, exchange rates themselves are by no means exclusively asset prices – real exchange rates are best seen as the relative price of domestic output in terms of foreign output which, depending on the situation, may have important but not easily measured effects on asset values.

---

of these countries constant would it make sense to invest a small fraction of the domestic portfolio in each of the many countries abroad.

[9] For a discussion of this puzzle and references to the literature, see Obstfeld and Rogoff [83].

8

Time Series Properties of Observed Exchange Rate Movements

In the theoretical analysis of Part I, and in the chapters that follow in Part III, the question of whether real and nominal exchange rates can be treated as random-walk series or near-random-walk series with low rates of mean reversion is of fundamental importance. This chapter presents the empirical work necessary to answer this question. The results that follow are consistent with, and extend using recent data, the work presented by Rogoff [91].

The annual average historical real exchange rates of the United Kingdom and Canada with respect to the United States and of Canada with respect to the United Kingdom are plotted in Fig. 8.1 while monthly real exchange rates of Canada, the United Kingdom, Japan, France and Germany with respect to the United States are plotted in Figs. 8.2a and 8.2b for the period 1957 through 2007. The nominal exchange rates and domestic/foreign price level ratios are also presented in these figures.

J.E. Floyd, *Interest Rates, Exchange Rates and World Monetary Policy*,
DOI 10.1007/978-3-642-10280-6_8, © Springer-Verlag Berlin Heidelberg 2010

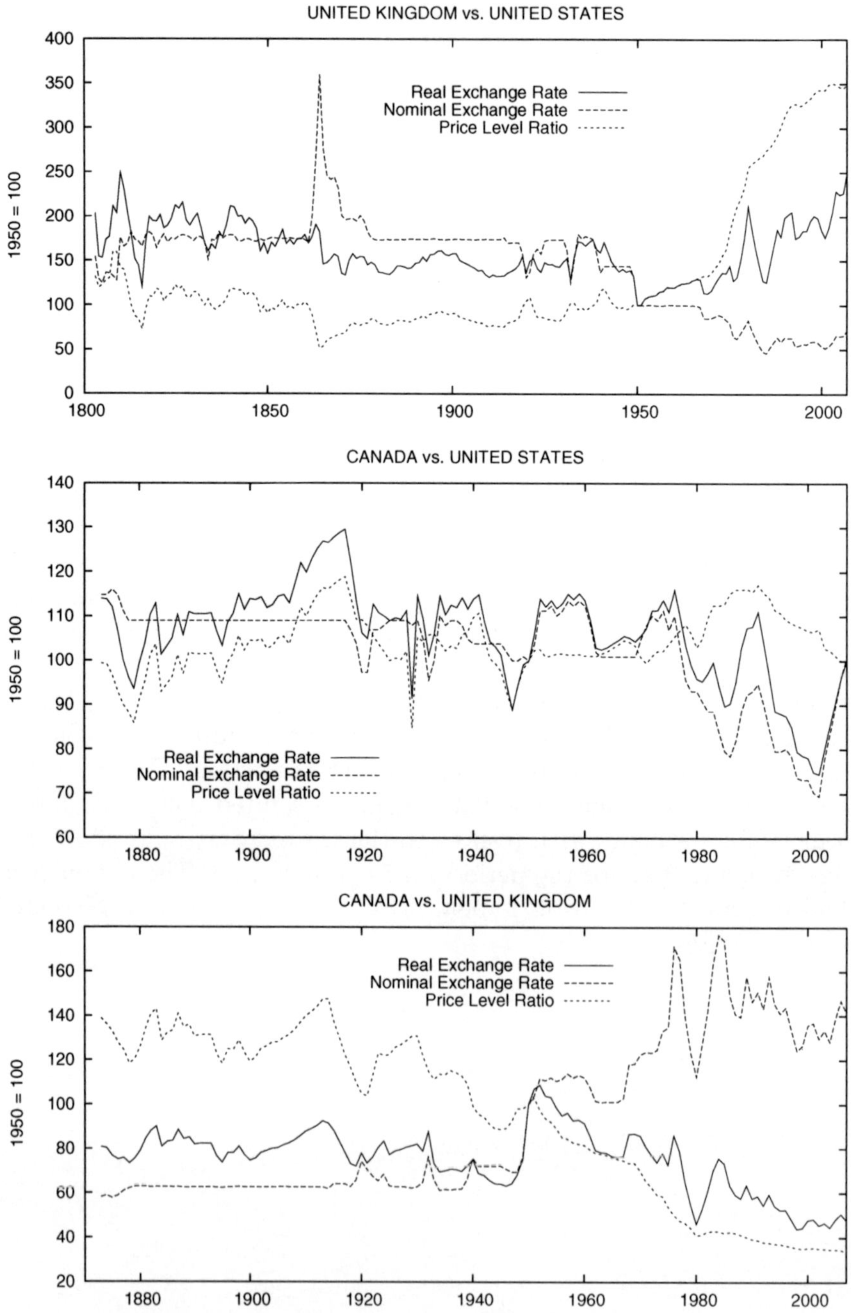

Fig. 8.1. Real exchange rates, nominal exchange rates and price level ratios: Annual data, 1950 = 100

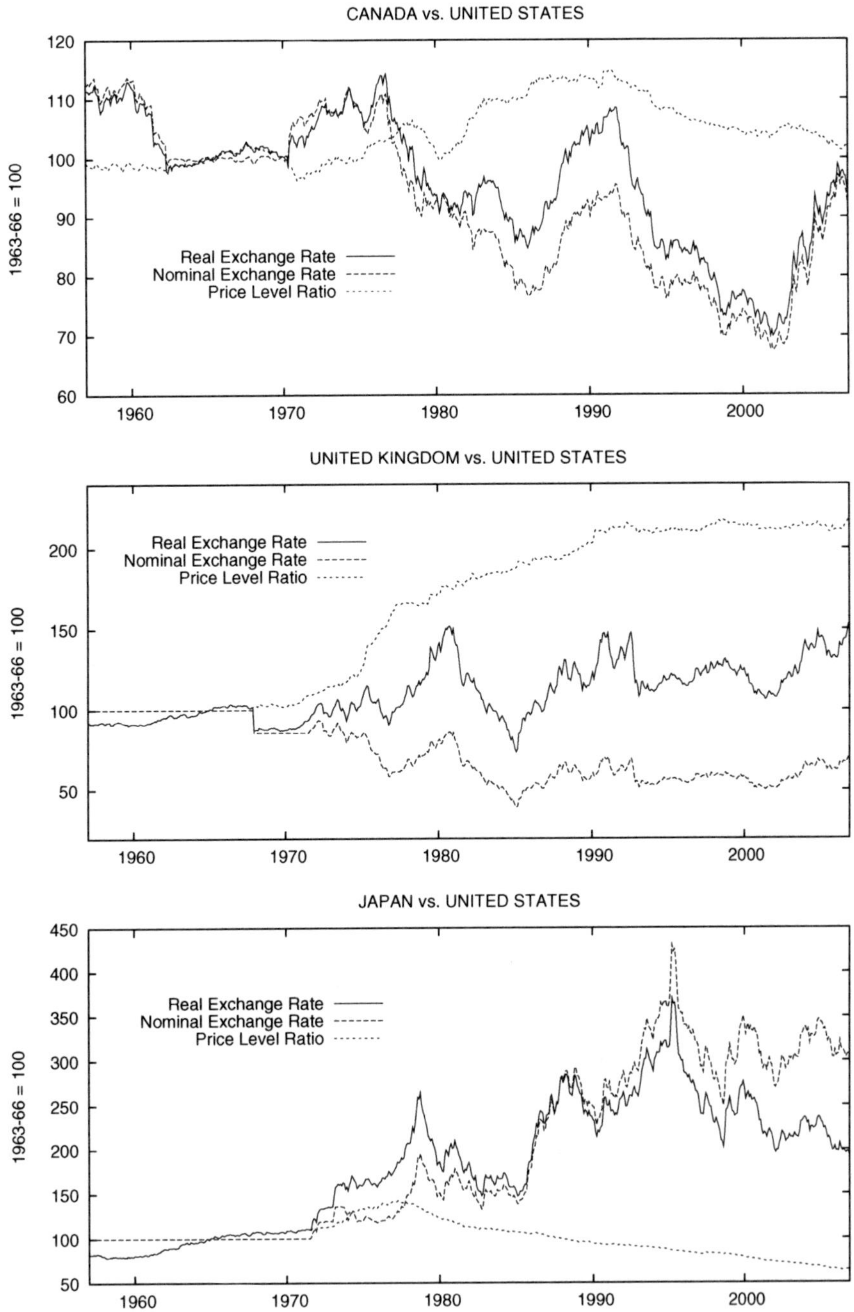

Fig. 8.2a. Real exchange rates, nominal exchange rates and price level ratios: Monthly data, 1963-66 = 100

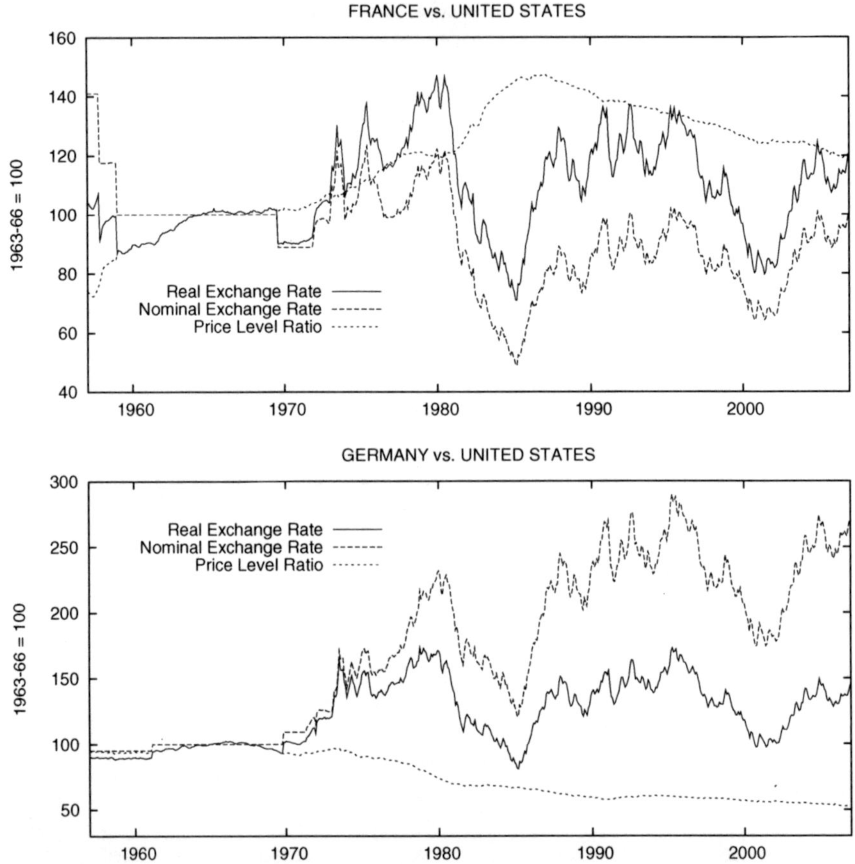

Fig. 8.2b. Real exchange rates, nominal exchange rates and price level ratios: Monthly data, 1963-66 = 100. After 1998 the Euro/Dollar exchange rate was spliced to the Franc/Dollar and Deutschmark/Dollar exchange rates.

8.1 Stationarity vs. Non-Stationarity of Time Series

It is necessary to begin with a review of some basic principles of time series analysis focusing on the question of stationarity and the methods of determining whether a particular series has that property.[1]

A time series can be thought of as a series of numbers indexed by time that portrays the time path of some variable. It is often convenient to imagine that these numbers are generated by some mathematical process and to attempt to discover which process best describes the behaviour of an observed series. For example a real exchange rate series might be generated by the equation

$$q_t = \beta\, q_{t-1} + \epsilon_t. \tag{8.1}$$

where q_t is the logarithm of a real exchange rate series, the units of which are manipulated so that the series equals unity in its first period, and its logarithm in that period therefore equals zero, and ϵ_t is a series of drawings of a zero-mean, constant-variance non-autocorrelated random variable. An alternative would be to visualize q_t as the percentage deviation from its initial level. Equation (8.1) is a first-order autoregressive process – first-order because there is only one lag of q_t on the right-hand side and autoregressive because the q_t are autocorrelated in the sense that the level of the variable in each period depends on its level in a previous period.

Lagging (8.1) repeatedly and then recursively substituting these lags back into (8.1) produces the expression

$$\begin{aligned} q_t = \beta^t\, q_0 + \epsilon_t + \beta\, \epsilon_{t-1} + \beta^2 \epsilon_{t-2} + \beta^3\, \epsilon_{t-3} \\ + \beta^4\, \epsilon_{t-4} + \cdots\cdots\cdots + \beta^{t-T}\, \epsilon_0. \end{aligned} \tag{8.2}$$

The time path of q_t depends critically on the parameter β. If this parameter equals zero then

$$q_t = \epsilon_t. \tag{8.3}$$

and q_t is itself a white noise process with mean equal to 0, showing the relative or percentage deviation of the particular real exchange rate in each period from its initial level which in this case turns out to be its mean level. The variance of q_t will equal the variance of ϵ_t which can be denoted here by σ^2. If $\beta = 1$, q_t becomes, utilizing (8.1),

[1] For a basic treatment of time series analysis, see Enders [33] and for a more advanced treatment, see Hamilton [50].

$$q_t = q_{t-1} + \epsilon_t. \tag{8.4}$$

The series is a random walk. It wanders without limit with q_t moving either up or down in each period compared to its previous value by a random amount ϵ_t, as can be seen by rewriting (8.4) as

$$q_t - q_{t-1} = \epsilon_t \tag{8.5}$$

or, by expansion, as

$$q_t = \epsilon_t + \epsilon_{t-1} + \epsilon_{t-2} + \epsilon_{t-3} + \cdots\cdots + \epsilon_0. \tag{8.6}$$

The variance of q_t will equal $(\sigma^2 + \sigma^2 + \sigma^2 + \cdots\cdots)$ which will grow in proportion to the number of periods over which the variance is being calculated.[2]

In this case where $\beta = 1$ the series is said to be non-stationary or have a unit root.[3] Its expected level at any point in time is its current level and its variance in the limit is infinity. Its future path need never pass through the level at which it started or any other level previously achieved, although there is no reason why it could not return to those levels. When $\beta > 1$ the series explodes, with the values of q_t getting increasingly larger with time.[4]

When $-1 < \beta < 1$ the series is stationary as can be seen from the fact that the absolute value of β^t gets smaller in (8.2) as t increases. If the ϵ_t are zero beyond some point, q_t will approach zero as t increases, with the speed of approach being greater, the smaller is $|\beta|$. The effects of each ϵ_t shock will thus dissipate with time. The variance of q_t will equal $[1 + (\beta)^2 + (\beta^2)^2 + (\beta^3)^2 + \cdots\cdots\cdots]\,\sigma^2$ which will be finite in the limit as t increases. In the case were $\beta = 0.9$, for example, this variance will equal $5.26\,\sigma^2$ in the limit.[5] The series will vary around zero with a persistence that will be greater as β gets larger.

---

[2] This follows from the fact that $Var\{u+v\} = Var\{u\} + Var\{v\}$ when u and v are uncorrelated variables.

[3] The root equals β.

[4] This can be seen from the fact that β^t will get bigger and bigger as t increases when $\beta > 1$. If β is negative the series oscillates around zero, doing so explosively if $\beta < -1$.

[5] This calculation uses the relationship $Var\{u + v\} = Var\{u\} + Var\{v\}$ in the footnote above plus the facts that $Var\{a\,x\} = a^2\,Var\{x\}$ and

$$1 + a + a^2 + a^3 + a^4 + \cdots\cdots = \frac{1}{1-a}$$

and then sets a equal to β^2.

Equation (8.1) is a first-order autoregressive process. A second-order autoregressive process would be represented by

$$q_t = \beta_1 \, q_{t-1} + \beta_2 \, q_{t-2} + \epsilon_t, \tag{8.7}$$

with two lags of q_t, and third and higher order processes can be similarly constructed.

Time series can also be moving average processes. An example would be an equation generating q_t of the form

$$q_t = \xi_0 \, \epsilon_t + \xi_1 \, \epsilon_{t-1} + \xi_2 \, \epsilon_{t-2} \tag{8.8}$$

which is a second-order moving average process – second-order because it contains two lags of the error term. Moving average processes are always stationary because ϵ_t is stationary and any average of stationary processes must itself be a stationary process.

Of course, time series processes can have both autoregressive and moving average components. Consider the equation

$$q_t = \beta_1 \, q_{t-1} + \beta_2 \, q_{t-2} + \xi_0 \, \epsilon_t + \xi_1 \, \epsilon_{t-1} + \xi_2 \, \epsilon_{t-2}. \tag{8.9}$$

This defines an ARMA(2,2) process – a process that is second-order autoregressive and second-order moving average. In general, ARMA(x, y) processes have x autoregressive lags and y moving average lags.

It is possible, of course, that q_t above could be a stationary process that is actually the first difference of another series z_t – that is, $q_t = z_t - z_{t-1}$ – and that the process z_t is a non-stationary autoregressive-moving-average process that has to be differenced once to produce the stationary ARMA(2,2) process. It is said to be integrated of order 1 because it has to be differenced once to produce a stationary process. If it had to be differenced twice to produce a stationary process it would be integrated of order 2, and so forth. The process z_t is thus an autoregressive-integrated-moving-average ARIMA(2,1,2) process – differencing it once produces an ARMA(2,2) process. In general, an ARIMA(x, d, y) process is one whose d-th difference is a stationary autoregressive-moving-average process with x autoregressive lags and y moving average lags.

As an example, take equation (8.9) with a constant term added.

$$q_t = \alpha + \beta_1 \, q_{t-1} + \beta_2 \, q_{t-2} + \xi_0 \, \epsilon_t + \xi_1 \, \epsilon_{t-1} + \xi_2 \, \epsilon_{t-2}. \tag{8.10}$$

Subtraction of q_{t-1} from both sides converts it to

$$\begin{aligned} q_t - q_{t-1} = \alpha - (1 - \beta_1) \, q_{t-1} + \beta_2 \, q_{t-2} \\ + \xi_0 \, \epsilon_t + \xi_1 \, \epsilon_{t-1} + \xi_2 \, \epsilon_{t-2} \end{aligned} \tag{8.11}$$

and a further addition and subtraction of $\beta_2\, q_{t-1}$ on the right side yields

$$\begin{aligned} q_t - q_{t-1} = \alpha - (1 - \beta_1 - \beta_2)\, q_{t-1} + \beta_2\, (q_{t-2} - q_{t-1}) \\ + \xi_0\, \epsilon_t + \xi_1\, \epsilon_{t-1} + \xi_2\, \epsilon_{t-2}. \end{aligned} \tag{8.12}$$

If $\beta_1 = \beta_2 = 0$, this series is stationary – equal, in fact, to the pure moving average series (8.8) with a constant added. In the case where $\alpha = 0$, the series will be stationary as long as $\beta_1 + \beta_2 < 1$ – a fraction $(1 - \beta_1 - \beta_2)$ of any change in Q_t will be removed in each subsequent period. A random-walk will only occur, given $\alpha = 0$, if $\beta_1 + \beta_2 = 1$. In this case, the expression reduces to

$$q_t - q_{t-1} = \xi_0\, \epsilon_t + \xi_1\, \epsilon_{t-1} + \xi_2\, \epsilon_{t-2} \tag{8.13}$$

and any change in q_t from period to period will be permanent. If α is unequal to zero, however, the series will never be stationary as long as the sum of β_1 and β_2 is different from zero. To see this, suppose that the error terms are all zero. Then the series will become

$$q_t - q_{t-1} = \alpha - (1 - \beta_1 - \beta_2)\, q_{t-1} + \beta_2\, (q_{t-2} - q_{t-1}) \tag{8.14}$$

and q_t will grow period by period by an amount α in addition to any change that occurs as a result of the other terms on the right side of the expression. If $\beta_1 + \beta_2 = 1$ the series can be described as a random walk plus drift, or trend, with the drift equal to α. If $\beta_1 + \beta_2 < 1$, the series is stationary around drift or trend. A further source of non-stationarity will arise if the series contains an additional term involving t such as, say, $\gamma\, t$. In this case, (8.14) will become

$$\begin{aligned} q_t - q_{t-1} = \alpha + \gamma\, t - (1 - \beta_1 - \beta_2)\, q_{t-1} \\ + \beta_2\, (q_{t-2} - q_{t-1}) \end{aligned} \tag{8.15}$$

and, even if there were no shocks, q_t will grow at an increasing or decreasing rate through time, eventually becoming infinitely large or small as $t \rightarrow \infty$. This will happen even if $\beta_1 + \beta_2 < 1$. An even more explosive result will arise if a term involving t^2 is added to the equation describing the process.

It turns out that an equation like (8.9) that includes autoregressive and moving-average terms can be expressed in the form of a pure autoregressive process containing an infinite number of autoregressive lags. Simply reorganize (8.9) to move ϵ_t to the left of the equality and q_t to the right, lag the resulting equation repeatedly to obtain expressions for e_{t-1}, e_{t-2}, e_{t-3} ... etc. and substitute these expressions successively into (8.9) and simplify. The resulting infinite order autoregressive process can then be converted into an equation like

$$\begin{aligned}\Delta q_t = -(1-\rho)\, q_{t-1} + \, (\beta_2 + \beta_3 + \beta_4 + \cdots + \beta_\infty)\, \Delta q_{t-1} \\ + (\beta_3 + \beta_4 + \cdots + \beta_\infty)\, \Delta q_{t-2} \\ + (\beta_4 + \cdots + \beta_\infty)\, \Delta q_{t-3} + \cdots\cdots\cdots + \epsilon_t \qquad (8.16)\end{aligned}$$

containing an infinite succession of lags of $\Delta q_t = (q_t - q_{t-1})$ where $\rho = \beta_1 + \beta_2 + \beta_3 + \cdots\cdots + \beta_\infty$.[6] The reader should note that in the next few pages ρ denotes a mean-reversion parameter and not a risk premium as elsewhere in book.

8.2 Testing for Stationarity

The problem here is to determine whether the time-series processes that can reasonably describe the evolution of actual real-world real exchange rates are stationary. And if they are stationary, it is useful to determine how fast the real exchange rate series return to their mean levels following a shock. The standard procedure, based on path-breaking work by David Dickey and Wayne Fuller [25] [26], uses ordinary-least-squares to estimate an equation of the form

$$\begin{aligned}\Delta q_t = \alpha + \gamma\, t - (1-\rho)\, q_{t-1} + \delta_1\, \Delta q_{t-1} + \delta_2\, \Delta q_{t-2} \\ + \delta_3\, \Delta q_{t-3} + \cdots\cdots\cdots + \epsilon_t \qquad (8.17)\end{aligned}$$

which is the infinite autoregressive process discussed above with the addition of a constant term and trend. It turns out that, under the null hypothesis that there is no mean reversion and $\rho = 1$, that process can be well approximated by an AR process containing no more than $T^{1/3}$ lags, where T is the number of observations.[7] The deterministic terms α and $\gamma\, t$ are dropped if there is no evidence of a trend in the series – if α is significantly different from zero, the rejection of the null-hypothesis of $\rho = 1$ indicates stationarity of the series around a drift or trend and if γ is significantly different from zero the series is stationary around an increasing or decreasing drift or trend.

In selecting the number of lags to be included, the appropriate procedure is to start with an unreasonably large number and progressively drop the longest lag if that lag turns out to be statistically insignificant. An alternative is to choose the number of lags that minimizes an

[6] See Enders [33], pages 225–227.

[7] This result was established by Said and Dickey [93].

information criterion such as the Akaike information criterion (AIC) or Schwartz Bayesian information criterion (SBC). These give calculated optimal balances between the gain associated with the reduction in the residual sum of squares when a lag is added and the loss associated with having one less degree of freedom. The relevant formulae calculated for each regression are

$$AIC(n) = ln\left(\frac{SSR(n)}{T}\right) + (n+1)\frac{2}{T} \tag{8.18}$$

$$SBC(n) = ln\left(\frac{SSR(n)}{T}\right) + (n+1)\frac{ln(T)}{T} \tag{8.19}$$

were $SSR(n)$ is the sum of squared residuals, n is the number lags and T is the number of observations and where $ln()$ is represents the natural logarithm of the expression in the brackets.[8] Of course, all these significance tests and criteria comparisons must apply to regressions estimated from the same number of observations.

It turns out that under the null-hypothesis that $\rho = 1$ the estimator of $(1-\rho)$ is not distributed according to the t-distribution. A table of critical values constructed by Dickey and Fuller [25] [26] must be used instead of the standard t-tables.[9]

A major problem here is that the test procedure just outlined has poor ability – statisticians use the term low power – to detect stationarity when the true value of ρ is close to unity, When one tests the null-hypothesis that $(1-\rho)$ equals zero one, in effect, uses the Dickey-Fuller table to obtain the appropriate critical value of the t-statistic for the estimate of $-(1-\rho)$. This critical value will be some negative number below which the estimated t-value has some small probability, say .05, of falling if ρ is really unity. So if ρ in fact equals unity there is only a 5% chance rejecting the null-hypothesis of non-stationarity and concluding that the series is stationary and a 95% chance of correctly concluding that the series is non-stationary. Now suppose that the true value of ρ is .999, implying stationarity with a very small degree of mean reversion. Application of the test, however, will nevertheless lead to the conclusion that the real exchange rate series is non-stationary almost 95% of the time because the t-statistic will still be below the

---

[8] See Stock and Watson [98], pages 453–467, for a discussion of these criteria. The authors recommend the AIC over the SBC for the purpose at hand because the former tends to overestimate the number of lags and studies of the performance of Dickey-Fuller tests suggest that having too many lags is better than having too few.

[9] A collection of these and other tables can be found in the file `statabs.pdf`.

critical value only very slightly more than 5% of the time. If ρ is .8 or .9, the estimated t-statistic will still lie above the critical value a high percentage of the time. So there a small risk, 5% in the example above, of concluding that the real exchange rate is stationary when it is not, and a very high risk of concluding that it is non-stationary when it is in fact stationary at true values of ρ not far below unity. These tests must therefore be viewed with caution.

The Dickey-Fuller tests assume that the errors ϵ_t are statistically independent of each other and have a constant variance. An alternative procedure, developed by Peter Phillips and Pierre Perron [89], can be used to conduct the tests under the assumption that there is some interdependence of the errors and they are heterogeneously distributed.[10] The following equations are estimated by ordinary-least-squares:

$$q_t = \alpha_1 + \rho_1\, q_{t-1} + \gamma\,(t - T/2) + \upsilon_t \tag{8.20}$$

$$q_t = \alpha_2 + \rho_2\, q_{t-1} + \nu_t \tag{8.21}$$

$$q_t = \rho_3\, q_{t-1} + \omega_t \tag{8.22}$$

where T is the number of observations and υ_t, ν_t and ω_t are error terms. Test statistics are then calculated based on modifications of the conventional t-statistics to allow for heterogeneity and interdependence of the error process. The critical values are the same as those for the corresponding statistics estimated using the Dickey-Fuller approach and the objective is to determine the circumstances, if any, under which the coefficient of q_{t-1} is significantly less than unity.

8.3 Some Stationarity Tests

Recent empirical work on real exchange rates has found that ρ is typically not far below unity – the null hypothesis that $\rho = 1$ usually cannot be rejected for short-sample periods at reasonable significance levels but can very often be rejected for long sample periods. The results of large-sample tests, together with the fact that the tests have low power when ρ is close to unity, have made it reasonable to conclude that there is generally some mean reversion.[11] It is nevertheless worthwhile to examine the stationarity of the real exchange rates being considered here using recent data.

Tables 8.1 and 8.2 present the results of tests performed on the real exchange rates of the U.K. with respect to the U.S., Canada with

[10] This procedure is discussed on pages 239, 240, 265 and 266 of Enders [33].

[11] See Rogoff [91].

respect to the U.S., and Canada with respect to the U.K. using annual data spanning periods longer than 100 years. Tables 8.3 and 8.4 present the results of tests using monthly real exchange rates for the years 1957 through 2007 for Canada, France, Germany, Japan and the U.K. with respect to the United States.

In all cases, the data are converted to percentage deviations from their means before the tests are run. The lag lengths are chosen to include all successive statistically significant lags – this turns out to also be consistent with the AIC and only very slightly out of line with the SBC. It turns out that the optimal numbers of lags was very small in both the annual and monthly calculations. The data sources are discussed in detail in Appendix F.[12] Longer series lengths were used in cases where the number of lags were smaller so as to use all data possible.

The annual Dickey-Fuller test results presented in Table 8.1 indicate that all three of the series are stationary with no drift or trend in annual data extending for 203 years in the U.K./U.S. case and 134 years in the series involving Canada. The same is true of the Phillips-Perron results in Table 8.2 except that in the non-stationarity of the real exchange rate of Canada with respect to the U.K. is only rejected at the 10% level, which is acceptable given the low power of the test. And, as shown in Tables 8.3 and 8.4, in the case of monthly data, non-stationarity of the real exchange rates with respect to the U.S. of all countries can be rejected in the Dickey-Fuller tests at the 10% level and in the cases of France and Germany also at the 5% level. The Phillips-Perron tests on monthly data indicate rejection of non-stationarity for Japan and Germany at the 10% level and France at the 5% level or better. While non-stationarity cannot be rejected at the 10% level for the real exchange rates of Canada and the U.K. with respect to the U.S., the t-statistics are only shy of the 10% critical value of 1.6 by a

[12] The annual data are in the files `jfdataan.gdt`, `jfdataan.xls`, `jfdataan.tab` and `jfdataan.lsp` and are described in Gretl data file `jfdataan.gdt` and in the textfile `jfdataan.cat`. The monthly data are in the files `jfdatamo.gdt`, `jfdatamo.xls`, `jfdatamo.tab` and `jfdatamo.lsp` and are described in Gretl data file `jfdatamo.gdt` and in the textfile `jfdatamo.cat`. The calculations for a range of lags for the Dickey-Fuller tests are performed in the XLispStat batch files `urootan.lsp` and `urootmo.lsp`, leading to the appropriate lag selections for the final results presented in the tables. The Dickey-Fuller tests are performed, using the lags so selected, in the Gretl and R scripts `urootan.inp`, `urootmo.inp`, `urootan.R` and `urootmo.R`. These batch or script files for XLispStat and R also contain the calculations for the Phillips-Perron tests using, alternatively, one and four lags. The output files have the same names as the input files except that the suffixes `.lou`, `.got` and `.Rot` replace `.lsp`, `.inp` and `.R`.

Table 8.1. Dickey-Fuller test results for real exchange rate series: Annual data

Dependent Variable Δq_t	Drift	q_{t-1}	Δq_{t-1}	Trend
U.K. / U.S. 1805–2007	0.504	-0.090	$0.145^{\circ\circ}$	-0.002
	(0.437)	(-2.715)	(2.063)	(-0.252)
	0.247	-0.087**	$0.142^{\circ\circ}$	
	(0.458)	(-2.803)	(2.054)	
		-0.087***	$0.142^{\circ\circ}$	
		(-2.821)	(2.063)	
Canada / U.S. 1874–2007	1.760	-0.145*		-0.013
	(1.558)	(-3.191)		(-1.655)
	-0.060	-0.104*		
	(-0.229)	(-2.711)		
		-.105***		
		(-2.722)		
Canada / U.K. 1875–2007	4.793	-0.108	$0.253^{\circ\circ\circ}$	-0.036
	(2.426)	(-3.008)	(2.962)	(-2.128)
	-0.238	-0.066	$0.239^{\circ\circ\circ}$	
	(-0.431)	(-2.174)	(2.771)	
		-0.067**	$0.241^{\circ\circ\circ}$	
		(-2.191)	(2.804)	

Notes and Sources: All series tested are expressed as percentage deviations from their means. The numbers in parentheses below the coefficients are the conventional t-statistics. The superscripts *, ** and *** indicate significance at the 10%, 5% and 1% levels, respectively, using the Dickey-Fuller tables and the superscripts $^{\circ}$, $^{\circ\circ}$ and $^{\circ\circ\circ}$ indicate significance at the 10%, 5% and 1% levels according to a standard t-test. For sources see Appendix F.

Table 8.2. Phillips-Perron test results for real exchange rate series: Annual Data

$$q_t = a_0 + a_1 q_{t-1} + a_2 (t - T/2) + u_t$$

$$q_t = \tilde{a}_0 + \tilde{a}_1 q_{t-1} + v_t \qquad q_t = \hat{a}_1 q_{t-1} + w_t$$

	$a_0 = 0$	$a_1 = 1$	$a_2 = 0$	$a_0 = 0$ & $a_1 = 1$	$\tilde{a}_1 = 1$	$\hat{a}_1 = 1$
U.K. / U.S. 1805–2002						
Lags = 1	0.137	-2.774	0.290	4.463	-2.985**	-3.002***
Lags = 4	0.145	-2.637	0.226	4.136	-2.876*	-2.894***
Canada / U.S. 1874–2002						
Lags = 1	-0.201	-3.090	-1.432	4.631	-2.620*	-2.639***
Lags = 4	-0.184	-3.325*	-1.068	5.010	-2.803*	-2.823***
Canada / U.K. 1874–2002						
Lags = 1	-0.547	-2.502	-1.513	2.923	-1.604	-1.628*
Lags = 4	-0.548	-2.498	-1.520	2.910	-1.582	-1.617*

Notes and Sources: All series tested are expressed as percentage deviations from their means. The superscripts *, ** and *** indicate significance at the 10%, 5% and 1% levels, respectively, using the Dickey-Fuller tables which are also appropriate for the Phillips-Perron test. The statistics in all columns but the fourth from the left are t-based. For sources see Appendix F.

Table 8.3. Dickey-Fuller test results for real exchange rate series: Monthly data, 1957–2007

Dependent Variable Δq_t	Drift	q_{t-1}	Trend	Δq_{t-1}	Δq_{t-2}	Δq_{t-3}
	-0.049	-0.005	0.0001	$0.207^{\circ\circ\circ}$		
	(-0.427)	(-0.859)	(0.404)	(5.136)		
Canada / U.S.	-0.006	-0.006		$0.209^{\circ\circ\circ}$		
	(-0.139)	(-1.622)		(5.262)		
		-0.006^{*}		$0.209^{\circ\circ\circ}$		
		(-1.623)		(5.266)		
	Estimation begins with March 1957					
	-0.556	-0.027^{*}	0.002	$0.338^{\circ\circ\circ}$	$-0.129^{\circ\circ\circ}$	$0.092^{\circ\circ}$
	(-2.239)	(-3.196)	2.700	(8.337)	(-3.038)	(2.263)
U.K. / U.S.	0.069	-0.010		$0.332^{\circ\circ\circ}$	$-0.136^{\circ\circ\circ}$	$0.083^{\circ\circ}$
	(0.768)	(-1.782)		(8.169)	(-3.214)	(2.028)
		-0.010^{*}		$0.333^{\circ\circ\circ}$	$-0.136^{\circ\circ\circ}$	$0.089^{\circ\circ}$
		(-1.791)		(8.206)	(-3.250)	(2.057)
	Estimation begins with May 1957					
	-0.349	-0.011	0.0014	$0.321^{\circ\circ\circ}$		
	(-0.922)	(-1.953)	(1.169)	(8.307)		
Japan / U.S.	0.072	-0.005		$0.316^{\circ\circ\circ}$		
	(0.620)	(-1.751)		(8.288)		
		-0.005^{*}		$0.317^{\circ\circ\circ}$		
		(-1.751)		(8.259)		
	Estimation begins with March 1957					

Continued on next page .....

Continued from previous page

Dependent Variable Δq_t	Drift	q_{t-1}	Trend	Δq_{t-1}	Δq_{t-2}	Δq_{t-3}
	-0.160	-0.018	0.0006	0.256$^{\circ\circ\circ}$	-.073°	.097$^{\circ\circ}$
	(-0.800)	(-2.705)	(1.085)	(6.325)	(-1.759)	(2.382)
France / U.S.	0.030	-0.016		0.256$^{\circ\circ\circ}$	-0.074°	0.096$^{\circ\circ}$
	(0.317)	(-2.501)		(6.321)	(-1.775)	(2.361)
		-0.016**		0.256$^{\circ\circ\circ}$	-0.073°	0.096$^{\circ\circ}$
		(-2.504)		(6.331)	(-1.774)	(2.367)
	Estimation begins with May 1957					
	-0.193	-0.014	0.0008	0.284$^{\circ\circ\circ}$		
	(-0.866)	(-2.465)	(1.280)	(7.303)		
Germany / U.S.	0.063	-0.104		0.282$^{\circ\circ\circ}$		
	(0.645)	(-2.105)		(7.256)		
		-0.010**		0.283$^{\circ\circ\circ}$		
		(-2.108)		(7.287)		
	Estimation begins with March 1957					

Notes and Sources: All the real exchange rate series are expressed as percentage deviations from their means. The numbers in the brackets below the coefficients are the conventional t-statistics. The subscripts containing the * and ° characters have the same meaning as in Table 8.1. For sources see Appendix F.

Table 8.4. Phillips-Perron test results for real exchange rate series: Monthly Data, 1957–2002

$$q_t = a_0 + a_1 q_{t-1} + a_2 (t - T/2) + u_t$$

$$q_t = \tilde{a}_0 + \tilde{a}_1 q_{t-1} + v_t \qquad q_t = \hat{a}_1 q_{t-1} + w_t$$

	$a_0 = 0$	$a_1 = 1$	$a_2 = 0$	$a_2 = 0$ & $a_1 = 1$	$\tilde{a}_1 = 1$	$\hat{a}_1 = 1$
Canada/U.S.						
Lags = 1	-0.136	-0.433	1.274	1.651	-1.458	-1.460
Lags = 4	-0.129	-0.614	1.348	1.740	-1.533	-1.534
U.K./U.S.						
Lags = 1	0.872	-2.669	1.423	2.861	-1.361	-1.369
Lags = 4	0.812	-2.897	1.034	3.043	-1.536	-1.547
Japan/U.S.						
Lags = 1	0.745	-1.440	-0.116	1.362	-1.581	-1.582
Lags = 4	0.680	-1.678	-0.405	1.601	-1.648	-1.649*
France/U.S.						
Lags = 1	0.350	-2.269	0.808	2.560	-2.068	-2.062**
Lags = 4	0.323	-2.466	0.644	2.739	-2.256	-2.260***
Germany/U.S.						
Lags = 1	0.753	-2.080	0.626	1.964	-1.769	-1.773*
Lags = 4	0.700	-2.234	0.427	2.194	-1.899	-1.905*

Notes and Sources: All the real exchange rate series are expressed as percentage deviations from their means. Estimation starts at February 1957 in the case of one lag and at May 1957 when two lags are used. The superscripts *, ** and *** indicate significance at the 10%, 5% and 1% levels, respectively, using the Dickey-Fuller tables which are also appropriate for the Phillips-Perron test. The statistics in all columns but the fourth from the left are t-based. For sources see Appendix F.

tiny amount. As in the annual data, no statistically significant drift or trend is found although an examination of the top panel of Fig. 8.2a leads one to conclude that a slight negative trend appears to be present in the real exchange rate of Canada with respect to the United States over the period 1957-2007.

These results are consistent with common sense economics in that non-stationarity would allow real exchange rates to vary without limit between zero and infinity – it is difficult to imagine that country's output could become worthless relative to that of another country under any reasonable circumstances.

An important conclusion arising from these results is the extremely low rates of mean-reversion of the real exchange rate series. A reasonable estimate of $1 - \rho$ from the annual data would be in the neighborhood of 0.9, implying that after 5 years nearly 60% of a shock to the real exchange rate will remain and after 10 years about 35% will still remain. In the case of monthly data the percentages are no smaller. This suggests that, barring knowledge of what future shocks will be, any short- or medium-term forecast of the real exchange rate should treat that variable as a random walk. Over a period of 100 years or so, of course, there is little reason to expect to observe a trend.

9

Efficient Markets and Exchange Rate Forecasts

It is important to examine, in the light of the analysis and empirical evidence presented in the previous two chapters, questions regarding whether foreign exchange rate movements have been consistent with asset market efficiency, and whether forward exchange rates are good predictors of future spot rates. After an examination of the properties of spot and forward exchange rates and forward premiums, the analysis will turn to the question of whether covered and uncovered interest parity hold, whether foreign exchange markets are efficient and whether forward exchange rates provide better forecasts of future spot rates than does the naive assumption of constancy of the current spot rate. What is often regarded as the 'forward premium puzzle' will be shown to be explainable within the bounds of rational behaviour subject to imperfect information.

Figure 9.1 presents a plot of the current spot and 90-day forward prices of the Canadian dollar in U.S. dollars in the top panel and plots the 90-day forward premium and the percentage changes in the spot rate over the subsequent 3 months in the bottom panel. The spot and forward rates move nearly in unison in the top panel, while it is clear in the bottom panel that the 3-month ahead changes in the spot rate are much more variable that the associated forward premiums. These results also hold for the U.S. dollar prices of the currencies of all countries here examined. The standard deviations of the 1-month forward premiums and percentage changes of spot rates to the next month, all at annual rates, are as follows:

	Standard Deviation	
One-Month	Forward Premium	% Change Spot Rate
Canada	1.98	18.92
U.K.	3.02	35.78
Japan	4.57	40.68
France	4.13	38.65
Germany	3.54	39.36

J.E. Floyd, *Interest Rates, Exchange Rates and World Monetary Policy*,
DOI 10.1007/978-3-642-10280-6_9,

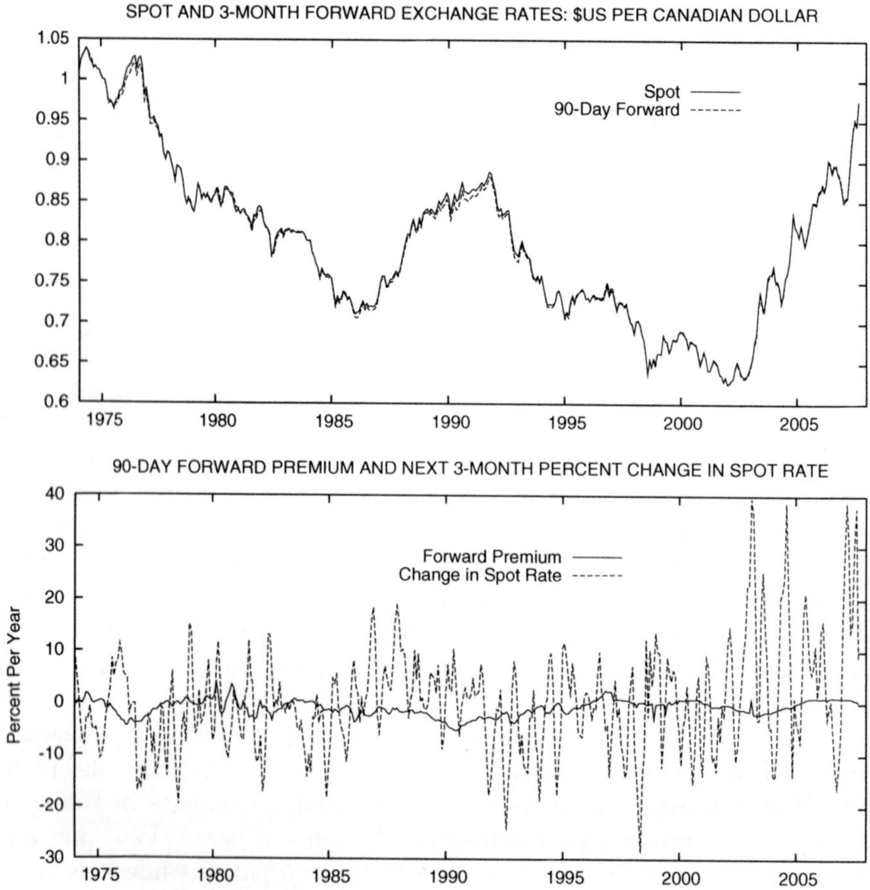

Fig. 9.1. Canada vs. United States: Spot and 90-day forward exchange rates, U.S. dollars per Canadian dollar (top panel) and 90-day forward premium and 3-month ahead percent change in spot rate (bottom panel). For sources see Appendix F.

The standard deviations of the one-month-ahead percentage changes in the spot rates are many times those of the forward premiums. The period of estimation of these standard deviations extends from June 1973 through November 2007 for Canada, the United Kingdom and Japan, and from June 1973 through December 1998 for France and Germany.[1]

[1] The standard deviations are calculated in Gretl and XLispStat using the input files `fprempuz.inp` and `fprempuz.lsp` and the results are in the output files `fprempuz.got` and `fprempuz.lou`. The data are in the files `jfdatamo.gdt` and

9.1 Covered Interest Parity

As noted in the preceding theoretical analysis, the interest parity condition is that the forward premium on a country's currency with respect to the U.S. dollar must equal the excess of U.S. over the domestic short-term interest rates minus a risk premium, positive or negative, that reflects any differential risk of holding capital in the domestic as opposed to the U.S. economy. Covered interest parity is said to hold when the interest rate differential is fully explained by the forward premium, and the country risk can therefore be ignored. Failure of covered interest parity to hold simply reflects the existence of differential country risk. A procedure to minimize the impact of country risk is to compare the interest rates on securities in the two countries' currencies issued by a single firm, or by issuers operating out of a third country. But even in these cases there will be some risk differential because, although the institution on which repayment depends is the same for both assets, or the assets are liabilities of the same institutions in third countries, future government intervention could still prevent ultimate repayment in one of the currencies.

Figures 9.2a and 9.2b present comparisons of the 3-month forward premium and the 3-month commercial paper rate differential for Canada vs. the United States and of the 1-month forward premiums and one-month off-shore euro-currency deposit rates for the U.S. relative to Canada, the United Kingdom, Japan, France and Germany. The observed fit is quite good even in the case of the 3-month commercial paper differential for Canada and much tighter in the case of the off-shore deposit rates. Nevertheless, there are substantial very short-run deviations from covered interest parity.

It turns out that these deviations are the result of problems with the collection of the spot and forward exchange rate data, as is illustrated by the case of the Japanese yen with respect to the U.S. dollar in recent years in Fig. 9.3. Two different monthly estimates of the spot and forward rates were obtained from *Datastream* for 1999 through 2007 – the mnemonics for the series are given below the charts in the top two panels. While the spot and forward rates are very similar in each of the two alternative estimates, the resulting 1-month forward premiums on the yen in terms of the dollar implied by the estimates, expressed in annual percentage rates, are strikingly different as shown

---

`jfdatamo.lsp` and in the Excel worksheet file `jfdatamo.xls` and are described in detail in the text file `jfdatamo.cat`. For more information about the data, see Appendix F.

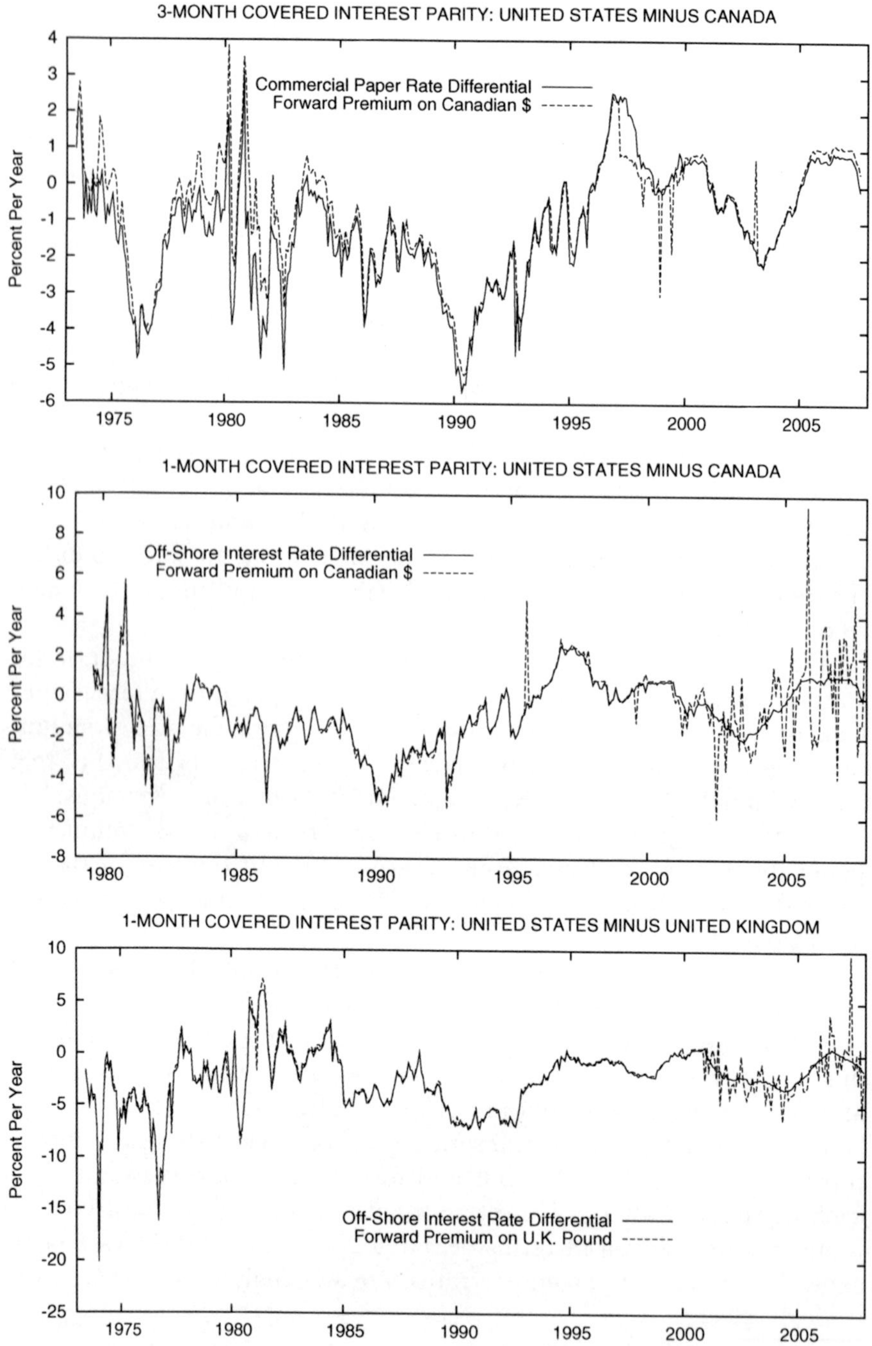

Fig. 9.2a. Covered interest parity for Canada and the United Kingdom with respect to the United States: For sources see Appendix F.

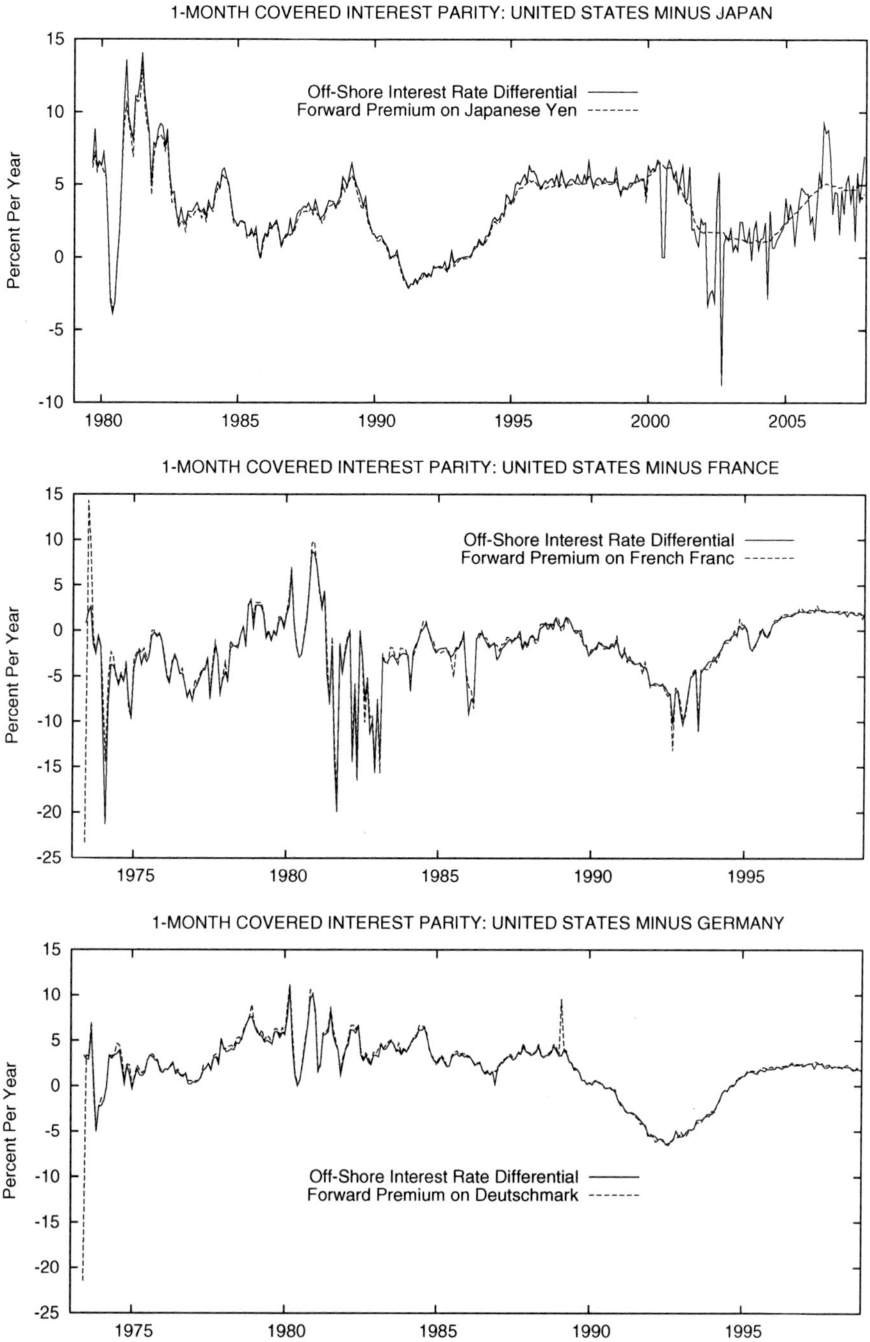

Fig. 9.2b. Covered interest parity for Japan, France and Germany with respect to the United States: For sources see Appendix F.

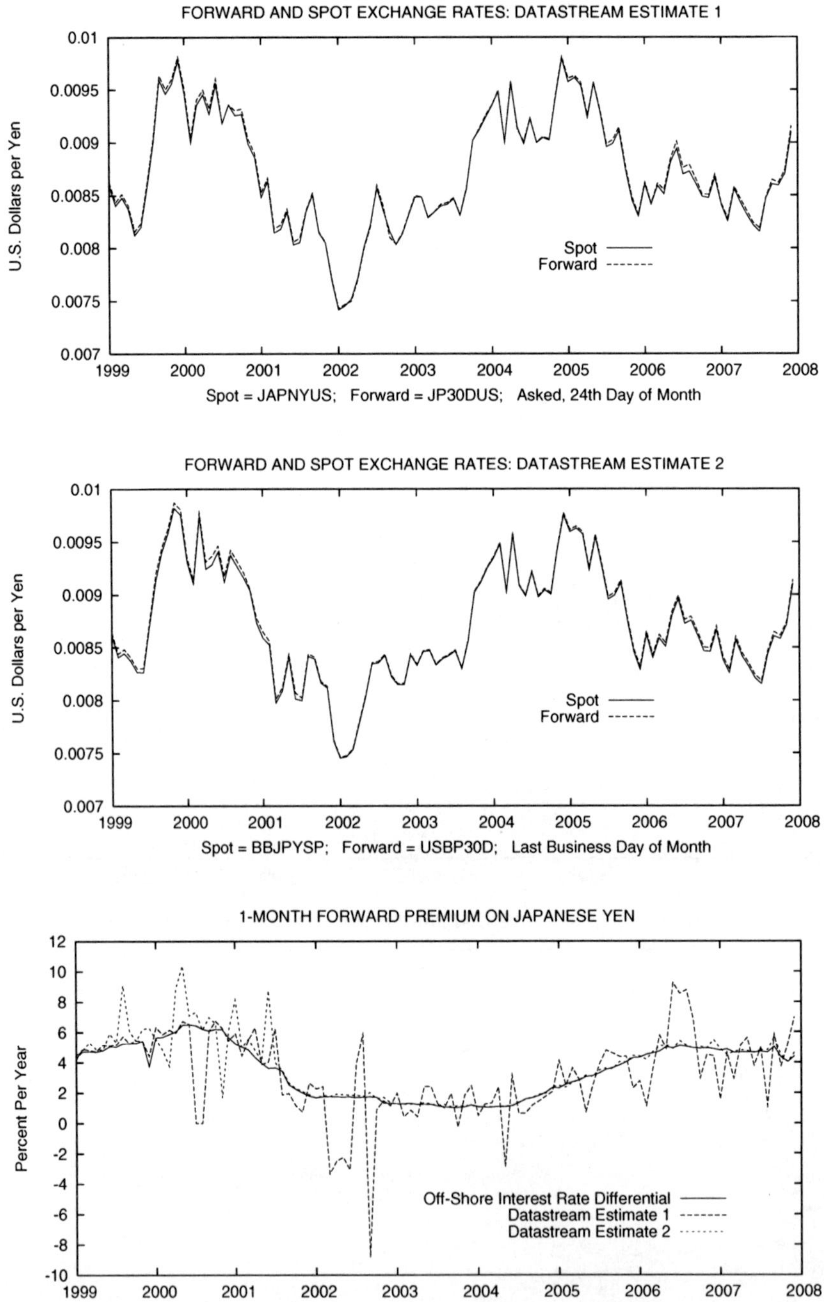

Fig. 9.3. Alternative off-shore interest differential and Datastream estimates of the Japanese spot and 1-month forward exchange rates with respect to the U.S. dollar, and the corresponding forward premia on the Yen. For sources see Appendix F.

in the bottom panel. There are two reasons for this. First, even slight differences between spot and forward rates have big effects on the forward premiums expressed in annual percentage rates. Second, it makes a difference whether the spot and forward exchange rate data pertain to prices asked, prices offered or actual contract prices, and whether the group of transactions that are averaged and the time interval over which they are averaged to obtain noon or closing prices for any given day is large or small.[2] These problems arise in the data for recent years with respect to all the currencies examined here. Indeed, as evident from the top panel of Fig. 9.2a, the problems also arise in Canadian exchange rate data that were collected by *Cansim* and not by *Datastream.*[3] For these reasons the 'implicit' forward premiums implied by the off-shore interest differentials are used instead of the actual forward premium estimates in all subsequent empirical analysis. Covered interest parity is thus assumed to hold to a reasonable approximation.

9.2 Uncovered Interest Parity

As previously noted, the interest parity condition given by equation (7.8) can be combined with the efficient markets condition (7.9) to yield

$$\tilde{i}_t - i_t \;=\; \Phi_t - \rho_c \;=\; E_\Pi - \rho_x - \rho_c \;=\; E_\Pi - \rho \tag{9.1}$$

where Φ_t is the forward premium and $\rho = \rho_x + \rho_c$ is the combined country and foreign exchange market risk premium on domestic assets. If enough people are risk-neutral so that the risk premiums disappear, this reduces to

$$\tilde{i}_t - i_t \;=\; \Phi_t \;=\; E_\Pi \tag{9.2}$$

which is known as the condition of uncovered interest parity – the foreign/domestic interest rate differential equals the expected rate of appreciation of the domestic currency.[4]

If expectations are formed rationally, in the sense that people take into account all information available to them, if market participants on average correctly anticipate future exchange rate movements, and if a sufficient fraction of those participants are risk neutral, the expected

---

[2] Alex Maynard and Peter Phillips [73] provide a discussion of these issues.

[3] For a complete discussion of the data sources, see Appendix F.

[4] Note that if uncovered interest parity holds so must covered interest parity since both risk premia are assumed to be zero.

rate of change in the exchange rate will equal the mean of the actual rate of change – prediction errors in the upward and downward directions will be equally likely. Forward exchange rates will then be unbiased predictors of future spot rates. Under these conditions, letting s_t and f_t be the logarithms of the spot and forward exchange rates, the regression

$$s_{t+1} = \alpha + \beta f_t + \epsilon_t \tag{9.3}$$

should produce estimates of α equal to zero and β equal to unity. If there is a constant risk premium, the estimate of α will differ from zero but that of β will still be unity. Alternatively, the change in the logarithm of the spot rate can be expressed as

$$s_{t+1} - s_t = \alpha + \beta\,(f_t - s_t) + \epsilon_t \tag{9.4}$$

which is identical to (9.3) when $\beta = 1.0$. The term $(s_{t+1} - s_t)$ is proportional to the percentage rate of change in the spot exchange rate and $(f_t - s_t)$ is proportional to the forward premium. Using (9.2) it can be seen that $\tilde{i}_t - i_t = f_t - s_t$ if the risk premium is zero and these two magnitudes will be on average proportional if α is a non-zero constant so that β will still be unity. Equation (9.3) can be defined as the 'forward rate' version of the 'unbiasedness hypothesis' and equation (9.4) as the 'forward premium' version.[5] Validity of the unbiasedness hypothesis is usually thought to imply uncovered interest parity.

Before turning to statistical estimation it is useful to examine what the principles developed in previous chapters and the evidence thus far observed imply about the magnitudes of α and β in the two expressions above. To start, assume that domestic and foreign inflation rates are zero, and known to be so, and that the real exchange rate is a random walk. If everyone correctly predicts the shocks ϵ_t and behaves rationally the magnitudes of α and β in both (9.3) and (9.4) will be 0 and 1 respectively. Under the more reasonable case where nobody can predict the ϵ_t, β will be zero in (9.4) because differences between f_t and s_t will only arise as a result of the random timing of individual transactions and those differences will be too small for arbitragers to profit from and will be uncorrelated with the movement of the spot exchange rate from the current to next period. The forward premium, and the excess of the foreign interest rate over the domestic rate, will not predict the change in the spot rate, or will do so only trivially in that $(s_{t+1} - s_t)$

[5] When the exchange rate is defined as the domestic currency price of foreign currency, the term 'forward discount version' should be used.

varies randomly around the predicted value of zero. Uncovered interest parity holds only in the sense that both Φ and E_{Π} equal a zero interest rate differential.

Nevertheless, the value of β in the 'forward rate' equation (9.3) will be very close to, but usually slightly less than, 1.0 as a consequence of the fact that the forward rate will almost exactly follow the spot rate with a one-period lag and the spot rate will be a random walk – only the slight random variation of f_t that is uncorrelated the next-period spot rate will reduce the estimate of β below unity and this, while likely, is not guaranteed. The estimated value of α will be close to, but usually very slightly greater than, zero. The presence of domestic/foreign inflation rate differences will not alter these conclusions as long as those differences are not of extreme magnitude. These issues with respect to estimates of α and β in the forward rate equation are explored more rigorously in Appendix E.

While it is quite clear that, in the absence of inflation differences, β will equal zero in the forward premium equation when the real exchange rate is a random walk, the forces determining the estimated value of β in the case of two or three decades of monthly data in situations where there is a degree of mean reversion are quite complex. In the pure random-walk case, the estimated level of β will be

$$b = \frac{Cov(s_{t+1} - s_t, u_t)}{Var(u_t)} = \frac{\sum[(s_{t+1} - s_t)(u_t)]}{\sum[u_t^2]} \tag{9.5}$$

where u_t is the percentage excess of the forward rate over the spot rate resulting from the normal hedging of traders' uncovered positions in the presence of transactions costs. When the domestic and foreign price levels vary randomly around constant expected values, the percentage change in the spot rate will be simply

$$s_{t+1} - s_t = \dot{p}_{ft} - \dot{p}_{dt} + \epsilon_t \tag{9.6}$$

where $\dot{p}_{ft}$ and $\dot{p}_{dt}$ are the percentage changes in the foreign and domestic price levels and ϵ_t is the random real exchange rate shock. Since the expectation of $s_{t+1} - s_t$ is zero, the forward premium becomes

$$\Phi_t = u_t. \tag{9.7}$$

Assuming on the basis of the empirical evidence presented earlier in this chapter that the standard deviation of month-to-month $(s_{t+1} - s_t)$ is 3 percent of the mean spot rate and the standard deviation of the random shock to the forward premium happens to be .0001, and letting the random and independent variations of the the domestic and foreign inflation rates each have standard deviations of .25 percent, one-thousand repetitions of calculations using a sample size of 360 (monthly for 30 years) with the shocks to the spot and forward rates normally distributed yields values of b that range roughly between -6000 and 6000, with approximately half of the estimates negative. The procedure for each repetition is to create the series $\dot{p}_{ft}$, $\dot{p}_{dt}$, ϵ_t and u_t as normal random variables with the variances specified, then use these series to create the series $s_{t+1} - s_t$ and Φ_t and, finally, regress $s_{t+1} - s_t$ on Φ_t to obtain an estimate of the coefficient β.[6] Increasing the sample size to 12000 reduces the range of estimates to roughly between -900 and 900. As the random variability of the forward rate becomes greater, b becomes better defined. Using a seemingly reasonable value for the standard deviation of u_t of a quarter of a percentage point, the estimated values of β in 1000 repetitions with a sample size of 360 range from around -2 to 2 with an average value in the range of -.05 to .05. The estimated standard deviations of b are still too large to enable rejection of the clearly false null-hypothesis that $\beta = 1$.

Increasing the average domestic and foreign inflation rates, known by market participants, from zero to .25 and .15 percent per month respectively, in which case the term

$$E\{\dot{p}_{ft} - \dot{p}_{dt}\}$$

is added to the right-hand side of (9.7), leads to no apparent change in the results – the forward premium and the percentage month-to-month changes in spot rates increase in proportion. Increasing the sample size to 12000 (1000 years), however, sufficiently reduces the standard deviations of the β estimates to make it possible to reject the null-hypothesis that $\beta = 1$ at much better than the 1% level.

Making allowance for a degree of mean reversion of the real exchange rates and the possibility of anticipated and unanticipated systematic increases and decreases of the real exchange rate and the domestic and foreign inflation rates through time complicates the analysis enormously. Yet it is possible to reach some useful conclusions using the simulation approach adopted above.

Given the statistical results of the preceding chapter, a monthly mean reversion parameter of no more than .01 would seem reasonable – this would imply an annual reversion of close to 12% of the deviation of the real exchange rate from its long-run mean. The equation

[6] These calculations are performed using the R script file `betacalc.R` and the XLispStat batch file `betacalc.lsp` and a particular run of the results discussed here is presented in the XLispStat output file `betacalc.lou`.

determining the relative change in the spot rate now becomes

$$s_{t+1} - s_t = -m\, q_{t-1} + \dot{p}_{ft} - \dot{p}_{dt} + \epsilon_t \tag{9.8}$$

where m is the mean reversion parameter, $\dot{p}_{ft}$ and $\dot{p}_{dt}$ are the percentage changes in the foreign and domestic price levels and, as before, ϵ_t is the random real exchange rate shock. And the forward premium becomes

$$\Phi_t = -m\, q_t + E\{\dot{p}_{ft} - \dot{p}_{dt}\} + u_t \tag{9.9}$$

where market participants correctly perceive the degree of mean reversion or

$$\Phi_t = E\{\dot{p}_{ft} - \dot{p}_{dt}\} + u_t \tag{9.10}$$

where they regard the real exchange rate as a pure random walk.

Using the same values of the remaining parameters, the results of 1000 simulation runs are essentially the same as before when the public does not realise that mean reversion is occurring. A correct perception of market participants that $m = .01$, however, leads to a substantial increase in the estimate of β to an average level roughly between 0.4 and 0.5 in the 1000 simulations with a sample size of 360. The coefficient standard errors are too large to permit rejection of the null-hypothesis that $\beta = 1$. Only about 16% of the estimated values of β are negative. Increasing the sample size to 12000 leads to estimates of β within the range of .227 to .668 and it becomes possible to reject both the null-hypotheses $\beta = 0$ and $\beta = 1$ in all 1000 simulation runs.

Given the slow rates of mean reversion and the substantial trends in the data examined in the previous chapter it would be plausible to argue that market participants, while being aware of the fact that real exchange rates will eventually return to their long-run mean levels, might reasonably project current trends in the short-run. While this violates the near-random-walk nature of observed past real exchange rate movements, it recognizes the fact that changes in real exchange rates arise from underlying real forces that vary persistently through time. Accordingly, it is useful to examine a situation where the public sets forward rates as moving averages of past realized relative changes in the real exchange rate plus the normal adjustment for expected differences between the foreign and domestic inflation rates. The equation determining the forward premium now becomes

$$\Phi_t = a_t + E\{\dot{p}_{ft} - \dot{p}_{dt}\} + u_t \tag{9.11}$$

where a_t is an n-period moving average of past real exchange rate changes – or, viewed alternatively, an adjustment to the expected change in the spot rate that would result from expected foreign and domestic inflation to incorporate underlying real exchange rate trends. Assuming that the true degree of mean reversion is .01 as before, but that the public ignores mean reversion in favour of projections of past real exchange rate growth, and using the same remaining parameters as before, 1000 simulations with a sample size of 360 produce negative estimates of β about 66 percent of the time when the expected change in the real exchange rate to next period is a 12 month moving average of past relative changes, falling to 57 percent of the time when the expected real exchange rate change is a 3-month moving average of past relative changes.

A substantial fraction of negative estimates of β can also arise when market participants fully take account of the mean reversion of the real exchange rate but are unaware of underlying deterministic real exchange rate shocks. For example, a situation where there is a uniform 1% per month upward shock for half of the period of estimation and a 1% per month downward shock for the other half will produce negative β estimates about 80 percent of the time. The fraction of negative β estimates reduces to around 25 percent, however, when the sample period is divided into four equal periods with shocks of equal magnitude in one direction in the first and third periods and in the other direction in the second and fourth periods.

Figure 9.4a provides plots of the real and nominal exchange rates generated by the above simulation model in the presence and absence of fully-anticipated mean reversion in cases where the estimated values of β are respectively positive and negative. In general it is impossible to predict the sign of the estimated β by looking at such graphs. Plots for simulations that involve unanticipated deterministic changes in the real exchange rate are shown in Fig. 9.4b. Although only cases with negative estimated values of β are shown, it should be remembered that negative coefficients occur only a small fraction of the time when the sign of the deterministic shocks alternates twice over the sample period. Plots for the cases where the public expects the next-period percentage change in the real exchange rate to be an average of previous changes over the past 3, 6 or 12 months are not shown because they exhibit identical patterns as plots of the form illustrated in Fig. 9.4a – the response of the forward premium is affected, but not the exchange rates themselves.

By way of comparison, Fig. 9.5 presents plots of the actual real and nominal exchange rates for Canada, the United Kingdom, Japan and Germany with respect to the United States. Taking into account the scales on the vertical axes, there is little apparent difference between

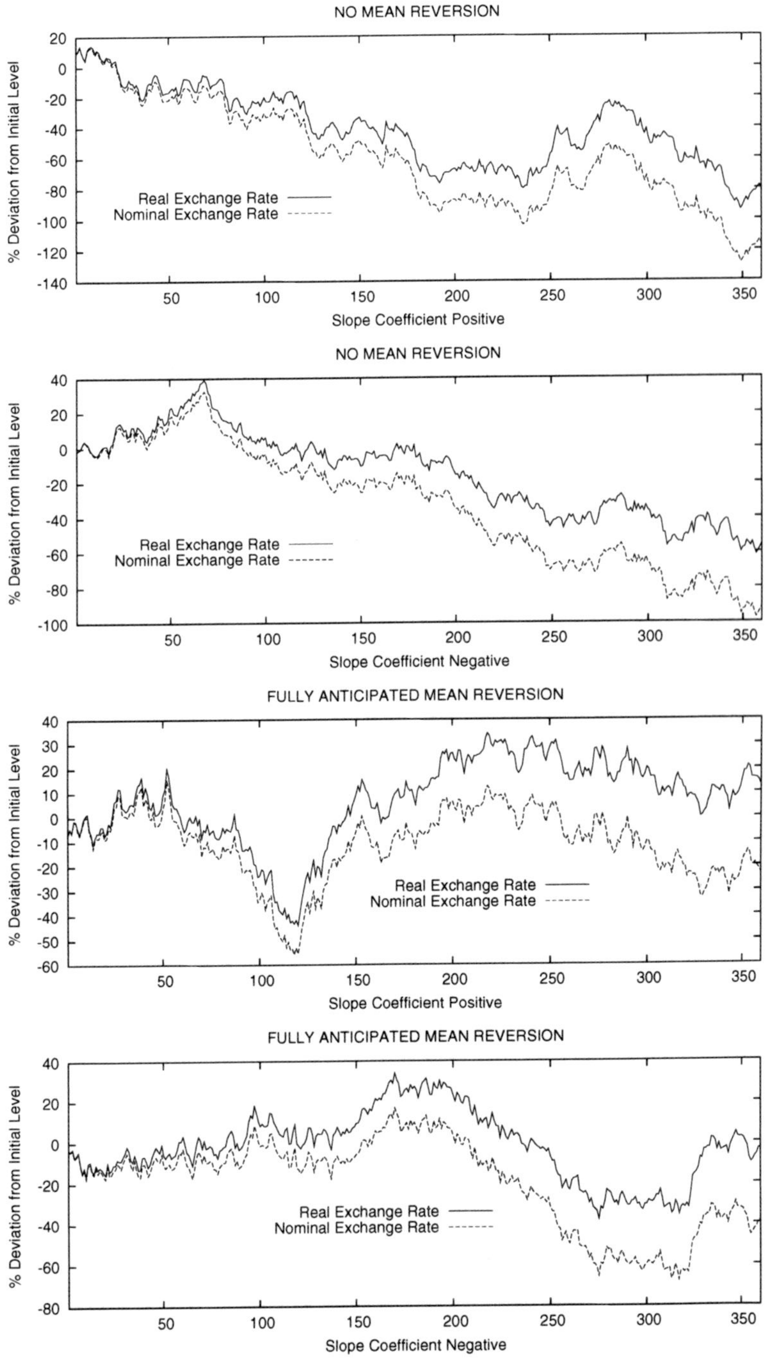

Fig. 9.4a. Simulated real and nominal exchange rate patterns with no deterministic shocks

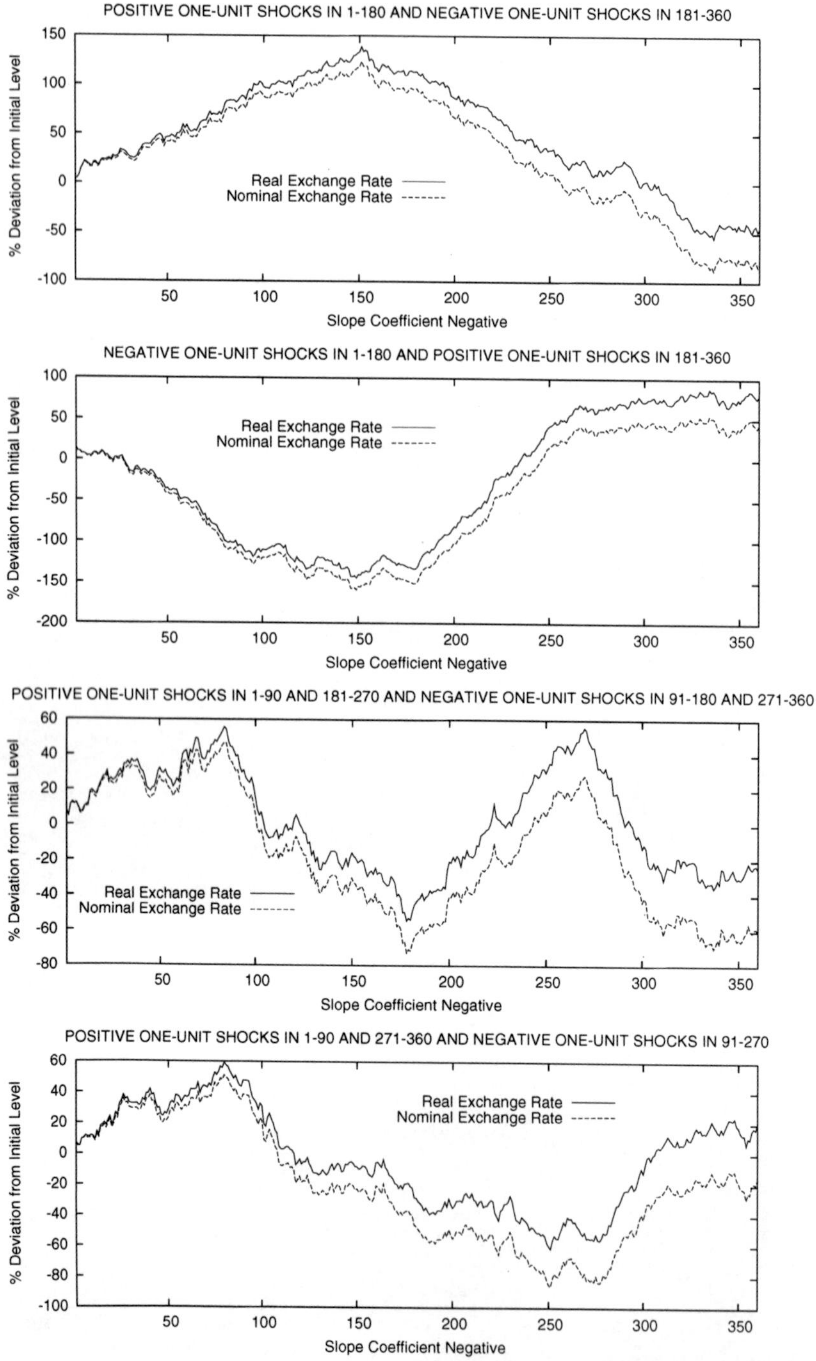

Fig. 9.4b. Simulated real and nominal exchange rate patterns with inclusion of deterministic shocks

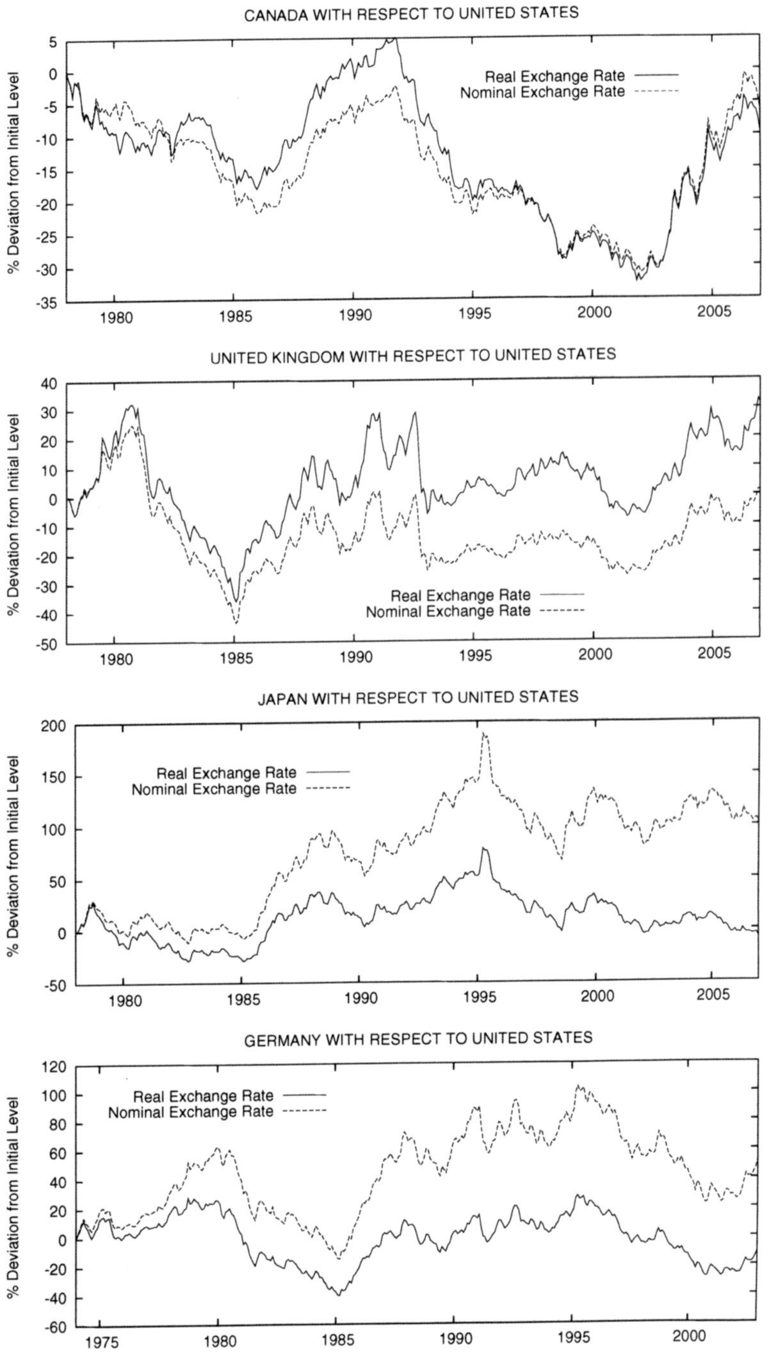

Fig. 9.5. Actual real and nominal exchange rate patterns for Canada, United Kingdom, Japan and Germany with respect to the United States

these plots and those generated by the simulation model presented in Fig. 9.4a and the bottom two panels of Fig. 9.4b.

Results of statistical estimation of the forward rate equation (9.3) are presented in Table 9.1. As expected, the coefficients of the lagged forward rate are close to but below unity, significantly so in most cases, and the constant terms are positive. Apart from the 3-month case involving the U.S. dollar price of the Canadian dollar, there is no evidence of serial correlation in the residuals. This suggests that in the 1-month forward rate equations there appear to be no autocorrelated left-out independent variables.

Table 9.2 presents estimation results for the forward premium equation (9.4). The estimated coefficient of the forward premium is everywhere negative and significantly so in the cases of Japan and the U.K.. There is no serial correlation in the residuals of the 1-month regressions and the constant terms are not statistically significant in the cases where the the coefficient of the forward premium is insignificant. In all five cases there is no basis for concluding that the coefficient of the forward premium is unity and the R-Squares are extremely low. The negative signs of the forward premiums in all regressions suggest that market participants may be basing their predictions of the future spot rate on the average of past rates of growth of the real exchange rate. But this notion is dispelled by results presented in Table 9.3. In every case where the current level of or past changes in the real exchange rate are significant determinants of the forward premium the sign is negative, indicating mean reversion. In the cases of France and the United Kingdom with respect to the United States there is no evidence of any effect on the forward exchange rate of current and past real exchange rates. In every case, the excess of the U.S. over the domestic inflation rate is a significant determinant of the forward premium with the correct sign – a lower domestic inflation rate relative to the U.S. rate leads to an increase in the forward premium.[7]

---

[7] The calculations for these tables were performed in Gretl and XLispStat using the input files `fprempuz.inp` and `fprempuz.lsp` and the results are in the respective output files `fprempuz.got` and `fprempuz.lou`. The estimates of serial correlation in the residuals were calculated only in XlispStat. The data are in the files `jefdatamo.gdt` and `jefdatamo.lsp` and in the Excel worksheet file `jefdatamo.xls` and are described in detail in the text file `jefdatamo.cat`. For additional discussion of these data see Appendix F.

Table 9.1. Regressions of spot exchange rates on lagged 1-month and 3-month forward rates

	Constant	Lagged Forward Rate	No. of Obs. T	R-Sq.	Serial Correlation Chi-Square – Order 1	< 6	$< T/4$
3-Month							
Canada/U.S.	0.015	0.984	414	0.961	631.5	941.6	977.9
1973:6–2007:11	(0.016)	(0.021)			[0.00]	[0.00]	[0.00]
1-Month							
Canada/U.S.	0.003	0.997	339	0.971	0.035	6.983	112.5
1979:9–2007:11	(0.009)	(0.012)			[0.85]	[0.22]	[0.02]
U.K./U.S.	0.043**	0.977***	414	0.964	3.859	5.606	87.51
1973:6–2007:11	(0.020)	(0.012)			[0.05]	[0.47]	[0.88]
Japan/U.S.	0.00009*	0.986**	339	0.982	0.748	6.049	57.68
1979:9–2007:11	(0.00006)	(0.007)			[0.39]	[0.30]	[0.99]
France/U.S.	0.004**	0.981**	319	0.970	0.012	5.507	66.97
1973:6–1999:12	(0.002)	(0.010)			[0.91]	[0.36]	[0.85]
Germany/U.S.	0.006	0.988*	319	0.973	1.303	4.743	71.11
1973:6–1999:12	(0.005)	(0.009)			[0.25]	[0.45]	[0.75]

Note: The test for serial correlation is a Lagrange Multiplier test based on work by Breusch [10] and Godfrey [48]. It involves regressing the residuals on lagged residuals together with the the matrix of independent variables and testing for significance of the lagged residuals. The figures in square brackets are P-values. When the residuals are serially correlated at the 10% level or worse, the coefficient standard errors, shown in the curved brackets, are adjusted for heteroscedasticity and autocorrelation with truncation lags equal to $.75\,T^{1/3}$ rounded to the nearest integer. The superscripts ** and * indicate significance at the 5% and 1% levels respectively of the null-hypotheses of zero values for the constant and unit values for coefficients of the forward rate.

Table 9.2. Regressions of percentage changes in spot exchange rates to next period on 1-month and 3-month forward premia

	Constant	Forward Premium	No. of Obs. T	R-Sq.	Serial Correlation Chi-Square – Order 1	< 6	$< T/4$
3-Month							
Canada/U.S.	0.210	-0.032	409	0.000	528.0	806.2	986.4
1973:9–2007:9	(0.980)	(0.437)			[0.00]	[0.00]	[0.00]
1-Month							
Canada/U.S.	-0.045	-0.900	339	0.006	0.138	4.038	96.35
1979:9–2007:11	(1.162)	(0.622)			[0.71]	[0.54]	[0.19]
U.K./U.S.	-3.118	-1.248**	414	0.010	0.638	1.576	89.84
1973:6–2007:11	(2.273)	(0.604)			[0.42]	[0.95]	[0.84]
Japan/U.S.	11.49***	-2.528***	339	0.024	0.033	2.399	67.73
1979:9–2007:11	(3.611)	(0.869)			[0.85]	[0.79]	[0.91]
France/U.S.	-2.392	-0.656	319	0.005	0.022	5.609	54.63
1973:6–1999:12	(2.338)	(0.537)			[0.88]	[0.35]	[0.99]
Germany/U.S.	2.763	-0.673	319	0.003	0.190	4.615	61.23
1973:6–1999:12	(2.579)	(0.712)			[0.66]	[0.46]	[0.94]

Note: The forward premia are based on off-shore interest rate differentials in the 1-month cases and on the corporate paper interest rate differential in the 3-month case. The percentage changes in the spot rates and the forward premia are expressed as annual rates. The superscripts *** and ** indicate signicance of the relevant coefficients at the 1% and 5% levels respectively. The test for serial correlation is the Lagrange Multiplier test discussed in the notes to the previous table. The figures in square brackets are the P-values and in those in curved brackets are the coefficient standard errors. In the Canadian 3-month case where the residuals are clearly serially correlated, the coefficient standard errors are adjusted for heteroscedasticity and autocorrelation with truncation lag equal to $.75\,T^{1/3}$ rounded to the nearest integer.

Table 9.3. Regressions of the 1-month forward premium on the past year's U.S. minus domestic inflation rate difference, the current real exchange rate and averages of percentage changes in real exchange rates during the past 1 to 3, 4 to 6 and 7 to 12 months

	Const.	Previous Years' Inflation	Real Exch. Rate	Average of Past Real Exch. Rate Changes 1-3	4-6	7-12	No. of Obs. R-Sq.
Canada/U.S.	5.417***	0.312***	-0.069***	0.012	0.017	0.021	340
1979:9–2007:12	(1.701)	(0.087)	(0.019)	(0.014)	(0.013)	(0.021)	0.238
U.K./U.S.	-4.665**	0.281***	0.024	-0.020	-0.000	-0.016	415
1973:6–2007:12	(2.340)	(0.081)	(0.020)	(0.013)	(0.009)	(0.017)	0.185
Japan/U.S.	2.053**	0.633**	-0.002	-0.026***	-0.009	-0.002	340
1979:9–2007:12	(1.021)	(0.249)	(0.005)	(0.010)	(0.007)	(0.014)	0.267
France/U.S.	-0.686	0.734***	-0.006	-0.021	0.012	-0.007	319
1973:6–1999:12	(2.868)	(0.149)	(0.025)	(0.019)	(0.013)	(0.023)	0.195
Germany/U.S.	7.542***	0.946***	-0.055***	0.003	0.005	-0.022**	319
1973:6–1999:12	(1.533)	(0.130)	(0.012)	(0.010)	(0.007)	(0.010)	0.544

Note: The forward premia are based on off-shore interest rate differentials and they and the percentage changes in the spot exchange rates are expressed as annual rates. The superscripts *** and ** indicate statistical significance at the 1% and 5% levels respectively. All coefficient standard errors, shown in the brackets below the coefficients, are adjusted for heterscedasticity and autocorrelation using the Gretl statistical program which chose a bandwidth of 5 and a bartlett kernel.

Clearly, there is no reason to be puzzled about the fact that the estimates of β in both the forward rate and forward premium equations are less than unity. And, it should not be surprising that in three out of the five cases the null-hypothesis that $\beta = 0$ cannot be rejected. That the estimated β coefficients in all the forward premium equations are negative is somewhat of a surprise although negative values in a fraction of the cases is extremely likely. This surprise is augmented by the fact that, as shown in Table 9.4, negative signs also occur in estimated forward premium equations for eight of the nine country-combinations

Table 9.4. Regressions of percentage changes in spot exchange rates to next period on 1-month forward premia: Canadian, British, Japanese, French and German currencies with respect to each other

	Constant	Forward Premium	No. of Obs. T	R-Sq.	Serial Correlation Chi-Square – Order 1	< 6	$< T/4$
Canada/U.K.	5.936***	-3.936***	339	0.044	0.567	2.152	72.83
1979:9–2007:11	(2.296)	(1.002)			[0.45]	[0.83]	[0.82]
Japan/U.K.	21.15***	-3.403***	339	0.017	0.401	1.691	58.93
1979:9–2007:11	(7.708)	(1.418)			[0.53]	[0.89]	[0.99]
France/U.K.	0.921	-0.712**	319	0.009	3.400	5.451	69.80
1973:6–1999:12	(1.951)	(0.534)			[0.06]	[0.36]	[0.78]
Germany/U.K.	-3.242	-0.064	319	.00003	3.791	5.619	73.78
1973:6–1999:12	(3.508)	(0.637)			[0.05]	[0.34]	[0.67]
Canada/Japan	-12.68	-2.844***	319	0.022	0.621	1.446	84.51
1973:6–1999:12	(4.778)	(1.038)			[0.43]	[0.92]	[0.49]
France/Japan	-3.630	0.349	244	0.001	0.002	5.944	39.58
1979:9–1999:12	(3.919)	(0.626)			[0.96]	[0.31]	[0.98]
Germany/Japan	-5.854*	-1.501	244	0.007	0.189	3.847	38.97
1979:9–1999:12	(3.011)	(1.122)			[0.66]	[0.57]	[0.99]
Canada/Germany	-2.590	-0.993	244	0.005	0.075	2.190	47.64
1979:9–1999:12	(3.601)	(0.899)			[0.78]	[0.82]	[0.89]
France/Germany	1.852	1.032***	319	0.149	2.907	6.082	57.80
1973:6–1999:12	(0.945)	(0.283)			[0.09]	[0.29]	[0.48]

Note: The forward premia, based on off-shore interest rate differentials, and the percentage changes in the spot rates are expressed as annual rates. The superscripts ***, ** and * indicate significance of the relevant coefficients at the 1%, 5% and 10% levels respectively. The test for serial correlation is the Lagrange Multiplier test discussed in the notes to Table 9.1. The figures in square brackets are the P-values and those in curved brackets are the coefficient standard errors. Where the residuals are serially correlated at the 10% level or worse, the coefficient standard errors are adjusted for heteroscedasticity and autocorrelation in the same fashion as in Table 9.1.

not involving the United States – the exceptions are France with respect to both Germany and Japan, with the positive coefficient for France with respect to Germany being statistically significant at the 1% level. Four of the negative slope coefficients – Canada with respect to Japan and the U.K. and Japan and France with respect to the U.K. – are statistically significant. It is interesting that all significant negative coefficients in the estimates of the forward premium equations in both Table 9.2 and Table 9.4 involve either Japan or the United Kingdom.

Is there a forward premium puzzle? Certainly one should not be puzzled by the fact that the estimates of the β coefficients in the forward premium equations are less than unity – these would be expected to be close to zero and can be negative a fraction of the time. There is still the question, however, of why negative coefficients occur a high fraction of the time. But this does not appear to be evidence of irrationality of market participants and consequent inefficiency of the foreign exchange market. In the simulation models it was easy to generate negative values for these coefficients – all that is necessary is a particular pattern of real exchange rate shocks. And negative values are even more probable if there happens to be, say, fully-anticipated increases in the domestic relative to foreign inflation rate, resulting in a fall in the forward premium, during a period in which the real exchange rate happens to unexpectedly rise sufficiently sharply to offset the downward effects of the changes in the inflation rate differences on the nominal exchange rate. Or there could be fully anticipated declines in the domestic relative to foreign inflation rate during periods when the real exchange rate is unexpectedly falling. Add to this the possibility that rational market participants can make mistakes in predicting domestic inflation rate changes on the basis of the inadequate information available to them. Scatter plots of the percent changes in exchange rates to next month against the current forward premiums in the cases of Canada, the United Kingdom, Japan, France and Germany with respect to the United States, shown in Figures 9.6a and 9.6b, indicate very weak relationships among the variables. The signs of the relationships are not obvious from the plots – a few outliers can make all the difference.

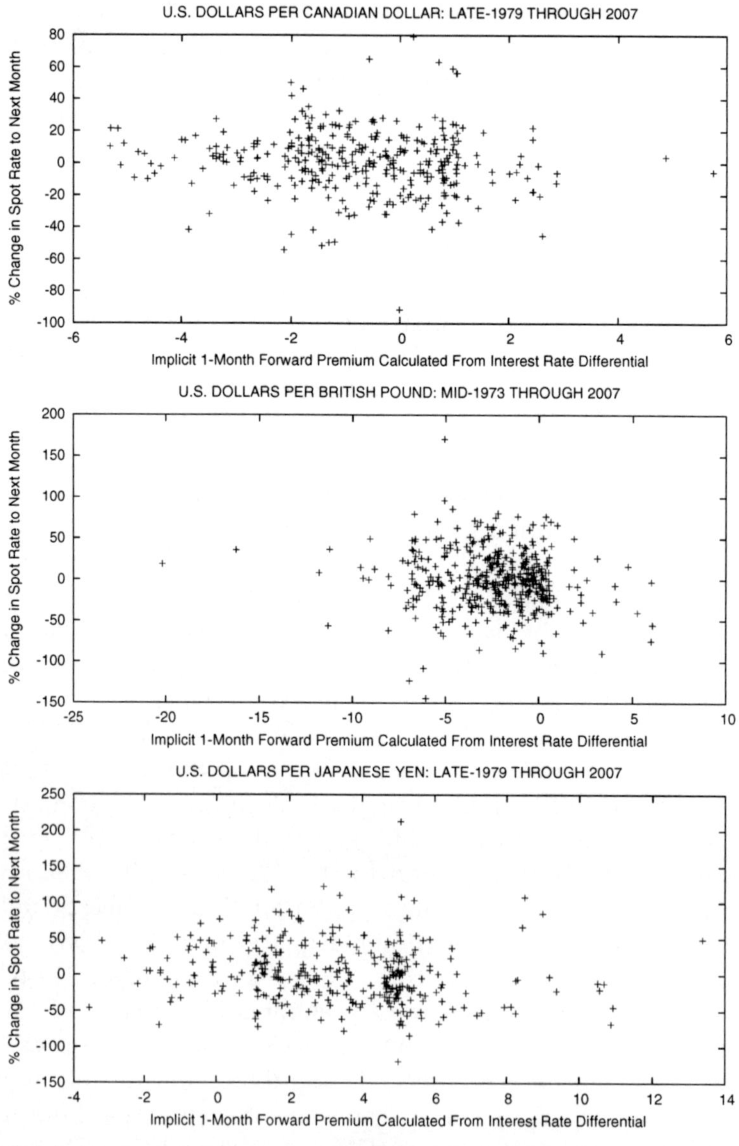

Fig. 9.6a. 1-Month forward discounts based on interest rate differentials and percentage changes of spot rates to next month – all interest rates and percentage changes are at annual rates

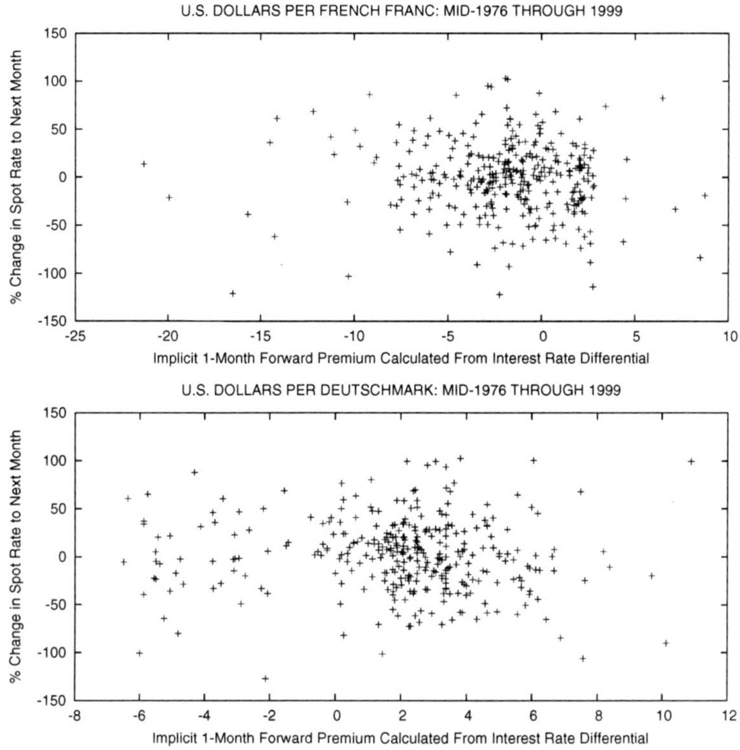

Fig. 9.6b. 1-Month forward discounts based on interest rate differentials and percentage changes of spot rates to next month – all interest rates and percentage changes are at annual rates

Kernel-density plots of the forecast errors resulting from naively using the current spot rate as the predictor of next-month's spot rate and, alternatively, using the current forward rate as the predictor are shown in Figures 9.7a and 9.7b. It is clear from these plots that there is little to choose between the two forecasting methods – indeed, this is consistent with the view that market participants have based their exchange-rate predictions largely on a naive assumption that over the next period the spot rate is equally likely to move in either direction. As shown in Table 9.5, the root-mean-square-errors of the two approaches are practically identical, with the forward rate forecast doing trivially worse than the naive spot projection.

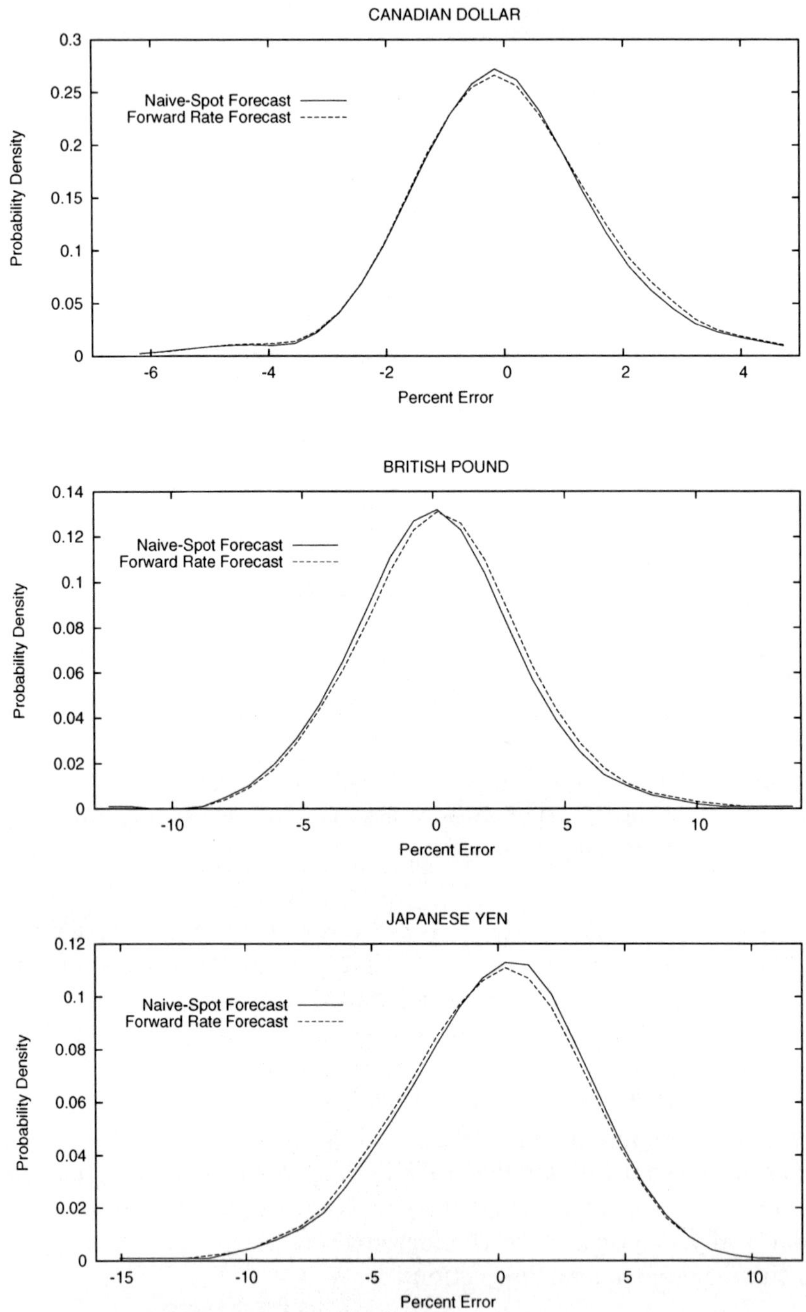

Fig. 9.7a. Kernel densities of the percentage errors of alternative forecasts of the U.S. dollar prices of the Canadian dollar, the British pound and the Japanese yen based on the naive assumption of constancy of the current spot rate and on the prediction implied by the current 1-month forward rate. For sources see Appendix F.

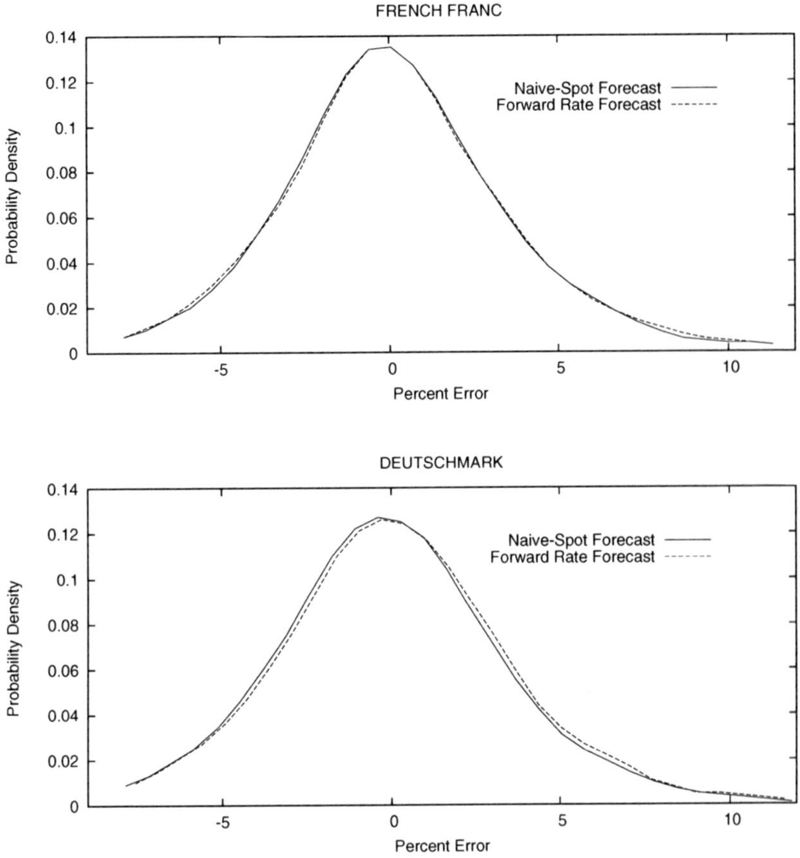

Fig. 9.7b. Kernel densities of the percentage errors of alternative forecasts of the U.S. dollar price of the French franc and German mark based on the naive assumption of constancy of the current spot rate and on the prediction implied by the current 1-month forward rate. For sources see Appendix F.

Table 9.5. Root-mean-square forecast errors of forward and naive current spot rate forecasts of next-period exchange rates expressed as U.S. dollars per unit of domestic currency

		Naive Spot Rate	Forward Rate
Canadian Dollar	1979:10 2007:11	1.574	1.594
U.K. Pound	1973:07 2007:11	2.999	3.025
Japanese Yen	1979:10 2007:11	3.381	3.434
French Franc	1973:07 2000:11	3.215	3.245
Deutschmark	1973:07 2000:11	3.243	3.279

It is reasonable to conclude that there is no basis for expecting unbiasedness of forward premium predictions of future changes in spot rates in the sense in which unbiasedness is usually thought of. And there appears to be no basis for concluding that foreign exchange markets are inefficient. This is especially the case since nothing rules out the possibility of variations through time in the risk premium which would make the estimates of β less than unity in the presence of market efficiency.[8]

[8] The kernel density estimates were calculated in the XLispStat file `fprempuz.lsp` and the statistics in the above table were calculated in Gretl using `fprempuz.inp` as well as in the XLispStat file. The data are in the files noted in previous footnotes in this chapter.

10

The Role of Real Shocks in Determining Real Exchange Rates: The Evidence

This chapter presents an empirical analysis of the role of real forces affecting the real exchange rates of several advanced industrial countries with respect to the United States – in particular, Canada, the United Kingdom, Japan, France and Germany. The task is to try to determine the extent to which observed real exchange rate changes are a consequence of real shocks to technology and capital accumulation. The lack of useful models of technological change makes this a difficult undertaking. One can only attempt to discern whether observed real exchange rate movements can be 'explained' by factors such as income growth, terms of trade changes, world oil and commodity price changes, shifts in world investment, and differential changes in government activity, that would obviously be expected to influence countries' real exchange rates. The real exchange rates with respect to the United States of Canada, the United Kingdom and Japan will be examined for the period 1974 through 2007. The real exchange rate of France with respect to the United States will be examined for the period 1974 through 1998, and that of Germany for the period 1974 through 1988. The sample periods for both France and Germany are shortened to end with European exchange market unification and the German analysis is further restricted to avoid data complications resulting from the merging of East Germany with West. All data are quarterly and explained in detail in Appendix F. The focus of this chapter will be entirely on real shocks with monetary shocks being the subject of the two chapters that follow. The analysis begins with the Canada/U.S. real exchange rate – it turns out that a full understanding of all the measurement and identification problems that arise with respect to all the real exchange rates examined can be best achieved by detailed study of this case.

J.E. Floyd, *Interest Rates, Exchange Rates and World Monetary Policy*,
DOI 10.1007/978-3-642-10280-6_10,

10.1 Canada vs. United States

The movements in Canada's real and nominal exchange rates with respect to the U.S. for the period 1974 through 2007, along with movements of the ratio of the Canadian to the United States price level are plotted in Figure 10.1 The trend of the real exchange rate from 1974 through 2002 has been downward, with a decline of around 25% between 1977 and 1985, a rise of more than 20% between 1985 and 1992 and a further fall of over 30% from 1992 through 2002. After 2002, the real exchange rate returned to its 1974 level. The nominal exchange rate shows the same pattern as the real exchange rate but differs on account of the higher average Canadian relative to U.S. inflation rate during the 1980s and the lower inflation rate in Canada relative to the U.S. after 1990.

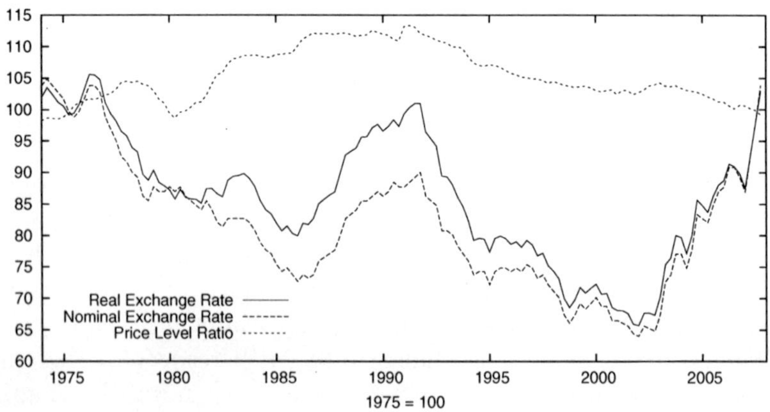

Fig. 10.1. Real and nominal exchange rates of Canada with respect to the United States and the ratio of the Canadian over United States price level, 1975 = 100.

The results of OLS regressions of the real exchange rate on various real variables are presented in the left-most column of Table 10.1.[1] The

[1] The entire set of regression results generated is shown in the XLispStat output file `rexcaus.lou` and in the Gretl output file `rexcaus.got`. These output files were generated by the respective input files `rexcaus.lsp` and `rexcaus.inp` using the data files `jfdataqt.lsp` and `jfdataqt.gdt`. The data are also in the Excel worksheet file `jfdataqt.xls`. The contents of these quarterly data files are explained in the text file `jfdataqt.cat`. For information on the data sources, see Appendix F.

Table 10.1. OLS regression analysis of real factors affecting the real exchange rate: Canada vs. United States, 1974:Q1 to 2007:Q4

Independent Variables	Dependent Variable Logarithm of Real Exchange Rate				
Constant	2.612 (0.187)***	2.369 (0.185)***	2.358 (0.184)***	2.292 (0.186)***	2.307 (0.197)***
Log of Commodity Prices	0.310 (0.065)***	0.372 (0.068)***	0.373 (0.067)***	0.388 (0.071)***	0.356 (0.063)***
Log of Energy Prices	0.154 (0.034)***	0.134 (0.034)***	0.135 (0.034)***	0.132 (0.034)***	0.163 (0.033)***
Real Net Capital Inflow	0.028 (0.004)***	0.022 (0.004)***	0.022 (0.004)***	0.021 (0.005)***	0.024 (0.004)***
		1-Month Corporate Paper	3-Month Corporate Paper	3-Month Tresury Bills	Long-Term Gov't Bonds
Interest Rate Differential		0.015 (0.004)***	0.016 (0.004)***	0.017 (0.004)***	0.032 (0.010) ***
Num. Obs.	136	136	136	136	136
R-Square	.775	.802	.805	.808	.796

Note: The commodity price variable is an index of world commodity prices, excluding energy, in U.S. dollars divided by an equal weighted index of U.S. export and import prices. The energy price variable is an index of world energy prices in U.S. dollars divided by the same index of U.S. export and import prices. The real net capital inflow variable is the negative of the Canadian current account balance as a percentage of domestic GDP minus the negative of the U.S. current account balance as a percentage of that country's GDP. The interest rate differential is Canada minus U.S. The figures in brackets are the heteroskedasticity and autocorrelation adjusted coefficient standard errors calculated in the Gretl statistical program, which chose a band width of 3 and a bartlett kernel. Significant serial correlation was present in the residuals of all regressions. The superscripts *** indicate significance at the 1% levels according to a standard t-test. For data sources, see Appendix F.

excess of Canadian government consumption expenditures as a percentage of GDP over the corresponding variable in the United States is not included in the regressions shown because it is statistically insignificant. The same is true of the logarithms of both countries' GDPs and the logarithm of Canada's terms of trade with respect to the rest of the world divided by the U.S. terms of trade with respect to the rest of the world. The logarithm of the energy price variable, which consists of the index of U.S. dollar prices of various forms of energy divided by an equally weighted average of U.S. export and import prices, explains the real exchange rate better than the logarithm of the oil price variable, which consists of U.S. crude oil prices divided by an equally weighted average of U.S. export and import prices, and so is included instead of the oil price variable. In every case substantial serial correlation is present in the residuals as evidenced by low Durbin-Watson statistics generated by Gretl and the LM-based tests for first-order autocorrelation and Ljung-Box Q-statistics for higher orders, calculated in Xlispstat.[2] This is, of course, not surprising because many technological forces that are correlated with time will not be captured by the crude regression analysis that could be applied. Accordingly, heteroskedasticity and autocorrelation consistent (HAC) standard-errors were calculated and are shown in the brackets below the coefficients.[3]

The regression result shown in the first column of Table 10.1 indicates what one would have expected. The logarithm of the Canadian real exchange rate with respect to the United States is positively related both to the logarithm of the ratio of U.S. commodity prices (excluding energy) over an equally weighted average of U.S. export and import prices and to the logarithm of the ratio U.S. dollar energy prices over the same average of U.S. export and import prices, as well as to the excess of the real net capital inflow into Canada over the real net capital inflow into the United States, both taken as percentages of the respective countries' GDPs. The real GDP variables were probably

[2] The LM-based test is an F-test of the significance of e_{t-1} in the regression

$$e_t = \alpha + \mathbf{X}\beta + \gamma e_{t-1} + u_t$$

where e_t are the residuals and $\mathbf{X}$ the matrix of regressors in the original regression and β is a column vector. This test has its origins in work by Breusch [10] and Godfrey [48]. The Ljung-Box test is a standard one available in most commercial econometric software programs.

[3] The HAC standard errors in the XLispStat output file were calculated using the formulas in Stock and Watson [98], page 505, and the truncation parameter was set equal to $0.75T^{1/3}$ rounded to an integer. The ones shown in the table were generated by Gretl.

insignificant because output growth does not differ much in the two countries and the effect of any trend of output growth is captured by the commodity and energy price variables. It would appear that the above rather crudely defined real factors explain almost 80 percent of the movements in the Canada/U.S. real exchange rate. The actual and fitted values are shown in Fig. 10.2. And it is clear from the plots in Fig. 10.3 of the portions of the real exchange rate movements captured by the individual included variables that, apart from trend, the excess of real net capital inflows into Canada as a percentage of GDP over real net capital inflows into the United States as a percentage of that country's GDP is the major distinctive factor explaining movements in Canada's real exchange rate with respect to the United States. This result is especially startling in that the importance of this determinant of movements in the Canadian real exchange rate with respect to the U.S. has been given little or no emphasis in professional discussion.

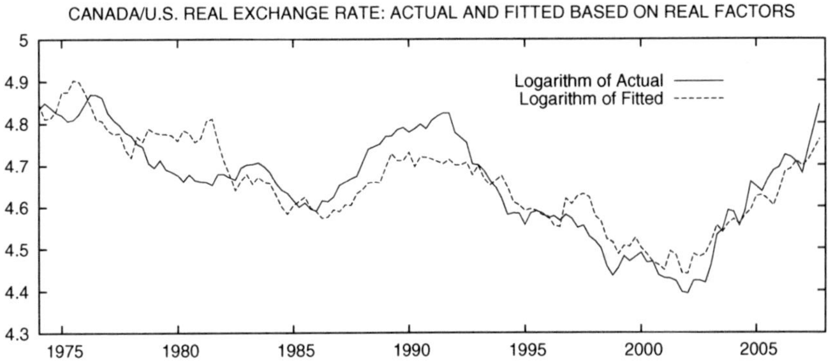

Fig. 10.2. The logarithm of the Canadian real exchange rate with respect to the United States and fitted values based on real factors.

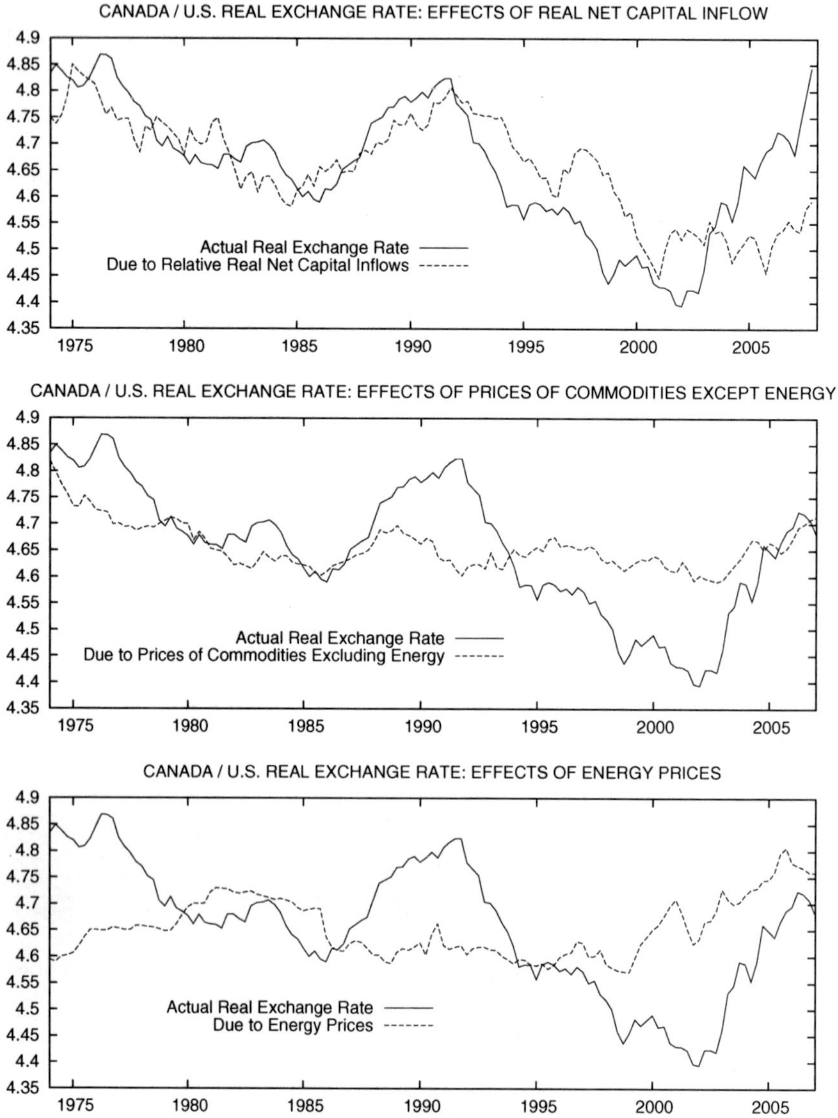

Fig. 10.3. The effects of real net capital inflows energy prices and the prices of commodities exclusive of energy on the Canadian real exchange rate with respect to the United States.

It is well known that statistically significant relationships often appear when unrelated non-stationary time-series variables are regressed on each other. It is necessary, therefore, to establish that the above regression result is not spurious. To check the stationarity of the relevant time series, Dickey-Fuller and Phillips-Perron stationarity tests were performed on all variables appearing in the above regressions. Three models were fit to each series:[4]

Model 1

Dickey-Fuller: $$\Delta y_t = a_0 + a_1\, y_{t-1} + a_2\, t + a_3\, \Delta y_{t-1} + a_4\, \Delta y_{t-2} + \ldots\ldots + a_{p+2}\, \Delta y_{t-p} + u_t$$

Phillips-Perron: $$y_t = \hat{a}_0 + \hat{a}_1\, y_{t-1} + \hat{a}_2\, (t - n/2) + \tilde{u}_t$$

Model 2

Dickey-Fuller: $$\Delta y_t = b_0 + b_1\, y_{t-1} + b_3\, \Delta y_{t-1} + b_4\, \Delta y_{t-2} + \ldots\ldots + b_{p+2}\, \Delta y_{t-p} + v_t$$

Phillips-Perron: $$y_t = \hat{b}_0 + \hat{b}_1\, y_{t-1} + \tilde{v}_t$$

Model 3

Dickey-Fuller: $$\Delta y_t = c_1\, y_{t-1} + c_3\, \Delta y_{t-1} + c_4\, \Delta y_{t-2} + \ldots\ldots + c_{p+2}\, \Delta y_{t-p} + w_t$$

Phillips-Perron: $$y_t = \hat{c}_1\, y_{t-1} + \tilde{w}_t$$

In all three models the null hypothesis is non-stationarity. The first model tests whether $a_1 < 0$, $a_0 \neq 0$ and $a_2 \neq 0$ and whether $\hat{a}_1 < 1$, $\hat{a}_0 \neq 0$ and $\hat{a}_2 \neq 0$. When these three conditions all hold the null hypothesis of non-stationarity can be rejected in favour of the alternative hypothesis of stationarity around drift, indicated by a constant term significantly different from zero and around trend, indicated by a coefficient of the time-trend variable significantly different from zero. The second model tests whether $a_1 < 0$ and $a_0 \neq 0$ and whether $\hat{a}_1 < 1$ and $\hat{a}_0 \neq 0$. When both conditions hold for a particular test, the null hypothesis of non-stationarity can be rejected in favour of the alternative

[4] The econometric work for the Canadian case was performed in XLispStat, Gretl, and R in the input files `rexcaus.lsp`, `rexcaus.inp` and `rexcaus.R` respectively and the relevant output is contained in the files `rexcaus.lou`, `rexcaus.got` and `rexcaus.Rot`. The data are in the Gretl and XLispStat files `jfdataqt.gdt` and `jfdataqt.lsp` respectively, in the Excel worksheet file `jfdataqt.xls` and, for use with R, also in the file `jfdataqt.tab`.

of stationarity around drift, indicated by the constant term significantly different from zero. Finally, the third model simply tests whether $a_1 < 0$ in the Dickey-Fuller test and $\hat{a}_1 < 1$ in the Phillips-Perron test. If so, the null hypothesis of non-stationarity can be rejected in favour of stationary without regard to drift and trend. The appropriate number of lags of Δy in the Dickey-Fuller tests performed using XLispStat was chosen on the basis of the Akaike and Bayes-Schwartz information criteria. In the estimation using Gretl, the lag-order was chosen by the program, working down from a maximum of 5.[5] The results are presented in Table 10.2, showing the Gretl results for the Dickey-Fuller test and the XLispStat results for the Phillips-Perron test, which could not be performed in Gretl.

Non-stationarity cannot be rejected in the case of the real exchange rate, the energy price variable and the net capital flow variable and can clearly be rejected for the commodity price variable. To establish that the regression in the left-most column of Table 10.1 is not spurious it must be shown that the real exchange rate, energy price the real net capital inflow variables are cointegrated – that is, that the residuals from the regression are stationary. The most effective procedure is to use a Johansen test.[6]

[5] In these tests the critical values are not those of the standard t-tests because the distributions of the statistics are non-standard when the null-hypothesis holds. Details of the tests together with the appropriate critical values can be found in Enders [33]. A table of critical values is reproduced in the file `statabs.pdf`.

[6] An alternative approach is to test the regression residuals for stationarity using a special set of critical values calculated by Engle and Yoo [37]. The problem with this test is that it, like the Dickey-Fuller and Phillips-Perron tests, has low power and therefore often fails to reject non-stationarity when stationarity in fact holds.

Table 10.2. The results of Dickey-Fuller and Phillips-Peron unit root tests for variables in the Canadian real exchange rate regressions

Model →		[1]			[2]		[3]
Variable	Test	Constant	Trend	Y_{t-1}	Constant	Y_{t-1}	Y_{t-1}
Log Real Exchange Rate	DF						
	PP				*nc*		
Log of Commodity Prices	DF				5%	1%	
	PP	5%	1%	10%	*nc*	1%	
Log of Energy Prices	DF						
	PP		1%		*nc*		
Real Net Capital Inflow	DF						
	PP				*nc*		
1-Mo. Corp. Paper Rate Differential	DF			5%		5%	5%
	PP			1%	*nc*	1%	1%
3-Mo. Corp. Paper Rate Differential	DF			5%		5%	5%
	PP			5%	*nc*	5%	5%
3-Mo. T-Bill Rate Differential	DF	5%		5%		10%	5%
	PP	10%		5%	*nc*	5%	5%
Long-Term Govt. Bond Rate Differential	DF					5%	10%
	PP				*nc*		

Notes: The percentages indicate the level at which the null hypothesis of nonstationarity can be rejected. Blank spaces indicate nonrejection and *nc* means that no calculation was recorded. DF refers to the Dickey-Fuller test and PP to the Phillips-Perron test. The calculations cover the period 1974 through 2007.

The Johansen procedure works with a VAR representation of the non-stationary variables[7]

$$\mathbf{y_t} = \mathbf{b} + \mathbf{B_1}\,\mathbf{y_{t-1}} + \mathbf{B_2}\,\mathbf{y_{t-2}} \ldots\ldots + \mathbf{B_p}\,\mathbf{y_{t-p}} + \mathbf{e_t}$$

where $\mathbf{y_t}$ is an m-dimensional vector containing the time-t values of the m variables in the VAR, $\mathbf{b}$ is an m-dimensional column vector, the $\mathbf{B_j}$ are $m \times m$ matrices of coefficients and $\mathbf{e_t}$ is an m-dimensional column vector of time-t error terms. This equation can be transformed into

$$\mathbf{\Delta y_t} = \mathbf{b} - \mathbf{Z_0}\,\mathbf{y_{t-1}} + \mathbf{Z_1}\,\mathbf{\Delta y_{t-1}} \ldots\ldots + \mathbf{Z_{p-1}}\,\mathbf{\Delta y_{t-p+1}} + \mathbf{e_t}$$

where

$$\begin{aligned}
\mathbf{Z_0} &= \mathbf{I_m} - \mathbf{B_1} + \mathbf{B_2} + \ldots\ldots + \mathbf{B_p} \\
\mathbf{Z_1} &= \mathbf{B_2} + \mathbf{B_3} + \ldots\ldots + \mathbf{B_p} \\
\mathbf{Z_2} &= \mathbf{B_3} + \mathbf{B_4} + \ldots\ldots + \mathbf{B_p} \\
\ldots &= \ldots\ldots\ldots \\
\mathbf{Z_{p-1}} &= \mathbf{B_p}
\end{aligned}$$

and $\mathbf{I_m}$ is an $m \times m$ identity matrix. For the variables to be cointegrated the rank of $\mathbf{Z_0}$, which is its number of non-zero characteristic roots or eigenvalues, must be positive. If the rank equals one there will be a single cointegrating vector which will be the eigenvector associated with the non-zero eigenvalue. If additional eigenvalues are positive there will be multiple cointegrating vectors but the total number cannot exceed $m - 1$. The Johansen procedure estimates $\mathbf{Z_0}$ and its eigenvalues along with two statistics called the L-max and the Trace statistics. The L-max statistic is used to decide whether the null hypothesis of h cointegrating vectors, where $(0 \leq h \leq m - 2)$, can be rejected in favour of $h + 1$ cointegrating vectors. The Trace statistic is used to decide whether the null hypothesis of h cointegrating vectors can be rejected in favour of more than h cointegrating vectors.

A Johansen test of the real exchange rate, real energy price and the real net capital inflow variables yields the following result:

[7] This procedure was developed by Johansen [58] [59] and Johansen and Juselius [60] [61].

Cointegration Vectors Under the Null Hypothesis	Eigen-Values	L-max	Trace
0	0.17008	25.534	36.121
		(0.0333)	(0.0377)
1	0.06452	9.075	10.766
		(0.4954)	(0.4169)
2	0.01236	1.691	1.691
		(0.1935)	(0.1935)
Lags = 8			

This is produced by Gretl with no restrictions on trend drift in the data. The P-values of the test are given in the brackets below the statistics. Lags ranging from 10 downward were tried and those in excess of 8 produced similar results both in Gretl and when the procedure was programmed in XLispStat.[8] It is reasonable to conclude that there is a single cointegrating vector. This conclusion is re-enforced by the fact that the real commodity price variable, which is stationary, is significant in the regression. Were the other variables not cointegrated, the residual from a regression including them alone would be non-stationary and could therefore could not be significantly correlated with the stationary commodity price variable.

Many contemporary analysts will argue that the Canada/U.S. interest rate differential should be added to the basic regression, their argument being that when the Bank of Canada tightens monetary policy by raising domestic interest rates capital inflows are attracted from the U.S., creating an excess demand for Canadian dollars and a rise in the domestic nominal and real exchange rates.[9] The excess of Canadian over U.S. interest rates on four types of assets were added to the basic regression and the results are presented in the right-most four columns of Table 10.1. In every case, the interest rate differential is statistically

---

8 Details of this test together with the appropriate critical values can be found in Chapter 6 of Enders [33] and tables giving these critical values are reproduced in `statabs.pdf`. The test was performed in Gretl and XLispStat using the input files `rexcaus.lsp` and `rexcaus.inp` that were used for the basic regressions.

9 For example, this is done routinely by John McCallum in a 1998 Royal Bank of Canada *Current Analysis* report [74].

significant at the 1% level with a positive sign. And the coefficients of the original variables do not change significantly.

It is clear from the theoretical analysis in previous chapters that there is no basis for concluding that the central bank of a small open economy like the Canadian one can significantly change the level of domestic interest rates by short-term monetary adjustments, provided that the expected rate of domestic inflation is not affected and the real exchange rate movement that would arise from any money supply shock is not expected to quicky reverse. And the notion that capital flows respond to international interest rate differentials has been shown to involve a fallacy of composition. To test whether money supply shocks affect the real exchange rate, unexpected money shocks rather than interest rate differentials should be added to the regression. This is the subject of the next chapter.

Why then are the interest differentials so statistically significant? Probably because the causation between interest rate differentials and the real exchange rate is the reverse of that specified by the regressions – it is likely that interest rate differentials are being explained by the other variables. A simultaneity bias would be expected with respect to all the variables – all that can be concluded is that the signs of the coefficients are in the direction expected by a rather crude general equilibrium analysis. Accordingly, the interest rate differentials are made the dependent variables in regression results shown in Table 10.3.[10]

In these regressions, all included independent variables are statistically significant at the 1% level. The remaining potential explanatory variables were dropped because they were not statistically significant, although the net capital flow variable turned out to be a statistically significant, but poor, substitute for the real exchange rate. Canadian real income has a positive sign and U.S. real income a negative one. The commodity and energy price variables both have negative signs and the log of the real exchange rate has a positive sign. A potential interpretation of these results is that increases in the real exchange rate and Canadian relative to U.S. real income increase the risk of holding Canadian as compared to U.S. assets while increases in commodity and energy prices reduce that relative risk. The problem with this interpretation is that it is difficult to imagine that the default risk on treasury bills and long-term government bonds would change as a result of the

[10] The calculations were performed in Gretl and XLispStat using the input files `idfcaus.inp` and `idfcaus.lsp` and the results can be found in the respective output files `idfcaus.got` and `idfcaus.lou`. The data files are those used in the input files `rexcaus.inp` and `rexcaus.inp`.

Table 10.3. OLS Regression analysis of real Factors affecting interest rate differentials: Canada vs. United States, 1974:Q1 to 2007:Q4

Independent Variables	Dependent Variables: Interest Rate Differentials			
	1-Month Corporate Paper	3-Month Corporate Paper	3-Month Treasury Bills	Long-Term Gov't Bonds
Constant	58.046 (12.988)***	57.794 (12.854)***	59.624 (13.865)***	26.423 (6.799)***
Log of Commodity Prices	-8.650 (1.133)***	-8.204 (1.050)***	-9.048 (1.297)***	-3.096 (0.508)***
Log of Energy Prices	-2.332 (0.576)***	-2.422 (0.552)***	-2.336 (0.598)***	-1.614 (0.248)***
Log of U.S. Real GDP	-23.321 (4.821)***	-23.237 (4.739)***	-22.440 (4.959)***	-9.041 (2.387)***
Log of Canadian Real GDP	22.764 (4.997)***	22.685 (4.896)***	21.645 (5.137)***	8.880 (2.457)***
Log of Real Exchange Rate	10.425 (1.758)***	10.081 (1.708)***	10.504 (1.971)***	3.668 (0.704)***
Num. Obs.	136	136	136	136
R-Square	.572	.607	.627	.586

Note: The variables are defined in Table 10.1. The figures in the brackets ( ) are the heteroskedastic and autocorrelation adjusted standard errors calculated in the Gretl statistical program, which chose a band width of 3 and a bartlett kernel. The superscripts *** indicate significance at the 1% levels according to a standard t-test. For data sources, see Appendix F.

magnitudes of changes in real exchange rates and commodity prices that have been observed. While the positive coefficient for the real exchange rate is consistent with mean reversion, such mean reversion has historically been very small. An alternative approach would explain the coefficients of the variables as reflecting the correlation of changes in those variables with expected future Canadian inflation relative to that in the United States. Expansion of income in a country, holding the conditions for full-employment equilibrium unchanged would tend to increase the prospect of domestic inflation. And increases in commodity and energy prices, holding real incomes and the price of domestic output in terms of foreign output constant would tend to increase full-employment output with the result that the upward pressure on domestic nominal prices will be smaller. And, holding other things constant, an increase in the real exchange rate – that is, the price of domestic in terms of foreign output – might be expected to exert upward pressure on domestic nominal prices.

Table 10.4. OLS Regression analysis of relationship between interest rate and inflation rate differentials: Canada vs. United States, 1974:Q1 to 2007:Q4

Independent Variables	Dependent Variables: Interest Rate Differentials			
	1-Month Corporate Paper	3-Month Corporate Paper	3-Month Treasury Bills	Long-Term Gov't Bonds
Constant	1.095 (0.238)***	1.144 (0.234)***	1.461 (0.249)***	0.986 (0.117)***
Inflation Rate Differential	0.362 (0.105)***	0.339 (0.102)***	0.335 (0.104)***	0.096 (0.047)***
Num. Obs.	136	136	136	136
R-Square	.130	.126	.115	.048

Note: The interest rate differentials are defined in Table 10.1 and the inflation differential is the excess of the Canadian over U.S. year-over-year CPI inflation rate. The figures in brackets are the heteroskedastic and autocorrelation adjusted standard errors calculated in the Gretl statistical program, which chose a band width of 3 and a bartlett kernel. The superscripts *** indicate significance at the 1% levels according to a standard t-test. For data sources, see Appendix F.

In this respect, it is interesting that the excess of the Canadian over the U.S. year-over-year inflation rate was insignificant when added to the Table 10.3 regressions. Yet this variable is always significant with the expected positive sign when it is the only explanatory variable, as shown in Table 10.4, but the R-squares, both unadjusted and adjusted for degrees of freedom, are very low compared to those in the Table 10.3 regressions.[11] This is consistent with the interpretation that the variables in the latter regressions are indeed capturing changes in the expected future inflation differential – they encompass all explanatory power contained in the inflation differential over the previous year, suggesting that the real variables encompass both the actual and expected differences in Canadian relative to U.S. inflation. Final conclusions regarding the determination of the Canada/U.S. interest rate differential must nevertheless wait until monetary shocks are introduced into the analysis in the next chapter.

10.2 United Kingdom vs. United States

The real and nominal exchange rates of the United Kingdom with respect to the United States for the period 1974 through 2007 are shown in Fig. 10.4. The British price level rose by more than 50% relative to the U.S. price level between 1974 and 1990, with the ratio of the two price levels being trendless from the latter year to the end of the period. Accordingly, the nominal exchange rate fell correspondlingly relative to the real rate before 1990 with the distance between them rather the same thereafter. Even before 1990, however, the real and nominal exchange rates varied together, with a trough after 1975, a peak around 1980, another trough in 1985, and a couple of peaks in the early 1990s.

The results of an OLS regression of the real exchange rate on the appropriate real factors that purport to explain it are shown in the leftmost column of Table 10.5.[12] The logarithms of the two countries' real outputs have the signs predicted by the Balassa-Samuelson hypothesis and a rise in the U.K. terms of trade with respect to the rest of the world relative to the U.S. terms of trade with respect to the rest of the world is positively related to the real exchange rate as would be expected. It is not clear what to make of the signs of the logs of the prices of commodities less energy and the price of oil. Since Britain imports commodities and produces oil, any interpretation one might make would seem to be ad-hoc. Given the crudeness of the available underlying theory of real exchange rate determination, it would probably be best to conclude that these variables are correlated with the

[11] The calculations in this table were performed using the same Gretl and XLispStat batch files that were used for the previous table.

[12] The U.K. vs. U.S. real exchange rate regressions and associated unit root tests were performed both in XLispStat and Gretl using the respective input files `rexukus.lsp` and `rexukus.inp` and the results are contained in the output files `rexukus.lou` and `rexukus.got`. The data files are the same as those used in the Canada vs. U.S. regressions.

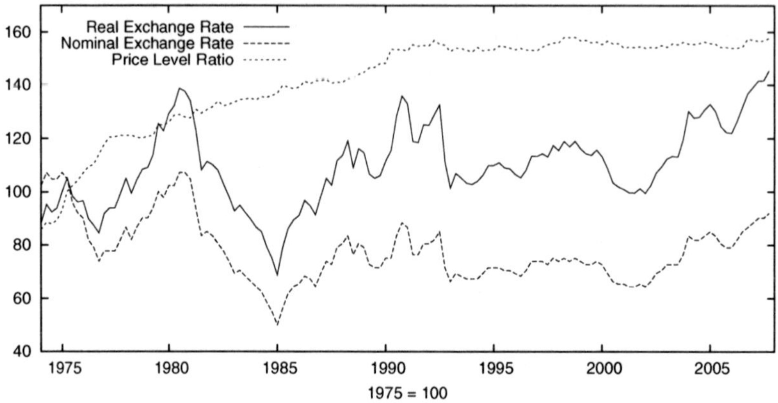

Fig. 10.4. Real and nominal exchange rates of the United Kingdom with respect to the United States and the ratio of the United Kingdom over United States price level, 1975 = 100.

plethora of real factors that could influence the real exchange rate. The excess government consumption expenditure in the U.K. as a fraction of output over the corresponding ratio for the U.S. and the magnitude of the net inflow of capital in to the U.K. relative to output less the corresponding magnitude for the U.S. were not statistically significant and therefore not included. The oil price variable yielded a better fit than an index of energy prices, with both divided by equally weighted average of U.S. export and import price indices and then expressed in logarithms.

Adding the U.K. minus U.S. interest rate differentials to the two right-most regressions in Table 10.5 weakens the effects of U.K. real output in both cases and that of U.S. real output in the case where the treasury-bill rate differential is used. And the treasury-bill rate differential is not statistically significant at the 5% level.

The actual and fitted values in the regression that excludes interest rate differentials are plotted in Fig. 10.5 and the contributions of the variables to explaining the real exchange rate movements are plotted in Fig. 10.6. The terms of trade ratio provides some explanation of the real exchange rate movements prior to 1985 as well as the increase that occurred after 2000. The commodity price variable also seems to explain the rise in the real exchange rate after 2000 although it is unclear what forces that variable is capturing. The income variables simply help explain the trend.

Table 10.5. OLS Regression analysis of real factors affecting the real exchange rate: United Kingdom vs. United States, 1974:Q1 to 2007:Q4

Independent Variables	Dependent Variable Logarithm of Real Exchange Rate		
Constant	-2.043 (1.282)	-3.609 (1.309)***	-4.391 (1.356)***
Log of Commodity Prices	0.466 (0.085)***	0.513 (0.072)***	0.359 (0.081)***
Log of Oil Prices	-0.206 (0.051)***	-0.184 (0.053)***	-0.174 (0.038)***
Log of Terms of Trade Ratio	1.835 (0.213)***	1.846 (0.225)***	1.932 (0.200)***
Log of U.K. Real GDP	2.216 (0.731)***	1.714 (0.786)**	1.432 (0.556)**
Log of U.S. Real GDP	-1.619 (0.586)***	-1.191 (0.632)*	-0.905 (0.451)**
		Treasury Bills	Long-Term Gov't Bonds
Interest Rate Differential		0.012 (0.006)*	0.027 (0.008)***
Num. Obs.	136	136	136
R-Square	.720	.748	.770

Note: The commodity price variable is an index of world commodity prices, excluding energy, in U.S. dollars divided by an equal weighted index of U.S. export and import prices. The oil price variable is U.S. crude oil prices divided by the same index of U.S. export and import prices. The terms of trade ratio is the U.K. terms of trade with respect to the rest of the world divided by the U.S. terms of trade with respect to the rest of the world. The interest rate differentials are U.K. minus U.S. The figures in brackets are the heteroskedasticity and autocorrelation adjusted coefficient standard errors calculated in the Gretl statistical program, which chose a band width of 3 and a bartlett kernel. Significant serial correlation was present in the residuals of all regressions. The superscripts ***, ** and * indicate significance at the 1%, 5% and 10% levels respectively. For data sources, see Appendix F.

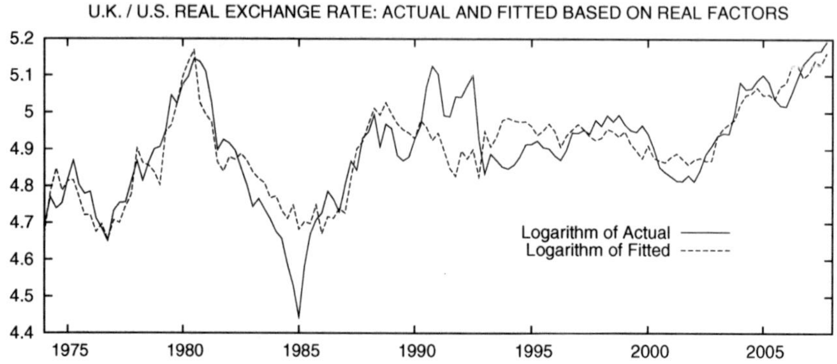

Fig. 10.5. The real exchange rate of the United Kingdom with respect to the United States: Actual and fitted levels in logarithms.

The question as to whether the above regression results could be spurious must now be addressed. Table 10.6 presents the results of stationarity tests of the variables involved. It is clear that the log of the commodity price variable and the log of U.S. real GDP are stationary and there is some evidence that the log of U.K. real GDP is also stationary. It thus turns out that the non-stationary variables in the above regressions must be cointegrated – otherwise the stationary variables would be insignificant. The results could thus not be spurious on the grounds of non-stationarity of the variables.

As noted above, once the standard errors of the coefficients are adjusted for heterskedasticity and autocorrelation, there is no significant effect of U.K. vs. U.S. treasury bill rate differentials on the real exchange rate. While the long-term government bond rate differential is statistically significant, those who view monetary policy as operating through interest rates would not be inclined to regard long-term rates as a policy tool. Given the statistical significance of the long-term interest rate differential, it is necessary to investigate the role of real factors in determining the excess of U.K. over U.S. interest rates to see if the real exchange rate is one of those factors. This is done in Table 10.7.[13] In the first and third columns, the included independent variables were selected by starting with all potential real variables plus the excess of the U.K. over the U.S. inflation rate and successively dropping the least significant. The log of the real exchange rate survived in the long-term

[13] The XLispStat and Gretl input files for these regressions are `idfukus.lsp` and `idfukus.inp` and the corresponding output files are `idfukus.lou` and `idfukus.got`. The data files are those used previously.

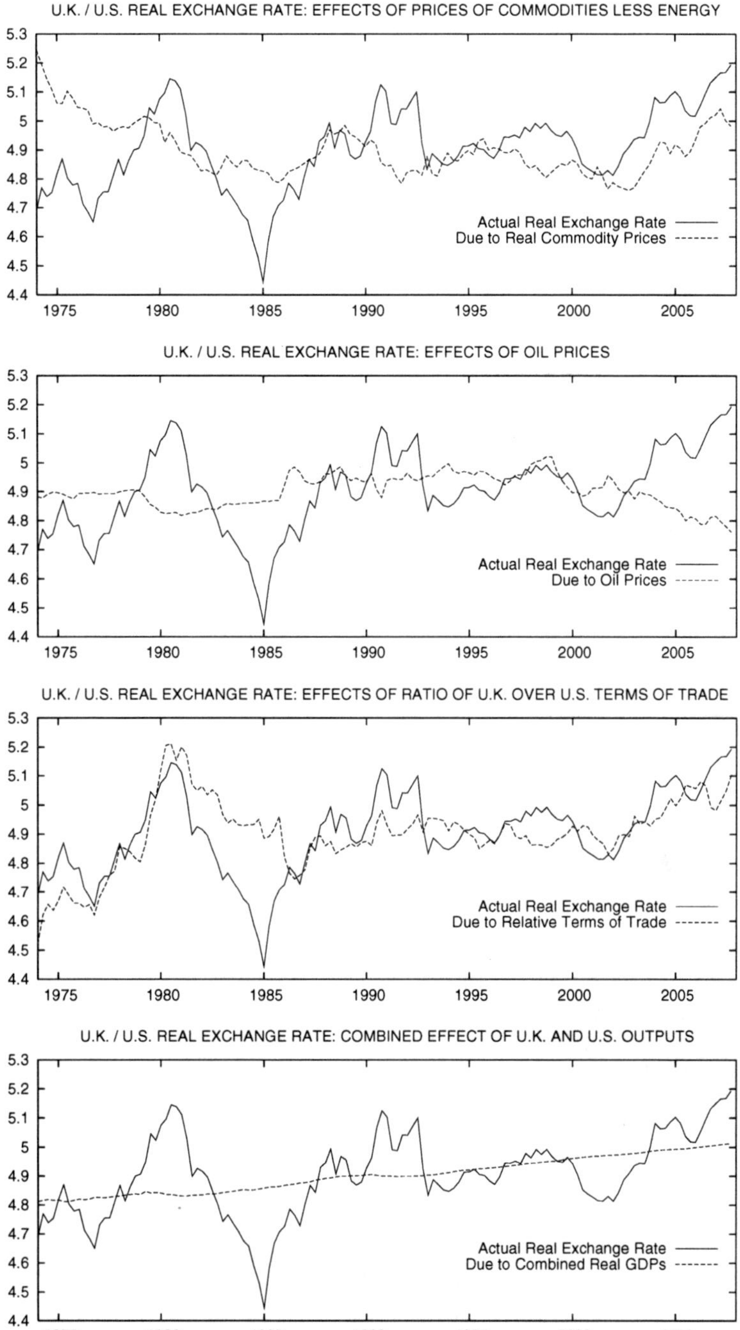

Fig. 10.6. The effects of oil prices, the prices of commodities exclusive of energy, the ratio of the U.K. to U.S. terms of trade and the combined effect of U.K. and U.S. outputs on the U.K. real exchange rate with respect to U.S.

Table 10.6. The results of Dickey-Fuller and Phillips-Peron unit root tests for variables in the United Kingdom real exchange rate and interest rate regressions

Model →		[1]			[2]		[3]
Variable	Test	Constant	Trend	Y_{t-1}	Constant	Y_{t-1}	Y_{t-1}
Log of Real Exchange Rate	DF						
	PP				*nc*		
Log of Commodity Prices	DF				1%	1%	
	PP	5%	1%	10%	*nc*	1%	
Log of Oil Prices	DF						
	PP		1%		*nc*		
Log of Ratio of Terms of Trade	DF				10%		
	PP	10%	1%		*nc*	5%	
Log of U.K. Real GDP	DF	10%	5%				
	DF	———	1%	———	——— 1%	———	
	PP		1%		*nc*		
Log of U.S. Real GDP	DF	5%	5%	5%			
	DF	———	1%	———	——— 1%	———	
	PP		1%		*nc*		
T-Bill Rate Differential	DF			1%	5%	1%	1%
	PP			5%	*nc*	5	5%
Long-Term Govt. Bond Rate Differential	DF						5%
	PP				*nc*		5%
U.K. minus U.S. Inflation Rate Differential	DF			1%		1%	1%
	PP			5%	*nc*	10%	5%

Notes: The percentages indicate the level at which the null hypothesis of non-stationarity can be rejected. Blank spaces indicate nonrejection and *nc* means that no calculation was recorded. DF refers to the Dickey-Fuller test and PP to the Phillips-Perron test. The null-hypotheses that the constant, trend coefficient, and coefficient of the log of real GDP lagged are jointly zero, and that the constant and coefficient of the log of real GDP lagged are jointly zero can be rejected at the 1% level for both countries using the Dickey-Fuller test performed with XLispStat. The calculations cover the period 1974 through 2007.

interest differential regression but not in the treasury bill rate differential regression. In the second column, the variables were selected by starting with those variables that were statistically significant in the real exchange rate regressions plus the inflation rate difference and successively dropping the least significant. The log of the real exchange rate survived as a statistically significant determinant of the treasury bill rate differential in this case.

In looking at the coefficients of the variables in Table 10.7 it is important to keep in mind that the risk premiums on government debt will represent the probability of default plus the probability of unexpected inflation. And the interest rate differentials themselves will directly reflect the excess of expected inflation in the U.K. over that in the U.S. It is therefore not surprising that the inflation rate difference is statistically significant with a positive sign in the treasury bill rate differential regression – greater past inflation tends to generate the expectation of greater future inflation in the short-run. In the case of the long-term government bond rate differential, the long-run expected inflation differential was better captured by the time patterns of the real variables than by the past inflation rate.

Any interpretation of the coefficients of the real variables in Table 10.7, however, will involve little more than an ad-hoc exercise of theoretical imagination. If one believes that the probabilities of default are very small and more or less constant, all that can be said is that a collection of real factors that would be expected to determine the real exchange rate are also correlated with the U.K. minus U.S. inflation rate differential. In contrast to the Canada vs. U.S. case, the inflation rate differential is the major factor affecting the U.K. minus U.S. interest rate differentials. This can be seen from the fact that the R-Square statistics, adjusted for degrees of freedom, in the regressions in Table 10.8 using the inflation rate difference as the only independent variable are one-third to one-half the magnitudes of the degrees-of-freedom-adjusted R-Squares in Table 10.7. A more complete analysis awaits the introduction of monetary shocks in the next chapter.

Table 10.7. OLS Regression analysis of real factors affecting interest rate differentials: United Kingdom vs. United States, 1974:Q1 to 2007:Q4

Independent Variables	Dependent Variables: Interest Rate Differentials		
	Treasury Bill Interest Rate Differential		Long-Term Gov't Bond Rate Differential
Constant	26.858 (8.825)***	59.373 (22.511)***	119.095 (11.000)***
Log of Commodity Prices	-5.766 (1.976)***	-4.553 (1.915)**	
Log of Energy Prices	1.534 (0.712)**		
Difference Gov't Cons.	-0.929 (0.370)**		0.441 (0.223)**
Difference Cap. Inflow	0.593 (0.169)***		
Terms of Trade Ratio		-13.452 (4.916)***	-18.875 (3.041)***
Log of U.K. Real GDP			15.302 (6.416)**
Log of U.S. Real GDP			-16.978 (5.263)***
Log of Real Exchange Rate		5.249 (2.532)**	7.643 (1.255)***
Inflation Rate Difference	0.244 (0.070)***	0.255 (0.089)***	
Num. Obs.	136	136	136
Adj. R-Square	.426	.297	.782

Note: The variables are defined in the text and in the notes to Table 10.5. The R-Square statistics are adjusted for degrees of freedom. The figures in brackets are the heteroskedasticity and autocorrelation adjusted standard errors calculated in the Gretl statistical program, and the significance levels shown, in the same way as in Table 10.5. For data sources, see Appendix F.

Table 10.8. OLS Regression analysis of relationship between interest rate and inflation rate differentials: United Kingdom vs. United States, 1974:Q1 to 2007:Q4

Independent Variables	Dependent Variables: Interest Rate Differentials Treasury Bills	Short-Term Gov't Bonds
Constant	1.889	2.352
	(0.302)***	(0.273)***
Inflation Rate Differential	0.257	0.264
	(0.067)***	(0.053)***
Num. Obs.	136	136
Adj. R-Square	.179	.262

Note: The interest rate differentials are defined in Table 10.5 and the inflation differential is the excess of the U.K. over U.S. year-over-year CPI inflation rate. The figures in brackets are the heteroskedastic and autocorrelation adjusted standard errors calculated in the Gretl statistical program, which chose a band width of 3 and a bartlett kernel. The superscripts *** indicate significance at the 1% levels according to a standard t-test. For data sources, see Appendix F.

10.3 Japan vs. United States

Figure 10.7 plots the real and nominal exchange rates of Japan with respect to the United States, along with the ratio of Japanese over the U.S. price level. The Japanese real exchange rate increased about 100 percent between 1974 and 1995 and then has declined by somewhat less than that amount by 2007. The Japanese price level fell rather steadily relative to the U.S. price level by about 50 percent from the late 1970s to 2007.

The results of an OLS regression analysis of real factors affecting the Japanese real exchange rate with respect to the U.S. are presented in Table 10.9.[14] The logarithm of the ratio of the Japanese terms of trade with respect to the rest of the world over the U.S. terms of trade with respect to the rest of the world is positively related to the real exchange rate and the logarithm of Japanese real GDP is positively related and that of U.S. real GDP is negatively related as consistent

[14] These regressions and the stationarity and cointegration tests discussed below are programmed in the XLispStat and Gretl input files `rexjnus.lsp` and `rexjnus.inp` and the outputs are in the files `rexjnus.lou` and `rexjnus.got`. The data files were those used previously in this chapter.

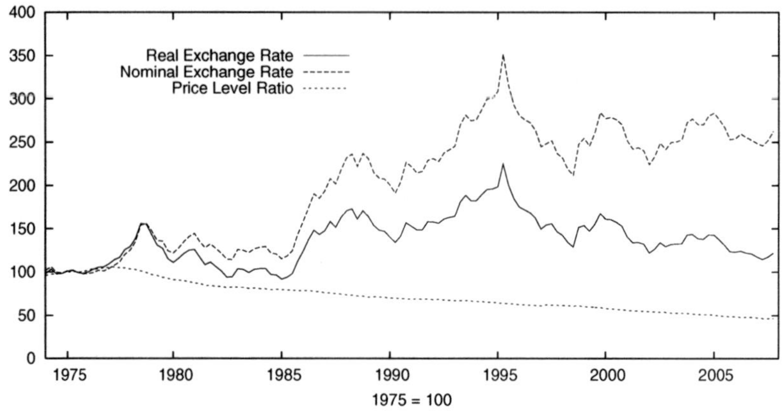

Fig. 10.7. Real and nominal exchange rates of the Japan with respect to the United States and the ratio of the Japanese over U.S. price level, 1975 = 100.

with the Balassa-Samuelson hypothesis. The logarithm of U.S. oil prices relative to the average of U.S. export and import prices and the excess Japanese government consumption expenditure as a percentage of GDP over U.S. government consumption expenditure as a percentage of that country's GDP are positively related and the excess of the negative of the Japanese trade balance – that is, real net capital inflow – as a percentage of GDP over the negative of the U.S. trade balance as a percentage of real GDP has, surprisingly, a negative sign. There is no obvious reason why the sign of the oil prices variable should be positive for Japan. In this respect it must be kept in mind that the results represent a relationship between the variables that undoubtedly suffers from simultaneity bias and left-out variables. When the Japanese less U.S. interest rate differential on long-term government bonds is added to the equation, it comes in with a negative sign and drives out the government consumption expenditure and real net capital inflow variables.

Figure 10.8 plots the actual and fitted values of the Japanese real exchange rate with respect to the U.S. and Figures 10.9a and 10.9b plot the measured effects of the various independent variables in the left-most regression in Table 10.9 on the real exchange rate. It is clear in third panel from the top of Fig. 10.9a that movements in the relative terms of trade account for a substantial part of the time pattern of the real exchange rate, and it is clear in the second panel from the bottom in Fig. 10.9b that Japanese real income growth has had an important

Table 10.9. OLS Regression analysis of real factors affecting the real exchange rate: Japan vs. United States, 1974:Q1 to 2007:Q4

Independent Variables	Dependent Variable Real Exchange Rate	
Constant	-9.610 (1.442)***	-10.038 (1.541)***
Log of Oil Prices	0.160 (0.051)***	0.123 (0.053)**
Log of Terms of Trade Ratio	1.237 (0.188)***	1.188 (0.166)***
Gov't Consumption Expenditure	0.033 (0.010)***	
Net Capital Inflow	-0.014 (0.006)**	
Log of Japanese Real GDP	1.224 (0.182)***	0.817 (0.153)**
Log of U.S. Real GDP	-1.868 (0.200)***	-0.272 (0.105)**
Interest Rate Differential		-0.028 (0.007)***
Num. Obs.	136	136
R-Square	.829	.841

Note: The construction of the variables is explained in the text. The figures in brackets are the heteroskedasticity and autocorrelation adjusted standard errors calculated in the Gretl statistical program, which chose a band width of 3 and a Bartlett kernel. Significant serial correlation was present in the residuals of all regressions. The superscripts ***, ** and *indicate significance at the 1%. 5% and 10% levels, respectively. For data sources, see Appendix F.

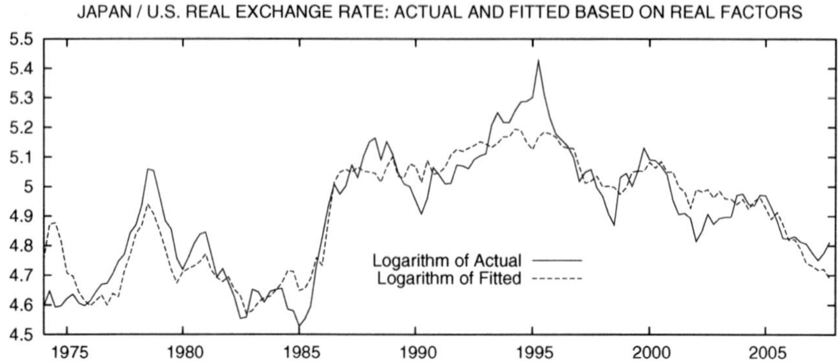

Fig. 10.8. Actual and fitted values of the logarithm of the Japanese real exchange rate with respect to the U.S.

influence. The effects of the other variables, apart from income growth in the U.S., are not observable on the graphs.

The next question that must be addressed is whether these regression results could be spurious on account of non-stationarity and lack of cointegration of the variables. Table 10.10 presents the results of Dickey-Fuller and Phillips-Perron tests of the stationarity of the variables that were not previously examined in the Canada vs. U.S. and U.K. vs. U.S. calculations. The government expenditure difference, the logarithm of Japanese real GDP and the long-term interest rate differential appear to be stationary, as does the inflation rate differential which will appear in the regressions in Table 10.11. The real exchange rate is non-stationary, as are the terms of trade ratio and real net capital inflow variables. It was established earlier that the oil price variable is non-stationary and the logarithm of U.S. real GDP appears to be stationary.

While the statistical significance of the stationary variables in a regression whose dependent variable is non-stationary clearly implies cointegration of the non-stationary variables, it is useful to perform a Johansen cointegration test on the latter variables. A Johansen test of the real exchange rate, oil price, terms of trade ratio, and real net capital inflow variables yields the following result, where the figures in brackets are the P-values.

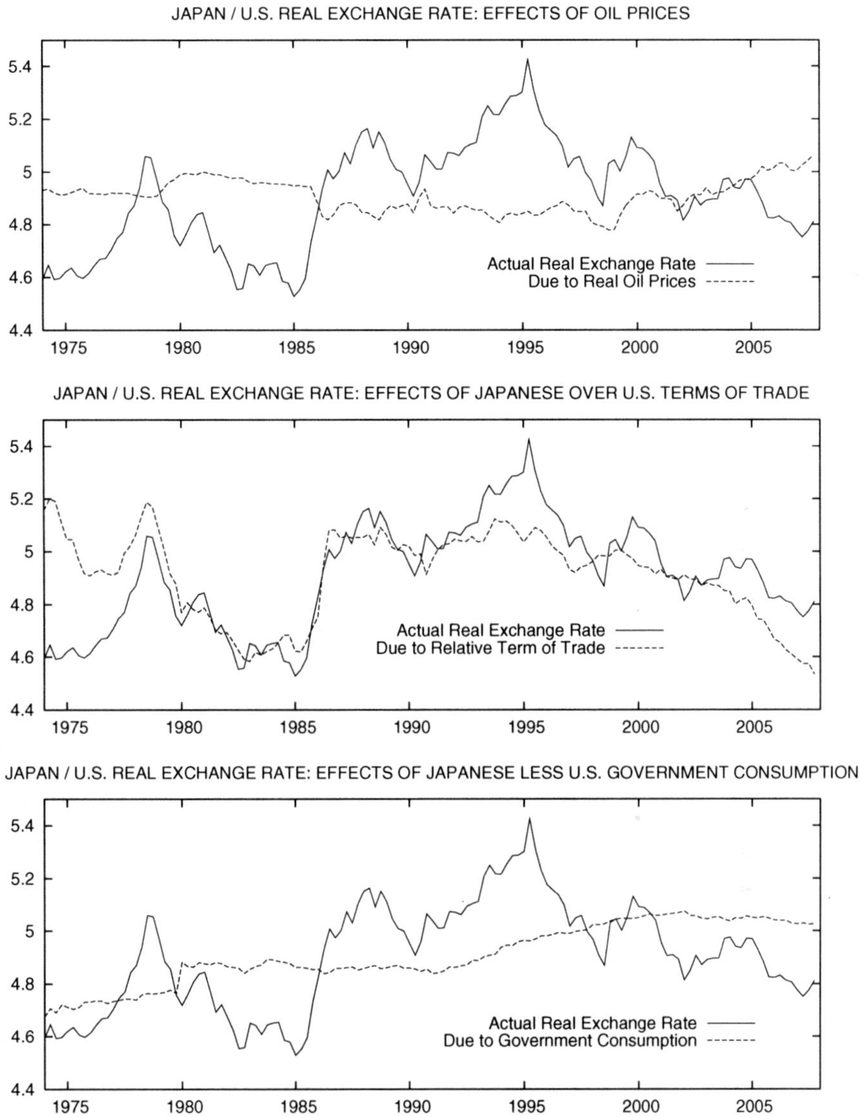

Fig. 10.9a. Effects on the logarithm of the Japanese real exchange rate with respect to the U.S. of oil prices, the ratio of the Japanese terms of trade with respect to the rest of the world over the U.S. terms of trade with respect to the rest of the world, and the excess of Japanese government consumption as a percentage of GDP over U.S. government consumption as a percentage of U.S. GDP.

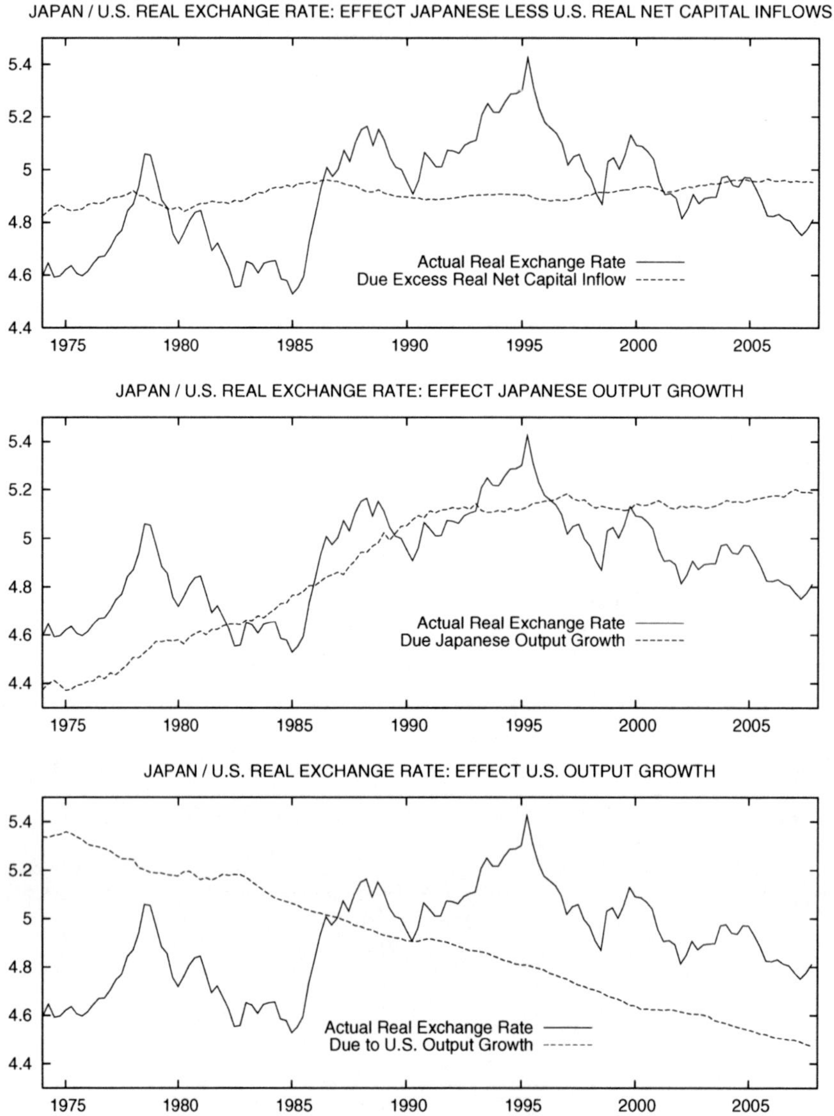

Fig. 10.9b. Effects on the Japanese real exchange rate with respect to the U.S. of the excess of Japanese real capital inflows as a percentage of GDP over U.S. real capital inflows as a percentage of U.S. GDP and of Japanese and U.S. real GDP growth.

Table 10.10. The results of Dickey-Fuller and Phillips-Peron unit root tests for variables in the Japanese real exchange rate and interest rate regressions

Model →		[1]			[2]		[3]
Variable	Test	Constant	Trend	Y_{t-1}	Constant	Y_{t-1}	Y_{t-1}
Log of Real Exchange Rate	DF						
	PP				*nc*		
Government Expenditure Difference	DF						5%
	PP				*nc*		1%
Real Net Capital Inflow Difference	DF						
	PP				*nc*		
Log of Ratio of Terms of Trade	DF						
	PP				*nc*		10%
Log of Japanese Real GDP	DF				5%	10%	
	DF				—— 1% —— (jointly)		
	PP				*nc*	10%	
Long-Term Interest Rate Differential	DF				5%	5%	
	PP				*nc*	5%	
Japan minus U.S. Inflation Rate Differential	DF				10%	10%	
	PP				*nc*		1%

Notes: Tests for variables tested in Tables 10.2 and 10.6 are not repeated here. The percentages indicate the level at which the null hypothesis of non-stationarity can be rejected. Blank spaces indicate nonrejection and *nc* means that no calculation was recorded. DF refers to the Dickey-Fuller test and PP to the Phillips-Perron test. The null-hypotheses that the constant and coefficient of the log of Japanese real GDP lagged are jointly zero can be rejected at the 1% level using the Dickey-Fuller test performed with XLispStat. The calculations cover the period 1974 through 2007.

Cointegration Vectors Under the Null Hypothesis	Eigen-Values	L-max	Trace
0	0.24854	37.145	71.135
		(0.0052)	(0.0008)
1	0.14202	19.912	33.990
		(0.1757)	(0.0647)
2	0.10172	13.945	14.077
		(0.1378)	(0.1835)
3	0.00102	0.13225	0.13225
		(0.7161)	(0.7161)
Lags = 6			

There is clearly a cointegrating vector.

Table 10.11 presents the results of regressions that purport to explain movements in the excess of the Japanese over the U.S. interest rates on long-term government bonds on the basis of the type of real factors that would be expected to explain movements in the Japanese vs. U.S. real exchange rate. An obvious explanatory variable, the Japanese minus U.S. year-over-year inflation rate difference, was added. The left-most regression was obtained by starting with all relevant real variables and dropping successively the least-significant variable until the remaining variables were all significant at the 5 percent level or better. The regression in the middle column was obtained by starting with the variables that were significant in explaining the real exchange rate movements and then dropping, in turn, the least significant variable other than the real exchange rate until all remaining variables were significant at the 5 percent level or better. The inflation differential when added turned out to be significant at only the 10 percent level and the real exchange rate variable was not significant at even the 10 percent level. The regression in the right-most column has the inflation differential as the only independent variable.[15]

[15] These statistical results are programmed in the XLispStat and Gretl input files **idfjnus.lsp** and **idfjnus.inp** with the outputs in the corresponding files **idfjnus.lou** and **idfjnus.got**. The data are in the files used previously.

Table 10.11. OLS Regression analysis of real factors on interest rate differentials: Japan vs. United States, 1974:Q1 to 2007:Q4

Independent Variables	Dependent Variable Long-Term Government Bond Rate Differential		
Constant	-14.301 (15.901)	-50.198 (11.304)***	-2.217 (0.249)***
Log of Commodity Prices	-3.890 (1.165)***		
Log of Oil Prices		2.496 (0.577)***	
Log of Terms of Trade Ratio		10.319 (2.098)***	
Difference Gov't Cons.	-1.095 (0.141)***		
Difference Capital Inflow	0.460 (0.080)***		
Log of Japanese Real GDP	-10.989 (1.620)***		
Log of U.S. Real GDP	19.355 (2.330)***		
Log of Real Exchange Rate		-2.215 (1.357)	
Inflation Rate Differential	0.198 (0.043)***	0.237 (0.087)*	0.359 (0.072)***
Num. Obs.	136	136	136
Adj. R-Square	.779	.597	.408

Note: The construction of the variables is explained in the text. The figures in brackets are the heteroskedasticity and autocorrelation adjusted coefficient standard errors calculated in the Gretl statistical program, which chose a band width of 3 and a bartlett kernel. The superscripts ***, ** and * indicate significance at the 1%, 5% and 10% levels respectively. For data sources, see Appendix F.

Since it is difficult to imagine that any significant probability of default exists for the public debt of either country, the most reasonable interpretation of the regression results is that they indicate the variables that are most correlated with the expected long-run inflation rate difference in Japan as compared to the U.S. While the positive sign of the terms of trade ratio variable in the middle regression is encouraging in that a rise in the price of traded output components in Japan relative to the United States might be expected to increase the probability of Japanese inflation, that variable is not statistically significant in the left-most regression, which has a much higher degrees-of-freedom-adjusted R-square. Any attempt to explain the signs of the variables would be ad-hoc – all that can be said is that they are correlated with the factors that determined the expected long-run inflation rate difference. Not surprisingly, the actual year-over-year inflation rate difference alone can explain over half the variation in the long-term interest rate differential. A fuller analysis awaits the incorporation of monetary shocks in the next chapter.

10.4 France vs. United States

The real and nominal exchange rates of France with respect to the United States are plotted, along with the ratio of the French over U.S. price levels in Fig. 10.10. The real exchange rate dropped sharply between 1980 and 1985 and then recovered by the late 1980s. France's price level rose about 30 percent relative the the U.S. price level between 1974 and 1985 and then declined gradually by about half that amount by the end of the period. The sample period ends in 1998 because after that year France was part of the European Currency Union and should not be viewed independently.

Table 10.12 presents the results of regressions of the logarithm of the French vs. U.S. real exchange rate on a set of real factors that would be expected to determine it.[16] The logarithm of energy prices in U.S. dollars divided by an equally weighted average of U.S. export and import prices provided a better fit than the logarithm of U.S. oil prices divided by the same U.S. traded goods price index. And the excess of net capital inflows and debt service flows into France – represented by the negative of the French trade balance – as a percentage of GDP over the

[16] The calculations for these regressions are performed in the XLispStat and Gretl batch files `rexfrus.lsp` and `rexfrus.inp` and the outputs are in the respective files `rexfrus.lou` and `rexfrus.got`. Again, the data are in the files used previously.

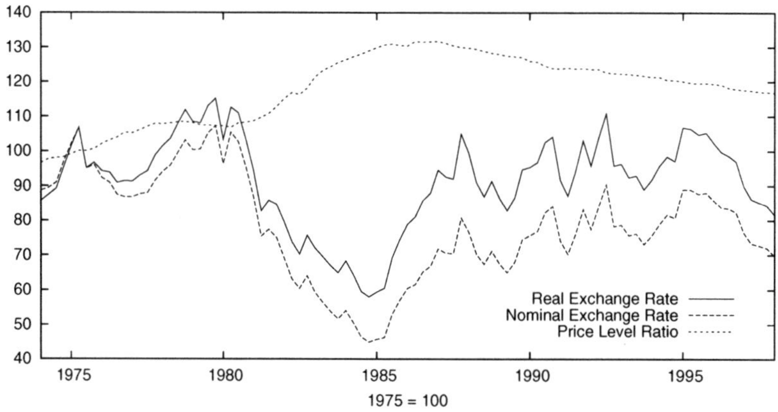

Fig. 10.10. Real and nominal exchange rates of France with respect to the United States and the ratio of the French over U.S. price level, 1975 = 100.

corresponding U.S. net inflows as a percentage of that country's GDP turned out to be statistically insignificant and was not included. The logarithm of the ratio of the French terms of trade with respect to the rest of the world over the U.S. terms of trade with respect to the rest of the world is positively related to the real exchange rate, as might be expected, and the effects of the logarithms of the French and U.S. real GDPs are positive and negative, respectively, as consistent with the Balassa-Samuelson hypothesis. The excess of French government consumption expenditure as a percentage of GDP over U.S. government consumption expenditure as a percentage of that country's GDP had the expected positive effect. The signs of the coefficients of the logarithms of U.S. dollar prices of energy and of commodities excluding energy, both deflated by U.S. traded goods prices, do not have an obvious non-ad-hoc interpretation.

Figures 10.11a and 10.11b plot the actual and fitted levels of the left-most regression in the table along with the separate effects of the individual included variables on the real exchange rate. An examination of these plots leads one to the conclusion that the main factor accounting for the decline in the real exchange rate between 1980 and 1985 and the increase thereafter was changes in the ratio of the French over the U.S. terms of trade.

The regressions in the two right-side regressions in Table 10.12 add the French minus U.S. interest rate differentials to the regression in deference to the common view that central bank imposed increases in domestic interest rates lead to an inflow of capital and an increase in

Table 10.12. OLS Regression analysis of real factors affecting the real exchange rate: France vs. United States, 1974:Q1 to 1998:Q4

Independent Variables	Dependent Variable Logarithm of Real Exchange Rate		
Constant	-3.901 (2.636)	-3.809 (2.580)	-4.048 (2.393)*
Log of Commodity Prices	0.313 (0.130)**	0.300 (0.121)**	0.343 (0.119)***
Log of Energy Prices	-0.279 (0.078)***	-0.283 (0.078)***	-0.272 (0.076)***
Gov't Cons. Difference	0.033 (0.018)*	0.032 (0.018)*	0.035 (0.018)*
Log of Terms of Trade Ratio	2.143 (0.144)***	2.129 (0.160)***	2.162 (0.162)***
Log of French Real GDP	1.778 (0.517)* * *	1.810 (0.551)**	1.564 (0.665)**
Log of U.S. Real GDP	-1.911 (0.432)***	-1.935 (0.446)***	-1.717 (0.557)***
		Treasury Bills	Long-Term Gov't Bonds
Interest Rate Differential		-0.001 (0.004)	0.015 (0.016)
Num. Obs.	100	100	100
R-Square	.803	.803	.809

Note: The construction of the variables is explained in the text. The figures in brackets are the heteroskedasticity and autocorrelation adjusted coefficient standard errors calculated in the Gretl statistical program, which chose a band width of 3 and a bartlett kernel. Significant serial correlation was present in the residuals of all the regressions. The superscripts ***, ** and * indicate significance at the 1%, 5% and 10% levels respectively. For data sources, see Appendix F.

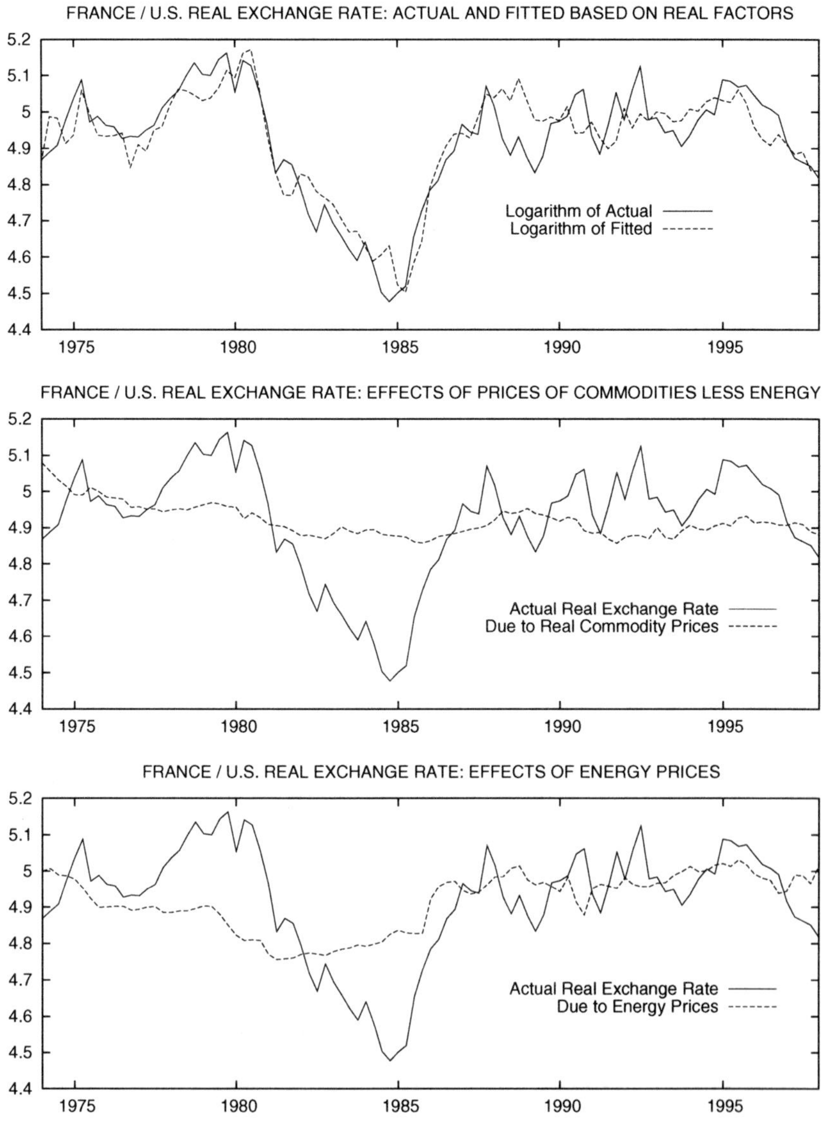

Fig. 10.11a. Actual and fitted values of the logarithm of the French real exchange rate with respect to the U.S. and the effects of of commodity prices and energy prices.

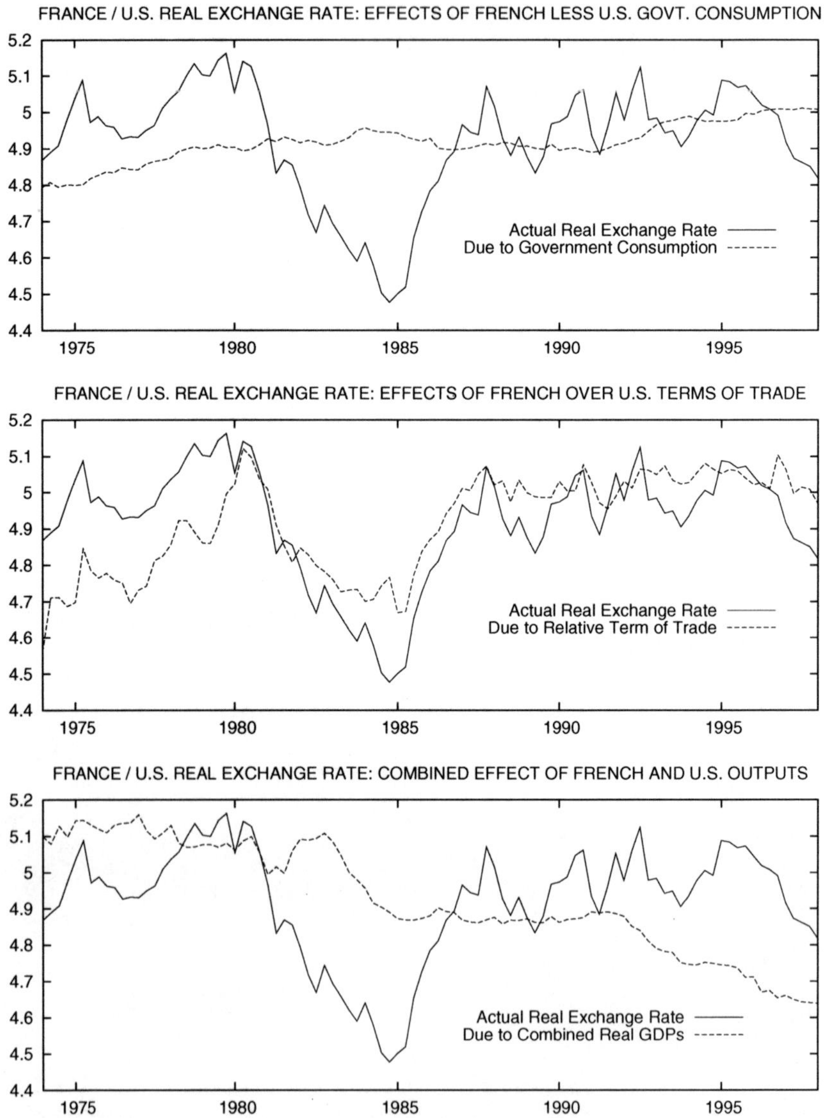

Fig. 10.11b. Effects on the logarithm of the French real exchange rate with respect to the U.S. of the excess excess of French government consumption as a percentage of GDP over U.S. government consumption as a percentage of U.S. GDP, of the logarithm of the ratio of the French terms of trade with respect to the rest of the world over the U.S. terms of trade with respect to the rest of the world and of combined French and U.S. real GDP growth.

the real exchange rate. It turns out that interest rate differentials on both treasury-bills and long-term government bonds are statistically insignificant and the former has a sign opposite to that required by the argument above.

Table 10.13 presents the results of tests of the stationarity of the variables used here that were not tested previously.[17] It turns out that the interest rate differentials, and the inflation rate differential which will be used in subsequent regressions, are the only variables that are clearly stationary. The commodity price variable and the log of U.S. real GDP were previously shown to be stationary and the energy price variable non-stationary.

A Johansen cointegration test of the real exchange rate, energy price, government expenditure difference, terms of trade ratio and French real GDP variables yields the following result:

Under the Null Hypothesis	Values	L-max	Trace
0	0.34837	42.827	97.192
		(0.0072)	(0.0009)
1	0.24364	27.924	54.365
		(0.1075)	(0.0580)
2	0.15535	16.883	26.141
		(0.3602)	(0.3108)
3	0.06852	7.0986	9.5578
		(0.7051)	(0.5312)
4	0.02429	2.4592	2.4592
		(0.1168)	(0.1168)
Lags = 7			

There is clearly a cointegrating vector.

[17] The Dickey-Fuller tests were performed in XLispStat and Gretl and the Phillips-Perron tests were performed using XLispstat. The code and results are in the files noted in the previous footnote.

Table 10.13. The results of Dickey-Fuller and Phillips-Peron unit root tests for variables in the French real exchange rate and interest rate regressions

Model →		[1]			[2]		[3]
Variable	Test	Constant	Trend	Y_{t-1}	Constant	Y_{t-1}	Y_{t-1}
Log of Real Exchange Rate	DF						
	PP				*nc*		
Government Expenditure Difference	DF						
	PP				*nc*		
Log of Ratio of Terms of Trade	DF						
	PP	10%	1%		*nc*	10%	
Log of French Real GDP	DF						
	DF						
	PP		1%		*nc*		
Treasury Bill Interest Rate Differential	DF						5%
	PP				*nc*		5%
Long-Term Interest Rate Differential	DF	1%	5%	1%	1%	1%	1%
	PP	5%			*nc*	10%	5%
French minus U.S. Inflation Rate Differential	DF						5%
	PP				*nc*		1%

Notes: Tests for variables tested in Tables 10.2, 10.6 and 10.10 are not repeated here. The percentages indicate the level at which the null hypothesis of non-stationarity can be rejected. Blank spaces indicate nonrejection and *nc* means that no calculation was recorded. DF refers to the Dickey-Fuller test and PP to the Phillips-Perron test. The calculations cover the period 1974 through 1998.

Regressions of the effects of real factors on the French minus U.S. interest rate differentials are presented in Table 10.14. The regression results are obtained by starting with all variables of interest and successively dropping the ones that are the least statistically significant until a completely significant set is obtained.[18] As in previous cases, with the exception of Canada, any attempt to interpret these regression results, which really show the effect of the variables on the excess of the expected French relative to U.S. inflation rates, would be ad-hoc. The proper interpretation of the underlying nature of the effects of the independent variables is not obvious with the exception of the logarithm of the terms of trade ratio in the first regression on the left. When this variable is dropped and replaced by the inflation rate differential, the R-Square improves slightly and the sign of the inflation rate differential is the one that would be expected. As shown in the right-most column of Table 10.15, the terms of trade ratio and the inflation differential happen to be highly negatively correlated. This occurs because of an increase and subsequent decline in French relative to U.S. inflation rates that happens to coincide with the decline and subsequent increase in the terms of trade ratio during the 1980s. It is also clear from that table that the inflation rate differentials alone are significantly positively related to the interest rate differentials although the correlation is only about 0.333 in the case of the treasury bill rate differential and around 0.5 in the case of the interest rate differential on long-term government bonds. Again, a better interpretation of the causes of changes in interest rate differentials awaits the introduction of monetary shocks in the next chapter.

[18] This process is carried out using XLispStat and Gretl in the files `idffrus.lsp` and `idffrus.inp` with the results contained in the respective output files `idffrus.lou` and `idffrus.got`.

Table 10.14. OLS Regression analysis of real factors on interest rate differentials: France vs. United States, 1974:Q1 to 1998:Q4

Independent Variables	Dependent Variable: Interest Rate Differential		
	Treasury Bills		Long-Term Gov't Bonds
Constant	141.163 (30.475)***	83.713 (17.291)***	1.822 (5.420)
Log of Commodity Prices	-13.899 (2.687)***	-12.795 (2.734)***	-2.762 (1.158)**
Log of Energy Prices	-3.789 (2.425)***	-4.223 (1.353)***	
Gov't Cons. Difference	-0.738 (0.247)***	-0.837 (0.228)***	-0.229 (0.064)***
Real Net Capital Inflow	0.667 (0.205)***	0.544 (0.217)**	0.211 (0.057)***
Log of Terms of Trade Ratio	-11.486 (4.894)**		
Log of Real Exchange Rate			2.641 (0.894)***
Intflation Rate Differential		0.333 (0.121)***	0.217 (0.054)***
Num. Obs.	100	100	100
R-Square	.473	.477	.661

Note: The construction of the variables is explained in the text. The figures in brackets are the heteroskedasticity and autocorrelation adjusted standard errors calculated in the Gretl statistical program, which chose a band width of 3 and a bartlett kernel. Significant serial correlation was present in the residuals of all the regressions. The superscripts ***, ** and * indicate significance at the 1%, 5% and 10% levels respectively. For data sources, see Appendix F.

Table 10.15. OLS Regression analysis of the effects of inflation rate differentials on interest rate differentials and the relationship between the terms of trade ratio and inflation rate differentials: France vs. United States, 1974:Q1 to 1998:Q4

Independent Variables	Dependent Variable		
	Interest Rate Differential		Inflation Rate Differential
	Treasury Bills	Long-Term Gov't Bonds	
Constant	1.874	0.848	147.323
	(0.493)***	(0.157)***	
Log of Terms of Trade Ratio			-31.236
			(4.152)***
Inflation Rate Differential	0.334	0.249	
	(0.128)**	(0.062)***	
Num. Obs.	100	100	100
R-Square	.111	.300	.660

Note: The construction of the variables is explained in the text. The figures in brackets are the heteroskedasticity and autocorrelation adjusted coefficient standard errors calculated in the Gretl statistical program, which chose a band width of 3 and a bartlett kernel. Significant serial correlation is present in the residuals of all the regressions. The superscripts ***, ** and * indicate significance at the 1%, 5% and 10% levels respectively. For data sources, see Appendix F.

10.5 Germany vs. United States

The real and nominal exchange rates of Germany with respect to the United States are plotted, along with the ratio of the German to the U.S. price level, in Fig. 10.12. The time period ends with 1988, prior to the unification of East and West Germany in 1990. The real exchange rate fell by close to 50 percent between the late 1970s and 1985 and then recovered very substantially by 1988. The German price level fell continually relative to the U.S. price level throughout the period by an amount totaling more than 30 percent.

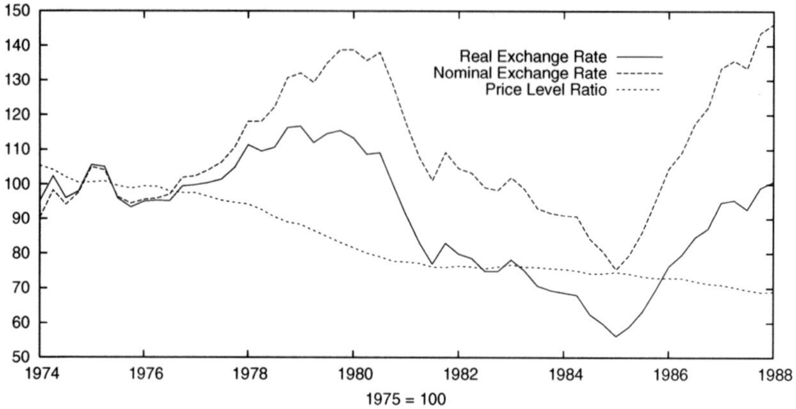

Fig. 10.12. Real and nominal exchange rates of Germany with respect to the United States and the ratio of the French over U.S. price level, 1975 = 100.

The results of a regression analysis of the real factors affecting the real exchange rate are presented in Table 10.16.[19] The coefficients of the logarithms of German and U.S. real GDP are positive and negative, respectively, as consistent with the Balassa-Samuelson hypothesis. The logarithm of the ratio of the German terms of trade with respect to the rest of the world over the corresponding U.S. terms of trade has a positive effect, reflecting the consequences of a rise in the prices of the traded components of output in Germany relative to the United States. The excess of German government consumption expenditure as a percentage of GDP over U.S. government consumption expenditure as a percentage of that country's GDP has a positive sign, as would be expected from a bias of public expenditure in the direction of domestic non-traded components. The logarithm of oil prices is negatively related to the real exchange rates as is consistent with the fact that Germany is not an oil producer. The logarithm of commodity prices excluding energy has a positive sign for reasons that are not clear.

Short-term and long-term interest rate differentials, when added to the regressions in the right-most two columns of the table have signs opposite to what would be expected by those who argue that a central bank induced increase in domestic interest rates attract capital and thereby raise the real exchange rate. The long-term government bond rate differential is not statistically significant and both it and

[19] These calculations were performed in Gretl and XLispStat using the batch files `rexgrus.inp` and `rexgrus.lsp` which produced the output files `rexgrus.got` and `rexgrus.lou` using the data files noted earlier in this chapter.

Table 10.16. OLS Regression analysis of real factors affecting the real exchange rate: Germany vs. United States, 1974:Q1 to 1988:Q4

Independent Variables	Dependent Variable Logarithm of Real Exchange Rate		
Constant	-1.243 (1.566)	0.170 (1.713)	-1.194 (1.560)
Log of Commodity Prices	0.259 (0.083)***	0.259 (0.114)**	0.292 (0.103)***
Log of Oil Prices	-0.126 (0.046)***	-0.130 (0.038)***	-0.134 (0.051)**
Gov't Cons. Difference	0.048 (0.022)**	0.015 (0.012)	0.041 (0.022)*
Log of Terms of Trade Ratio	1.370 (0.219)***	1.504 (0.249)***	1.362 (0.228)***
Log of German Real GDP	2.283 (0.620)***	1.942 (0.672)***	2.331 (0.654)***
Log of U.S. Real GDP	-2.105 (0.365)***	-2.036 (0.386)***	-2.161 (0.404)***
		Treasury Bills	Long-Term Gov't Bonds
Interest Rate Differential		-0.014 (0.006)**	-0.006 (0.011)
Num. Obs.	60	54	60
R-Square	.925	.945	.926

Notes: The regression that includes the treasury bill interest rate differential begins in the third quarter of 1975. The construction of the variables is explained in the text. The figures in brackets are the heteroskedasticity and autocorrelation adjusted standard errors calculated in the Gretl statistical program, which chose a band width of 3 and a bartlett kernel. Significant serial correlation is present in the residuals of all the regressions. The superscripts ***, ** and * indicate significance at the 1%, 5% and 10% levels respectively. For data sources, see Appendix F.

the treasury bill rate differential are obvious substitutes for the difference between German and U.S. government consumption expenditures, taken as percentages of their respective GDPs. It should be noted that the regression using the treasury bill rate differential begins in the third-quarter of 1975 rather than at the beginning of 1974.

The actual and fitted values of the left-most regression in Table 10.16 are plotted in the top panel of Fig. 10.13a and effects of the variables used as regressors are plotted, along with the actual series, in the bottom two panels of that figure and in Fig. 10.13b. The results are very similar to what occurred in the cases of France, Japan, and the United Kingdom. Of all the variables, only the logarithm of the ratio of the German terms of trade to the U.S. terms of trade has had a quantitative effect easily visible to the naked eye. The terms of trade ratio obviously significantly accounted for the observed pattern of real exchange rate movements.

The next issue to be faced is that of spurious regression. Table 10.17 gives the results of Dickey-Fuller and Phillips-Perron tests of the stationarity of the variables in the regression that were not tested previously.[20] The commodity price variable was previously found to be stationary and the oil price variable non-stationary. U.S. real GDP was also previously found to be stationary. As can be seen from the table, the remaining variables in the left-most regression are non-stationary, although non-stationarity of the government expenditure variable can be rejected at the 10 percent level.

[20] The Dickey-Fuller tests were performed in XLispStat and Gretl and the Phillips-Perron tests were performed using XLispStat. The code and results are in the files noted in the previous footnote.

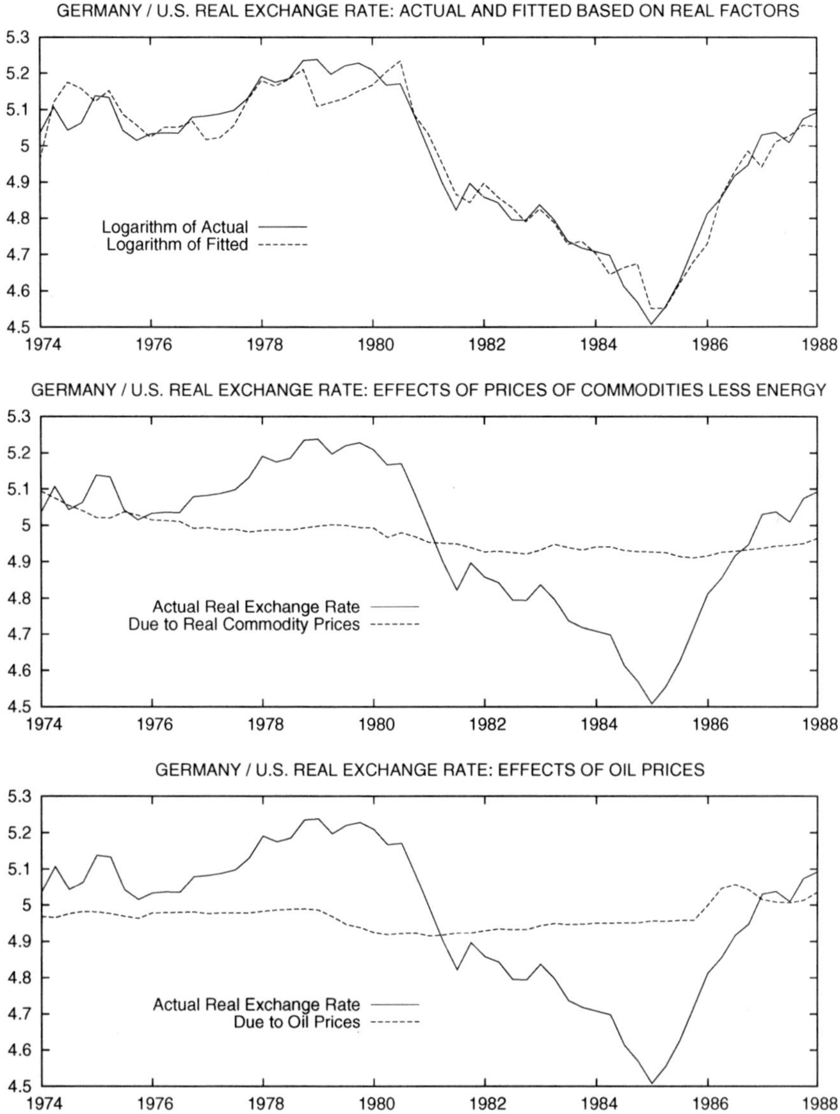

Fig. 10.13a. Actual and fitted values of the logarithm of the German real exchange rate with respect to the U.S. and the effects of of commodity prices and oil prices.

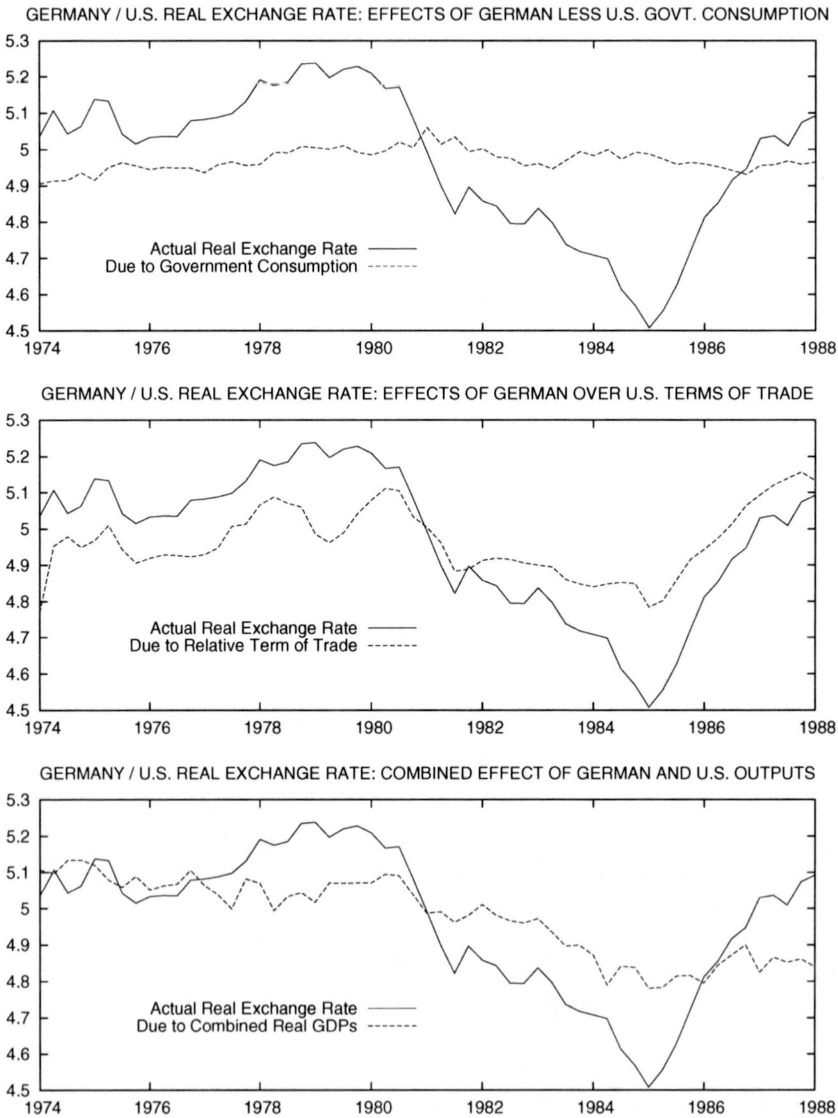

Fig. 10.13b. Effects on the logarithm of the German real exchange rate with respect to the U.S. of the excess excess of German government consumption as a percentage of GDP over U.S. government consumption as a percentage of U.S. GDP, of the logarithm of the ratio of the German terms of trade with respect to the rest of the world over the U.S. terms of trade with respect to the rest of the world and of combined German and U.S. real GDP growth.

Table 10.17. The results of Dickey-Fuller and Phillips-Peron unit root tests for variables in the German real exchange rate and interest rate regressions

Model →		[1]			[2]		[3]
Variable	Test	Constant	Trend	Y_{t-1}	Constant	Y_{t-1}	Y_{t-1}
Log of Real	DF				10%		
Exchange							
Rate	PP		1%		*nc*		
Government	DF				5%	10%	
Expenditure							
Difference	PP		1%		*nc*	10%	
Log of	DF						
Ratio of							
Terms of Trade	PP		1%		*nc*		
Log of	DF						
German	DF						
Real GDP	PP		1%		*nc*		
Treasury Bill	DF	10%			1%	5%	
Interest Rate							
Differential	PP				*nc*	10%	
Long-Term	DF				5%	10%	
Interest Rate							
Differential	PP				*nc*	10%	
German minus U.S.	DF				10%		
Inflation Rate							
Differential	PP				*nc*		

Notes: Tests for variables tested in Tables 10.2, 10.6 10.10 and 10.13 are not repeated here. The percentages indicate the level at which the null hypothesis of non-stationarity can be rejected. Blank spaces indicate nonrejection and *nc* means that no calculation was recorded. DF refers to the Dickey-Fuller test and PP to the Phillips-Perron test. The calculations cover the period 1974 through 1988 for all variables except the treasury-bill interest rate differential which begins in the third quarter of 1975.

A Johansen cointegration test of the real exchange rate, oil price, government expenditure, terms of trade ratio and German real GDP variables yielded the following result:

Under the Null Hypothesis	Values	L-max	Trace
0	0.59055	50.005	101.32
		(0.0004)	(0.0003)
1	0.37625	26.432	51.318
		(0.1586)	(0.1053)
2	0.22867	14.150	24.885
		(0.5536)	(0.3976)
3	0.10337	6.1355	10.346
		(0.8013)	(0.4554)
4	0.07243	4.2103	4.2103
		(0.0402)	(0.0402)
Lags = 4			

The variables are clearly cointegrated.

As can be seen from Table 10.17, the treasury bill rate differential is stationary – the fact that it is significant when added to the real exchange rate regression further confirms the cointegration of the non-stationary variables in that regression. The long-term government bond rate differential, for which non-stationarity can be rejected at the 10 percent level, is insignificant when added to the real exchange rate regression and therefore not significantly related to the dependent variable.

Table 10.18 presents the results of an OLS regression analysis of the relationship between the treasury bill and long-term government bond interest rate differentials and the set of real factors potentially affecting the real exchange rate.[21] The logarithm of the prices of commodities excluding energy was statistically insignificant and therefore excluded,

[21] These calculations were performed using XLispStat and Gretl in the files `idfgrus.lsp` and `idfgrus.inp` with the results contained in the respective output files `idfgrus.lou` and `idfgrus.got`.

Table 10.18. OLS Regression analysis of real factors on interest rate differentials: Germany vs. United States

Independent Variables	Dependent Variable: Interest Rate Differential				
	Treasury Bills		Long-Term Gov't Bonds		
	1975:Q3 to 1988:Q4		1974:Q1 to 1988:Q4		
Constant	61.252 (10.794)***	-1.666 (0.477)***	79.367 (11.362)***	81.606 (12.405)***	-2.446 (0.592)***
Log of Energy Prices	-1.670 (0.756)**		-4.153 (0.534)***	-4.035 (0.507)***	
Gov't Cons. Difference	-0.943 (0.346)***		-0.641 (0.289)**	-0.737 (0.363)**	
Log of Terms of Trade Ratio			-4.575 [2.173]**	-4.813 [2.187]***	
Log of German Real GDP			13.594 (4.920)***	11.853 (6.111)*	
Log of U.S. Real GDP	-6.112 (1.019)***		-16.402 (2.935)***	-15.063 (4.114)***	
Intflation Differential	0.250 (0.101)**	0.322 (0.103)***		-0.044 (0.076)***	-0.105 (0.130)
Num. Obs.	54	54	60	60	60
R-Sq. (Adj.)	.594	.222	.883	.882	-.002

Note: The construction of the variables is explained in the text. The figures in brackets are the heteroskedasticity and autocorrelation adjusted standard errors calculated in the Gretl statistical program, which chose a band width of 3 and a bartlett kernel. Significant serial correlation is present in the residuals of all the regressions. The superscripts ***, ** and * indicate significance at the 1%, 5% and 10% levels respectively. For data sources, see Appendix F.

while the logarithm of energy prices provided a better fit than, and was therefore substituted for, the logarithm of oil prices. As in the corresponding interest rate differential regressions for the other countries with respect to the United States, about all that can be said about the signs of the coefficients is that they somehow capture the relationship between the independent variables and the expected inflation rate in Germany relative to the United States. As can be seen from the R-Squares adjusted for degrees of freedom, the inflation rate differential can account for a rather small fraction of the variation in the treasury bill rate differential and for virtually none of the variation in the long-term government bond rate differential. Indeed, in the case of the latter variable, the inflation rate differential has the wrong sign and in the regression by itself is statistically insignificant. When included along with the other variables, the inflation rate differential tends to capture the effects of, and thereby displace, the German real GDP variable. As in the case of the other countries, it will be interesting to see what will happen when money supply shock variables are added in the next chapter.

One final matter needs attention. With the shortening of the sample period to end with 1988 combined with the fact that the treasury bill rate differential starts in the third quarter of 1975, the regressions which include that variable are based on only 54 observations – less than 14 years of quarterly data. One might argue that this sample is too small, given that the distributions of OLS regression coefficients, standard-errors and t-ratios approach their true values in the limit.[22] Accordingly, a boot-strap procedure is adopted to check the coefficients and t-values in the case of the regression explaining the treasury bill interest rate differential. The residuals from the initial regression were resampled 10000 times and, in each case, added to the initial fitted values to obtain a new series for the dependent variable. A regression was run on each of these new series and coefficients and t-ratios obtained.[23]

Table 10.19 presents the original coefficients and t-ratios, the average of the coefficients obtained for each variable in the 10000 bootstrap regressions and the first and third quartiles and medians of the 10000 t-ratios obtained for each variable. The averages of the bootstrapped coefficients were very close to those of the original regression. And the original t-ratios were well within the first and third quartiles of the

[22] The author thanks his colleague John Maheu for suggesting this problem and its solution.

[23] These calculations were performed in XLispStat using the batch file `idfgrus.lsp` with the results in `idfgrus.lou`.

Table 10.19. Actual OLS and bootstrapped coefficients and t-ratios in regression analysis of real factors affecting the treasury bill rate differential: Germany vs. United States, 1975:Q3 to 1988:Q4

Independent Variables		Dependent Variable: T-Bill Rate Differential			
		Coefficient	T-Ratio		
			1st Quartile	Median	3rd Quartile
Constant	Bootstrap	61.133	1.755	5.273	6.118
	Original	61.252		— 4.980 —	
Log of Energy Prices	Bootstrap	-1.669	-3.049	-2.345	-1.637
	Original	-1.670		— -2.197 —	
Government Expenditure Difference	Bootstrap	-0.941	-3.108	-2.396	-1.692
	Original	-0.943		— -2.246 —	
Log of U.S. Real GDP	Bootstrap	-6.099	-6.017	-5.173	-4.382
	Original	-6.112		— -4.889 —	
Intflation Rate Differential	Bootstrap	0.252	2.431	3.147	3.876
	Original	0.250		— 2.932 —	

bootstrapped t-ratios and not far from the respective median values. The small sample size does not seem to present a problem.

10.6 Conclusions

The results obtained in this chapter can now be summarized. First, it is clear that a range of plausible real forces can explain major fractions of the movements of the real exchange rates with respect to the United States of the countries examined. In all cases the domestic and U.S. income variables have the signs that would be predicted from the work of Balassa and Samuelson. In the case of Canada vs. the U.S., domestic real net capital inflows as a percentage of GDP less U.S. real net capital inflows as a percentage of GDP can explain the major movements of the real exchange rate, with energy and commodity prices being highly statistically significant and accounting for the upward movements after 2002. With respect to the other four countries vs. the United States, the factor having an observed quantitatively obvious effect on pattern of the real exchange rate movements turns out to be the ratio of the domestic terms of trade with respect to the rest of the world over the U.S. terms of trade with respect to the rest of the world.

Only in the cases of Canada and the U.K. with respect to the U.S. was a statistically significant positive relationship found between domestic-U.S. interest rate differentials and the real exchange rate, as is predicted by those who make the claim, shown to be misleading elsewhere in this book, that an increase in interest rates generated by the central bank will lead to an inflow of capital and thereby have a positive effect on the real exchange rate. In all other cases the interest rate differential had a negative sign and/or was insignificant.

Real factors that would plausibly affect real exchange rates turn out in every case to have an observed relationship to the excess of domestic over U.S. interest rates on treasury bills and long-term bonds and, in the case of Canada, one- and three-month corporate paper. While the relationship between the relevant real factors and the corporate paper rate differentials can be viewed, along with uncertainty about the magnitude of the domestic as opposed to U.S. expected inflation rate, as effects on the risk of holding the Canadian as opposed to the U.S. commercial paper, in all other cases the results must be interpreted as effects that operate via expected inflation rates alone, given that the probabilities of default on the government debt obligations involved are surely little affected by changes in these observed real variables. In every case but Germany vs. the United States, the excess of the domestic over the U.S. inflation rate had a significant positive effect on interest rate differentials although in the case of Canada the interest rate differentials were statistically insignificant when added to the regression that included the significant real factors.

Finally, it was clearly established that the above observed regression results cannot have been spurious on account of lack of cointegration.

11

The Role of Money Supply Shocks in Determining Real Exchange Rates: The Evidence

This chapter extends the previous one by adding money supply shocks to the set of previously established real shocks affecting real exchange rates to determine whether these monetary factors have also had significant effects. Given the propensity for overshooting, one would expect positive unanticipated domestic money supply shocks to have negative effects on real exchange rates as home residents re-balance their portfolios by buying assets abroad. In addition, it is necessary to determine whether such positive exogenous unanticipated monetary shocks have had downward effects on domestic relative to U.S. interest rates as is widely claimed in the financial press. Monetary shocks that are fully anticipated should affect the domestic inflation rate relative to that in the United States in the same direction and these effects should appear in the interest rate differential as soon as the expectations are formed. The nominal exchange rate and price levels, but not the real exchange rate, will change through time as a result of correctly anticipated monetary shocks.

The empirical analysis below will establish that observed unanticipated money supply shocks have had no significant effects on the real exchange rates with respect to the U.S. of the five countries being examined. And, without such effects on real exchange rates, there is no basis for concluding that they have had effects on domestic vs. United States interest rate differentials. The absence of real exchange rate effects, given that observed money supply changes did in fact occur, leads one to conclude that that such money supply shocks were generated by the authorities to offset shocks to the demand for money that would otherwise have resulted in overshooting changes in real and nominal exchange rates. There could not have been portfolio adjustment pressures on interest rate differentials in the absence of corresponding portfolio

J.E. Floyd, *Interest Rates, Exchange Rates and World Monetary Policy*,
DOI 10.1007/978-3-642-10280-6_11, © Springer-Verlag Berlin Heidelberg 2010

adjustment pressures on real exchange rates. Thus, in the few cases where a negative relationship between unanticipated domestic money supply shocks and domestic relative to U.S. interest rates is evident, this relationship must be interpreted as a policy response by the monetary authorities to interest rate changes rather than a response of interest rates to money supply shocks.

The major analytical issue that must first be faced is the identification of the portions of observed changes in the monetary aggregates that are unanticipated. These can be represented by the percentage deviations of the monetary aggregates from their expected levels. The question is how to determine what the expected levels of the aggregates were at each date. Five alternative methods of establishing the expected levels of each monetary aggregate are adopted and will be referred to in later statistical analysis by numbers assigned to them below. Logarithms of the levels of all available base money, M1 and M2 aggregates and the nominal GDPs of the U.S., Canada, the U.K., Japan, France and Germany are first obtained. The alternative expected levels of each monetary aggregate in each quarter are the predicted values generated by one of the following five processes:

[1] The expected levels are those predicted by 10-year running regressions of the actual level of the monetary aggregate on the levels of itself and nominal GDP in the previous eight quarters.

[2] The expected levels are those predicted by 10-year running regressions of the level of the monetary aggregate on its own levels in the previous eight quarters.

[3] The expected levels are those predicted by regressions of the current level of the aggregate on those of the eight past periods of itself and of GDP that are statistically significant. For each regression the statistically significant lags are obtained by starting with 8 lags and successively dropping the least significant of these lags in repeated test runs of the regression until all remaining lags are significant at the 5% level. The first period's regression, which produces the expected level of the relevant monetary aggregate for the first quarter of 1974, uses all available data prior to that date, with an additional quarter of data added for each subsequent period's regression.

[4] The expected level of each aggregate is determined by a process identical to **[3]** above except that no more than 10 years of data are used in each period's regression. Once a date is reached for which the running regression uses 10 years of data, the addition of the each subsequent quarter of data is accompanied by the removal of the earliest quarter to maintain the sample size at 40 quarters.

[5] The expected levels are determined by running trend projections of the level of the aggregate using its values in the previous 8 quarters.

The five alternative unanticipated money shock series are obtained by taking the percentage deviations of the actual from the expected values generated above. The percentage deviations are approximated by multiplying the excess of the logarithms of the actual values over the calculated expected values of those logarithmic levels by 100. As should be clear the five alternative processes differ with respect to the assumed degree of sophistication of market participants. An analysis of relationship between unanticipated money supply shocks and the real exchange rates and interest rate differentials of the five countries with respect to the United States can now proceed.

11.1 Canada vs. the United States

The signs and statistical significance of the Canadian and U.S. unanticipated money supply shocks in the real exchange rate equations for each of the five expectation generating processes above for all nine combinations of the two countries' monetary aggregates are presented in Table 11.1.[1] In only 10 of the 45 cases does the Canadian monetary aggregate have the hypothesized negative sign. And the U.S. aggregate has the hypothesized positive sign in 19 of the 45 cases. In all of the 7 cases where the money shock coefficient is significant, the sign is opposite to that consistent with negative effects of Canadian unanticipated money shocks and positive effects of United States ones on the real exchange rate of Canada with respect to the United States. And, since the coefficients are statistically significant in only 7 of the 90 cases, it is clear that there is no basis for concluding that unanticipated money supply shocks have had effects of importance on the real exchange rate.

[1] The empirical work in this section was performed in both Gretl and XLispStat using the respective input files `rexcaus.inp`, `idfcaus.inp`, `rexcaus.lsp` and `idfcaus.lsp` with the outputs contained in the corresponding files `rexcaus.got`, `idfcaus.got`, `rexcaus.lou` and `idfcaus.lou`. The data used throughout this chapter can be viewed in the Gretl files `jfdataqt.gdt` and `jfumdata.gdt`, and are contained in the XLispStat data files `jfdataqt.lsp` and `jfumdata.lsp` for use with that program. These data are also available in the Excel files `jfdataqt.xls` and `jfumdata.xls` and the descriptions of the variables are reproduced in the text files `jfdataqt.cat` and `jfumdata.cat`. The unanticipated money supply shock data in the data files with the root name `jfumdata` are calculated in the XLispStat files `uamonus.lsp`, `uamonca.lsp`, `uamonuk.lsp`, `uamonjn.lsp`, `uamonfr.lsp`, and `uamongr.lsp` and the outputs are in files with the same root names and the suffix `.lou`.

Table 11.1. The signs and statistical significance of unanticipated money shocks added to the basic Canada vs. U.S. real exchange rate regression.

Expectations Formation	Canadian Base	U.S. Base	Canadian M1	U.S. Base	Canadian M2	U.S. Base
[1]	$+^{**}$	+	+	+	+	+
[2]	+	+	+	+	−	+
[3]	+	+	+	+	$+^{*}$	+
[4]	+	+	+	+	+	+
[5]	−	+	+	+	−	+
		U.S. M1		U.S. M1		U.S. M1
[1]	$+^{***}$	−	+	−	$+^{*}$	−
[2]	+	−	+	−	−	−
[3]	+	+	−	+	$+^{*}$	+
[4]	$+^{*}$	−	+	−	+	+
[5]	−	−	+	−	−	−
		U.S. M2		U.S. M2		U.S. M2
[1]	$+^{***}$	$-^{*}$	+	$-^{*}$	+	−
[2]	+	−	+	−	−	−
[3]	+	−	+	−	$+^{*}$	−
[4]	$+^{*}$	$-^{*}$	+	$-^{**}$	+	$-^{*}$
[5]	−	$-^{**}$	+	$-^{***}$	−	$-^{***}$

Notes: The superscripts *, ** and *** denote significance at the 10 percent, 5 percent and 1 percent levels respectively. The five alternative processes by which the expected levels of the money stocks are determined are discussed in the text. The base regression to which the uanticipated money shocks are added is presented in the left-most column of Table 10.1. The magnitudes and statistical significance of the original variables in that regression are not much affected by the addition of the unanticipated money shock variables.

With respect to the effects of money supply shocks on interest rate differentials, the first question that arises is whether previous periods' quarter-over-quarter and year-over-year rates of money growth have affected expectations of inflation and thereby Canadian relative to U.S. interest rates. Accordingly, each of the nine combinations of Canadian and U.S. quarter-over-quarter and year-over-year base money, M1 and M2 growth, lagged one period, were added in turn to the four basic interest rate differential regressions that were presented in Table 10.3. The signs and statistical significance of these lagged money growth variables are shown in Table 11.2. No statistically significant effects were

Table 11.2. The signs and statistical significance of 1-period lagged quarter-over-quarter and year-over-year money growth added to the basic Canada vs. U.S. interest rate differential regressions.

Monetary Aggregate		Interest Rate Differential: Canada minus U.S.							
		1-Month Corporate Paper		3-Month Corporate Paper		Treasury Bill		Long-Term Government Bonds	
Canada	U.S.	Quarter-Over-Quarter: Lagged One Quarter							
Base	Base	−	−	−	−	−	−	$-^{**}$	+
	M1	−	−	−	+	−	−	$-^{**}$	+
	M2	−	+	−	+	−	−	$-^{**}$	$-^{**}$
M1	Base	−	−	−	−	−	−	−	−
	M1	−	−	−	+	−	−	$-^{*}$	+
	M2	−	+	−	+	−	+	−	−
M2	Base	$+^{**}$	−	$+^{**}$	−	$+^{***}$	−	+	−
	M1	$+^{**}$	−	$+^{**}$	−	$+^{***}$	−	+	+
	M2	$+^{**}$	−	$+^{**}$	−	$+^{***}$	−	+	$-^{*}$
		Year-Over-Year: Lagged One Quarter							
Base	Base	+	−	+	−	+	−	−	+
	M1	+	−	+	+	+	+	−	$+^{*}$
	M2	+	−	+	−	+	−	−	$-^{**}$
M1	Base	−	−	−	−	−	−	−	+
	M1	−	+	−	+	$-^{*}$	+	−	$+^{*}$
	M2	−	−	−	−	−	−	−	$-^{***}$
M2	Base	+	−	+	−	$+^{**}$	−	$+^{**}$	−
	M1	+	+	+	+	$+^{**}$	+	$+^{**}$	$-^{*}$
	M2	+	−	+	−	$+^{**}$	−	$+^{*}$	$-^{**}$

Notes: The superscripts *, ** and *** denote significance at the 10 percent, 5 percent and 1 percent levels respectively. The magnitudes and statistical significance of the original variables in that regression are not much affected by the addition of the lagged money growth variables.

found in case of the 1-month and 3-month corporate paper and treasury bill rate differentials except for the effects of quarter-over-quarter Canadian M2 growth which were in every case significantly positive. In the long-term government bond rate differential regressions, Canadian quarter-over-quarter base money growth had significant negative signs and year-over-year Canadian M2 growth had positive and statistically significant effects in the two regressions that also included U.S. year-over-year base money and M1 growth respectively while year-over-year U.S. M2 growth had a negative and statistically significant effect in all three regressions containing it. In all cases the signs, magnitudes and significance of the coefficients of the original variables in the regressions were not much affected.

Overall, a one-period lagged Canadian quarter-over-quarter money growth variable was statistically significant in 12 of the 36 regressions – positively in all nine cases involving M2 growth and negatively in the three long-term government bond rate differential equations that included base money growth. A one-period lagged U.S. quarter-over-quarter money growth variable was statistically significant in only 1 of the 36 regressions. A Canadian year-over-year money growth variable was statistically significant in only 5, and a U.S. year-over-year money growth variable was significant in only 3, of the 36 regressions. And in only one regression was both a Canadian and U.S. money growth variable significant – this was the long-term government bond rate differential regression that included one-period lagged quarter-over-quarter growth of Canadian base money and U.S. M2, both having negative signs.

It is worth noting that the signs of the previous period's quarter-over-quarter Canadian base money growth were negative in all the regressions that included it but these negative signs were statistically significant in only the long-term government bond rate differential regressions. An explanation of these negative signs will be presented below when the effects of unanticipated base money shocks are discussed. The large number of statistically significant positive signs of the previous period's quarter-over-quarter Canadian M2 growth suggests that it was a good predictor of expected Canadian inflation. There is little evidence that, holding Canadian money growth constant, last period's U.S. money growth had any significant effects on the interest rate differentials. This suggests that one-period-lagged quarter-over-quarter and year-over-year U.S. money growth was either poorly related to inflationary expectations in the United States, which would seem unlikely, or equally affected inflation expectations in both countries, therefore leaving Canada vs. U.S. interest rate differentials unaffected.

Table 11.3. The signs and statistical significance of unanticipated money shocks added to the basic Canada vs. U.S. interest rate differential regressions.

	1-Month Corporate Paper Rate					
Expectations Formation	Canadian Base	U.S. Base	Canadian M1	U.S. Base	Canadian M2	U.S. Base
[1]	$-^{**}$	+	−	−	+	−
[2]	$-^{***}$	−	$-^{*}$	−	+	−
[3]	$-^{***}$	+	$-^{**}$	−	+	−
[4]	−	+	$-^{**}$	−	−	−
[5]	$-^{***}$	+	−	−	+	−
		U.S. M1		U.S. M1		U.S. M1
[1]	$-^{**}$	+	−	+	+	−
[2]	$-^{***}$	−	−	−	+	−
[3]	$-^{**}$	−	$-^{**}$	+	+	−
[4]	$-^{*}$	+	$-^{***}$	+	−	+
[5]	$-^{***}$	+	−	−	+	−
		U.S. M2		U.S. M2		U.S. M2
[1]	$-^{**}$	$+^{*}$	−	$+^{**}$	+	+
[2]	$-^{***}$	+	$-^{*}$	+	+	+
[3]	$-^{**}$	+	$-^{*}$	+	+	+
[4]	$-^{*}$	$+^{*}$	$-^{**}$	$+^{**}$	−	$+^{**}$
[5]	$-^{***}$	+	−	+	+	+

Continued on Next Page

Table 11.3 presents the signs and statistical significance of unanticipated Canadian and U.S. money supply shocks, calculated in all five ways, when added to the basic interest rate differential regressions in Table 10.3. It is interesting to note that unanticipated Canadian base money shocks are always negatively related to the Canada-U.S. interest rate differentials, significantly so in 36 of the 45 cases involving short-term interest rate differentials and 10 of the 15 cases involving long-term interest rate differentials. The signs of unanticipated Canadian M1 shocks are also everywhere negative but are significantly so in only 20 of the 60 cases. Unanticipated Canadian M2 shocks are negatively related to the interest rate differential variables in 15 of the

Table 11.3 continued from previous page.

	3-Month Corporate Paper Rate					
Expectations Formation	Canadian Base	U.S. Base	Canadian M1	U.S. Base	Canadian M2	U.S. Base
[1]	$-^{**}$	$-$	$-$	$-$	$+$	$-$
[2]	$-^{***}$	$+$	$-$	$-$	$+$	$-$
[3]	$-^{***}$	$+$	$-^{**}$	$-$	$+$	$-$
[4]	$-^{*}$	$+$	$-^{**}$	$-$	$-$	$-$
[5]	$-^{***}$	$+$	$-$	$-$	$+$	$-$
		U.S. M1		U.S. M1		U.S. M1
[1]	$-^{**}$	$+$	$-$	$+$	$+$	$+$
[2]	$-^{***}$	$+$	$-$	$-$	$+$	$-$
[3]	$-^{***}$	$+$	$-^{**}$	$+$	$+$	$-$
[4]	$-^{*}$	$+$	$-^{**}$	$+$	$-$	$+$
[5]	$-^{***}$	$+$	$-$	$-$	$+$	$-$
		U.S. M2		U.S. M2		U.S. M2
[1]	$-^{**}$	$+^{*}$	$-$	$+^{**}$	$+$	$+^{**}$
[2]	$-^{***}$	$+$	$-$	$+$	$+$	$+$
[3]	$-^{**}$	$+$	$-^{**}$	$+$	$+$	$+$
[4]	$-^{*}$	$+$	$-^{**}$	$+^{**}$	$+$	$-^{*}$
[5]	$-^{***}$	$+$	$-$	$+$	$+$	$+$

Continued on Next Page

60 cases, with none of those negative relationships statistically significant and positive relationships significant twice. One would have to conclude that there is strong evidence that unanticipated Canadian base money shocks were negatively related to the excess of Canadian over U.S. interest rates as would be expected by most popular analyses of domestic monetary policy. Even though the negative relationship between unanticipated Canadian M1 shocks and the interest rate differentials is weaker and a negative relationship of Canadian M2 shocks and the interest rate differentials essentially non-existent, this empirical evidence is important because it is the stock of base money that the Bank of Canada directly controls.

Unanticipated U.S. base money shocks were positively related to Canada-U.S. interest rate differentials in only 22 of the 60 cases, significantly so in only 4 cases involving the interest rate differential on long-term government bonds. None of the 38 negative relationships were statistically significant. Unanticipated U.S. M1 shocks were pos-

Table 11.3 continued from previous page.

	Treasury Bill Rate					
Expectations Formation	Canadian Base	U.S. Base	Canadian M1	U.S. Base	Canadian M2	U.S. Base
[1]	$-^{*}$	$+$	$-^{*}$	$-$	$+^{**}$	$-$
[2]	$-^{***}$	$-$	$-^{**}$	$-$	$+$	$-$
[3]	$-^{***}$	$-$	$-^{***}$	$-$	$+^{***}$	$-$
[4]	$-^{*}$	$-$	$-^{**}$	$-$	$+$	$-$
[5]	$-^{***}$	$-$	$-$	$-$	$+$	$-$
		U.S. M1		U.S. M1		U.S. M1
[1]	$-^{**}$	$+$	$-^{*}$	$+$	$+$	$+$
[2]	$-^{***}$	$-$	$-^{*}$	$+^{*}$	$+$	$-^{*}$
[3]	$-^{***}$	$+$	$-^{***}$	$+$	$+$	$-$
[4]	$-^{*}$	$+$	$-^{**}$	$+$	$-$	$+$
[5]	$-^{***}$	$-$	$-$	$-$	$+$	$-$
		U.S. M2		U.S. M2		U.S. M2
[1]	$-^{**}$	$+$	$-^{*}$	$+^{*}$	$+$	$+^{*}$
[2]	$-^{***}$	$+$	$-^{*}$	$+$	$+$	$+$
[3]	$-^{**}$	$+$	$-^{**}$	$-$	$+$	$-$
[4]	$-^{**}$	$+$	$-^{*}$	$+$	$-$	$+$
[5]	$-^{***}$	$+$	$-$	$+$	$+$	$+$

Continued on Next Page

itively related to the interest rate differentials in 38 of the 60 cases, significantly so only in 9 of the 12 times a positive sign occurred in the cases involving the interest differential on long-term government bonds. With regard to unanticipated U.S. M2 shocks, positive signs occurred in 56 out of 60 cases with those signs statistically significant in only 7 cases. Support for the argument that unanticipated U.S. money supply shocks drove down U.S. interest rates and thereby increased the Canada vs. U.S. interest rate differentials is not strong. The matter of concern here, however, is the rather clear negative effects of unanticipated Canadian base money shocks on the four interest rate differentials. These effects are consistent with the uniformly negative, though mostly statistically insignificant, effects of one-period lagged quarter-over-quarter Canadian base money growth on Canadian minus U.S. interest rate differentials.

Table 11.3 continued from previous page.

	Long-Term Government Bond Rate					
Expectations Formation	Canadian Base	U.S. Base	Canadian M1	U.S. Base	Canadian M2	U.S. Base
[1]	$-^{**}$	$+^{**}$	$-$	$+$	$+$	$+^{*}$
[2]	$-^{**}$	$+$	$-$	$+$	$+$	$+$
[3]	$-^{***}$	$+$	$-^{**}$	$+$	$+$	$+$
[4]	$-^{*}$	$+^{**}$	$-$	$+^{**}$	$-$	$+^{***}$
[5]	$-^{***}$	$+$	$-$	$-$	$-$	$-$
		U.S. M1		U.S. M1		U.S. M1
[1]	$-^{*}$	$+^{***}$	$-$	$+^{***}$	$+$	$+^{***}$
[2]	$-^{**}$	$+^{**}$	$-$	$+^{***}$	$-$	$+^{**}$
[3]	$-^{**}$	$+$	$-^{***}$	$+^{**}$	$+^{*}$	$+$
[4]	$-$	$+^{**}$	$-$	$+^{**}$	$-$	$+^{*}$
[5]	$-^{***}$	$-$	$-$	$-$	$-$	$-$
		U.S. M2		U.S. M2		U.S. M2
[1]	$-$	$+$	$-$	$+^{**}$	$+$	$+$
[2]	$-^{**}$	$+$	$-$	$+$	$-$	$+$
[3]	$-^{**}$	$+$	$-^{**}$	$+$	$+^{*}$	$+$
[4]	$-$	$+$	$-$	$+$	$-$	$+$
[5]	$-^{***}$	$+$	$-$	$-$	$-$	$+$

Notes: The base regressions to which the uanticipated money shocks are added are presented in Table 10.3. The magnitudes and statistical significance of the original variables in those regressions are not much affected. Regarding other details, see the notes to Table 11.1.

Based on the above evidence, can one make a case that the Bank of Canada controls domestic interest rates by making changes in base money that are unanticipated by market participants? The answer has to be no because of the complete absence of effects of such base money shocks on Canada's real exchange rate with respect to the U.S. Any negative effect on interest rates of a positive base money shock has to arise because resulting excess money holdings lead to attempts to re-balance portfolios by purchasing non-monetary assets. In an open world capital market, this has to lead to purchases of assets abroad and resulting downward pressure on nominal and real exchange rates. The fact that no effects on the real exchange rate can be found implies that such re-balancing of portfolios was not necessary which, in turn, implies that no unanticipated money shock in fact occurred. This means that the observed unanticipated base money shocks must have been undertaken to maintain portfolio equilibrium in the face of movements in domestic relative to U.S. interest rates that occurred as a result of other forces. That is, the observed money supply shocks should be viewed as Bank of Canada responses to changes in domestic interest rates, not the other way around. This might also explain the observed, negative signs of lagged quarter-over-quarter Canadian base money growth although the implication would be that current and lagged base money growth are positively correlated. That correlation is about 0.3, positive but low enough to possibly account for the fact that the negative signs of the Canadian base money growth variable are not statistically significant.

The reason for this response of base money to interest rates is the avoidance of overshooting effects on the real exchange rate that changes in the demand for money associated with these interest rate changes would cause. The observed changes in Canadian relative to U.S. interest rates would be interpreted as responses of the excess of expected Canadian over U.S. inflation to the range of factors originally included in the regressions referred to in Table 10.3 plus lagged quarter-to-quarter Canadian M2 growth together with other factors that cannot be measured and included.

Is there a clear negative relationship between unanticipated Canadian base money shocks and Canadian interest rates? As can be seen from the regression results shown in Table 11.4, the answer is yes. Nevertheless, it must be concluded from the very low R-squares in those regressions that very small proportions of shocks to the demand for liquidity that the Bank of Canada is responding to by adjusting base money have resulted from changes in domestic interest rates.

Table 11.4. OLS Regression analysis of the relation between unanticipated Canadian base money shocks, Canadian interest rates and Canada minus U.S. interest rate differentials, 1974:Q1 to 2007:Q4

Independent Variables	Dependent Variable Unanticipated Canadian Base Money Shock			
Constant	0.076 (0.104)	0.503 (0.173)***	0.097 (0.104)	0.521 (0.176)***
1-Month Corporate Paper Rate Differential	-0.103 (0.050)**			
Canadian 1-Month Corporate Paper Rate		-0.070 (0.020)***		
3-Month Corporate Paper Rate Differential			-0.117 (0.051)**	
Canadian 3-Month Corporate Paper Rate				-0.072 (0.020)***
Number of Observations	136	136	136	136
R-Square	.020	.051	.024	.053

Continued on Next Page

In conclusion, the evidence strongly suggests that unanticipated money supply shocks have had little effect on Canada's real exchange rate with respect to the U.S. And, in the absence of such effects, the observed negative relationship between such shocks and the differential of Canadian over U.S. interest rates makes it reasonable to believe that the Bank of Canada has avoided monetary shocks to the real exchange rate, that would surely have been overshooting, by appropriately adjusting base money in response to demand for money shocks.

Table 11.4 continued from previous page.

Independent Variables	Dependent Variable Unanticipated Canadian Base Money Shock			
Constant	0.143 (0.105)	0.503 0.174***	0.126 (0.154)	0.558 (0.280)**
Treasury Bill Rate Differential	-0.122 (0.050)**			
Canadian Treasury Bill Rate		-0.072 (0.021)***		
Long Term Government Bond Rate Differential			-0.166 (0.116)	
Canadian Long-Term Government Bond Rate				-0.070 (0.033)**
Number of Observations	136	136	136	136
R-Square	.028	.051	.010	.027

Notes: The data sources are to be found in Appendix F. The unanticipated money supply shock is the percentage deviation from an expected level calculated process [3] in the text. The figures in brackets are the heteroskedastic and autocorrelation adjusted standard errors calculated by the Gretl statistical program, which chose a band width of 3 and a bartlett kernel. The superscripts ***, ** and * indicate significance at the 1%, 5% and 10% levels, respectively, according to a standard t-test. For data sources, see Appendix F.

11.2 United Kingdom vs. United States

The signs and statistical significance of U.K. unanticipated M0 and M2 shocks when included in the basic real exchange rate regression shown in the left-most column of Table 10.5 are presented in Table 11.5. The sample period was shortened to end with the first quarter of 2006 because the British monetary aggregate series were unavailable beyond that quarter.[2]

The signs of the unanticipated shock to the U.K. M0 aggregate were negative in 10 of the 15 regressions and those of the U.K. M2 aggregate were everywhere negative. Statistically significant negative coefficients for the unanticipated M0 shock occurred only when the two crude measures of expectations generation were adopted – regressions using eight lags of the aggregate itself, and eight quarter trend projections. The unanticipated U.K. M2 shock was never statistically significant at the 5% level or better. It mattered not which U.S. unanticipated money shock was paired with the U.K. M0 shocks. Since there are six statistically significant negative coefficients and no statistically significant positive ones, the case for concluding that U.K. unanticipated money shocks have impacted on the real exchange rate, while weak, has some merit. As can be seen from Figure 11.1, however, even in the strongest case a trivial portion of the variations of the real exchange rate of the United Kingdom with respect to the United States is accounted for by these unanticipated U.K. M0 shocks. If, as argued in the situation with regards to Canada, the Bank of England is adjusting base money to offset overshooting effects of variations of the U.K. demand for money on the exchange rate, which would be the only reason to make seemingly random adjustments of the M0 aggregate, only the portion of the observed M0 shock that does not offset a corresponding shock to the demand for the aggregate will represent an excess supply shock and thereby affect the real exchange rate. The negative coefficient suggests that the Bank of England has tended to over-compensate for demand-for-money shocks, thereby introducing some minor excess money supply shocks to the real exchange rate in the same direction as the demand-for-money shock.

The unanticipated U.S. money shocks have the expected positive signs in 15 of the 30 cases though only 3 of these are statistically sig-

[2] All the statistical calculations referred to in this section were performed using the Gretl input files `rexukus.inp` and `idfukus.inp` and the XLispStat input files `rexukus.lsp` and `idfukus.lsp`. The corresponding output files are `rexukus.got`, `idfukus.got`, `rexukus.lou` and `idfukus.lou`. The data files are the ones used in the previous analysis of the Canada vs. U.S. case.

Table 11.5. The signs and statistical significance of unanticipated money shocks added to the basic United Kingdom vs. United States real exchange rate regression for the sample period 1974:Q1 through 2006:Q1.

Expectations Formation	U.K. M0	U.S. Base	U.K. M2	U.S. Base
[1]	+	+	−	+
[2]	$-^{***}$	+	−	−
[3]	−	+	$-^{*}$	+
[4]	−	+	−	+
[5]	$-^{***}$	$+^{**}$	−	+
		U.S. M1		U.S. M1
[1]	+	−	−	−
[2]	$-^{***}$	+	−	+
[3]	−	+	$-^{*}$	+
[4]	+	$-^{*}$	−	$-^{*}$
[5]	$-^{***}$	$+^{***}$	−	$+^{***}$
		U.S. M2		U.S. M2
[1]	+	$+^{*}$	−	$-^{*}$
[2]	$-^{***}$	−	−	−
[3]	−	−	$-^{*}$	−
[4]	+	$-^{**}$	−	$-^{**}$
[5]	$-^{***}$	−	−	−

Notes: The superscripts *, ** and *** denote significance at the 10 percent, 5 percent and 1 percent levels respectively. The five alternative processes by which the expected levels of the money stocks are determined are discussed in the text. The base regression to which the uanticipated money shocks are added is presented in the left-most column of Table 10.5. The magnitudes and statistical significance of the original variables in that regression are not much affected by the addition of the unanticipated money shock variables.

nificant and 2 of the 15 negative signs are also significant. There is little reason to conclude that U.S. unanticipated money shocks have impacted the U.K. real exchange rate with respect to that country.

Turning now to the question of whether U.K. money growth has had an observable effect on the excess of U.K. over U.S. short-term interest rates, the results of adding the growth of the the monetary aggregates to the treasury bill and short-term government bond interest rate differentials regressions are presented in Table 11.6. Quarter-over-quarter and year-over-year U.K. M0 growth is negatively related to the treasury bill rate differential and positively related to the long-term government

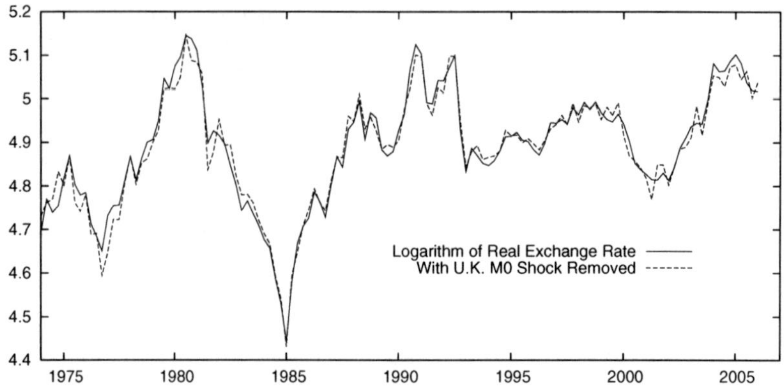

Fig. 11.1. Effects of observed unanticipated United Kingdom M0 shocks, generated using expectations estimation form [2], on that country's real exchange rate with respect to the United States.

bond rate differential, but none of these relationships are statistically significant. The negative signs in the case of the treasury bill rate differential are consistent with a relationship between the unanticipated money shock and the underlying real interest rate differential while the positive signs in the other case suggest a relationship of British M0 growth to the expected rate of British relative to U.S. inflation. The complete lack of statistical significance of the coefficients, however, suggests that little can be concluded from these results.

The signs and statistical significance of unanticipated shocks to U.K. M0 and M2 when these are added, along with the unanticipated shocks to the U.S. monetary aggregates, to the left-most and right-most U.K. minus U.S. interest rate differential regressions in Table 10.7 are presented in Table 11.7. The U.K. M0 shock bears a negative relationship to both U.K. minus U.S. interest rate differentials in every regression in which it is included although it is statistically significant at the 5% level or better in only five of the 30 regressions, all of which involve the treasury bill rate differential. And all of these five cases involve the same two crude measures of the unanticipated M0 shock as had statistically significant negative coefficients in the real exchange rate regressions. The unanticipated U.K. M2 shocks had negative coefficients in 20 of the 30 regressions in which they appeared but those coefficients were statistically significant at the 5% level or better in only 3 of those regressions, all of which had the long-term government bond rate differential as the dependent variable. The coefficients of the unan-

Table 11.6. The signs and statistical significance of 1-period lagged quarter-over-quarter and year-over-year money growth added to the basic U.K. vs. U.S. interest rate differential regressions for the sample period 1974:Q1 through 2006:Q1.

Monetary Aggregate		Interest Rate Differential: U.K. minus U.S.							
		Treasury Bill		Long-Term Government Bonds		Treasury Bill		Long-Term Government Bonds	
U.K.	U.S.	Quarter-Over-Quarter Lagged One Quarter				Year-Over-Year Lagged One Quarter			
M0	Base	−	+	+	−	−	+	+	−
	M1	−	$+^{***}$	+	+	−	$+^{***}$	+	+
	M2	−	−	+	$-^{**}$	−	−	$+^{*}$	$-^{***}$
M2	Base	+	+	−	−	−	+	−	−
	M1	+	$+^{***}$	−	+	−	$+^{**}$	−	−
	M2	+	$-^{*}$	−	$-^{**}$	−	−	−	$-^{***}$

Notes: The superscripts *, ** and *** denote significance at the 10 percent, 5 percent and 1 percent levels respectively. The magnitudes and statistical significance of the original variables in that regression are not much affected by the addition of the unanticipated money shock variables.

ticipated U.S. base money shocks were positive in all the regressions that contained them, statistically significantly so in 5 of the 10 cases involving the treasury bill rate differential but none of the 10 cases involving the government bond rate differential. Positive coefficients also appeared in all 20 regressions involving U.S. M1 but were significant only in 4 of the cases involving the treasury bill rate differential. The coefficients of the unanticipated U.S. M2 shocks were positive in only 4 of the 10 regressions involving the treasury bill rate differential and in 9 of the 10 regressions involving the long-term government bond rate differential. None of these coefficients, regardless of sign, was statistically significant at the 5% level or better.

These U.K. results differ in an important way from the Canadian results in the preceding section. There it was concluded that the failure of Canadian unanticipated base money shocks to have observable negative effects on that country's real exchange rate with respect to the United States ruled out the possibility that their observed negative coefficients in the Canada minus U.S. interest rate differentials regressions

Table 11.7. The signs and statistical significance of unanticipated money shocks added to the basic U.K. vs. U.S. interest rate differential regressions for the sample period 1974:Q1 through 2006:Q1.

	Treasury Bill Rate					
Expectations Formation	U.S. Base	U.K. M0	U.S. M1	U.K. M0	U.S. M2	U.K. M0
[1]	+***	−	+	−	+	−
[2]	+	−***	+	−***	+	−***
[3]	+	−	+***	−*	−	−
[4]	+**	−	+	−	−	−
[5]	+**	−**	+**	−**	−	−*
		U.K. M2		U.K. M2		U.K. M2
[1]	+***	−	+	−	+	−
[2]	+	+	+	+	+	+
[3]	+	−	+***	−	−	−
[4]	+**	+	+	−	−	−
[5]	+	+	+**	+	−	+
	Long-Term Government Bond Rate					
Expectations Formation	U.S. Base	U.K. M0	U.S. M1	U.K. M0	U.S. M2	U.K. M0
[1]	+	−	+	−	+	−
[2]	+	−	+	−	+*	−
[3]	+	−	+*	−	−	−
[4]	+	−	+	−	+	−
[5]	+	−	+	−	+	−
		U.K. M2		U.K. M2		U.K. M2
[1]	+	−	+	−	+	−
[2]	+	−	+	−	+*	−
[3]	+	−*	+*	−*	+	−*
[4]	+	−**	+	−**	+	−**
[5]	+	+	+	+	+	+

Notes: The base regressions to which the uanticipated money shocks are added are presented in Table 10.7. In the case of the treasury bill rate differential, the left-most regression is used. Although the signs of the original variables those regressions were unaffected and the magnitudes of the coefficients not substantially affected, the statistical significance of the energy price variable was eliminated in almost every treasury bill rate differential regression. The signs and statistical significance of the variables in the long-term government bond rate differential regression were unaffected and the magnitudes of the coefficients were not much affected. Regarding other details, see the notes to Table 11.1.

could represent the effect of unanticipated base money shocks on interest rates. Instead, it was concluded that the observed variations of base money were a response by the Bank of Canada to prevent overshooting exchange rate movements arising from the demand-for-money effects changes in interest rates arising from other causes. Here in the U.K. situation, the observed negative relationship between unanticipated M0 shocks and the real exchange rate with respect to the U.S. rules is consistent with base money shocks having negative effects on both the real exchange rate and short-term U.K. minus U.S. interest rate differentials, as consistent with conventional arguments in the popular press although those arguments rarely mention the exchange rate.

Table 11.8. OLS Regression analysis of the relation between unanticipated United Kingdom base money shocks and the U.K. treasury bill rate and U.K. minus U.S. treasury bill rate differential, 1974:Q1 to 2006:Q1

Independent Variables	Dependent Variable Unanticipated U.K. Base Money Shock [2]		[5]	
Constant	0.099 (0.133)	0.262 (0.225)	0.112 (0.249)	0.975 (0.332)***
Treasury Bill Rate Differential	-0.084 (0.043)*		-0.074 (0.060)	
U.K. Treasury Bill Rate		-0.043 (0.028)		-0.122 (0.040)***
Number of Observations	129	129	129	129
R-Square	.041	.027	.021	.138

Notes: The unanticipated money supply shocks are the percentage deviations from expected levels calculated according to processes [2] and [5] in the text. The figures in brackets are the heteroskedastic and autocorrelation adjusted standard errors calculated by the Gretl statistical program, which chose a band width of 3 and a bartlett kernel. The superscripts ***, ** and * indicate significance at the 1%, 5% and 10% levels, respectively, according to a standard t-test. For data sources, see Appendix F.

While the observed results do not permit a rejection of the popular view noted above, it also not possible to reject the view suggested by the theory developed here, that unanticipated base money shocks were a response to shocks to the demand for money in order to avoid overshooting. This view requires that the observed unanticipated U.K. M0 shocks be a response of the Bank of England to demand for money changes, some arising from interest rate changes occurring in response to other forces in the world economy. Results of regressions of unanticipated M0 shocks on the treasury bill interest rate differential and the U.K. treasury bill rate alone are shown in Table 11.8. Only the two crude measures of the unanticipated M0 shock that were significant in the earlier regressions are used. The expected negative coefficients appear but the results are not strong. A strong negative relationship appears only when the expected M0 level from which unanticipated M0 shocks are derived is a simple eight quarter trend projection.

Given that the negative coefficients of the unanticipated M0 shock are statistically significant in the real exchange rate and interest rate differential regressions when only two of the five measures of that shock are used, the support for either of these two hypotheses is weak. Nevertheless, one solid conclusion does emerge. Only tiny portions of observed real exchange rate variability can be accounted for by money supply shocks.

11.3 Japan vs. United States

The signs and statistical significance of unanticipated Japanese and U.S. money shocks when added to the basic regression of the Japanese real exchange rate with respect to the United States on the range of real factors that would be expected to determine it are presented in Table 11.9.[3] The regression to which the unanticipated money shock variables are added is presented in the left-most column of Table 10.9. The alternative unanticipated money shock variables were calculated using the five different measures of expected money stock levels used for the other countries and explained near the beginning of this chapter.

In contrast to the Canadian and British cases, the signs of the domestic unanticipated base money shock variable is positive in all but one case, but significantly so only once at even the 10% level. The U.S. base money shock variables have negative signs in all 15 cases and are statistically significant in four of the five regressions in which the

[3] The statistical calculations presented in this section are performed in the respective Gretl and XLispStat files `rexjnus.inp`, `idfjnus.inp`, `rexjnus.lsp` and `idfjnus.lsp` for which the respective output files are `rexjnus.got`, `idfjnus.got`, `rexjnus.lou`, and `idfjnus.lou`. The data files used are the prevously noted ones used throughout this chapter.

Table 11.9. The signs and statistical significance of unanticipated money shocks added to the basic Japan vs. U.S. real exchange rate regression.

Expectations Formation	Japanese Base	U.S. Base	Japanese M1	U.S. Base	Japanese M2	U.S. Base
[1]	+	$-^{**}$	+	$-^{*}$	$-$	$-^{*}$
[2]	+	$-^{**}$	+	$-^{*}$	$+^{***}$	$-^{*}$
[3]	+	$-^{**}$	+	$-$	+	$-^{*}$
[4]	$+^{*}$	$-^{***}$	+	$-^{*}$	$+^{*}$	$-^{*}$
[5]	+	$-^{*}$	$-$	$-$	+	$-$
		U.S. M1		U.S. M1		U.S. M1
[1]	+	$-$	+	$-$	$-$	+
[2]	+	$-$	+	$-$	$+^{***}$	$-$
[3]	+	$-$	+	$-$	+	$-$
[4]	+	$-$	+	$-$	$+^{*}$	$-$
[5]	+	$-^{***}$	+	$-^{**}$	+	$-^{**}$
		U.S. M2		U.S. M2		U.S. M2
[1]	+	$-$	+	$-$	$-$	$-$
[2]	+	+	+	+	$+^{***}$	+
[3]	$-$	$-$	+	$-$	+	$-$
[4]	+	$-$	+	$-$	$+^{*}$	$-$
[5]	+	+	+	$-$	$+^{*}$	+

Notes: The superscripts *, ** and *** denote significance at the 10 percent, 5 percent and 1 percent levels respectively. The five alternative processes by which the expected levels of the money stocks are determined are discussed in the text. The base regression to which the uanticipated money shocks are added is presented in the left-most column of Table 10.9. The magnitudes and statistical significance of the original variables in that regression are not much affected by the addition of the unanticipated money shock variables.

Japanese unanticipated base money shock also appears. The Japanese unanticipated M1 shock variables are positively signed, but never statistically significant, in all but one of the 15 cases and the corresponding unanticipated M2 shock variables are positively signed in 12 of the 15 cases, significantly so in three of them. The signs of the unanticipated U.S. M1 and M2 shocks are negative in all regressions in the case of M1 and in 10 of the 15 regressions involving M2. There are three statistically significant negative coefficients in the case of U.S. M1, all involving the determination of the expected level by 8 quarter trend projections, and no statistically significant coefficients for U.S. M2.

The positive relationships between the unanticipated Japanese base money shocks and that country's real exchange rate with respect to the U.S. are consistent with an association of positive unexpected domestic money shocks with decreases, not increases in the excess supply of money. This would imply that the Japanese authorities adjusted base money to offset shocks to the demand for money but fell short on average from the full adjustment required. In other words, base money was adjusted in the same direction as changes in the demand for money but by not quite enough to offset completely effect of the changes in the demand for money on the exchange rate. This is in contrast to the British case where the Bank of England seemingly over-adjusted base money by a slight amount.

The negative effects of U.S. money shocks on the Japanese real exchange rate with respect to the U.S. are a bit of a puzzle. One would expect that an unanticipated U.S. money expansion would reduce, not increase, the U.S. real exchange rate with respect to all countries. While negative signs of unanticipated U.S. base money shocks added to the Canadian real exchange rate with respect to the U.S. were frequent, the signs of this variable were typically positive in the case of the U.K. real exchange rate with respect to the U.S. All that can be concluded here is that unanticipated U.S. monetary expansion typically occurred during periods when the Japanese real exchange rate with respect to that country was falling.

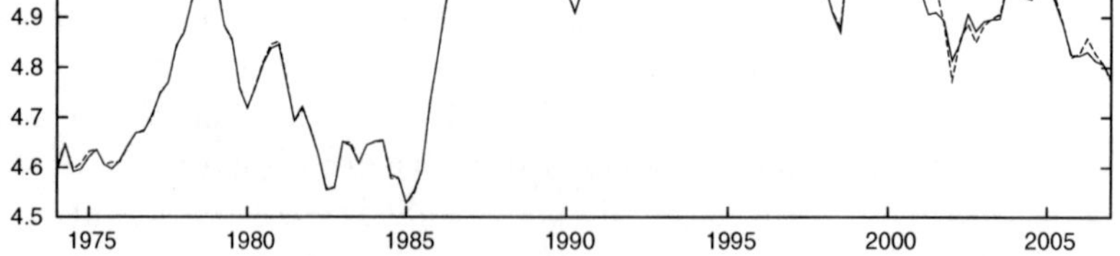

Fig. 11.2. Effects of observed unanticipated Japanese base money shocks, generated using expectations estimation form [5], on that country's real exchange rate with respect to the United States.

As can be seen in Fig. 11.2, one clear conclusion does emerge. The effects of unanticipated money supply shocks on the Japanese real exchange rate with respect to the U.S. were of trivial magnitude as compared to the effects of real shocks. The anticipated level of Japanese base money used in generating the data was obtained using procedure [4] – OLS forecasts based on the significant lags of base money and nominal GDP over the previous 10 years. This was the only case in which the unanticipated base money shock was statistically significant at the 10% level or better.

Table 11.10. The signs and statistical significance of one-period lagged quarter-over-quarter and year-over-year money growth added to the basic Japan minus U.S. interest rate differential regression.

Monetary Aggregate		Long-term Government Bond Rate Differential			
Japan	U.S.	Quarter-Over-Quarter Lagged One Quarter		Year-Over-Year Lagged One Quarter	
Base	Base	$-^{**}$	$+^{**}$	$-$	$+^{**}$
	M1	$-^{*}$	$+^{***}$	$+$	$+^{***}$
	M2	$-$	$+$	$+$	$-$
M1	Base	$-$	$+$	$-$	$+^{**}$
	M1	$-$	$+^{***}$	$-$	$+^{***}$
	M2	$-$	$+$	$-$	$-$
M2	Base	$+^{***}$	$+$	$+$	$+^{**}$
	M1	$+^{**}$	$+^{***}$	$-$	$+^{***}$
	M2	$+^{***}$	$+$	$+$	$-$

Notes: The superscripts *, ** and *** denote significance at the 10 percent, 5 percent and 1 percent levels respectively. The magnitudes and statistical significance of the original variables in the regression are not much affected by the addition of the lagged money growth variables.

Table 11.10 presents the signs and statistical significance of one-period lagged quarter-over-quarter and year-over-year Japanese and U.S. money growth when added to the regression of the Japanese minus U.S. long-term government bond interest rate differential on various real factors presented in the left-most column of Table 10.11. Japanese quarter-over-quarter M2 growth was positive and statistically significant, as consistent with it having a positive effect on expectations of

Japanese inflation. Japanese quarter-over-quarter base money growth, lagged one period, had negative signs and was statistically significant at the 5% level in one of the three cases, suggesting the possibility of negative effects on real interest rates consistent with the popular view of the effects of monetary expansion. It turns out, however, that the correlation between quarter-over-quarter base money growth in the current period and lagged one period is not statistically significantly different from zero, eliminating any support for this view.

Japanese M1 growth, both quarter-over-quarter and year-over-year always has a negative sign but is never statistically significant. United States quarter-over-quarter money growth is always positive and statistically significant at the 5% level or better in 4 of the 9 cases while U.S. year-over-year base money and M1 growth both have statistically significant positive signs in every case. This says that higher expected Japanese relative to U.S. inflation was associated with more rapid U.S. money growth, which makes no sense from a causal point of view.

The Japanese and U.S. unanticipated money shock variables were added to the basic Japanese minus U.S. long-term interest rate differential regression in the left-most column of Table 10.11 and the signs and statistical significance of the unanticipated money shock variables are presented in Table 11.11. The Japanese unanticipated base money shock has everywhere a negative sign but is statistically significant at the 5% level or better in only 1 of the 15 cases, which uses 8 quarter trend projections as the estimate of the expected base money levels. Because of the positive relationship of these unanticipated base money shocks to the Japanese real exchange rate with respect to the U.S., one cannot conclude that this represents evidence for the popular view of the negative effects of domestic unanticipated money expansion on domestic relative to foreign interest rates.

The evidence is consistent with the view that the Japanese monetary authorities have tended to adjust base money in response to changes in the demand for money to avoid overshooting effects on the exchange rate. Table 11.12 indicates a statistically significant negative relationship between the Japanese unanticipated base money shock and the Japan minus U.S. interest rate differential on long-term government debt, and a negative though not statistically significant relationship between the unanticipated base money shock and the level of Japanese long-term government bond rates. The overall lack of statistical significance of the Japanese unanticipated base money shock in Table 11.11, however, weakens the conclusion that the Japanese authorities have adjusted base money in response to changes in domestic interest rates.

Table 11.11. The signs and statistical significance of unanticipated money shocks added to the basic Japan minus U.S. interest rate differential regression.

	Long-Term Government Bond Rate					
Expectations Formation	Japanese Base	U.S. Base	Japanese M1	U.S. Base	Japanese M2	U.S. Base
[1]	$-$	$+$	$-$	$+$	$-^{***}$	$+$
[2]	$-$	$-$	$-$	$-$	$+$	$-$
[3]	$-$	$+$	$-$	$+$	$-^{***}$	$+$
[4]	$-$	$+$	$-$	$+$	$-^{***}$	$+$
[5]	$-^{**}$	$+^{**}$	$-$	$+$	$-$	$+$
		U.S. M1		U.S. M1		U.S. M1
[1]	$-$	$+$	$-$	$+$	$-^{***}$	$+$
[2]	$-$	$+^{**}$	$-$	$+^{**}$	$+$	$+^{**}$
[3]	$-$	$+^{*}$	$-$	$+^{*}$	$-^{***}$	$+$
[4]	$-$	$+$	$-$	$+$	$-^{***}$	$+$
[5]	$-^{*}$	$+^{**}$	$-$	$+^{**}$	$-$	$+$
		U.S. M2		U.S. M2		U.S. M2
[1]	$-^{*}$	$-$	$-$	$-$	$-^{***}$	$-$
[2]	$-$	$+$	$-$	$+$	$-$	$+$
[3]	$-$	$-$	$-$	$-$	$-^{**}$	$-$
[4]	$-$	$-$	$-$	$-$	$-^{***}$	$-$
[5]	$-$	$+^{***}$	$-$	$+^{***}$	$-$	$+^{***}$

Notes: The superscripts *, ** and *** denote significance at the 10 percent, 5 percent and 1 percent levels respectively. The five alternative processes by which the expected levels of the money stocks are determined are discussed in the text. The base regression to which the uanticipated money shocks are added are presented in the left-most column of Table 10.11. The magnitudes and statistical significance of the original variables in the regression are not much affected by the addition of the unanticipated money shock variables.

The effects of U.S. unanticipated base money shocks on the Japan minus U.S. long-term government bond rate differential were positive in 12 of the 15 cases but statistically significantly so in only one case. Positive signs for unanticipated U.S. M1 shocks were present in all relevant regressions but the relationship was statistically significant in only 5 of the 15 cases. For unanticipated U.S. M2 shocks, there were positive signs in only 6 of the 15 cases with 3 of these statistically significant. This evidence is too weak to permit any conclusion regarding the effects of unanticipated U.S. money supply shocks.

Table 11.12. OLS Regression analysis of the relation between unanticipated Japanese base money shocks and the interest rate on Japanese long-term government bond and the Japan minus U.S. interest rate differential on long-term government bonds.

Independent Variables	Dependent Variable Unanticipated Japanese Base Money Shock Expectations Generating Process [5]	
Constant	-1.899 (0.831)**	0.688 (1.419)
Long-Term Gov't Bond Rate Differential	-0.507 (0.235)**	
Japanese Long-Term Gov't Bond Rate		-0.238 (0.156)
Number of Observations	135	135
R-Square	.031	.017

Notes: The unanticipated money supply shocks are the percentage deviations from expected levels calculated according to processes [5] in the text. The figures in brackets are the heteroskedastic and autocorrelation adjusted standard errors calculated using XLispStat with a truncation lag of 4. The superscripts ***, ** and * indicate significance at the 1%, 5% and 10% levels, respectively, according to a standard t-test. For data sources, see Appendix F.

As in the cases of Canada and the United Kingdom vs. the United States, the main conclusion of this section is that Japanese unanticipated money supply shocks can explain only a trivial proportion of the variations of country's observed real exchange rate with respect to the United States.

11.4 France vs. United States

The signs and statistical significance of unanticipated French and U.S. money supply shocks when added to the factors determining the French real exchange rate with respect to the U.S. that were presented in the left-most column of Table 10.12 are shown in Table 11.13.[4] The unanticipated French money supply shocks are never statistically significant at the 5% level or better. And, as shown in Fig. 11.3, the magnitudes of the effects are trivial although a careful examination indicates that the real exchange rate was observably higher as a result of the presence of unanticipated French base money shocks during the 1990s when the country was adjusting its inflation rate downward in preparation for joining the European Monetary System. With respect to the U.S. unanticipated money suppy shocks, statistical significance occurs at the 5% level only 3 times. The signs of the French unanticipated base money shocks are negative in all but one statistically insignificant case as would be consistent with the conclusion that the French authorities slightly over-compensated for demand for money adjustments in changing the stock of base money. They might better be explained, however, by the tightening in the 1990s in preparation for European monetary union. Apart from this important situation, unless one were to believe that the response of the real exchange rate to exogenous base money changes is virtually zero, there is no basis for believing that the observed shocks were exogenous and independent of demand for money changes.

Unlike the cases involving Canada, the United Kingdom and Japan, the addition of one-period-lagged quarter-over-quarter and year-over-year money growth rates to the French interest rate differential regressions in Table 10.14 substantially changed the statistical significance of the originally present variables in many cases. Accordingly, insignificant variables were dropped and new equations thereby formed. The equations with the highest degrees-of-freedom-adjusted R-Squares are presented in Table 11.14 along with the original basic regressions. It turned out that the best regression of the long-run government bond rate differential was one whose original variables were not much affected by the addition of year-over-year money growth. In that case French year-over-year money growth came in with a positive sign and

[4] The statistical calculations in this section were performed in the Gretl and XLispStat input files `rexfrus.inp`, `idffrus.inp`, `rexfrus.lsp` and `idffrus.lsp` and the results are in the respective output files `rexfrus.got`, `idffrus.got`, `rexfrus.lou` and `idffrus.lou`. The data files are those used throughout this chapter.

Table 11.13. The signs and statistical significance of unanticipated money shocks added to the basic France vs. U.S. real exchange rate regression.

Expectations Formation	French Base	U.S. Base	French M1	U.S. Base	French M2	U.S. Base
[1]	$-^{*}$	+	+	+	−	+
[2]	−	+	$+^{*}$	+	−	+
[3]	$-^{*}$	+	+	+	+	+
[4]	−	+	+	+	−	+
[5]	−	+	−	+	−	+
		U.S. M1		U.S. M1		U.S. M1
[1]	$-^{*}$	+	+	−	−	−
[2]	−	+	$+^{*}$	+	−	+
[3]	$-^{*}$	+	+	+	+	+
[4]	−	−	+	−	−	−
[5]	−	$+^{**}$	−	$+^{**}$	−	$+^{**}$
		U.S. M2		U.S. M2		U.S. M2
[1]	$-^{*}$	−	−	−	−	−
[2]	−	+	+	+	−	+
[3]	−	+	+	+	+	+
[4]	−	+	+	+	−	+
[5]	+	+	−	+	−	+

Notes: The superscripts *, ** and *** denote significance at the 10 percent, 5 percent and 1 percent levels respectively. The five alternative processes by which the expected levels of the money stocks are determined are discussed in the text. The base regression to which the uanticipated money shocks are added is presented in the left-most column of Table 10.12. The magnitudes and statistical significance of the original variables in that regression are not much affected by the addition of the unanticipated money shock variables.

the sign of U.S. year-over-year money growth was negative, as would be expected by positive effects of domestic and foreign money growth on domestic and foreign expected inflation rates. In the best regression having the treasury bill differential as the dependent variable, French year-over-year M2 growth took a negative sign. This is consistent with the occurrance of monetary expansion by the French authorities in response to declines in the domestic interest rate resulting from other causes – the simple correlation between the current and one-period lagged French year-over-year money growth rates is over 0.95 and statistically significant at the 1% level. Yet one also cannot reject the popular notion that the change in the treasury bill rate in France com-

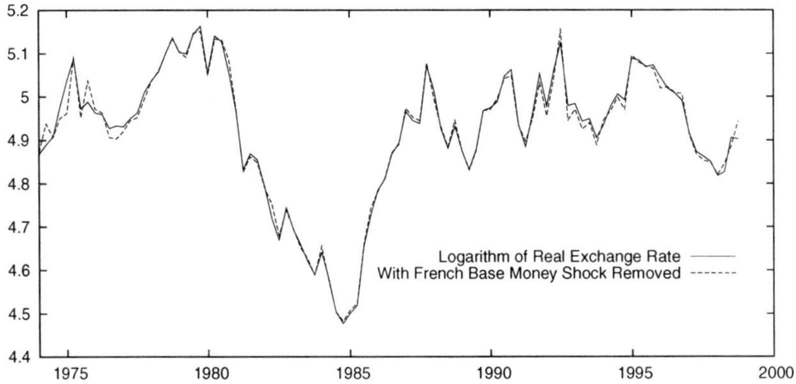

Fig. 11.3. Effects of observed unanticipated French base money shocks, generated using expectations estimation form [3], on that country's real exchange rate with respect to the United States.

pared to the U.S. was the consequence of French monetary expansion although, as shown in Part I, there is little theoritical basis for that view.

Table 11.15 presents the signs and statistical significance of unanticipated French and U.S. money supply shocks when added to the regressions containing year-over-year money growth in Table 11.14. French unanticipated base money shocks had negative signs in all but 7 of the 30 regressions but none of the signs were statistically significant. French unanticipated M1 shocks had negative signs in all of the treasury bill differential regressions and these were statistically significant at the 5% level or better in 8 of the 15 regressions. Negative signs occurred in only 6 of the long-term government bond rate differential regressions and the unanticipated M1 shocks were never statistically significant. In the case of unanticipated French M2 shocks, negative signs occurred in all but 2 of the 15 treasury bill rate differential regressions and 5 of these negative signs were statistically significant at the 5% level or better. In the 15 long-term government bond rate differential regressions, unanticipated French M2 supply shocks had positive signs in 12 of the 15 cases and these signs were statistically significant about half the time.

The question arises as to whether the evident effects of the quite possibly exogenous French unanticipated base money shocks on the real exchange rate in the 1990s are matched by corresponding effects on the treasury bill rate differential that would indicate the positive effect of

Table 11.14. OLS Regression analysis of real and monetary factors on interest rate differentials: France vs. United States, 1974:Q1 to 1998:Q4

Independent Variables	Dependent Variable: Interest Rate Differential Treasury Bills		Long-Term Gov't Bonds	
Constant	83.713 (17.291)***	7.589 (0.978)***	1.822 (5.420)	1.333 (5.083)
Log of Commodity Prices	-12.795 (2.734)***		-2.762 (1.158)**	-2.779 (0.834)***
Log of Energy Prices	-4.223 (1.353)***			
Gov't Expenditure Difference	-0.837 (0.228)***	-0.868 (0.123)***	-0.229 (0.064)***	-0.304 (0.056)***
Real Net Capital Inflow	0.544 (0.217)**		0.211 (0.057)***	0.173 (0.053)***
Log of Real Exchange Rate			2.641 (0.894)***	2.897 (0.813)***
Intflation Rate Differential	0.333 (0.121)***	0.860 (0.121)***	0.217 (0.054)***	0.307 (0.058)***
Year-Over-Year Base Money Growth: France				0.021 (0.009)**
Year-Over-Year M2 Growth: France		-0.366 (0.063)***		
Year-Over-Year M2 Growth: U.S.		-0.225 (0.091)**		-0.115 (0.030)***
Observations	100	100	100	100
Adjusted R-Square	.449	.610	.643	.701

Note: The construction of the variables is explained in the text. The figures in brackets are the heteroskedastic and autocorrelation adjusted standard errors calculated in the Gretl statistical program, which chose a band width of 3 and a bartlett kernel. The first and third regressions from the left are reproductons from Table 10.14. The superscripts ***, ** and * have the usual meaning.

Table 11.15. The signs and statistical significance of unanticipated money shocks added to the basic France vs. U.S. interest rate differential regressions.

	Treasury Bill Rate					
Expectations Formation	French Base	U.S. Base	French M1	U.S. Base	French M2	U.S. Base
[1]	$-$	$+^{***}$	$-$	$+^{***}$	$-$	$+^{***}$
[2]	$-$	$+^{***}$	$-^{*}$	$+^{***}$	$-$	$+^{***}$
[3]	$-$	$+^{***}$	$-^{**}$	$+^{***}$	$-$	$+^{***}$
[4]	$-$	$+^{***}$	$-$	$+^{***}$	$-$	$+^{***}$
[5]	$+$	$+^{***}$	$-$	$+^{**}$	$-^{**}$	$+^{***}$
		U.S. M1		U.S. M1		U.S. M1
[1]	$-$	$+$	$-$	$+$	$+$	$+$
[2]	$-$	$+$	$-^{**}$	$+$	$-^{**}$	$+$
[3]	$-$	$+$	$-^{***}$	$+$	$-$	$+$
[4]	$-$	$-$	$-^{**}$	$-$	$-$	$-$
[5]	$+$	$+$	$-^{**}$	$+$	$-^{***}$	$+$
		U.S. M2		U.S. M2		U.S. M2
[1]	$-$	$-$	$-$	$-$	$+$	$-$
[2]	$-$	$-$	$-^{**}$	$-$	$-^{**}$	$-$
[3]	$-$	$-$	$-^{***}$	$+$	$-$	$-$
[4]	$-$	$-$	$-^{**}$	$+$	$-$	$-$
[5]	$+$	$-^{*}$	$-^{*}$	$-$	$-^{***}$	$-^{*}$

Continued on Next Page

monetary contraction on that interest rate differential predicted by the popular view of the operation of monetary policy. The effect on the T-bill rate differential of the same base money shocks as were used for Fig. 11.3 are shown in Fig. 11.4. No obvious persistent positive effect on the T-bill rate differential during the 1990s is present, although it must be kept in mind that the coefficient of the monetary shock here is not statistically significant. And the overall effects of monetary shocks are trivial although, because of a few extreme instances, the standard-deviation of the associated difference in the treasury bill rate differential is about 25 basis points.

Again, the strong basic conclusion is that unanticipated money shocks had trivial effects on the French real exchange rate with respect to the United States. And again, one cannot reject empirically either the popular view that the monetary authority influenced interest rates or the view espoused here that the French authorities adjusted

Table 11.15 continued from previous page.

	Long-Term Government Bond Rate					
Expectations Formation	French Base	U.S. Base	French M1	U.S. Base	French M2	U.S. Base
[1]	−	+***	+	+***	+***	+***
[2]	−	+**	+	+**	+	+**
[3]	−	+**	−	+**	+**	+**
[4]	−	+***	+	+***	+***	+***
[5]	−	+***	−	+***	−	+***
		U.S. M1		U.S. M1		U.S. M1
[1]	−	+	+	+	+***	+
[2]	−	+	+	+	+	+
[3]	−	+	−	+	+*	+
[4]	+	+	+	+	+**	+
[5]	+	+	−	+	−	+
		U.S. M2		U.S. M2		U.S. M2
[1]	−	−	+	−	+**	−
[2]	−	+	+	−	+	−
[3]	−	−	−	−	+*	−
[4]	+	−	+	−	+**	−
[5]	+	+	−	+	−	−

Notes: The base regressions to which the uanticipated money shocks are added are presented in Table 11.14. For each interest rate differential, the right-most regression is used as the base. The superscripts *, ** and *** have the usual meaning.

the money stock in response to demand for money shocks, some due to interest rate changes, in order to prevent exchange rate overshooting. As in the cases of Canada, the U.K. and Japan vs. the U.S., the interest rate differential regressions are too weak statistically for firm conclusions to be drawn – unanticipated money suppy shock variables are not statistically significant and the independent variables in the regression are present because of their apparent correlation with the domestic and U.S. expected inflation rates rather than their direct causal relationship to the interest rate differentials.

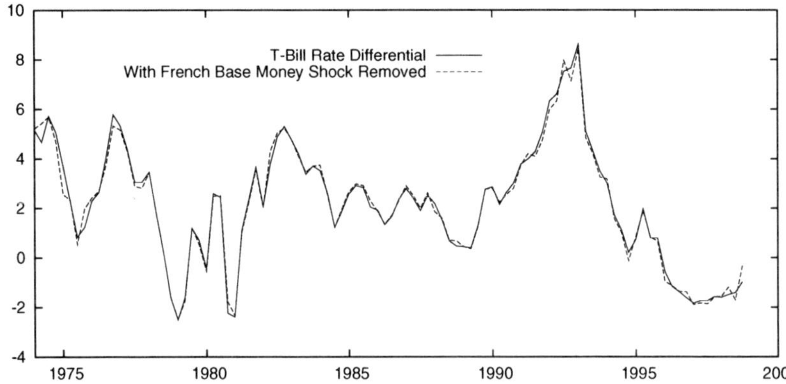

Fig. 11.4. Effects of observed unanticipated French base money shocks, generated using expectations estimation form [3], on that country's T-bill rate differential with respect to the United States.

11.5 Germany vs. United States

The addition of unantipated German and U.S. money supply shocks to the real exchange rate regressions in the left-most column of Table 10.16 yield the signs of these shocks shown in Table 11.16. No statistically significant effects of German unanticipated base money shocks are found and the signs are for the most part positive. Unanticipated German M1 shocks are statistically significant only in the cases where the expected level of M1 is a linear trend projection of past values and the signs are negative in these cases. Only in these plus two additional cases are the corresponding unanticipated U.S. money supply shocks statistically significant, and in both the additional cases the signs are positive.

The effects of the unanticipated German M1 shocks on the real exchange rate in the statistically significant case where unanticipated U.S. base money also appears in the regression are plotted in Fig. 11.5. The effects are more pronounced than in the relevant plots for the other four countries but the unanticipated money supply shocks are not a major determinant of movements in the German real exchange rate with respect to the United States. And it must be kept in mind that unanticipated shocks to German base money, which is the aggregate that the domestic authorities directly control, are everywhere statistically insignificant.

The signs and statistical significance of one-period-lagged quarter-over-quarter and year-over-year German and U.S. money growth when added to the two basic interest rate differential regressions, first and

Table 11.16. The signs and statistical significance of unanticipated money shocks added to the basic Germany vs. U.S. real exchange rate regression.

Expectations Formation	German Base	U.S. Base	German M1	U.S. Base	German M2	U.S. Base
[1]	+	+	+	+	$+^{*}$	+
[2]	−	+	+	+	+	+
[3]	+	+	−	+	+	+
[4]	+	$+^{*}$	+	$+^{*}$	+	$+^{*}$
[5]	−	$+^{**}$	$-^{***}$	$+^{***}$	$-^{*}$	$+^{**}$
		U.S. M1		U.S. M1		U.S. M1
[1]	+	−	+	−	+	−
[2]	+	+	+	+	+	+
[3]	+	−	−	−	+	−
[4]	+	−	+	−	+	−
[5]	−	+	$-^{***}$	$+^{**}$	$-^{*}$	+
		U.S. M2		U.S. M2		U.S. M2
[1]	+	−	+	−	$+^{*}$	−
[2]	+	−	+	−	+	−
[3]	+	−	−	−	+	−
[4]	+	−	+	−	+	−
[5]	+	−	$-^{**}$	−	−	−

Notes: The superscripts *, ** and *** denote significance at the 10 percent, 5 percent and 1 percent levels respectively. The five alternative processes by which the expected levels of the money stocks are determined are discussed in the text. The base regression to which the uanticipated money shocks are added is presented in the left-most column of Table 10.16. The magnitudes and statistical significance of the original variables in that regression are not much affected by the addition of the unanticipated money shock variables.

third from the left in Table 10.18, are shown in Table 11.17. The coefficients of the German money growth variables are always negative, but statistically significantly so in 6 of the 36 cases. The U.S. lagged quarter-over-quarter money growth variables are positive in 24 of the 36 cases, significantly so in only 6 of those instances. Only 2 of the negative signs are statistically significant. Given the absence of any statistically significant effects of German unanticipated money shocks on the country's real exchange rate with respect to the United States, the best interpretation of the negative signs of German money growth is as a response of the money stock to interest rate changes generated by other forces, not as a response of interest rates to money growth.

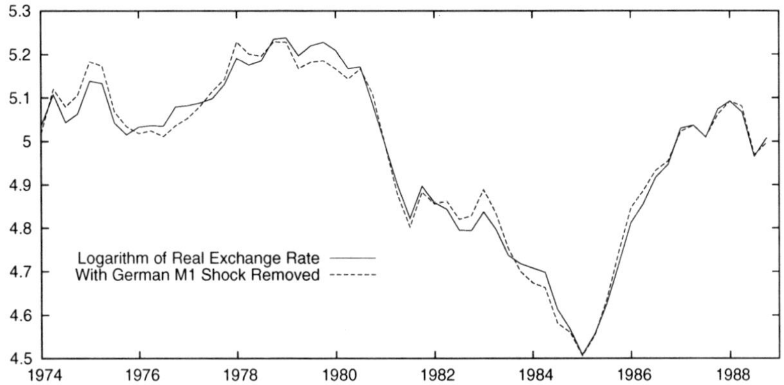

Fig. 11.5. Effects of observed unanticipated German base M1 shocks, generated using expectations estimation form [5], on that country's real exchange rate with respect to the United States.

It should be kept in mind that if the observed German money growth rates were fully anticipated by market participants their effects on the interest rate differential would have been positive.

The signs and significance of unanticipated German and U.S. money supply shocks when added to the basic interest rate differential regressions are shown in Table 11.18. The unanticipated German base money shock is negative in 29 of the 30 cases but statistically significantly so at the 5% level in only one case. The unanticipated German M1 shock is negative in 27 of the 30 cases but significantly so in only 3 of those cases. German unanticipated M2 shocks are everywhere negative and significant at the 5% level in 9 of the 30 cases. Unanticipated shocks to the U.S. monetary aggregates are positive in about one-third of the 30 cases representing each aggregate – the only instance of statistical significance occurs in one of these cases.

The fact that German unanticipated money supply shocks are positively related to that country's real exchange rate with respect to the United States, and not significantly so, in the majority of the 45 cases and statistically significantly negative in only three cases where the anticipated level of the money stock is estimated as a trend projection of the past eight values, suggests that any negative relationships between the money shock and interest rates must have resulted from a response of the German monetary authorities to interest rate changes arising from other sources, and not from a response of interest rates to money supply shocks. Moreover, the high fraction of positive relation-

Table 11.17. The signs and statistical significance of 1-period lagged quarter-over-quarter and year-over-year money growth added to the basic Germany vs. U.S. interest rate differential regressions.

Monetary Aggregate		Interest Rate Differential: Germany minus U.S.							
		Treasury Bill		Long-Term Government Bonds		Treasury Bill		Long-Term Government Bonds	
Germany	U.S.	Quarter-Over-Quarter Lagged One Quarter				Year-Over-Year Lagged One Quarter			
Base	Base	$-$	$-^{**}$	$-$	$+$	$-$	$-$	$-$	$+^{*}$
	M1	$-^{**}$	$-^{*}$	$-$	$+^{**}$	$-$	$-$	$-$	$+^{***}$
	M2	$-^{*}$	$-$	$-$	$+$	$-$	$+$	$-$	$+$
M1	Base	$-^{**}$	$-^{*}$	$-$	$+$	$-^{*}$	$+$	$-$	$+^{*}$
	M1	$-^{***}$	$-$	$-$	$+^{**}$	$-^{**}$	$+$	$-$	$+^{***}$
	M2	$-^{***}$	$-$	$-$	$+$	$-^{**}$	$+$	$-$	$+$
M2	Base	$-$	$-^{**}$	$-$	$+$	$-$	$-$	$-$	$+^{*}$
	M1	$-$	$-$	$-$	$+^{**}$	$-^{*}$	$+$	$-$	$+^{***}$
	M2	$-^{*}$	$-$	$-$	$+$	$-^{*}$	$+$	$-$	$+$

Notes: The superscripts *, ** and *** denote significance at the 10 percent, 5 percent and 1 percent levels respectively. The magnitudes and statistical significance of the original variables in that regression are not much affected by the addition of the unanticipated money shock variables.

ships between the money shocks and the real exchange rate suggests that the German authorities tended to bring about adjustments of the money stocks that were slightly insufficient to compensate for demand for money changes resulting from the whole range of factors that resulted in demand for money shocks.

Again, the inescapable conclusion is that, as was the case with respect to the other countries, a trivial portion of the overall changes in the German real exchange rate with respect to the United States can be accounted for by unanticipated money supply shocks.

Table 11.18. The signs and statistical significance of unanticipated money shocks added to the basic German vs. U.S. interest rate differential regressions.

	Treasury Bill Rate					
Expectations Formation	German Base	U.S. Base	German M1	U.S. Base	German M2	U.S. Base
[1]	−	−	+	−	−	−
[2]	−*	−	−	−	−	−
[3]	−	−	−	−	−*	−
[4]	−	−*	−	−*	−*	−
[5]	−	−	−	−	−	−
		U.S. M1		U.S. M1		U.S. M1
[1]	−	−	+	−	−	−
[2]	−*	−	−	−	−	−
[3]	−	−	−	−	−**	−
[4]	−*	−	−	−	−	−
[5]	−*	−	−	−	−*	−
		U.S. M2		U.S. M2		U.S. M2
[1]	−	+	+	+	−	+
[2]	−	+	−	+	−	+
[3]	−*	+	−	+	−**	+
[4]	−	+	−	+	−*	+
[5]	−**	+	−*	+	−*	+

Continued on Next Page

11.6 Conclusions

The main conclusion of this chapter is that unanticipated money supply shocks have accounted for trivial portions of the variations in the real exchange rates of the five countries studied with respect to the United States. While negative relationships between the countries' unanticipated money shocks and the excesses of their domestic interest rates over corresponding U.S. rates are frequently present, though largely statistically insignificant, the absence of effects on the respective real exchange rates with respect the United States renders unsupportable the popular view that the monetary authorities in countries other than the U.S. control domestic interest rates by varying domestic base money. On the contrary, it appears that the authorities are responding to interest rate changes as well as other forces affecting the demand for money by adjusting the domestic money supply. The reason for doing so is the prevention of overshooting effects of demand for money shocks on the

Table 11.18 continued from previous page.

	Long-Term Government Bond Rate					
Expectations Formation	German Base	U.S. Base	German M1	U.S. Base	German M2	U.S. Base
[1]	−	+	−	−	$-^{**}$	−
[2]	−	−	−	−	−	−
[3]	−	−	−	−	$-^{**}$	−
[4]	−	−	$-^{**}$	−	$-^{**}$	−
[5]	+	+	−	+	−	+
		U.S. M1		U.S. M1		U.S. M1
[1]	−	−	$-^{*}$	−	$-^{**}$	−
[2]	−	+	−	+	−	+
[3]	−	−	−	−	$-^{*}$	−
[4]	−	−	$-^{**}$	−	$-^{*}$	−
[5]	−	+	−	+	$-^{**}$	$+^{**}$
		U.S. M2		U.S. M2		U.S. M2
[1]	−	−	−	−	$-^{*}$	−
[2]	−	−	−	−	−	−
[3]	−	−	−	−	$-^{**}$	−
[4]	−	−	$-^{**}$	−	$-^{**}$	−
[5]	−	+	−	+	$-^{*}$	$+^{*}$

Notes: The base regressions to which the uanticipated money shocks are added are presented in Table 10.18. For each interest rate differential, the right-most regression is used as the base. The superscripts *, ** and *** have the usual meaning.

domestic nominal and real exchange rate with respect to the U.S. and, as a result, with respect to other countries as well. Such overshooting would be expected to be substantial in view of the fact that asset markets adjust much faster to desired portfolio changes than does the balance of trade in response to real exchange rate movements. As argued earlier, even in the absence of pricing to market independently of exchange rates, the response of the nominal exchange rate would be expected to be at least double any percentage shock to the demand for liquidity.

The absence of effects of unanticipated money supply shocks on real exchange rates has to be consequent on either a trivial magnitude of such shocks or on the fact that these shocks are offsetting demand for money changes so that the excess money supply shocks are trivial even though the observed shocks are not. Table 11.19 presents the average

Table 11.19. Averages of the standard deviations of the alternatively calculated unanticipated money supply shocks for each country for the time periods used in the regressions.

Country	Money Supply Shocks Percentages of Expected Levels		
	Base	M1	M2
United States	0.954	1.242	0.801
Canada	1.395	2.528	1.462
United Kingdom	1.278		3.131
Japan	6.675	2.640	1.899
France	6.430	1.834	1.263
Germany	0.989	1.683	0.911

Notes: The unanticipated money supply shocks are the percentage deviations from expected levels calculated according to the five processes outlined in the text. For each monetary aggregate, the standard deviations were calculated for each of the five measures of the unanticipated shock and then averaged. For data sources, see Appendix F.

standard deviations of the quarterly percentage unanticipated shocks of the monetary aggregates of the six countries, where the standard deviations being averaged are those associated with the five methods of calculating unanticipated money shocks outlined at the beginning of the chapter.[5] The standard deviations of the percentage base money shocks are in excess of unity for all countries other than Germany and the United States, and are as high as 6 percent for Japan and France. The standard deviations of the unanticipated M1 shocks as percentages of expected levels everywhere substantially exceed unity as do those of unanticipated M2 shocks for Canada, the U.K., Japan and France.

It is difficult to imagine how unanticipated exogenous liquidity shocks of this magnitude would not substantially affect real exchange

[5] These statistics are calculated in the XLispStat and Gretl files `stdmshks.lsp` and `stdmshks.inp` and the results can be found in `stdmshks.lou` and `stdmshks.got`.

Table 11.20. Average percentage changes in the real exchange rate with respect to the United States associated with one percent unanticipated monetary shocks in Canada, United Kingdom, Japan, France and Germany, together with the number of positive and negative changes and their statistical significance, using five alternative measures of the unanticipated shock to each monetary aggregate and holding constant the corresponding unanticipated shocks to the U.S. monetary aggregates.

	Canada	U.K.	Japan	France	Germany
Base Money					
% Change	0.314	-1.057	0.111	-0.144	0.279
Positive	12	5	14	1	12
Significant	3	0	0	0	0
Negative	3	10	1	14	3
Significant	0	6	0	0	0
M1					
% Change	0.104		0.213	0.161	-0.092
Positive	14		14	11	9
Significant	0		0	0	0
Negative	1		1	4	6
Significant	0		0	0	3
M2					
% Change	0.242	-0.279	0.710	-0.203	0.522
Positive	9	0	12	3	7
Significant	0	0	1	0	1
Negative	6	15	3	12	8
Significant	0	0	0	0	0

Notes: The unanticipated money supply shocks are the percentage deviations from expected levels calculated according to the five processes discussed in the text. The numbers of positive and negative effects and their statistical significance are obtained from Tables 11.1, 11.5, 11.9, 11.13 and 11.16. For data sources, see Appendix F.

rates. Table 11.20 presents the average of the percentage shocks to the real exchange rate resulting from one percent changes in the five alternative measures of each unanticipated money supply shock calculated in the regressions referred to in this chapter.[6] The table also gives the number of coefficients taking each sign and the number with each sign being statistically significant. The averages of the point estimates of

[6] These calculations were performed in the Gretl and XLispStat files in which the regression results obtained in this chapter were produced.

these exchange rate effects are negative in only 4 of the 14 cases and exceed unity only in the case of U.K. base money. In all but three of the cases the percentage change is less than one-third the magnitude of the percentage unanticipated money supply shock. This is, of course, consistent with the observation that real exchange rate are not much affected by unanticipated money supply shocks, as opposed to shocks to the range of real variables studied in the previous chapter. It appears that countries' monetary authorities could generate unanticipated money supply shocks of the magnitudes observed without having major effects on real and nominal exchange rates. But if they did so, where is the evidence of overshooting?

It is reasonable to believe that not all of the observed unanticipated money supply shocks represent shocks to the excess supply – that is, changes in the excess of the supply of liquidity over the demand for it. If, to take an example, the authorities of a country adjust the domestic base money aggregate upward by 0.9% in response to a 1% increase in the demand for base money, an excess demand for money of a tenth of one percent will arise. If the resulting percentage increase in the real exchange rate is one percent, the associated overshooting will be in the order of 10 times the excess money demand shock. The fact that most of the average percentage changes in the real exchanges rates with respect to the U.S. are positively, not negatively, related to the individual countries' unanticipated money shocks suggests that these shocks cannot be the result of an attempt to pursue monetary policy – they are in the wrong direction! The conclusion that observed money shocks are responses of the authorities to demand for money changes to prevent overshooting would seem inescapable.

12

Further Evidence from a Blanchard-Quah VAR Analysis

As an extension to the conclusion of the previous chapter that money supply shocks have had essentially no effects on observed real exchange rate movements, this chapter addresses the issues using the vector autoregression technique developed by Olivier Blanchard and Danny Quah [8]. The application of this technique can incorporate the possibility that demand for money shocks may have had effects on the real exchange rates quite apart from unanticipated changes in the countries' monetary aggregates.

12.1 Vector Autoregression Analysis

In order to understand the procedure developed by Blanchard and Quah it is necessary review briefly the basics of vector autoregression analysis.[1] Consider two time series, each of which is a function of the current value of the other, p lagged values of itself and the other time series, and an *iid* error term:

$$\begin{aligned} y_{1(t)} &= a_{10} + a_{12}\, y_{2(t)} + a_{111}\, y_{1(t-1)} + a_{112}\, y_{1(t-2)} + \ldots + a_{11p}\, y_{1(t-p)} \\ &\quad + a_{121}\, y_{2(t-1)} + a_{122}\, y_{2(t-2)} + \ldots + a_{12p}\, y_{2(t-p)} + e_{1(t)} \qquad (12.1) \end{aligned}$$

$$\begin{aligned} y_{2(t)} &= a_{20} + a_{21}\, y_{1(t)} + a_{211}\, y_{1(t-1)} + a_{212}\, y_{1(t-2)} + \ldots + a_{21p}\, y_{1(t-p)} \\ &\quad + a_{221}\, y_{2(t-1)} + a_{222}\, y_{2(t-1)} + \ldots + a_{22p}\, y_{2(t-p)} + e_{2(t)} \qquad (12.2) \end{aligned}$$

This system can be written in matrix notation as

[1] Readers unfamiliar with VAR analysis should work through pages 291-353 of Walter Enders' textbook [33] and pages 257-372 of James Hamilton's book on time series analysis [50] as well as through pages 9-27, 43-58 and 97-117 of Helmut Lütkepohl's introductory book on multiple time series analysis [72].

J.E. Floyd, *Interest Rates, Exchange Rates and World Monetary Policy*,
DOI 10.1007/978-3-642-10280-6_12,

$$\begin{bmatrix} y_{1(t)} \\ y_{2(t)} \end{bmatrix} = \begin{bmatrix} a_{10} \\ a_{20} \end{bmatrix} + \begin{bmatrix} 0 & a_{12} \\ a_{21} & 0 \end{bmatrix} \begin{bmatrix} y_{1(t)} \\ y_{2(t)} \end{bmatrix} + \begin{bmatrix} a_{111} & a_{121} \\ a_{211} & a_{221} \end{bmatrix} \begin{bmatrix} y_{1(t-1)} \\ y_{2(t-1)} \end{bmatrix}$$
$$+ \begin{bmatrix} a_{112} & a_{122} \\ a_{212} & a_{222} \end{bmatrix} \begin{bmatrix} y_{1(t-2)} \\ y_{2(t-2)} \end{bmatrix} + \begin{bmatrix} a_{113} & a_{123} \\ a_{213} & a_{223} \end{bmatrix} \begin{bmatrix} y_{1(t-3)} \\ y_{2(t-3)} \end{bmatrix} + \ldots$$
$$\cdots\cdots\cdots + \begin{bmatrix} a_{11p} & a_{12p} \\ a_{21p} & a_{22p} \end{bmatrix} \begin{bmatrix} y_{1(t-p)} \\ y_{2(t-p)} \end{bmatrix} + \begin{bmatrix} e_{1(t)} \\ e_{2(t)} \end{bmatrix} \tag{12.3}$$

or, alternatively,

$$\mathbf{y}_t = \mathbf{a} + \mathbf{A_0}\,\mathbf{y}_t + \mathbf{A_1}\,\mathbf{y}_{t-1} + \mathbf{A_2}\,\mathbf{y}_{t-2} + \mathbf{A_3}\,\mathbf{y}_{t-3} + \cdots$$
$$\cdots\cdots\cdots + \mathbf{A_p}\,\mathbf{y}_{t-p} + \mathbf{e}_t \tag{12.4}$$

where $\mathbf{y}_t$, $\mathbf{a}$ and $\mathbf{e}_t$ are 2×1 column vectors and $\mathbf{A_0}$, $\mathbf{A_1}$, $\mathbf{A_2}$, $\cdots$ $\mathbf{A_p}$ are 2×2 matrices of coefficients. The vector $\mathbf{e}_t$ is a 2-element vector of white noise residuals that satisfies $E\{\mathbf{e}_t\mathbf{e}_t'\} = \mathbf{D}$, where $\mathbf{D}$ is a diagonal matrix which, with appropriate scaling of the elements of $\mathbf{y}$, becomes an identity matrix.

The system given by (12.4), which is called a *structural* VAR or a *primitive system*, can be solved simultaneously to yield the *reduced form* or *standard form* of the VAR:

$$(\mathbf{I} - \mathbf{A_0})\,\mathbf{y}_t = \mathbf{a} + \mathbf{A_1}\,\mathbf{y}_{t-1} + \mathbf{A_2}\,\mathbf{y}_{t-2} + \mathbf{A_3}\,\mathbf{y}_{t-3} + \cdots\cdots\cdots\cdots\cdots$$
$$\cdots\cdots\cdots + \mathbf{A_P}\,\mathbf{y}_{t-p} + \mathbf{e}_t \tag{12.5}$$

which reduces to

$$\mathbf{y}_t = (\mathbf{I} - \mathbf{A_0})^{-1}\mathbf{a} + (\mathbf{I} - \mathbf{A_0})^{-1}\mathbf{A_1}\,\mathbf{y}_{t-1} + (\mathbf{I} - \mathbf{A_0})^{-1}\mathbf{A_2}\,\mathbf{y}_{t-2}$$
$$+ (\mathbf{I} - \mathbf{A_0})^{-1}\mathbf{A_3}\,\mathbf{y}_{t-3} + \cdots\cdots\cdots\cdots\cdots\cdots$$
$$\cdots\cdots\cdots\cdots + (\mathbf{I} - \mathbf{A_0})^{-1}\mathbf{A_P}\,\mathbf{y}_{t-p} + (\mathbf{I} - \mathbf{A_0})^{-1}\mathbf{e}_t. \tag{12.6}$$

Letting $\mathbf{b} = (\mathbf{I} - \mathbf{A_0})^{-1}\mathbf{a}$, $\mathbf{B_1} = (\mathbf{I} - \mathbf{A_0})^{-1}\mathbf{A_1}$, $\mathbf{B_2} = (\mathbf{I} - \mathbf{A_0})^{-1}\mathbf{A_2}$, $\cdots$ etc., and $\mathbf{u}_t = (\mathbf{I} - \mathbf{A_0})^{-1}\,\mathbf{e}_t$, the standard form VAR can be written as

$$\mathbf{y}_t = \mathbf{b} + \mathbf{B_1}\,\mathbf{y}_{t-1} + \mathbf{B_2}\,\mathbf{y}_{t-2} + \mathbf{B_3}\,\mathbf{y}_{t-3} + \cdots + \mathbf{B_P}\,\mathbf{y}_{t-p} + \mathbf{u}_t. \tag{12.7}$$

All this assumes, of course, that the matrix $(\mathbf{I} - \mathbf{A_0})$ has an inverse. Given that $E\{\mathbf{e}_t\mathbf{e}_t'\} = \mathbf{D}$, the variance-covariance matrix of the vector of residuals $\mathbf{u}_t$ equals

$$\begin{aligned}\mathbf{\Omega} &= E\{\mathbf{u}_t\mathbf{u}_t{}'\}\\ &= E\{[(\mathbf{I}-\mathbf{A_0})^{-1}\mathbf{e}_t][(\mathbf{I}-\mathbf{A_0})^{-1}\mathbf{e}_t]'\}\\ &= E\{[(\mathbf{I}-\mathbf{A_0})^{-1}]\mathbf{e}_t\mathbf{e}_t{}'[(\mathbf{I}-\mathbf{A_0})^{-1}]'\}\\ &= [(\mathbf{I}-\mathbf{A_0})^{-1}]E\{\mathbf{e}_t\mathbf{e}_t{}'\}[(\mathbf{I}-\mathbf{A_0})^{-1}]'\\ &= [(\mathbf{I}-\mathbf{A_0})^{-1}]\,\mathbf{D}\,[(\mathbf{I}-\mathbf{A_0})^{-1}]'\end{aligned}$$

The two equations in (12.7) are estimated by ordinary least squares, with the appropriate lag length chosen on the basis of likelihood-ratio tests and the Akaike and Schwartz-Bayesian criteria.[2]

The standard form system given by (12.7) can be manipulated to express the current value of each variable as a function solely of the vector of residuals $\mathbf{u}_t$. This is called its *moving average representation*— $\mathbf{y}_t$ is a moving average of the current and past values of $\mathbf{u}_t$.

$$\mathbf{y}_t = \mathbf{C_0}\,\mathbf{u}_t + \mathbf{C_1}\,\mathbf{u}_{t-1} + \mathbf{C_2}\,\mathbf{u}_{t-2} + \cdots\cdots + \mathbf{C_s}\,\mathbf{u}_{t-s} + \mathbf{y_0}. \quad (12.8)$$

where $\mathbf{y_0}$ is some initial value of $\mathbf{y}_t$ and s is the chosen length of the moving average representation.

The above moving average representation does not give a proper indication of how the system responds to shocks to the individual structural equations. The problem is that the shocks to the equations contained in the vector $\mathbf{u}_t$ are correlated with each other. One therefore cannot determine what the effects on the two variables of a shock to one structural equation alone would be—an observed u_t will represent the combined shocks to both equations. This can be seen from the fact that from (12.6)

$$\mathbf{u}_t = (\mathbf{I}-\mathbf{A_0})^{-1}\,\mathbf{e}_t.$$

In order to determine the effects of a shock to an individual structural equation of the system one has to be able to solve the system for $\mathbf{A_0}$ and thereby obtain $(\mathbf{I}-\mathbf{A_0})^{-1}$. This will enable an operation on (12.8) to transform the $\mathbf{u}_{t-j}$ in into $\mathbf{e}_{t-j}$. In the process, of course, the matrices $\mathbf{C_j}$ will also be transformed into a useful representation of the impulse-responses – the responses of the two variables through time to a shock to one of them in some past period.

[2] Likelihood ratio tests are performed on the estimated system of equations first with long lags and then with progressively shorter lags, testing the restriction of leaving out lags in comparing each set of lag lengths. Alternatively one can select the lag length that minimizes Akaike and Schwartz-Bayesian criteria calculated for each potential lag-length. It is better to err by choosing lag lengths that are too long rather than too short.

The approach used to identify $\mathbf{A_0}$ in VAR analysis is to find the matrix that will orthogonalize the errors – that is, transform the $\mathbf{u}_{t-j}$ into $\mathbf{e}_{t-j}$ which are uncorrelated with each other. Given any matrix $\mathbf{G}$ that has an inverse, equation (12.8) can be rewritten

$$\mathbf{y}_t = \mathbf{C_0}\,\mathbf{G}\mathbf{G}^{-1}\,\mathbf{u}_t + \mathbf{C_1}\,\mathbf{G}\mathbf{G}^{-1}\,\mathbf{u}_{t-1} + \mathbf{C_2}\,\mathbf{G}\mathbf{G}^{-1}\,\mathbf{u}_{t-2} + \cdots\cdots + \mathbf{C_s}\,\mathbf{G}\mathbf{G}^{-1}\,\mathbf{u}_{t-s} + \mathbf{y_0}. \qquad (12.9)$$

The task is to find the $\mathbf{G}$ for which

$$\mathbf{G} = (\mathbf{I} - \mathbf{A_0})^{-1}.$$

Then

$$\mathbf{y}_t = \mathbf{Z_0}\,\mathbf{e}_t + \mathbf{Z_1}\,\mathbf{e}_{t-1} + \mathbf{Z_2}\,\mathbf{e}_{t-2} + \cdots\cdots + \mathbf{Z_s}\,\mathbf{e}_{t-s} + \mathbf{y_0} \qquad (12.10)$$

where

$$\mathbf{Z_j} = \mathbf{C_j}\,\mathbf{G}$$

and

$$\mathbf{e}_{t-j} = \mathbf{G}^{-1}\,\mathbf{u}_{t-j} \quad \Longrightarrow \quad \mathbf{u}_{t-j} = \mathbf{G}\,\mathbf{e}_{t-j}$$

Suppose that

$$\mathbf{A_0} = \begin{bmatrix} 0 & 0 \\ a_{21} & 0 \end{bmatrix}$$

so that the current level of y_1 is not affected by the current level of y_2 while the current level of y_2 does depend on the current level of y_1 – the system is recursive. Both y_1 and y_2, of course, continue to be affected by their own and each other's past values. The standard approach to identifying the elements of $\mathbf{A_0}$ in VAR analysis is to make this assumption and decompose the matrix of reduced form residuals

$$\mathbf{u_t}\,\mathbf{u_t'} = \boldsymbol{\Omega} = \mathbf{G}\,\mathbf{e_t}(\mathbf{G}\,\mathbf{e_t})' = \mathbf{G}\,\mathbf{e_t}\mathbf{e_t'}\,\mathbf{G}' = \mathbf{G}\,\mathbf{D}\,\mathbf{G}'$$

choosing implicit units of measurement for the variables for which the standard deviations of the structural errors are unity so that $\mathbf{D} = \mathbf{I}$. The problem is to obtain the matrix $\mathbf{G}$ for which

$$\mathbf{G}\,\mathbf{G}' = \boldsymbol{\Omega}.$$

This simply involves doing a Choleski decomposition of the matrix $\boldsymbol{\Omega}$ which yields the result

$$(\mathbf{I} - \tilde{\mathbf{A}}_0)^{-1} = \mathbf{G}$$

and, hence,

$$\tilde{\mathbf{A}}_0 = \mathbf{I} - \mathbf{G}^{-1}$$

where $\tilde{\mathbf{A}}_0$ is a representation of $\mathbf{A}_0$ after scaling of the variables to render $\mathbf{D} = \mathbf{I}$. The matrix $\mathbf{G}$ so obtained can then be used to obtain the $\mathbf{Z}_j$ matrices in equation (12.10) with the errors $\mathbf{e}_t$ having unit variance. The assumption that $a_{12} = 0$ can be replaced with an assumption that $a_{21} = 0$, reversing the direction of recursiveness, by simply reversing the ordering of the two variables so that y_2 becomes the first variable in the system and y_1 becomes the second.

The problem with the assumptions required for a Choleski decomposition in the analysis here, which uses the real and nominal exchange rates as the two variables, is that it is clear that the two exchange rates will move together in the current period regardless of which one is shocked – the system is not recursive.

12.2 The Blanchard-Quah Decomposition

The approach developed by Blanchard and Quah replaces the Choleski assumption that either a_{12} or a_{21} equals zero with an alternative identifying assumption – that one shock, in this case the monetary shock, has only a temporary effect on one of the variables, in this case the real exchange rate, but a permanent effect on the other variable, here the nominal exchange rate, while the other shock, in this case called the real shock, has permanent effects on both variables. Letting the real exchange rate be the first variable and the monetary shock the first shock, the requirement is imposed that the top-left elements in $\mathbf{Z}_0 = \mathbf{C}_0\,\mathbf{G}$, $\mathbf{Z}_1 = \mathbf{C}_1\,\mathbf{G}$, $\mathbf{Z}_2 = \mathbf{C}_2\,\mathbf{G}$, $\cdots\cdots\cdots\cdots$, $\mathbf{Z}_s = \mathbf{C}_s\,\mathbf{G}$, sum to zero.[3] The Blanchard-Quah decomposition yields the appropriate $\mathbf{Z}_i$ matrices in equation (12.10). Using these matrices, it is then possible to obtain impulse-response functions giving the sequence of responses of the real and nominal exchange rates over a future time horizon to monetary and real shocks of one standard-deviation magnitude in an initial period. And the variances of the forecast errors in predicting the real and nominal exchange rates in each period over a future time horizon resulting from unforseen one standard-deviation monetary and

[3] It matters not which shock is assumed to be the monetary one. If the second shock is the monetary one then the requirement is simply that the sum of the top right elements of the above matrices equal zero.

real shocks in each period can also be obtained. This makes it possible to determine the percentages of the future error variances of current forecasts of future real and nominal exchange rates that will result from unforseen monetary and real shocks of average magnitude in every period. Finally, it is possible to decompose the actual movements of the real and nominal exchange rates over the sample period into the movements that have resulted from real and monetary shocks respectively.

12.3 The Results

A Blanchard-Quah analysis of the real and nominal exchange rates with respect to the United States of the countries being studied was performed using the procedure outlined above.[4] The responses of the real exchange rates to monetary shocks are shown in the top panels of Figures 12.1 through 12.5. The historical decompositions of the real and nominal exchange rates into the portions due to monetary and real shocks are shown in the middle and bottom panels.

It is clear from the top panels of the first, second and fourth figures that no statistically significant responses to monetary shocks of the real exchange rates of Canada, the U.K. and France with respect to the U.S. are found. In the cases of Japan and Germany, in the third and fifth figures, there is some evidence of a response. Essentially the same conclusion arises with respect to the historical decompositions of the real exchange rate movements. In the cases of Canada, the U.K. and France, the portions of the real exchange rate movements that can be ascribed to monetary shocks are tiny. Apart from some small effects of nominal shocks on the real exchange rate during the late 1970s, the same is true of Japan. In the German case quite significant effects of monetary shocks on the real exchange rate with respect to the United

[4] All the calculations in this chapter were performed in XLispStat using the batch files `bqvarcau.lsp`, `bqvaruku.lsp`, `bqvarjnu.lsp`, `bqvarfru.lsp` and `bqvargru.lsp` for Canada, the U.K., Japan, France and Germany, respectively, with respect the the U.S. and the results are in files having the same names except for the suffix `.lou`. Gretl could not be used because that program does not support Blanchard-Quah VAR analysis. Accordingly, as a cross-check, the calculations were also performed using the commercial program Rats. The relevant Rats batch and output files have the same root names as those previously mentioned with the suffixes `.prg` and `rou` respectively. The relevant data are in the Rats data file `jfdatamo.rat`. A discussion of the XLispStat functions, written by the present author, can be found in Chapter 11 of a rough manual entitled "Statistics and Econometrics Using XLispStat" that can be found, along with a smaller short manual, on the author's web-site.

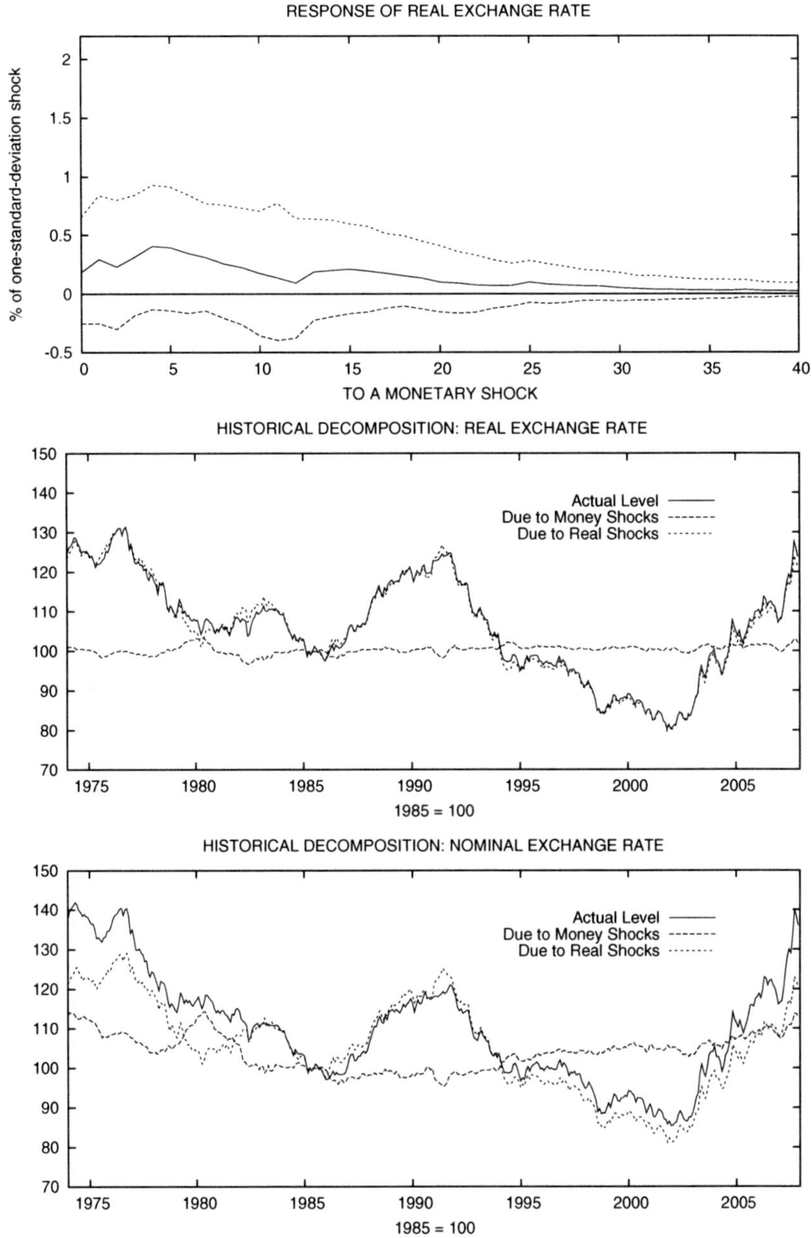

Fig. 12.1. Blanchard-Quah-VAR historical decompositions of Canada's real and nominal exchange rates with respect to the U.S. dollar into the movements attributable to real and money shocks and the response of the real exchange rate to money shocks.

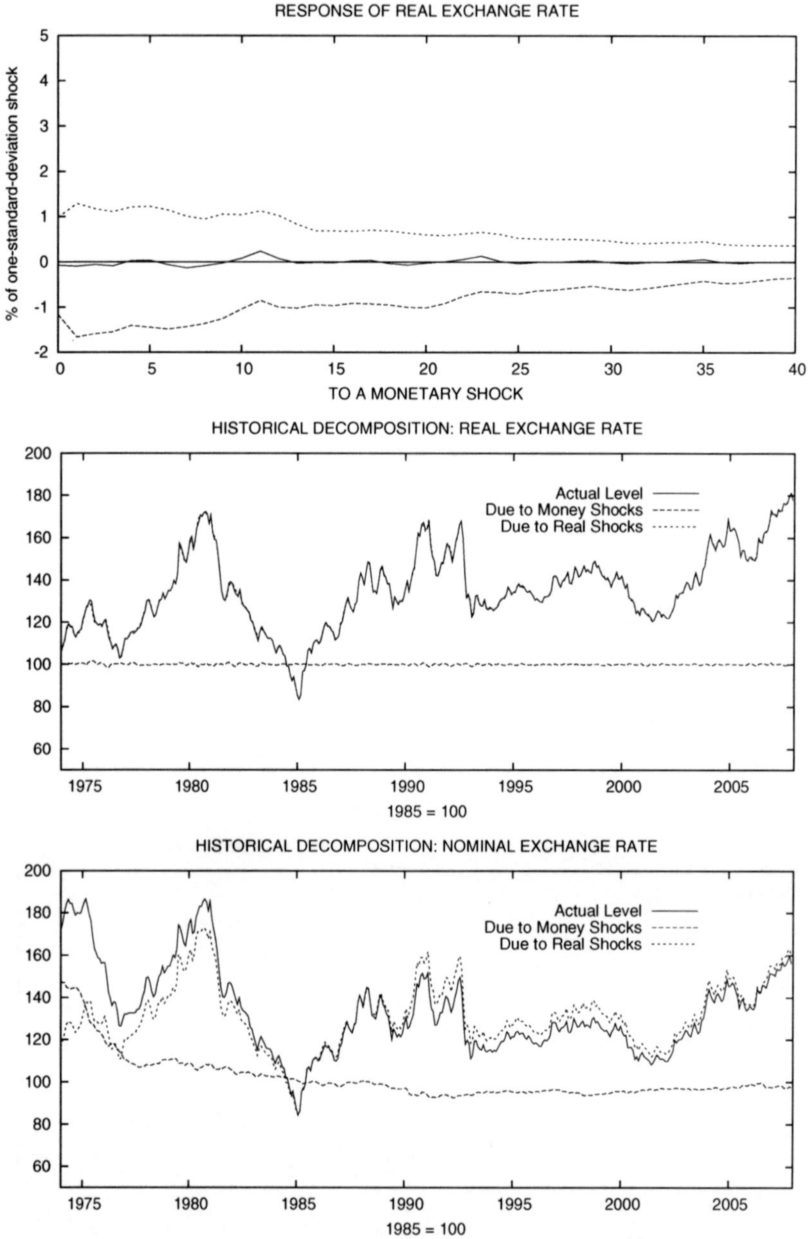

Fig. 12.2. Blanchard-Quah-VAR historical decompositions of Britain's real and nominal exchange rates with respect to the U.S. dollar into the movements attributable to real and money shocks and the response of the real exchange rate to money shocks.

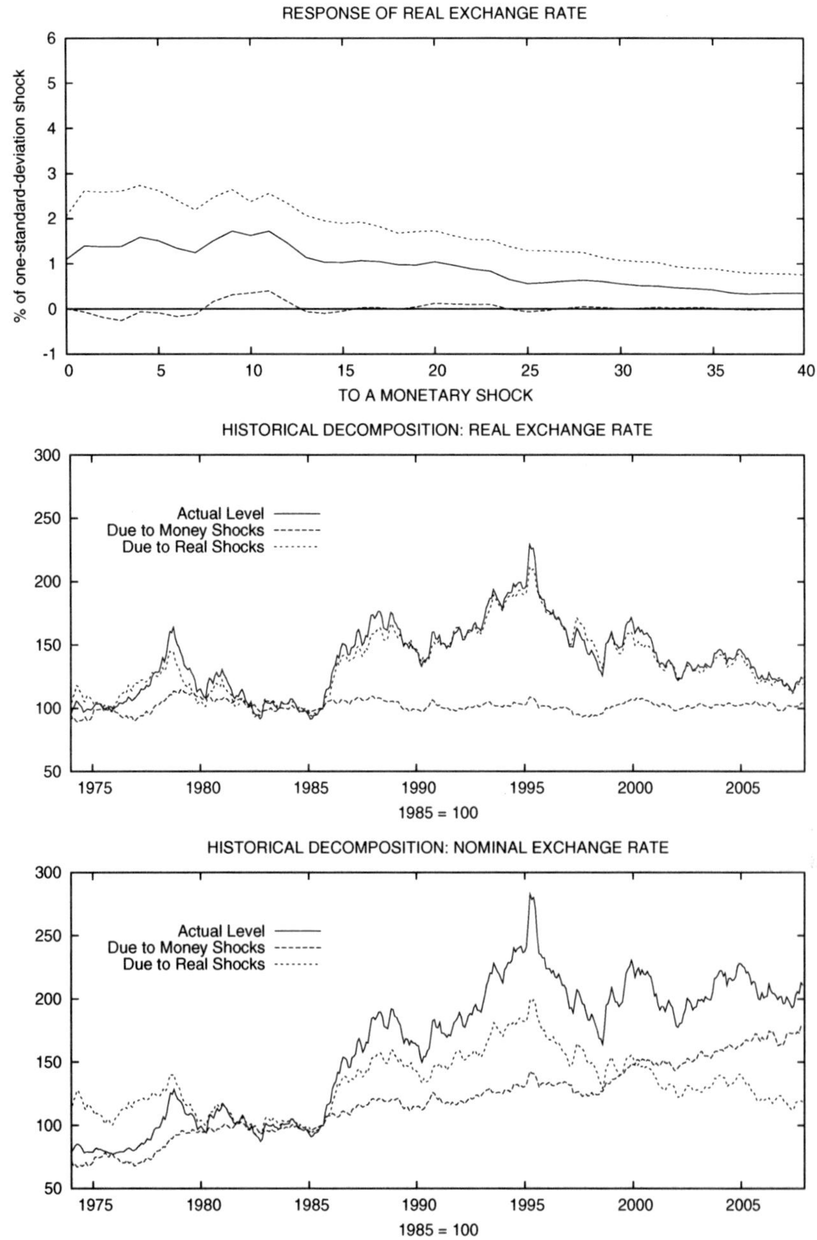

Fig. 12.3. Blanchard-Quah-VAR historical decompositions of Japanese real and nominal exchange rates with respect to the U.S. dollar into the movements attributable to real and money shocks and the response of the real exchange rate to money shocks.

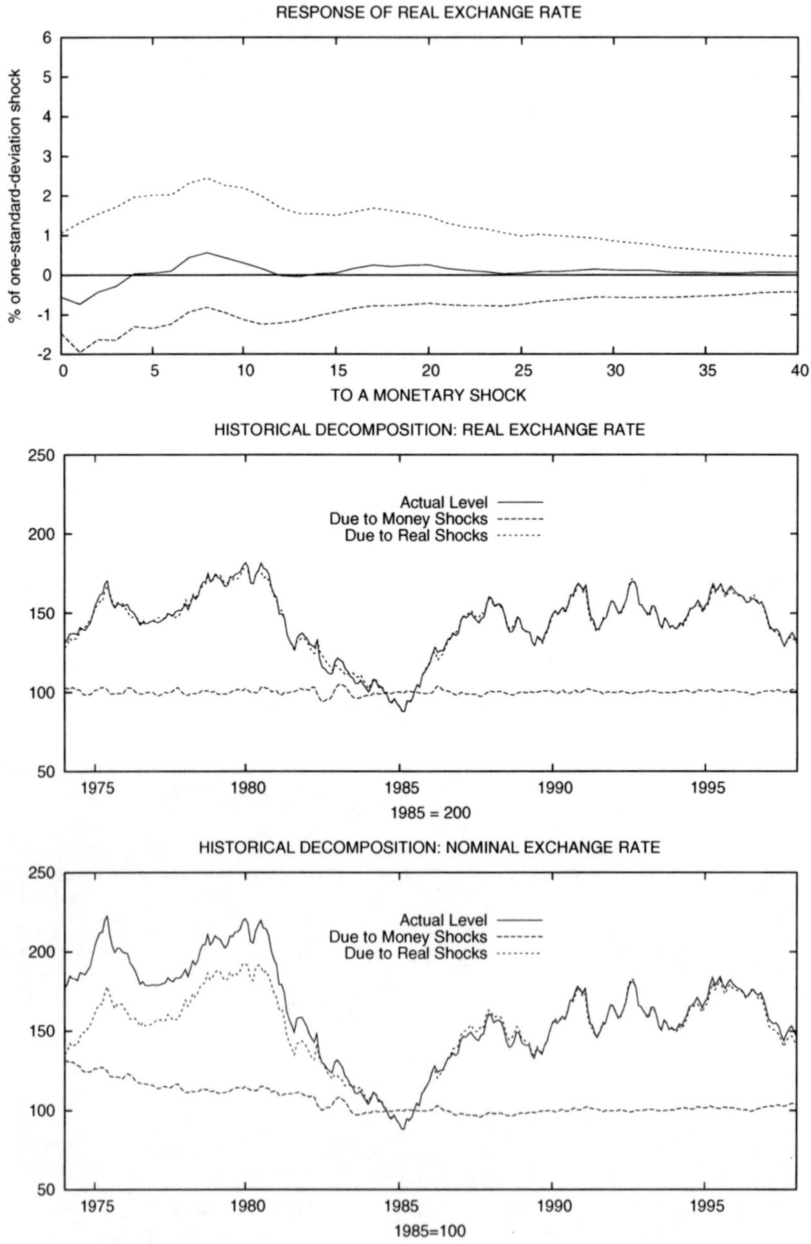

Fig. 12.4. Blanchard-Quah-VAR historical decompositions of French real and nominal exchange rates with respect to the U.S. dollar into the movements attributable to real and money shocks and the response of the real exchange rate to money shocks.

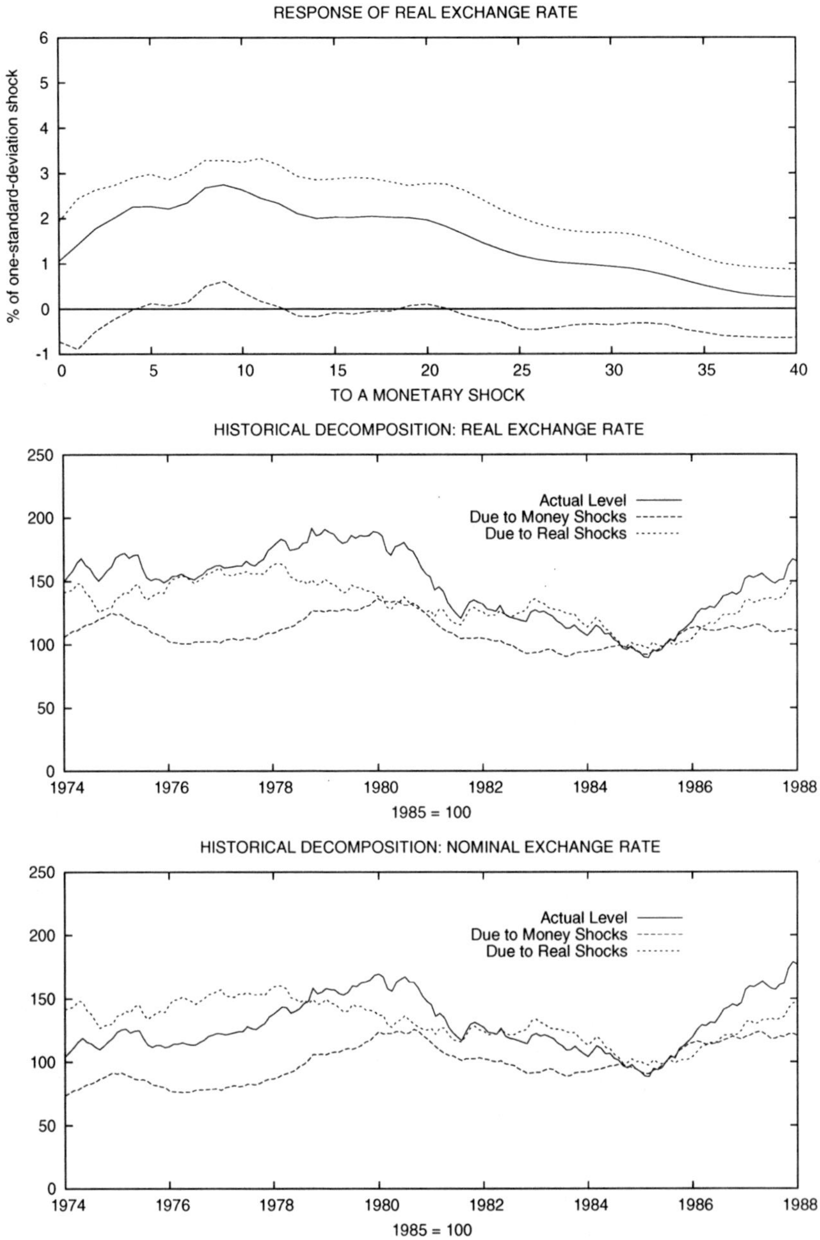

Fig. 12.5. Blanchard-Quah-VAR historical decompositions of German real and nominal exchange rates with respect to the U.S. dollar into the movements attributable to real and money shocks and the response of the real exchange rate to money shocks.

States are evident. These effects are very smooth, with no evidence of sharp movements that one would associate with overshooting.

With respect to the effects of monetary shocks on the nominal exchange rate, the German historical decomposition indicates that monetary shocks were every bit as important as real shocks. In the case of Japan, monetary shocks were also important but their effect was almost completely confined to trend – real shocks were clearly responsible for all major year-to-year movements in the nominal exchange rate with respect to the U.S. With respect to Britain and France, the monetary shocks had very smooth effects on the nominal exchange rates, reflecting increased control over the domestic inflation rates relative to U.S. inflation in the late 1970s and early 1980s. Monetary shocks also had important effects on the Canadian nominal exchange rate with respect to the U.S. during the late 1970s and early 1980s – the negative and then positive effects of real shocks on the nominal exchange rate over a five year period were offset by nominal shocks. Apart from this short period in the case of Canada, real shocks were clearly the major determinant of year-to-year nominal exchange rate movements in every country examined other than Germany.

Table 12.1. Historical Decomposition: Changes in Real Exchange Rate Levels Due to Monetary Shocks

	Maximum Level	Minimum Level	Maximum Less Minimum
Canada	103.078	96.405	6.674
U.K.	101.609	98.379	3.231
Japan	112.628	87.703	24.925
France	104.958	93.759	11.120
Germany	124.692	82.576	42.116

Table 12.1 presents the differences between the maximum and minimum levels of the decomposed real exchange rates produced by monetary shocks for the five countries – the maximum and minimum levels

Table 12.2. Percentages of the forecast-error-variances of the Real Exchange Rate Due to Monetary Shocks for monthly horizons

Horizon	U.K.	Canada	France	Japan	Germany
0	0.101	2.388	5.364	18.121	18.101
1	0.097	3.072	5.458	17.832	19.252
2	0.119	3.336	6.825	17.818	20.851
3	0.132	3.787	7.039	17.731	21.414
4	0.343	4.297	8.470	18.192	21.979
5	0.343	4.299	8.462	18.253	21.958
6	0.496	4.448	8.498	18.487	21.993
7	0.567	4.523	10.110	18.525	22.197
8	0.605	4.626	10.265	19.312	23.431
9	0.662	4.685	10.472	19.742	23.426
10	0.838	4.740	10.669	19.843	23.099
11	1.221	4.733	10.942	19.751	23.283
12	1.621	4.841	11.360	20.073	23.398
13	1.781	5.339	11.358	21.099	23.760
14	1.784	5.348	11.433	21.191	23.870
15	1.784	5.352	11.437	21.175	23.873
16	1.812	5.367	11.623	21.169	23.872
17	1.814	5.384	11.704	21.171	23.867
18	1.891	5.410	11.719	21.215	23.864
19	1.908	5.428	11.732	21.215	23.856
20	1.937	5.490	11.732	21.263	23.878
21	1.950	5.493	11.840	21.314	24.045
22	1.998	5.507	11.872	21.382	24.349
23	2.074	5.508	11.882	21.397	24.649
24	2.272	5.508	11.921	21.695	24.857
25	2.314	5.552	11.924	21.781	25.025
26	2.326	5.568	11.950	21.782	25.104
27	2.327	5.571	11.950	21.787	25.133
28	2.333	5.573	11.959	21.791	25.129
29	2.336	5.574	11.971	21.797	25.122
30	2.366	5.584	11.978	21.828	25.124

are expressed as percentages of the average levels. For Japan the difference between the maximum and minimum effect of monetary shocks on the real exchange rate with respect to the United States is about 25 percent of the average level and for Germany the difference is 42 percent of the average level. It is clear from the middle panel of Fig. 12.3 that the minimum and maximum for Japan both occurred during the late 70s when real shocks were affecting the real exchange rate in the same direction. In the German case, the minimum and maximum were separated by about four years during the same general period – from about 1977 through 1981. Since no sharp within-year movements of the real exchange rates of the sort one might associated with overshooting are apparent during this period, it would seem that the authorities of the two countries were essentially 'leaning against the exchange rate' in their conduct of monetary policy during these years. Indeed, the smooth yet substantial observed monetary effects on the German real exchange rate with respect to the U.S. over all the years examined suggest that the Bundesbank may have been operating in this way during the entire period.

The percentages of the forecast-error-variances of the real exchange rates of the five countries with respect to the U.S. that were due to monetary shocks are presented in Table 12.2. While these are substantial – in the order of 20 to 25 percent – for Japan and Germany, one would have to conclude that real shocks still account for the major fraction of the forecast error variances of these countries as well as Canada, the U.K. and France.

Part III

Implications for Monetary Policy

The empirical analysis of Part II generated some important results. It established that the Post-Bretton-Woods real exchange rates of major countries with respect to the United States – and, correspondingly, also with respect to each other – were determined almost entirely by real factors relating to world technological change and capital accumulation and their consequent effects on international capital movements, oil and commodity prices, real income growth, and international terms-of-trade changes. And it was clearly evident that unanticipated shocks to the supply of money had no effects of consequence on real exchange rates. The fact that non-trivial unpredictable changes in the supplies of money of the countries examined did occur leads one to believe that monetary policies were followed that financed demand-for-liquidity shocks to prevent their affecting exchange rates. Of relevance here is the conclusion of Part I, and the literature there referred to, that there are strong reasons to expect overshooting movements in exchange rates in response to shocks to the excess demand for liquidity.

Another result from Part II is the tendency of forward premia to be very small in relation to the typical period-to-period movements of nominal exchange rates. This is a direct consequence of the near-random-walk character of real exchange rate movements combined with the stability of core inflation rates in the countries examined. Period-to-period movements of real exchange rates are unpredictable, being as likely in one direction as the other, apart from slight mean-reversion that will depend upon whether the real exchange rate is above or below its historical mean value. And inflation rates, though quite variable, tend to revert towards some longer-term inflation tendency. While forward and spot exchange rates tend to be highly correlated, with the former lagging the latter by one period, the forward premiums or discounts cannot be expected to predict the next period's change in spot exchange rates with any accuracy, given the lack of current information about the forces that will determine future real exchange rates, except under circumstances where the average inflation rates of the countries involved are, and can be expected to continue to be, substantially different.

The above evidence is thus consistent with the observed tendency of real and nominal exchange rates to move closely together under flexible exchange rate regimes with the difference between them being the typically stable path of the ratio of the respective countries' price levels.

This third part of the monograph develops a theory that explains the evidence of Part II within the framework of behaviour of countries' monetary authorities that is consistent with both their own self-interest and that of the general public, and provides further tests of this theory. Chapter 13 constructs a model based on the framework developed in Part I. A theory of *stochastic monetary interdependence* is then developed in Chapter 14 and its implications for world-wide monetary policy, target zones, and monetary unions explored. Finally, Chapter 15 brings forth further evidence to test this theory and provides suggestions for future analysis.

13

The Model

13.1 Basic Equations and Diagrams

The model used in what follows focuses on the problem of a small country that faces domestic technology and demand for money shocks and operates in an international economy in which the other countries also experience technology, demand for money, and supply of money shocks. The basic model is a two-country one, consisting of the small country and a big country which can be treated, as the situation requires, either as a rest-of-world aggregate or as a major component of that aggregate. When the rest-world-aggregate consists entirely of small countries that do not cooperate explicitly in the setting of monetary policy, the solution of the individual country's policy problem defines world monetary policy in the sense that all countries have to solve the same problem. When the world consists of a big country and a collection of small countries, world monetary policy involves an interaction between the big country and many small countries that are substantively identical to the one modeled.

Under conditions where full employment is continually maintained the foreign (big) economy produces $\tilde{Y}_{ft}$ units of output and the domestic (small) economy produces Y_{ft} units of output. The relative price of domestic output in terms of rest-of-world output is denoted by Q_{ft} which thus represents the small country's full-employment real exchange rate with respect to the big country. It is assumed that one unit of foreign output can be transformed costlessly into one unit of foreign-employed capital, and one unit of domestic output into one unit of domestically employed capital, although adjustment costs will be involved in putting the resulting capital into productive use.

J.E. Floyd, *Interest Rates, Exchange Rates and World Monetary Policy*,
DOI 10.1007/978-3-642-10280-6_13,

World residents are assumed to be free to exchange ownership of existing stocks of capital, and finance new capital formation, across international borders. World asset or portfolio equilibrium is thus determined by the demand functions for money together with the Euler condition determining the relationship between domestic and foreign interest rates. The demand functions for money are standard with all variables but interest rates expressed in logarithms, denoted by lower-case arabic letters.

$$\begin{aligned} m_t &= p_t + \psi_t + \eta\, i_t + \epsilon\, y_t \\ &= p_t + \psi_t + \eta\, r_t + \eta\,(E_{t-1}p_{t+1} - E_{t-1}p_t) + \epsilon\, y_t \qquad (13.1) \\ \tilde{m}_t &= \tilde{p}_t + \tilde{\psi}_t + \tilde{\eta}\, \tilde{i}_t + \tilde{\epsilon}\, \tilde{y}_t \\ &= \tilde{p}_t + \tilde{\psi}_t + \tilde{\eta}\, \tilde{r}_t + \tilde{\eta}\,(E_{t-1}\tilde{p}_{t+1} - E_{t-1}\tilde{p}_t) + \tilde{\epsilon}\, \tilde{y}_t \qquad (13.2) \end{aligned}$$

where p_t is the price level, m_t is the nominal money stock, i_t and r_t are, respectively, the nominal and real interest rates, ψ_t is a the logarithm of a demand-for-money shift variable, E_{t-1} is the expectations operator based on the information available in the period $t-1$ and η (< 0) and ϵ (> 0) are, respectively, the interest semi-elasticity and the income elasticity of demand for real money balances.[1] A $\tilde{}$ over a variable always denotes the large rest-of-world economy. The relationships between the nominal and real interest rates are given by

$$i_t = r_t + (E_{t-1}p_{t+1} - E_{t-1}p_t)$$

and

$$\tilde{i}_t = \tilde{r}_t + (E_{t-1}\tilde{p}_{t+1} - E_{t-1}\tilde{p}_t).$$

In contrast to nominal interest rates, real interest rates are unobservable to private individuals and governments. For simplicity it is everywhere assumed that the home residents in all countries hold only home money.

Each country's securities are denominated in their own output goods and the domestic real interest rate differs from the foreign real rate by a risk differential ρ_t minus the expected rate of change in the real exchange rate, represented by the expected change in the logarithm of the real exchange rate q_t.[2] Hence,

---

[1] The interest semi-elasticity of demand for money is the relative change in the quantity of real money balances demanded divided by the change in the level of the interest rate.

[2] As explained in Part I, an expected rise in the real exchange rate represents an expected capital gain on holding domestically employed capital, causing the domestic net-of-capital-gain real interest rate to fall.

$$r_t = \tilde{r}_t + \rho_t - (E_{t-1}q_{t+1} - E_{t-1}q_t). \tag{13.3}$$

Since each country's residents must hold their existing stocks of wealth as either monetary or non-monetary assets, zero excess demands for money in both countries implies a zero excess demand for the world aggregate of non-monetary assets. Equations (13.1) and (13.2) thus imply that domestic and foreign residents hold their desired mixes of monetary and non-monetary assets. Equation (13.3) ensures that the existing mix of domestic and foreign non-monetary assets is willingly held by world residents. A situation where domestic and foreign residents together want to hold a greater ratio of domestic to foreign securities in their portfolios than the ratio of domestic to foreign securities in actual existence, for example, will result in a rise in the price of domestic securities relative to foreign securities and a fall in the domestic interest rate relative to the foreign interest rate.

The real exchange rate is defined in logarithms as

$$q_t = p_t + \pi_t - \tilde{p}_t \tag{13.4}$$

where π_t is the logarithm of the nominal exchange rate defined as the foreign currency price of domestic currency. Individuals and governments can observe nominal but not real exchange rates.

The deviation of the real exchange rate from its full-employment level can be expressed as

$$q_t - q_{ft} = \sigma\left[(y_t - y_{ft}) - (\tilde{y}_t - \tilde{y}_{ft})\right] \tag{13.5}$$

where $\sigma < 0$. The real exchange rate is at its full-employment level when output is at its full-employment level although the full-employment real exchange rate may vary independently of changes in the full-employment output levels as a result of changes in the expected future return to domestically employed capital relative to capital employed abroad and ongoing changes in technology and tastes that affect the relative valuation of the two countries' outputs. When domestic output and employment rise relative to rest-of-world output and employment at given technology and tastes and unchanged full-employment output levels, an excess supply of domestic output on the world market occurs and the value of domestic output in terms of rest-of-world output declines, reducing the domestic real exchange rate relative to its full-employment level.

Finally, the deviation of the rest-of-world real interest rate from its full employment level is negatively related to the deviation of rest-of-world output from its full-employment level according to

$$\tilde{r}_t - \tilde{r}_{ft} = \tilde{\phi}\,(\tilde{y}_t - \tilde{y}_{ft}) \tag{13.6}$$

where $\tilde{\phi} < 0$. This relationship results from the fact that, say, an increase in output above its full-employment level, being temporary, will feed into savings in order to intertemporally smooth consumption. The price of capital will be bid up and the interest rate will be bid down with the increase in output thereby channeled into investment. Or, viewed in more conventional terms, a fall in the real interest rate relative to its full-employment level will increase the price of capital goods relative to their cost of production and thereby result in an increase in investment which will produce a temporary increase in output relative to its full-employment level until such time as the price level can adjust.

The six equations, (13.1) through (13.6) contain eight endogenous variables, y_t, $\tilde{y}_t$, p_t, $\tilde{p}_t$, r_t, $\tilde{r}_t$, q_t and π_t, with the full-employment levels of the interest rates, outputs, and the real exchange rate being exogenous along with the nominal money stocks, ρ_t, $(E_{t-1}q_{t+1} - E_{t-1}q_t)$, $(E_{t-1}p_{t+1} - E_{t-1}p_t)$, $(E_{t-1}\tilde{p}_{t+1} - E_{t-1}\tilde{p}_t)$, $\tilde{\psi}_t$ and ψ_t.

Ideal closure of the model would require the addition of relationships between the deviations of outputs from full-employment and the sequence of subsequent-period price level adjustments, allowing for exogenous price level shocks in response to changes in expectations about future shocks to the demand for and supply of money and real interest rate shocks in response to changes in the risk of holding domestic as opposed to foreign assets and in the expected future time path of the real exchange rate. The model would then become an explicitly intertemporal one, driven by the time-paths of exogenous shocks to the demand for and supply of money as well as the time paths of full-employment outputs and interest rates and the full-employment real exchange rate resulting from ongoing accumulation of capital inclusive of technology. Realistic incorporation of dynamics would also require modifications of the structural equations (13.5) and (13.6) to include lagged deviations of domestic and foreign outputs from their full-employment levels to take account of the fact that that commitments to changes in capital stocks and output cannot be costlessly reversed and require time to complete.

Unfortunately, such ideal modifications will produce an infinity of potential dynamic paths depending on how fast people learn about each individual period's particular real and monetary shocks and policy changes and on the relevant firms' optimal intervals between successive adjustments of product prices and wage levels. And there is no basis for assuming that learning processes will be the same for a particular shock occurring at one point in time and a shock of the same type occurring at another point in time – appropriate assumptions in one situation may turn out to be inappropriate in another.

The only satisfactory approach in terms of present analytical objectives is to adopt two alternative assumptions for each country: a) one that imposes zero price flexibility by setting the logarithm of the normalized price level at zero, and b) one that imposes complete price flexibility by setting the deviation of output from its full employment level at zero. The first enables an approximate analysis of the short-run consequences of an exogenous shock when prices cannot fully adjust while the second produces the long-run results that will occur after prices have fully adjusted. While the length-of-run cannot be precisely known, one can operate on the assumption that price level adjustment eventually will occur. Accordingly, the following two equations are added to the model.

$$\tilde{p}_t = 0 \quad \text{or} \quad \tilde{y}_t = \tilde{y}_{ft} \tag{13.7}$$

$$p_t = 0 \quad \text{or} \quad y_t = y_{ft} \tag{13.8}$$

The eight equations (13.1) through (13.8) now solve for all eight variables, y_t, $\tilde{y}_t$, p_t, $\tilde{p}_t$, r_t, $\tilde{r}_t$, q_t and π_t in the case where the exchange rate is flexible. With a fixed exchange rate the number of equations exceeds the remaining seven above-listed endogenous variables, so a new variable must be made endogenous. That variable is the nominal money supply of the country that chooses to fix the exchange rate – its authorities automatically adjust the domestic money stock when they buy and sell foreign exchange reserves to maintain the chosen exchange rate parity.

The model has a simple diagrammatic presentation. Consider first the large rest-of-world economy. Equation (13.2) can be presented as an upward sloping curve in $(\tilde{r}, \tilde{y})$ space, yielding the combinations of the real interest rate and output for which the markets for domestic assets are in equilibrium. This is presented as the $\tilde{\text{A}}\tilde{\text{A}}$ curve in Fig. (13.1) An increase in the nominal money supply or decline in the price level or reduction in the demand for money, possibly resulting from an increase in the expected rate of inflation, shifts the curve to the right. The vertical line $\tilde{\text{Y}}_{\text{f}}\tilde{\text{Y}}_{\text{f}}$ denotes the full employment level of output. And equation (13.6) can be presented as the downward sloping curve $\tilde{\text{G}}\tilde{\text{G}}$ in $(\tilde{r}, \tilde{y})$ space giving the combinations of the real interest rate and output for which the market for the flow of output is in equilibrium. This curve shifts along with the vertical $\tilde{Y}_{\text{f}}\tilde{Y}_{\text{f}}$ line in response to changes in the full-employment levels of the interest rate and income.[3] Equilibrium

[3] It would be convenient, though unconventional, to set the origin at $\tilde{\text{Y}}_{\text{f}}$.

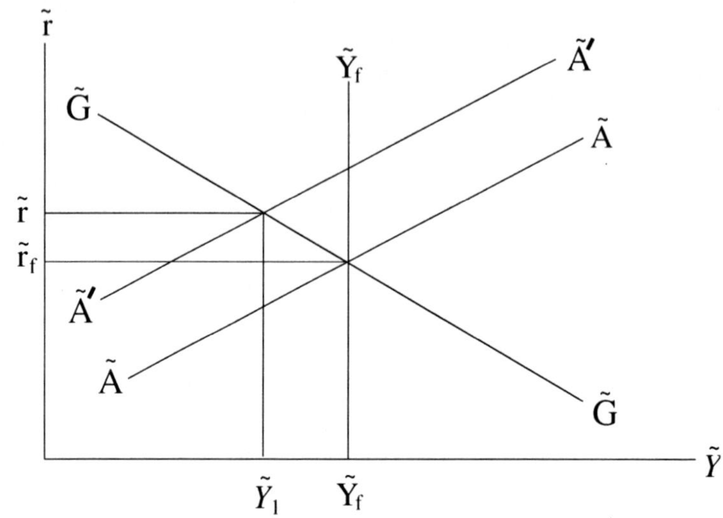

Fig. 13.1. The large rest-of-world economy

is determined by the intersection of these two curves – that is, by the solution of equations (13.2) and (13.6) for $\tilde{r}$ and $\tilde{y}$. With price flexibility and full employment, $\tilde{p}$ will be such that $\tilde{y} = \tilde{y}_f$ and $\tilde{\mathrm{A}}\tilde{\mathrm{A}}$ will have moved to intersect $\tilde{\mathrm{G}}\tilde{\mathrm{G}}$ at its intersection with $\tilde{\mathrm{Y}}_{\mathrm{f}}\tilde{\mathrm{Y}}_{\mathrm{f}}$, at which point $\tilde{r} = \tilde{r}_f$.

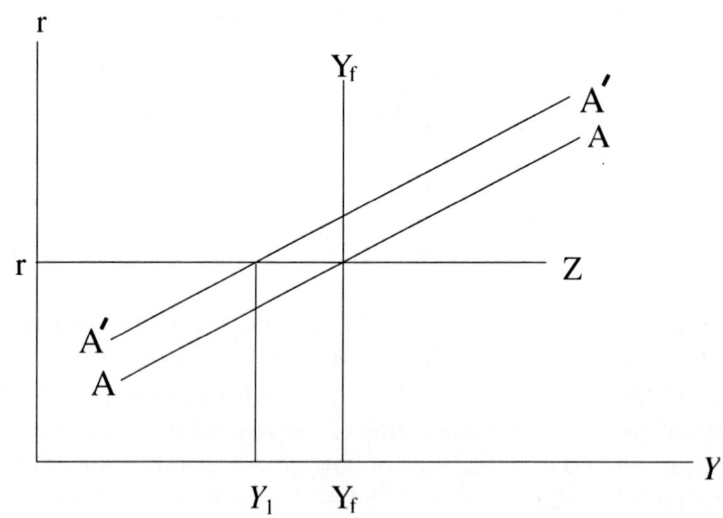

Fig. 13.2. The small domestic economy

The equilibrium of the small domestic economy can be portrayed in Fig. 13.2. The equilibrium level of $\tilde{r}$ determined in Fig. 13.1 plus the risk premium ρ minus the expected future change in the log of the real exchange rate yields the horizontal line r Z determining the domestic real interest rate. And the vertical line $\mathrm{Y_f Y_f}$ denotes the full-employment level of output. Domestic asset equilibrium will be determined at the intersection of the line AA, which represents equation (13.1), and the r Z line. Under full-employment conditions the domestic price level must be such that AA passes through the intersection of r Z and $\mathrm{Y_f Y_f}$.

The variable y_f and the existing levels of $\tilde{y}$ and $\tilde{y}_f$ substitute along with q_f into equation (13.5) to determine the equilibrium level of q. Under a floating exchange rate, this value of q together with the levels of p and $\tilde{p}$ substitute into equation (13.4) to yield the equilibrium level of the nominal exchange rate π. Under a fixed exchange rate with full employment, the domestic nominal money supply will have had to be adjusted to produce a level of p sufficient to maintain the fixed value of π in equation (13.4) given the equilibrium real exchange rate q – such proportional variations in m and p will not affect the level of AA, which depends on movements of m relative to p.

When the price level is fixed in the small domestic economy and the exchange rate is flexible, output is determined at the internationally determined domestic real interest rate by equation (13.1) – that is, by the intersection of AA with the r Z line. That output level feeds into equation (13.5) along with the full-employment real exchange rate and the levels of y_f, $\tilde{y}$ and $\tilde{y}_f$ to produce the equilibrium level of q which, in turn, feeds into equation (13.4) along with $\tilde{p}$ and the fixed level of p to produce the equilibrium level of π. Expansionary monetary policy operates by reducing π and q and thereby increasing y – that is, by shifting AA to the right. Real sector policies that shift the full-employment level of the real exchange rate will cause the actual real exchange rate to move in proportion, with the equilibrium level of output determined in equation (13.1) being unaffected.

If the country's authorities impose a fixed exchange rate, the above equilibrating process works in reverse. The fixed levels of π and p in equation (13.4) result in a fixed level of q which when substituted into (13.5) yields the equilibrium level of y. That level of y together with the fixed level of p, when plugged into equation (13.1), produces the level of m the authorities must create if the exchange rate parity is to be maintained. In terms of Fig. 13.2, the position of output along the r Z line is determined by equations (13.4) and (13.5) and m adjusts endogenously to make the AA curve pass through that point. Monetary policy is therefore ineffective while policies that increase the full-employment equilibrium level of the real exchange rate will, by reducing the current real exchange rate relative to its equilibrium level, increase the equilibrium level of output as can be seen from equation (13.5).

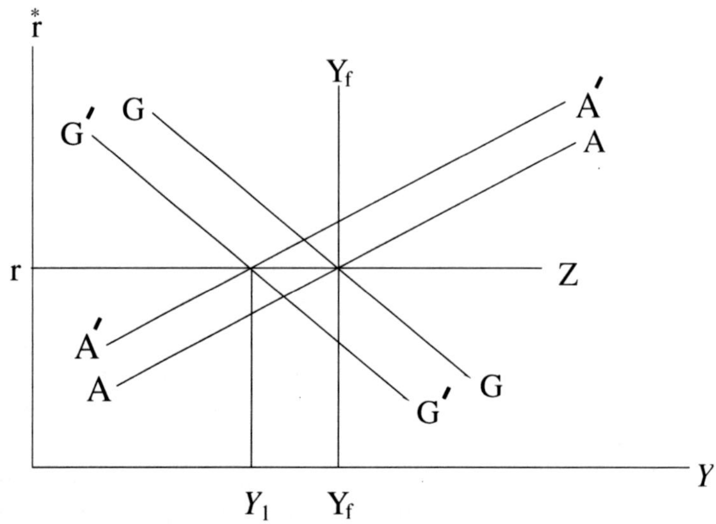

Fig. 13.3. The small domestic economy with graphic portrayal of real goods market equilibrium

The graphical analysis in Fig. 13.2 in the fixed price level and fixed exchange rate case is rather sparse – equilibrium along the r Z line is determined, not by a curve that shifts, but by mathematical action in the background. The exposition can be improved by noting that equation (13.5) can be modified into the virtually equivalent form

$$y_t - y_{ft} = \frac{1}{\phi}(r_t - r_{ft}) + \frac{1}{\sigma}(q_t - q_{ft}) + (1 - \frac{\tilde{\phi}}{\phi})(\tilde{y}_t - \tilde{y}_{ft}) \quad (13.9)$$

and, where ϕ is negative, portrayed as the downward sloping curve GG in Fig. 13.3. For comparison, equation (13.6) can be written as

$$\tilde{y}_t - \tilde{y}_{ft} = \frac{1}{\tilde{\phi}}(\tilde{r}_t - \tilde{r}_{ft}). \quad (13.10)$$

Where $\phi = \tilde{\phi}$ the slopes of GG and $\tilde{G}\tilde{G}$ are identical and the term involving $(\tilde{y}_t - \tilde{y}_{ft})$ drops out of equation (13.9). Since r and $\tilde{r}$ vary in the same direction by the same amount at given levels of ρ and

$(E_{t-1}q_{t+1} - E_{t-1}q_t)$, a fall in world interest rates relative to full-employment levels would then increase output in both countries by the same amount relative to full-employment levels. A decline in the real exchange rate relative to its full-employment level will cause the small country's output to increase relative to its full-employment level, shifting GG to the right.

Equation (13.9) can be expressed as (13.5) by replacing r and r_f with $\tilde{r}$ and $\tilde{r}_f$, in recognition of the fact that the risk premium and expected rate of change in the real exchange rate will equally affect the current and full employment domestic interest rates, and then substituting equation (13.6) into (13.9) to eliminate the real interest rate term and rearranging the result.

Fig. 13.3 has a simple Fleming-Mundell interpretation [39][79], equivalent in result to that of the standard textbook IS-LM model. Under a flexible exchange rate, output is determined by the intersection of the AA curve and r Z line with the GG curve adjusting automatically to pass through that intersection as a result of changes in the nominal and real exchange rates. With price level flexibility, the domestic price level adjusts to drive AA through the intersection of r Z and $\mathrm{Y_f Y_f}$ with GG automatically following suit through whatever adjustments of π and q are required. Under a fixed exchange rate, output is determined by the intersection of the GG curve and the r Z line, with the AA curve adjusting automatically to pass through that intersection as a result of changes in the money supply produced by the authorities to defend the exchange rate peg. With price flexibility, the price level and real exchange rate will adjust in proportion to drive GG through the intersection of r Z and $\mathrm{Y_f Y_f}$ with AA automatically following suit as a result of money supply adjustments required to maintain the fixed nominal exchange rate. Monetary policy works only under flexible exchange rates while fiscal-policy induced shifts in full-employment output and real exchange rates and, hence the GG curve, are possible only under fixed exchange rates.

13.2 Consolidated Four-Equation System

13.2.1 Flexible Price Levels: Full-Employment

When the price level is flexible and full-employment holds, equations (13.5) and (13.6) disappear and equations (13.1), (13.2), (13.3) and (13.4) reduce to the following three-equation system when the actual levels of output, the real exchange rate and real interest rates are replaced by their full-employment levels.

$$p = (m - \psi) - \eta\,(\tilde{r}_f + \rho - E_{\dot{q}} + E_{\dot{p}}) - \epsilon\, y_f \tag{13.11}$$

$$\tilde{p} = (\tilde{m} - \tilde{\psi}) - \tilde{\eta}\,(\tilde{r}_f + E_{\dot{\tilde{p}}}) - \tilde{\epsilon}\,\tilde{y}_f \tag{13.12}$$

$$\pi = q_f - p + \tilde{p} \tag{13.13}$$

The domestic price level will vary in direct proportion to the domestic stock of money relative to the demand for it. The demand for money can decline directly in response to a decline in ψ or indirectly in response to an increase in the risk premium on domestic assets, an increase in the expected rate of inflation, an expected future decline in the real exchange rate or an increase in full-employment output and income. The rest-of-world price level will vary in direct proportion to an expansion of the stock of money relative to the demand for it, where the demand for money can rise directly in response to an increase in $\tilde{\psi}$ and indirectly in response to falls in the real interest rate and the expected rate of rest-of-world inflation, and to an increase in the full-employment level of rest-of-world output. If determined freely in the market, the nominal exchange rate will be higher, the higher the full-employment real exchange rate and the lower the domestic price level relative to the price level in the rest-of-the world. If the nominal exchange rate is fixed, the domestic price level will be determined by the real exchange rate and the price level abroad, and the authorities will have to continually keep the domestic nominal money stock at whatever level will validate that price level and thereby maintain the exchange rate parity.

13.2.2 Fixed Price Levels

Consolidation of the model under conditions of fixed output prices and less-than-full employment can be accomplished by taking the first-difference of equations (13.1), (13.2), (13.4), (13.5) and (13.6). In doing so, the first differences of y, $\tilde{y}$, $\tilde{r}$ and q are modified as follows, using y as an example of the nature of the calculations.

$$\begin{aligned} y_t - y_{t-1} &= y_t - y_{t-1} + y_{ft} - y_{ft} + y_{f(t-1)} - y_{f(t-1)} \\ &= (y_t - y_{ft}) - (y_{t-1} - y_{f(t-1)}) + (y_{ft} - y_{f(t-1)}) \\ &= \Delta y + \Delta y_f \qquad (13.14) \\ \tilde{y}_t - \tilde{y}_{t-1} &= \Delta \tilde{y} + \Delta \tilde{y}_f \qquad (13.15) \\ \tilde{r}_t - \tilde{r}_{t-1} &= \Delta \tilde{r} + \Delta \tilde{r}_f \qquad (13.16) \\ q_t - q_{t-1} &= \Delta q + \Delta q_f \qquad (13.17) \end{aligned}$$

The operator Δ refers in the case of y, $\tilde{y}$, $\tilde{r}$ and q to the change in the deviation of the respective variable from its full-employment level. In all other cases, Δ signifies simply the change in the actual level of the variable.

Differencing equations (13.1) and (13.2) and making the above substitutions yields the first two equations of the consolidated model.

$$\begin{aligned} \Delta y &= \frac{1}{\epsilon}(\Delta m - \Delta\psi) - \frac{\eta}{\epsilon}(\Delta\tilde{r} + \Delta\tilde{r}_f) \\ &\quad - \frac{\eta}{\epsilon}(\Delta\rho - \Delta E_{\hat{q}} + \Delta E_{\hat{p}}) - \Delta y_f \qquad (13.18) \\ \Delta\tilde{y} &= \frac{1}{\tilde{\epsilon}}(\Delta\tilde{m} - \Delta\tilde{\psi}) - \frac{\tilde{\eta}}{\tilde{\epsilon}}(\Delta\tilde{r} + \Delta\tilde{r}_f) \\ &\quad - \frac{\tilde{\eta}}{\tilde{\epsilon}}\Delta E_{\tilde{\hat{p}}} - \Delta\tilde{y}_f \qquad (13.19) \end{aligned}$$

The first difference of equation (13.4) yields

$$\Delta q = \Delta\pi - \Delta q_f \qquad (13.20)$$

Substitution of this into the first difference of equation (13.5) yields the third equation of the consolidated model.[4]

$$\Delta\pi = \sigma\,(\Delta y - \Delta\tilde{y}) + \Delta q_f \qquad (13.21)$$

[4] It is important here to remember that, as established above, the first differences of the deviations of q, y, $\tilde{y}$, and $\tilde{r}$ from their full-employment levels are simply Δq, Δy, $\Delta\tilde{y}$, and $\Delta\tilde{r}$.

Finally, the last equation of the four equation system follows directly from the first difference of equation (13.6).

$$\Delta\tilde{r} = \tilde{\phi}\,\Delta\tilde{y} \tag{13.22}$$

Equation (13.20) performs the supplementary role of replacing, if desired, the variable $\Delta\pi$ with Δq.

The interpretation of the four equation system, (13.18), (13.19), (13.21) and (13.22), is straight forward. When the exchange rate is flexible, domestic output will increase relative to its full-employment level in response to an increase in the supply of money relative to the demand for it. The demand for money can increase as a result of exogenous shocks and in response to decreases in the rest-of-world interest rate, the risk premium on domestic assets and the expected future rate of domestic inflation and in response to an expected future increase in the real exchange rate and an increase in the full-employment output level. Similarly, foreign output will increase relative to its full-employment level in response to an increase in the rest-of-world money supply relative to the demand for it. And the demand for money can increase exogenously or as a result of decreases in the rest-of-world interest rate and in the expected rate of rest-of-world inflation and an increase in the rest-of-world full-employment output level. The deviation of the world interest rate from its full-employment level will depend inversely upon the deviation of rest-of-world output from its full-employment level. The nominal exchange rate will increase in response to a decline in domestic output relative to its full-employment level, decline in response to an increase in foreign output relative to its full-employment level, and increase in response to an increase in the full-employment level of the real exchange rate. When the nominal exchange rate is fixed, the deviation of domestic output from its full-employment level will respond directly in equation (13.21) to the deviation of rest-of-world output from its full-employment level and to changes in the full-employment level of the real exchange rate. The domestic authorities will then have to produce the change in the nominal money stock required to finance any change in the deviation of domestic output from its full-employment level, accomodating any current changes in rest-of-world and domestic real interest rates and domestic full-employment output.

Of particular interest are overshooting effects on the exchange rate when it is flexible. A critical factor in the exchange rate movement in equation (13.21) is the magnitude of σ, the inverse of which is the elasticity of the response of domestic real output, via changes in the current account balance, to a change in the real exchange rate. If in the very short run this response elasticity is very low, σ will be very high and the resulting exchange rate movement in response to a domestic output shock will be enormous. Any movement in excess of what would occur under full-employment conditions represents overshooting. The formulation in this chapter assumes that the price level of goods produced in each country is also the price level of goods absorbed. This implies that changes in the exchange rate do not cause domestic prices in domestic currency to change – that is, there is pricing to market. Thus, over a length of run so short that $1/\sigma \Rightarrow 0$, the only possible limit on the degree of exchange rate movement is the expectation that the underlying real exchange rate change due to overshooting will eventually be reversed as complete adjustment eventually takes place. This means that when π overshoots in a downward direction in response to an excess supply of money, and q falls correspondingly, investors will expect a future rise in q with the result that $E_{\dot{q}}$ rises and the interest rate falls, increasing the quantity of money demanded to offset the initial positive shock to the excess supply. An additional factor limiting the degree of overshooting, discussed in detail in the last chapter of Part I, is the effect of the exchange rate change on the domestic currency prices of domestically produced traded goods – ignoring this issue here simplifies the analysis without affecting the conclusions.

13.3 Formal Equilibrium Conditions

The full-employment equilibrium values of p, $\tilde{p}$ and π are given directly by equations (13.11), (13.12) and (13.13), respectively. The equations of the fixed price level model, (13.18),(13.19), (13.21) and (13.22), need to be formally solved to produce the equilibrium values of Δy, $\Delta \tilde{y}$, $\Delta \tilde{r}$ and $\Delta \pi$ in response to the real and monetary shocks incorporated in those equations.

13.3.1 Rest-of-World Equilibrium

The equilibrium shock to the rest-of-world interest rate is obtained by substituting (13.19) into (13.22) to yield

$$\left(1 + \frac{\tilde{\phi}\tilde{\eta}}{\tilde{\epsilon}}\right) \Delta \tilde{r} = \frac{\tilde{\phi}}{\tilde{\epsilon}} (\Delta \tilde{m} - \Delta \tilde{\psi}) - \frac{\tilde{\phi}\tilde{\eta}}{\tilde{\epsilon}} \left(\Delta \tilde{r}_f + \Delta E_{\dot{\tilde{p}}}\right) - \tilde{\phi}\, \Delta \tilde{y}_f \qquad (13.23)$$

which reduces to

$$\Delta\tilde{r} = \frac{\tilde{\phi}}{\tilde{\epsilon} + \tilde{\phi}\,\tilde{\eta}}\,(\Delta\tilde{m} - \Delta\tilde{\psi}) - \frac{\tilde{\phi}\,\tilde{\eta}}{\tilde{\epsilon} + \tilde{\phi}\,\tilde{\eta}}\left(\Delta\tilde{r}_f + \Delta E_{\tilde{\dot{p}}}\right) - \frac{\tilde{\phi}\,\tilde{\epsilon}}{\tilde{\epsilon} + \tilde{\phi}\tilde{\eta}}\,\Delta\tilde{y}_f \tag{13.24}$$

Substitution of (13.22) into (13.24) to eliminate $\Delta\tilde{r}$ yields the equilibrium shock to rest-of-world real output.

$$\Delta\tilde{y} = \frac{1}{\tilde{\epsilon} + \tilde{\phi}\,\tilde{\eta}}\,(\Delta\tilde{m} - \Delta\tilde{\psi}) - \frac{\tilde{\eta}}{\tilde{\epsilon} + \tilde{\phi}\,\tilde{\eta}}\left(\Delta\tilde{r}_f + \Delta E_{\tilde{\dot{p}}}\right) - \frac{\tilde{\epsilon}}{\tilde{\epsilon} + \tilde{\phi}\tilde{\eta}}\,\Delta\tilde{y}_f \tag{13.25}$$

13.3.2 Domestic Equilibrium With a Flexible Exchange Rate

The equilibrium shock to domestic output under a flexible exchange rate is obtained by substituting the equilibrium shock to the world interest rate, given by (13.24), into equation (13.18).

$$\begin{aligned}
\Delta y &= \frac{1}{\epsilon}\,(\Delta m - \Delta\psi) - \frac{\eta}{\epsilon}\,\Delta\tilde{r}_f - \frac{\eta}{\epsilon}\,(\Delta\rho - \Delta E_{\dot{q}} + \Delta E_{\dot{p}}) - \Delta y_f \\
&\quad - \frac{\eta\,\tilde{\phi}}{\epsilon\,(\tilde{\epsilon} + \tilde{\phi}\,\tilde{\eta})}\,(\Delta\tilde{m} - \Delta\tilde{\psi}) + \frac{\eta\,\tilde{\phi}\,\tilde{\eta}}{\epsilon\,(\tilde{\epsilon} + \tilde{\phi}\,\tilde{\eta})}\left(\Delta\tilde{r}_f + \Delta E_{\tilde{\dot{p}}}\right) \\
&\quad + \frac{\eta\,\tilde{\phi}\,\tilde{\epsilon}}{\epsilon\,(\tilde{\epsilon} + \tilde{\phi}\tilde{\eta})}\,\Delta\tilde{y}_f \\
&= \frac{1}{\epsilon}\,(\Delta m - \Delta\psi) - \frac{\eta\,\tilde{\phi}}{\epsilon\,(\tilde{\epsilon} + \tilde{\phi}\,\tilde{\eta})}\,(\Delta\tilde{m} - \Delta\tilde{\psi}) \\
&\quad - \frac{\eta}{\epsilon}\left(1 - \frac{\tilde{\phi}\,\tilde{\eta}}{\tilde{\epsilon} + \tilde{\phi}\,\tilde{\eta}}\right)\Delta\tilde{r}_f - \Delta y_f + \frac{\eta\,\tilde{\phi}\,\tilde{\epsilon}}{\epsilon\,(\tilde{\epsilon} + \tilde{\phi}\tilde{\eta})}\,\Delta\tilde{y}_f \\
&\quad - \frac{\eta}{\epsilon}\,(\Delta\rho - \Delta E_{\hat{q}}) - \frac{\eta}{\epsilon}\,\Delta E_{\hat{p}} + \frac{\eta\,\tilde{\phi}\,\tilde{\eta}}{\epsilon\,(\tilde{\epsilon} + \tilde{\phi}\,\tilde{\eta})}\Delta E_{\tilde{\hat{p}}}
\end{aligned} \tag{13.26}$$

In the special case where $(\Delta m - \Delta\psi) = (\Delta\tilde{m} - \Delta\tilde{\psi})$, $\Delta y_f = \Delta\tilde{y}_f$, $\Delta E_{\dot{p}} = \Delta E_{\tilde{\dot{p}}}$ and the domestic and rest-of-world economies are identical except for scale so that $\eta = \tilde{\eta}$ and $\epsilon = \tilde{\epsilon}$, the above expression reduces to

$$\begin{aligned}\Delta y &= \left(\frac{1}{\epsilon + \tilde{\phi}\eta}\right)(\Delta m - \Delta\psi) - \left(\frac{\eta}{\epsilon + \tilde{\phi}\eta}\right)(\Delta\tilde{r}_f + \Delta E_{\dot{p}}) \\ &\quad - \left(\frac{\epsilon}{\epsilon + \delta\phi\eta}\right)\Delta y_f - \frac{\eta}{\epsilon}(\Delta\rho - \Delta E_{\hat{q}}) \qquad (13.27)\end{aligned}$$

which, apart from the terms involving the risk premium on domestic assets and the expected rate of change in the real exchange rate, is identical to equation (13.25).

Equations (13.25) and either (13.26) or (13.27) can be substituted into equation (13.21) to obtain the resulting $\Delta\pi$. In the case where the domestic and rest-of-world shocks are identical and the economies are identical apart from scale, and the risk premium on domestic assets and the expected rate of change in the real exchange rate are unchanged, the domestic and foreign outputs will change relative to their full-employment levels in the same proportion and the nominal exchange rate will be unaffected.

13.3.3 Domestic Equilibrium With a Fixed Exchange Rate

When the exchange rate is fixed, the shock to domestic output can be obtained by substituting equation (13.25) into (13.21) to produce

$$\begin{aligned}\Delta y &= \Delta\tilde{y} - \frac{1}{\sigma}\Delta q_f \\ &= \frac{1}{\tilde{\epsilon} + \tilde{\phi}\tilde{\eta}}(\Delta\tilde{m} - \Delta\tilde{\psi}) - \frac{\tilde{\eta}}{\tilde{\epsilon} + \tilde{\phi}\tilde{\eta}}\left(\Delta\tilde{r}_f + \Delta E_{\tilde{\dot{p}}}\right) \\ &\qquad - \frac{\tilde{\epsilon}}{\tilde{\epsilon} + \tilde{\phi}\tilde{\eta}}\Delta\tilde{y}_f - \frac{1}{\sigma}\Delta q_f . \qquad (13.28)\end{aligned}$$

The required adjustment of the domestic nominal money stock to protect the exchange rate parity can be obtained by equating the right-hand-side of this equation with the right-hand-side of equation (13.26) and solving for Δm. The only avenue under which the domestic authorities can eliminate a deviation of domestic output from its full-employment level is through tax and expenditure policies that increase or reduce the full-employment-equilibrium real exchange rate. For example, government expenditure policies that increase current real output toward its full-employment level operate by increasing the full-employment real exchange rate. As can be seen from equation (13.28), an increase in the full-employment real exchange rate at a given level of full-employment output will lead to an increase in domestic output relative to its full-employment level. If the economy was initially at full employment the domestic price level will eventually rise in the long run, increasing the real exchange rate to match the increase in its full-employment level and driving output back down to its full-employment level.

Real shocks to the long-run equilibrium real exchange rate of the sort found in Part II will therefore lead to temporary increases in output at given levels of the current real exchange rate when the nominal exchange rate is fixed, thereby making the real exchange rate shock unobservable in the data in the short-run. In the long-run, when the price level can adjust, it will increase, increasing the observed real exchange rate to its long-run full-employment level and reducing output back to its full-employment level.

13.4 Response of the Domestic Economy to Domestic and Foreign Shocks

At this point is is useful to summarize the above results graphically. Foreign shocks are portrayed in Fig. 13.4. Starting at full-employment equilibrium, a monetary shock, here specified as an increase in the demand for money, shifts the $\tilde{\mathrm{A}}\tilde{\mathrm{A}}$ curve to the left to $\tilde{\mathrm{A}}'\tilde{\mathrm{A}}'$. The interest rate rises in response to the attempt of the country's residents to sell non-monetary assets in return for money, leading to a reduction in output to $\tilde{Y}_1$. A positive real shock shifts the $\tilde{\mathrm{G}}\tilde{\mathrm{G}}$ curve to the right to $\tilde{\mathrm{G}}'\tilde{\mathrm{G}}'$. The interest rate rises as a result of the attempt of home residents to sell non-monetary assets in order to increase their money holdings as output and income rise above the full employment level.

The domestic response to domestic monetary and real shocks can be seen with reference to Fig. 13.5. When the exchange rate is flexible, an increase in the demand for money shifts the AA curve to the left to A′A′. Domestic residents' excess demand for money causes them to try to sell non-monetary assets to foreigners in return for money. This causes the domestic currency to appreciate and the real exchange rate with respect to the rest of the world to rise, eventually shifting the GG curve to the left to G′G′ and reducing the level of income and output to Y_1. The the nominal and real exchange rates may rise very substantially during the time interval required for these exchange rate changes to reduce the current account balance and the level of output. When the exchange rate is fixed the leftward shift of AA will not occur – to maintain the fixed exchange rate, the domestic authorities will be forced to buy foreign exchange reserves in return for domestic currency to finance the private sector purchase of non-monetary assets.

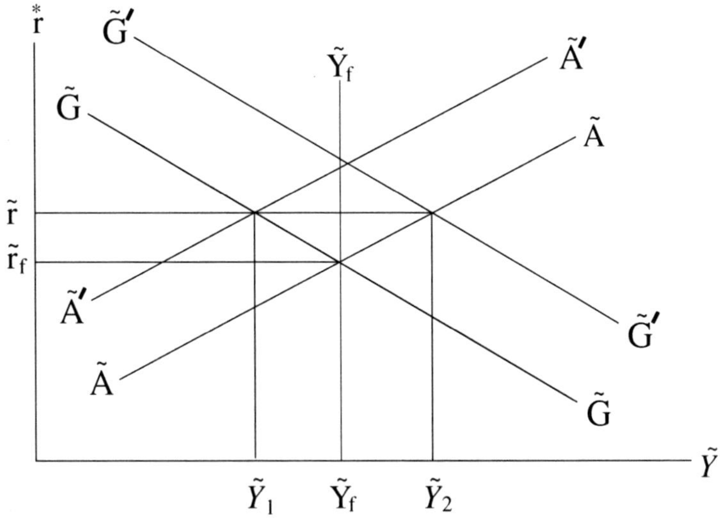

Fig. 13.4. Real and monetary shocks in the large rest-of-world economy

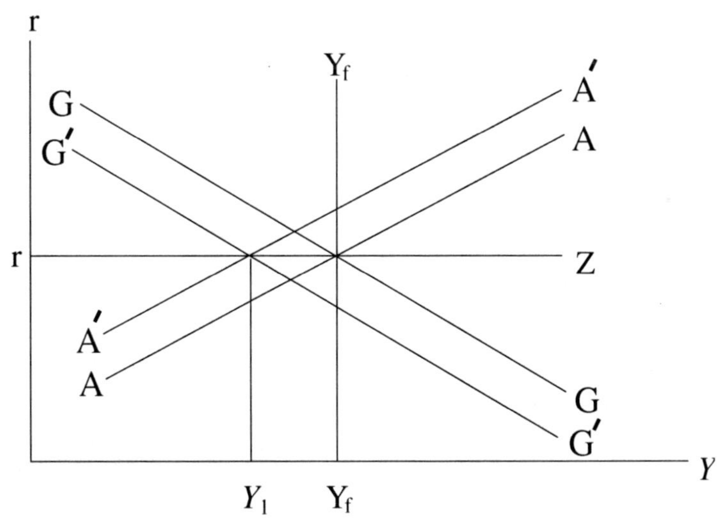

Fig. 13.5. Domestic response to domestic real and monetary shocks

The AA curve and output will remain at the full-employment level, unaffected by the private sector's increased demand for liquidity. When the exchange rate is fixed, an adverse real shock will shift the GG curve to the left to G′G′. An example would be an increase in the domestic full-employment real exchange rate with respect to the rest of the world. As output and income fall, domesitic residents' demand for liquidity declines leading to an attempt to purchase non-monetary assets from foreigners. To maintain the exchange rate, the domestic authorities have to finance the resulting balance of payments deficit by selling foreign exchange reserves for domestic currency – this shifts the AA curve to the left to A′A′, financing the decline in domestic output and employment. If the exchange rate were flexible the domestic currency would devalue, reducing the real exchange rate to its new equilibrium level and thereby preventing the leftward shift of the GG curve from occurring – output and income will remain at the full-employment level. As noted in Part I, flexible exchange rates neutralize the effects of real shocks on domestic output and employment while fixed exchange rates neutralize the effects of monetary shocks.

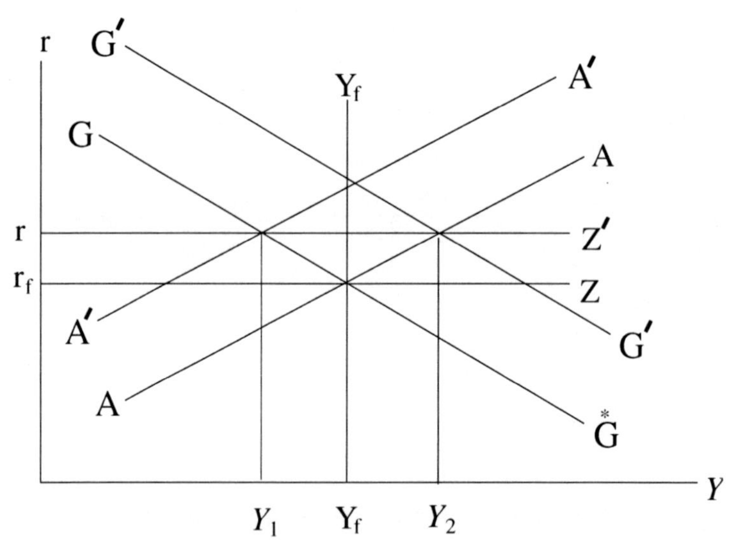

Fig. 13.6. Domestic response to shocks in the large rest-of-world economy

Finally, the response of the domestic economy to rest-of-world monetary and real shocks can be seen with reference to Fig.13.6. These shocks operate on the domestic economy by changing the rest-of-world and, hence, the domestic interest rate. Consider the case where the domestic real interest rate rises as a result of either negative monetary shocks or positive real shocks in the rest of the world. If the exchange rate is fixed, domestic equilibrium will occur at the intersection of the GG curve and the horizontal line rZ′ – the authorities will have to reduce the money supply to maintain the fixed exchange rate, shifting the AA curve to the left to A′A′. If the interest rate rose as a result of a negative monetary shock in the rest of the world, the domestic and rest-of-world outputs and incomes will be affected in the same direction. If the interest rate rose as a result of a foreign real shock, foreign output and income will rise, moving in the opposite direction to the effect on domestic income and output.

Now suppose that the domestic authorities let the exchange rate float. If they hold domestic liquidity constant in the face of the rise in the world interest rate, domestic output will increase. The excess supply of money at the new higher interest rate will cause domestic residents to try to purchase non-monetary assets from foreigners, leading to a devaluation of the domestic nominal and real exchange rates with respect to the rest of the world. The GG curve will shift to the right to G′G′, raising domestic income and output to Y_2. If the increase in the world interest rate was caused by a monetary shock in rest of the world, income there will have fallen, moving in the opposite direction to domestic income. Also, the devaluation of the domestic real and nominal exchange rates could be very large during the early part of the time interval over which domestic income increases, reflecting the tendency of the exchange rate to overshoot. If the increase in rest-of-world interest rates was due to a real shock, domestic and rest-of-world income will move in the same direction under a flexible exchange rate.

Thus, domestic and foreign incomes move in opposite directions in response to foreign monetary shocks when the exchange rate is flexible and in the same direction when it is fixed. And domestic and foreign incomes move in the same direction in response to foreign real shocks when the exchange rate is flexible and in opposite directions when it is fixed.

14

Monetary Policy and Exchange Rates

Given that the monetary authorities are confident of the basic structure of the above model, know the signs but not the exact magnitudes of the parameters, and have no clear grasp over the dynamics, what is the best way for them to conduct monetary policy? Broadly viewed, the objectives of monetary policy are three in number. First, monetary growth must be such as to make the domestic price level grow at a stable rate over the long run – for developed economies that need not use an inflation tax to finance public expenditure, this inflation rate would normally be on the positive side of, but very close to, zero. Second, the stock of liquidity should, ideally, be varied around its long-term growth path in a manner that will prevent deviations of output and employment from their full-employment levels. Third, although central banks should be independent of political control, they nevertheless have to maintain public credibility – this means that they cannot appear to be creating, or allowing, unstable conditions in domestic foreign exchange and capital markets. Historically, the danger has been that this third objective might dominate the other two.

14.1 Large vs. Small Open Economies

Consider first the case of a big world economy that has little concern for its tiny trading partners. To do their job perfectly, its authorities would have to know the time paths of the full-employment levels of output and interest rates and the magnitudes and timing of short-run real shocks and demand for money shocks, as well as the magnitudes of the coefficients in the underlying model together with its dynamic properties. Forecasts of the underlying full-employment paths of income and interest rates are clearly possible but subject to error, particularly

J.E. Floyd, *Interest Rates, Exchange Rates and World Monetary Policy*,
DOI 10.1007/978-3-642-10280-6_14,

in view of the fact that these full-employment paths may be cyclical. Forecasts of future short-term real and money demand shocks are virtually impossible and it is usually only possible to observe the current levels of output, employment, wages and prices with hindsight. While nominal interest rates can be observed on a daily basis, the real interest rates relevant for domestic investment cannot be observed at all. And, of course, the magnitudes of the parameters in any credible basic model like the one developed here are not known with any precision, and the same is true of prospective dynamic paths of the variables.

Two alternative rules of operation in this morass have traditionally been promoted. The first would have the authorities continually adjust nominal interest rates to keep domestic investment at levels that will continually maintain output as close as possible to its full-employment level. The second would have the authorities continually maintain an appropriate rarely-changing rate of growth of nominal liquidity, thereby ensuring that major inflations and depressions will not occur, while giving up on the prospect of fine-tune corrections of short-term movements in the levels of output and employment. Both rules face a similar problem. In the case of interest rate control, the authorities can only observe nominal interest rates, and these can deviate substantially from the relevant unobservable real interest rates as a result of changing public views concerning future inflation. In the case of liquidity growth rules, the authorities do not observe the level of nominal liquidity – they only observe the monetary base and a number of monetary aggregates, all of which give only partial information about liquidity growth. Moreover, they can learn only with considerable hindsight about changing trends in the demand for the various monetary aggregates and in output growth.

In terms of a goal of perfect implementation, the problems facing a big world-dominant economy pale to insignificance in comparison to those of a small open economy. The authorities in the small economy, like those in the big one, need information about their domestic variables. In addition, however, they need virtually the same information about the rest-of-world aggregates. Moreover, the objective of controlling domestic real interest rates by manipulating a short-term nominal call-money rate is largely mythological, involving either manipulation of the risk premiums on domestic real assets by imposing minor short-term portfolio adjustments on domestic and foreign asset holders or generating real exchange rate movements so large as to create public expectations of their reversal in the near future. Imposed on all this is the fact that monetary policy in small open economies operates via its effects on nominal and real exchange rates and consequent trade balance adjustments in an environment in which there is every reason to believe that significant monetary shocks, from either the supply or demand side, will lead to substantial overshooting movements in real and nominal exchange rates. Accusations of creating or allowing market disorder represent a nightmare that few central bankers will be inclined to entertain.

The modern practice, in small open economies as well as big ones, has been to muddle along using the best current information obtainable about a wide variety of variables, with publicly-stated emphasis on interest rate control combined with the maintenance of orderly markets while, in many cases, using inflation rate targets as the measure of performance.

14.2 Fixed vs. Flexible Exchange Rates

One way the small country's authorities can try to work around the above-noted problems is to adopt a fixed exchange rate, tying their currency to that of a big neighboring country. Assume for the moment that purchasing-power-parity holds in the extreme sense that the real exchange rate never varies from a constant full-employment level. This implies that all short-run and long-run real shocks facing the two economies are symmetric. From the definition of the real exchange rate it is clear that the domestic and rest-of-world price levels must vary in proportion— choosing the units of the real and nominal exchange rates appropriately, both q_f and π in equation (13.13) can be set equal to zero.[1] In addition, since Δq_f becomes zero in equation (13.28) all deviations of domestic and rest-of-world output from their full-employment levels will also be the same. The small country's authorities can simply free-ride off the big country's monetary policy, ending up with the same time-paths of short-run economic conditions and long-term inflation as exist abroad. By fixing the exchange rate, they force themselves to automatically adjust Δm_t in equation (13.18) to preserve its parity—the stock of domestic liquidity becomes endogenous. When the big neighbor country is politically stable and hires its economic advisors from the same pool as does the small country, there is little reason to presume that, on average, the small country could do better on its own.

The problem lies, of course, with the assumption of purchasing power parity. The empirical results in Part II indicate clearly that

[1] That is, their values when not expressed in logarithms can be set equal to unity.

the typical industrial country's real exchange rate is a near random walk, exhibiting wide swings over the long run. Canada's real exchange rate with respect to the United States, for example, fell about 20 percent between the late 1970s and mid-1980s, then rose about 15 percent between the mid-1980s and the early 1990s, and then fell about 30 percent between the early 1990s and the early years of the twenty-first century, finally rising to about the late-1970s level by the time of this writing. Had the nominal exchange rate been fixed, the Canadian price level would have had to move relative to the U.S. price level by these percentages for full-employment to have been maintained. Given that prices tend to be rigid in the short-run, it is reasonable to expect that during substantial periods a negative Δq_f would have resulted in negative values for Δy, accompanied by substantial levels of Canadian unemployment. Also, even if purchasing power parity held in the long run, stochastic variations in q_f and Δy would still have occurred. By fixing its exchange rate a country loses important short- and long-run *insulation advantages of flexible exchange rates*, which protect domestic output and prices from asymmetric domestic/foreign real shocks that result in variations in q_f.

The alternative is to let the exchange rate float, but then the authorities have to decide how to manage the growth of liquidity. The process of achieving a stable average rate of price-level growth over four or five year horizons should not be too daunting since it is possible to maintain a stable rate of base money growth that can be adjusted from time to time to compensate for emerging trends in the ratios of various monetary aggregates to base money, in full-employment real income and in various measures of the velocity of money. The problem is that, whatever the potential benefits of maintaining a constant rate of monetary growth in a large world-dominant economy might be, such a policy is completely out of the question for a small open economy. The problem is not one of maintaining a stable average rate of inflation. Rather, it is one of maintaining acceptable variances of the deviations of output, employment and exchange rates around their full-employment levels.

Suppose that, by some astounding coincidence, it is possible to maintain constant rates of growth of liquidity both in the small country and in the rest of the world that would stabilize their five year moving average inflation rates at constant levels. From equation (13.25) the variance of the deviations of rest-of-world output around its full-employment levels becomes

$$Var\{\Delta\tilde{y}\} = \left(\frac{1}{\tilde{\epsilon} + \tilde{\phi}\,\tilde{\eta}}\right)^2 Var\{\Delta\tilde{\psi}_m\} + \left(\frac{\tilde{\eta}}{\tilde{\epsilon} + \tilde{\phi}\,\tilde{\eta}}\right)^2 Var\{\Delta\tilde{r}_f\}$$
$$+ \left(\frac{\tilde{\epsilon}}{\tilde{\epsilon} + \tilde{\phi}\,\tilde{\eta}}\right)^2 Var\{\Delta\tilde{y}_f\} \qquad (14.1)$$

where the expected future inflation rate is assumed to be constant and the shocks, $\Delta\tilde{\psi}_m$, $\Delta\tilde{r}_f$, and $\Delta\tilde{y}_f$, are assumed to be uncorrelated with each other. The variance of the small open economy's output around its full-employment levels, obtained from equation (13.26), is

$$Var\{\Delta y\} = \left(\frac{1}{\epsilon}\right)^2 Var\{\Delta\psi_m\} + \left(\frac{\eta\,\tilde{\phi}}{\epsilon\,(\tilde{\epsilon} + \tilde{\phi}\tilde{\eta})}\right)^2 Var\{\Delta\tilde{\psi}_m\}$$
$$+ \left(\frac{\tilde{\epsilon}\,\eta}{\epsilon\,(\tilde{\epsilon} + \tilde{\phi}\tilde{\eta})}\right)^2 Var\{\Delta\tilde{r}_f\} + Var\,\{\Delta y_f\}$$
$$+ \left(\frac{\tilde{\epsilon}\,\eta\,\tilde{\phi}}{\epsilon\,(\tilde{\epsilon} + \tilde{\phi}\tilde{\eta})}\right)^2 Var\{\Delta\tilde{y}_f\} \qquad (14.2)$$

where $\Delta\psi_m$, $\Delta\tilde{\psi}_m$, $\Delta\tilde{r}_f$, $\Delta\tilde{y}_f$ and Δy_f are uncorrelated with each other, the expected domestic inflation rate and the risk premium on domestic assets are constant, and period-to-period movements of the real exchange rate are indistinguishable from a random-walk so that $\Delta E_{\dot{q}} = 0$.

Suppose for the sake of argument that the two economies are structurally identical except for scale so that $\eta = \tilde{\eta}$ and $\epsilon = \tilde{\epsilon}$, and that $Var\{\Delta\psi_m\} = Var\{\Delta\tilde{\psi}_m\}$ and $Var\{\Delta y_f\} = Var\{\Delta\tilde{y}_f\}$. Then it will clearly be the case that

$$Var\{\Delta y\} > Var\{\Delta\tilde{y}\}$$

since

$$\frac{1}{\tilde{\epsilon}} > \frac{1}{\tilde{\epsilon} + \tilde{\phi}\,\tilde{\eta}}$$

$$\frac{\tilde{\epsilon}}{\tilde{\epsilon} + \tilde{\phi}\tilde{\eta}} < 1$$

and

$$\frac{\tilde{\eta}\,\tilde{\phi}}{\tilde{\epsilon} + \tilde{\phi}\tilde{\eta}} \neq 0$$

The variance of output around the full-employment level will be greater in the small country than in the rest of the world even when the variances of their respective liquidity-demand and full-employment output level shocks are the same and both economies are identical except for scale. Finally, the variance of the nominal exchange rate can be obtained from equation (13.21).

$$\begin{aligned} Var\{\Delta\pi\} = \sigma^2 \, [Var\{\Delta y\} + Var\{\Delta\tilde{y}\} \\ - 2\, Cov\{\Delta y\, \Delta\tilde{y}\}] + Var\{\Delta q_f\} \end{aligned} \quad (14.3)$$

where Δq_f can reasonably be assumed to be uncorrelated with Δy and $\Delta\tilde{y}$, given that it does not appear in equations (14.1) and (14.2). And substitution of this expression into equation (13.20) yields the variance of the deviation of the real exchange rate from its full-employment level.

$$Var\{\Delta q\} = \sigma^2 \, [Var\{\Delta y\} + Var\{\Delta\tilde{y}\} \; - 2\, Cov\{\Delta y\, \Delta\tilde{y}\}] \quad (14.4)$$

Here it should be remembered that in the very short run σ would be expected to be quite large.

It turns out that, quite apart from these results, the variances of the small-country liquidity demand and full-employment output shocks are likely to be many times larger than the variances of the corresponding big-country shocks. Think of the world as consisting of n equal-sized areas each with a variable S_t^i (not in logarithms) subject to random shocks. Let one of these areas be the small country and denote the magnitude of its variable by S_t^1 and let the remaining $n-1$ areas be the big country whose aggregate level of the variable is denoted by $S_t^R = \sum_{i=2}^n S_t^i$. The deviation of the big-country's aggregate variable from its initial value taken as a proportion of that initial value will equal

$$\begin{aligned} \Delta S_t^R &= \sum_{i=2}^n \left[\frac{(S_t^i - S_{t-1}^i)}{S_{t-1}^R} \right] = \sum_{i=2}^n \frac{S_{t-1}^i}{S_{t-1}^R} \left[\frac{(S_t^i - S_{t-1}^i)}{S_{t-1}^i} \right] \\ &\simeq \sum_{i=2}^n \frac{1}{n-1} \left[\frac{(S_t^i - S_{t-1}^i)}{S_{t-1}^i} \right] = \frac{1}{n-1} \sum_{i=2}^n \Delta S_t^i \end{aligned} \quad (14.5)$$

When the shocks in the different areas are independent and have the same variance, the variance of this aggregate shock will equal

$$\begin{aligned} Var(\Delta s_R) &= \frac{1}{(n-1)^2} \sum_{i=2}^n Var(\Delta s_i) = \frac{(n-1)}{(n-1)^2} \, Var(\Delta s_i) \\ &= \frac{1}{n-1} \, Var(\Delta s_i). \end{aligned} \quad (14.6)$$

where s_R and s_i are the logarithms of S^R and S^i.

The variance of the shock in the small country will be $(n-1)$ times the variance of the shock in the big country. By pegging its currency to the large-country's currency, the small country in effect pools its overall demand for money shocks with the big-country shocks – the average percentage shock over a large area will always be smaller than the percentage shocks of the individual small areas that comprise it.[2] There is thus a *pooling advantage of fixed exchange rates.* A classic example is the Canada/U.S. case during the period 1962:Q4 through 1970:Q1 when the Canadian dollar was pegged to the U.S. dollar. The standard deviations of the quarter-to-quarter percentage changes in Canadian base money, M1 and M2 were around than 3, 8 and 10 times the standard deviations of the quarter-to-quarter percentage changes of the corresponding U.S. variables. These monetary aggregates should be viewed simply as indicators of the degrees of liquidity in the respective economies.[3] During the fixed exchange rate period the Canadian money supply can be assumed to have been adjusted endogenously in response to demand for money shocks to maintain the fixed exchange rate. By tying the Canadian dollar to the U.S. dollar, the Canadians essentially pooled their demand for money shocks with those in the U.S. so that unanticipated domestic output and price level changes became dependent on the U.S. shocks rather than their own. Of course, not all the observed changes in the U.S. monetary aggregates need have been the result of underlying shocks to the demand for liquidity. Since the U.S. can be presumed to have been conducting monetary policy, the supply changes in that country could have been different from the underlying demand changes. This would have resulted in interest rate changes sufficient to create ultimate changes in quantities demanded equal to those changes in supply. And those interest rate changes would have had an effect on the quantities of the Canadian monetary aggregates demanded in the same direction that, given the fixed exchange rate, would have induced equivalent changes in the supplies of those Canadian aggregates. Apart from differences in the interest elasticities of the comparable Canadian and U.S. aggregates, therefore, the U.S. pursuit of monetary policy would not have reduced the standard deviations of the U.S. aggregates relative to the standard deviations of

---

[2] Note that all shocks to $\varDelta y$ and $\varDelta\tilde{y}$ in the equations above under flexible exchange rates are, directly or indirectly, shocks to the demand for money.

[3] These calculations are performed in the XLispStat and Gretl batch files `mshkcaus.lsp` and `mshkcaus.inp` and the results are in the output files `mshkcaus.lou` and `mshkcaus.got`. The data are in the files `jfdataqt.gdt`, `jfdataqt.lsp` and `jfdataqt.xls` and described in the text file `jfdataqt.cat`.

their Canadian counterparts. Indeed, because of the fixed exchange rate the Canadian authorities are forced to generate a domestic monetary policy comparable to that in the United States. The higher standard deviations of the Canadian aggregates as compared to their U.S. counterparts thus necessarily reflects excess variability of the demand for money in Canada as compared to the United States.

Small countries' monetary policy problem is to try to simultaneously achieve the pooling advantages of fixed exchange rates together with the insulation advantages of flexible exchange rates. It turns out that a small country's authorities could do this to a highly satisfactory degree if they can determine which market shocks to the domestic exchange rate are portfolio shocks and continually adjust domestic liquidity to neutralize them. All asymmetric demand-for-liquidity shocks result in an attempt by domestic residents to adjust their liquidity holdings to the desired level. They do this by selling assets to or buying them from foreign residents in return for money. If the authorities can sense when this is happening they can supply the necessary liquidity or mop up the excess liquidity to offset the effects of these private portfolio adjustments on the exchange rate. This is what would happen automatically if the exchange rate were fixed. When the exchange rate is flexible it will then move entirely on the basis of real factors, with all monetary shocks being neutralized. Monetary conditions will be the same in the small domestic economy as in the rest of the world and the domestic and rest-of-world business cycles, to the extent that they arise from monetary factors, will be the same. There will be no overshooting movements in exchange rates – indeed, the ability of the authorities to create the same monetary conditions at home as abroad implies an ability to recognize when overshooting movements of the exchange rate are about to take place and neutralize them. Essentially, the task facing the small country's authorities is to maintain an 'orderly' foreign exchange market. To the extent that asset holders can sense when overshooting is occurring and would thereby put pressure on forward exchange rates and domestic interest rates, this also leads to the maintenance of orderly domestic asset markets.

The continual creation by the domestic authorities of the same monetary conditions at home as exist abroad will not necessarily result in the same inflation rate in the domestic economy as abroad. The reason is that, by offsetting domestic portfolio shocks the authorities, in effect, create whatever supply of liquidity domestic residents wish to hold. If the domestic inflation rate is higher, and expected to continue to be higher, than the inflation rate abroad, the domestic authorities will end up automatically creating the additional liquidity trough time to finance that higher inflation rate. Moreover, an increase in the expected rate of domestic inflation will cause the demand for liquidity to decline immediately and then grow at a more rapid rate thereafter than the current growth rate. The above-noted process of preventing exchange rate overshooting will lead the domestic authorities to mop up this initial excess stock of liquidity and then provide the greater future liquidity growth desired by domestic residents. Shifts in inflation expectations will thus become self-fulfilling. For this reason it is necessary for the authorities to constantly make clear their intentions to maintain the current core inflation rate, thereby attempting to keep domestic residents' inflation expectations unchanged at the appropriate level.

The only way the authorities could deal with an unwanted shift in domestic residents' inflation expectations is to use the nominal exchange rate as a policy instrument – that is, constantly adjust the domestic stock of base money to maintain the current and future growth of the nominal exchange rate equal to the underlying growth of the full-employment real exchange rate minus the excess of the desired domestic inflation rate over the foreign inflation rate. Letting $\bar{p}_t$ and $\bar{\pi}_t$ be the logarithms of desired price level and the target exchange rate, equation (13.4) yields

$$\bar{\pi}_t = q_{ft} + \tilde{p}_t - \bar{p}_t, \tag{14.7}$$

where q_{ft} and $\tilde{p}_t$ have to be replaced by forecasted values for the current year. The problem is that, since the full-employment real exchange rate is a near random walk, its time-path is unpredictable. And the observed level of the real exchange rate in period $t-1$, which would be the best forecast of q_{ft}, will differ from that period's true full-employment level by an amount that will depend on the deviations of domestic and foreign output and employment from their full-employment levels. If domestic output is below its full-employment level there is a clear advantage to forcing the nominal exchange rate below the level that would result from using observed q_{t-1} as the forecast of q_{ft}.

If prices were flexible, the domestic authorities could continually force the nominal exchange rate in equation (14.7) towards rough equality with the previous period's real exchange rate minus the excess of the desired domestic price level over a prediction of the current price level abroad.[4] The nominal exchange rate would then become a near random walk, approximately one period behind the real exchange rate, and the domestic price level would exhibit a more or less constant trend. The problem is that price-level rigidity will hide the period-to-period movement of the full-employment real exchange rate, whose current variability will be translated into period to-period changes in the level of employment rather than changes in the price level. The authorities would then have to use observed output and employment changes as indicators of the direction in which the full-employment real exchange rate must have changed and base their period-to-period pressures on the nominal exchange rate on this evidence. An increase in the unemployment rate would indicate that the full-employment real exchange rate has fallen and a decline in the unemployment rate would indicate that it has risen – the authorities must push the nominal exchange rate downward in the former case and upward in the latter, in both cases by amounts that would be extremely difficult to estimate correctly, especially in view of the possibility that domestic real shocks may also have been occurring.

Probably the best procedure the authorities could follow would be to continually adjust domestic monetary conditions to keep movements of the nominal exchange rate within 'a normal trading range' with the result that the gradual movements in the equilibrium full-employment real exchange rate would automatically be financed and the overshooting consequences of portfolio shocks could reasonably be offset. Then, if the price level begins creeping above or below its target level, appropriate upward or downward pressure on the nominal exchange rate can be applied. The problem, of course, is that once the authorities begin controlling the nominal exchange rate, they lose sight of its equilibrium level. The practical aspects of central banking are beyond the scope of this monograph. All that can be said here is that the evidence in Part II strongly suggests that the authorities of several major countries have in fact performed the above suggested tasks to a reasonable approximation. Major difficulties only occur when a substantial fraction of the large rest-of-world economy is exhibiting unstable monetary conditions, as was the case in the 1930s, but minor difficulties will arise more frequently.

When the domestic real exchange rate with a major trading partner is changing only gradually and by small amounts as time passes, the

[4] Obviously, this could be done using inflation rates and rates of real and nominal exchange rate growth or using calculations of the ratio of the domestic price level to the foreign price level where both are measured in a single currency.

small open economy's authorities can bypass problems of managing the float by simply adopting a fixed exchange rate with respect to that country.

14.3 Implications for the World Monetary System

The above analysis suggests that, whether or not small countries adopt fixed exchange rates with a single large economy, cyclical deviations of output from full-employment levels and persistent deviations of price levels from individual countries' core inflation rates will be roughly the same over the entire world. And, in the event that there is a single large country that is uninterested in its exchange rates with respect to trading partners, that country will run world monetary policy. When no such self-centered country exists and all countries, or large groups of them let their exchange rates float, world monetary policy will be a blind-leading-the-blind situation. All countries, by maintaining orderly foreign exchange markets with respect to the rest of the world, will end up financing all changes in the domestic relative to the foreign demand for liquidity. To the extent that the world demand for liquidity increases, however, downward pressure on world output, employment and prices will typically result. Countries whose demand for liquidity has increased will expand their money supplies to smooth out the appreciation of their currencies, but those whose demand for liquidity has not increased will tighten their domestic credit conditions to smooth out the depreciation of their currencies. The net effect will be an overall excess demand for world liquidity, causing world interest rates to rise and world output and employment to fall in the short run and all countries' price levels to fall in the long run. To the extent that those countries experiencing an increased demand for liquidity ignore the effects on their exchange rates with respect to other countries, the latter will end up reducing the world supply of liquidity to keep their exchange rates from depreciating, accentuating the effect on world real interest rates, output, employment and prices. To the extent that the countries whose demand for liquidity has not increased do nothing while the authorities in the country whose demand for liquidity has increased provide the liquidity to eliminate the portfolio shock to the exchange rate, the increased demand for liquidity will be fully financed and nothing will happen to world interest rates, output, employment and prices.

It is evident, therefore, that world price levels will typically rise and fall through time in response to changes in the world demand for money consequent on technological factors that change transaction costs and shifts in expectations about what is likely to happen in the future. If most countries are politically stable and multi-country banking crises can be avoided, there is little reason to believe that major inflations and depressions will arise. Nevertheless, there is also little reason to expect that significant business cycles will be avoided. In cases where a country of major size ignores developments in its foreign exchange market, monetary shocks in that country will be transmitted abroad and have world-wide effect. The avoidance of major world problems will then hinge on the stability of conditions in that dominant country. In cases where there are a couple of dominant countries – say, for example, the United States and the European Union – conditions in the one that cares least about its exchange rate will determine world monetary conditions. One would hope that, in such situations, appropriate cooperation between the two countries' monetary authorities would be forthcoming.

14.3.1 Foreign Exchange Crises

In situations where its real exchange rate with respect to a large major trading partner is moving extremely slowly through time, a country can avoid the difficult problems of monetary management by adopting a fixed exchange rate with respect to that partner. In fixed-exchange-rate situations, and in some cases when exchange rates are flexible, speculative crises in a country's foreign exchange market can arise. The analysis here leads to the conclusion that such crises can arise from only two basic causes. One is a situation where the country's real exchange rate begins falling and it is reasonable to expect that its government will allow the nominal exchange rate to float rather than live with the downward pressures on output, employment and prices that would otherwise arise. Since real exchange rates are near-random-walks, major speculative pressures of this sort are unlikely to arise then the exchange rate is flexible. The second basic cause of foreign exchange crises is a situation where it might be reasonable to believe that, for political reasons, a country's government is likely to finance future government expenditure by money creation. This type of situation can occur under flexible as well as fixed exchange rates.

Contrary to what has traditionally been believed, when capital is internationally mobile there is no reason for an apparent shortage of foreign exchange reserves to lead to a crisis under fixed exchange rates. A country can accumulate reserves, costlessly in terms of any effects on output, employment and prices, by simply drawing base money out of circulation—the attempts of asset holders to restore their liquidity levels by selling assets to foreigners will lead to an accumulation of foreign exchange reserves in return for a restoration of that base money stock as the authorities take the necessary measures to keep the domestic currency from appreciating above its fixed parity. Since monetary policy is ineffective under fixed exchange rates with international capital mobility, the stock of foreign exchange reserves can be costlessly adjusted to whatever level desired.

14.3.2 Exchange Rate Target Zones

The above analysis has important implications for the practice of setting target zones within which the authorities commit themselves to maintain future levels of the the nominal exchange rate. Advocacy of target zones has had a long history and the practice was followed in the European community at times since the breakdown of the Bretton-Woods system.

Let us define the nominal exchange rate fundamental as the level the nominal exchange rate that would occur at each point in time in response to the economy's underlying full-employment real exchange rate together with the desired course of monetary policy. Suppose it happens that the nominal exchange rate fundamental for the next 100 periods behaves as plotted in Fig. 14.1 – that is, as a white noise shock about a constant mean. Suppose that a credible target zone extending 7.5% on either side of the exchange rate parity, set as 1.0 in the figure, is established. As long as it is believed that the authorities will intervene in the foreign exchange market as necessary to keep the exchange rate within the target zone, the actual exchange rate will automatically remain within the zone. As the exchange rate approaches the upper (lower) bound, investors will anticipate that, given the potential action by the authorities, it will be more likely to fall (rise) than rise (fall). As a result, the exchange rate will approach the bound asymptotically.[5] Note that it is essential to this argument that the bands be credible – that investors have no doubt that the authorities will behave as they promise.

Is it is a good idea for the authorities to establish target zones and make these commitments? If the shocks to the exchange rate fundamental appearing in Fig. 14.1 are the result of demand for money shocks which the authorities are not offsetting with appropriate adjustments

[5] See Krugman [65] for an elaboration of this point.

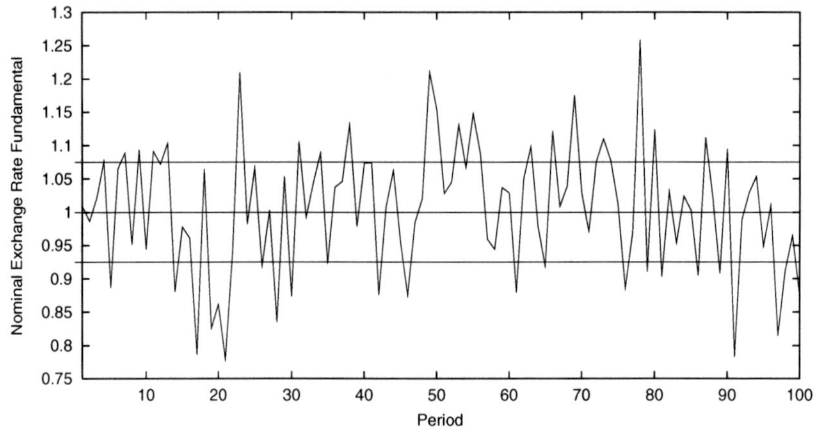

Fig. 14.1. A target zone of ± 7.5% when the nominal exchange rate is fundamental a stationary normal random process with mean of 1 and variance of 0.2

of the supply of liquidity, then limiting the extent to which these fluctuations can occur and the resulting shocks to output, employment and prices that will result from them is good. But it would be even better for the authorities to fix the exchange rate at its parity level 1.0 – the optimal target zone is of zero width. When the shocks to the exchange rate fundamental are purely monetary shocks it is in the public interest to eliminate them entirely. This can be done by fixing the exchange rate – the authorities will thereby be committed to financing all exogenous demand-for-money shocks with appropriate adjustments of the money supply.

On the other hand, suppose that the shocks to the exchange rate fundamental appearing in Fig. 14.1 are the result of shocks to the full-employment real exchange rate and that the authorities are able to verify that no demand-for-liquidity shocks are occurring. In this case it is not in the public interest to in any way limit the resulting nominal exchange rate movements. The exchange rate is insulating the domestic economy from asymmetric real shocks. Capping nominal exchange rate movements will divert these unanticipated shocks onto domestic output, employment and prices.

The situation becomes more complicated when both monetary and real asymmetric shocks are occurring. To not lose the insulating effects of exchange rate flexibility on real shocks one would be inclined to set the target zone boundaries outside the limits of fundamental exchange rate variations resulting from asymmetric real shocks so that the additional range of variability resulting from asymmetric monetary shocks would be endogenously eliminated. But if the authorities know the bounds beyond which exchange rate movements will surely be the result of monetary shocks, they can smooth out a large fraction shocks that exceed these bounds by appropriate monetary and exchange rate management without setting a target zone. Furthermore, there is the problem that monetary as well as real shocks will be causing variability of the exchange rate fundamental within the target zone, so the authorities still have to decide whether it would be better to fix the exchange rate at the unitary par value and give up the insulating advantage of flexible exchange rates in return for the pooling advantage of fixed rates. If the decision is to go for the insulating properties of flexible exchange rates within the bounds of variability due to real shocks, then there would seem to be little advantage in setting a target zone because if the authorities know the appropriate target zone they know enough to substantially eliminate the exchange rate fluctuations in excess of these bounds without setting a target zone. And should an unexpectedly large real shock occur, no credibility will be lost by letting the real exchange rate move beyond its normal bounds to neutralize it.

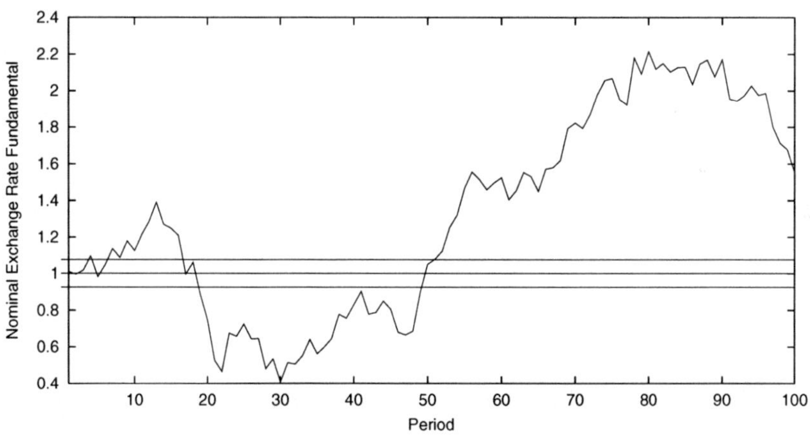

Fig. 14.2. A target zone of ± 7.5% when the nominal exchange rate fundamental is a random walk starting at a value of unity with innovations generated by the random process in Fig. 14.1

All of the above discussion has been predicated on the assumption that the exchange rate fundamental deviates randomly around a constant mean value. In fact, full-employment real exchange rates are near random walks and, even with appropriate control over long-term domestic inflation rates, exchange rate fundamentals will wander far and wide as indicated in Fig. 14.2. Unless the innovations to the full-employment real exchange rate are extremely small, any reasonable fixed target zone will be quickly violated. The alternative is to adopt a flexible target zone—that is to move the zone periodically so that it will always bracket the expected asymmetric shocks to the full-employment real exchange rate. The flexible target zone so established would have the advantage of neutralizing major monetary shocks while insulating the domestic price level from both current period and cumulative innovations to the real exchange rate. Again, however, if the authorities have enough information to set an appropriate target band beyond which the exchange rate should not be allowed to fluctuate, then they have the information to neutralize the offending asymmetric monetary shocks without setting a target zone.

The only reason for setting a target zone would appear to be to establish credibility in the eyes of the public that there will be limits to the asymmetric monetary shocks – in particular, domestic monetary finance of government expenditure – that will be allowed to affect the exchange rate. The central bank does not have to establish credibility with the public that it can neutralize random monetary shocks because it clearly must be able to recognize such shocks if it has sufficient information to continually adjust the flexible target zone as the full-employment real exchange rate evolves and the government has no self-interest in not neutralizing these shocks. It is in situations where the authorities may face tempting political pressures to finance government expenditures by printing money that they need to establish a commitment to maintain the nominal exchange rate within a band dictated by the evolving full-employment real exchange rate. But as long as they allow themselves to adjust the target zone, as the random walk nature of the real exchange rate requires that they must do from time to time, it will be difficult for them to maintain credibility that the zone will be adjusted only in response to real exchange rate movements and never in anticipation of future inflationary finance. This is especially the case because governments that might reap short-run political gains from inflationary finance can always point to 'evidence' of potential real exchange rate movements that led them to inappropriately lower their target zone for the international value of the domestic currency or mistakenly fail to raise that zone when the full-employment real exchange rate increased. To maintain credibility in the face of political pressures to engage in inflationary finance, the only real option is to fix the exchange rate using a currency board or other credible institutional arrangement that will guarantee that the authorities will have no discretion regarding monetary policy. The opportunity cost of this is a price level that will be a near random walk. To eliminate these random walk price level movements, the monetary authorities have to have an appropriate degree of independence from the political pressures for inflationary finance. If they have that independence then there is no reason for them to set a flexible target zone. If they do not have that independence, then flexibility of the target zone will make it difficult to establish credibility.

In the context of the present analysis, therefore, exchange rate target zones do not appear to be useful. To establish monetary policy credibility in a world where the full-employment real exchange rate is a near random walk, it would be wiser to commit to an inflation rate target zone rather than an exchange rate target zone.

14.3.3 Currency Unions

One way a country can commit to non-monetary finance of government expenditure is to adopt the currency of a stable neighboring country as its own, taking what was originally its domestic currency completely out of circulation. The problem with this approach is that, as noted above, the domestic price level will become a near-random-walk, possibly ranging far and wide from any initial position. And, to the extent that prices are sticky, output and employment will be affected. The insulating advantages of flexible exchange rates will be lost.[6]

If this is such a bad idea, however, why would a large group of European countries abandon their home currencies for a single European currency, managed by a European central bank? There are two basic reasons. First, there are resource gains from not having to constantly switch between currencies when engaging in trade. Second, there were deep desires among the members for an important degree of political as well as economic union. But how can the near-random-walk nature of real exchange rate movements and the related price level movements be avoided?

It is crucial that, before creating a currency union, these countries made a prior agreement to allow, along with free capital mobility, free mobility of labour among all common-currency members. Inter-country migration will eliminate a major source of real exchange rate variation by substantial equalization of real wages, for equivalent tasks, across the countries – otherwise it would undoubtedly be beneficial for the

---

[6] See the author's paper with colleague Jack Carr [12] concerning the advisability of Canada adopting the U.S. dollar as its currency.

provinces of Canada and states in the U.S. to each have separate currencies.

Under circumstances where wages differ across countries solely on the basis of location preference and the returns to capital differ solely on the basis of risk premiums, real exchange rates movements will not reflect changes in real wage differentials for equivalent occupations. Even if there are substantial cultural barriers to migration, all that is required to equalize wages is substantial inter-country movements of workers at the margin. But free migration of labour will be insufficient to eliminate significant real exchange rate movements through time. Wages can be higher on average in one country than others, and this will be reflected in the prices of non-traded output components and the country's real exchange rate, if that country happens to specialize in products that require high human-skill inputs. Also, the prices of the products in which particular countries specialize may vary substantially through time to the extent that technological growth favors, for extended periods, natural resources with which particular countries happen to be exclusively endowed. But resulting movements in real exchange rates need not result in wage differences that would not otherwise occur on the basis of the skill-compositions of the respective labour forces, except insofar as those wage differences reflect utility gains or losses – that is, rents – from living in particular areas rather than others.

Ultimately, four factors would seem to be relevant in the decision as to whether a particular country should join a currency union. The first is the expected degree of variability over time of its real exchange rate with respect to that union and the ease with which the necessary domestic price adjustments in response to such real exchange rate movements can occur without leading to changes in employment. The second is the amount of resources that can be saved by not having to engage in constant currency exchange in the ordinary course of business – an important issue here will be the fraction of the country's output that is traded, which will probably vary inversely with the size of the country. The third is the resources that can be saved by not having to conduct domestic monetary policy and thereby risk variations in domestic output and employment and prices from mistakes in neutralizing the effects of monetary shocks on the real and nominal exchange rates. Again, the smaller the country, the bigger these costs are likely to be as a fraction of income. Finally, of course, the country's residents must agree to permit unrestricted migration of people to and from the other countries in the currency union.

15

Corroborating and Other Evidence

The two immediately preceding chapters provide a theory to explain the absence of observed effects on real and nominal exchange rates of monetary shocks. Under flexible exchange rates, central banks find it in the public interest, as well as their own interest, to continually finance demand-for-liquidity shocks by adjusting the stock of liquidity so as to prevent overshooting movements of the exchange rate. As a result, monetary conditions in all countries will tend to be the same, and all will experience roughly the same medium-term deviations of domestic inflation from its politically acceptable core rate and roughly the same business cycles to the extent that the latter are influenced by monetary conditions.[1] By following this policy of neutralizing portfolio shocks to their exchange rates, countries simultaneously obtain the insulation properties of flexible exchange rates against asymmetric real shocks and at least some of the portfolio smoothing properties of fixed exchange rates against asymmetric monetary shocks. Because such 'orderly markets' or 'even keel' policies cannot be implemented without error, however, it will pay countries to adopt fixed exchange rates with respect to important trading partners if their real exchange rates with respect to those countries are sufficiently stable through time. In the absence of such real exchange rate stability, movements in real exchange rates in response to ongoing real shocks will be transmitted under a fixed exchange rate regime to output and employment and the domestic price level rather than being absorbed by nominal exchange rate movements.

[1] Business cycles resulting entirely from the interaction of real forces will also be correlated across countries due to the coordinating effects of trade and capital movements.

J.E. Floyd, *Interest Rates, Exchange Rates and World Monetary Policy*,
DOI 10.1007/978-3-642-10280-6_15, © Springer-Verlag Berlin Heidelberg 2010

While this theory of stochastic monetary interdependence is fully consistent with the evidence presented in Part II, it is important in concluding this work to check its consistency with additional evidence regarding the historical behavior of real exchange rates, the comparability of business cycles and inflation episodes across countries, and other details about the correspondence of countries' monetary policies. Following an analysis of this additional evidence, the chapter closes with an unavoidably speculative preliminary application of the results obtained in this study to the prospects for success of the European Monetary Union.

15.1 The Historical Evidence Regarding Real Exchange Rates

A clear implication of the above analysis is that countries will tend to adopt fixed exchange rates when the underlying full-employment real exchange rates vary little through time, reverting to flexible rates when, as in recent years, real exchange rates are highly variable. This, of course, is quite the opposite of the frequently-heard argument that the adoption of flexible exchange rates leads to real exchange rate variability that would not be present under a fixed exchange rate regime.

Figure 15.1a plots the annual historical percentage deviations from base levels of the real exchange rates of Canada, the United Kingdom, France and Germany with respect to the United States, and Fig. 15.1b gives similar plots for Canada, France and Germany with respect to the United Kingdom and for France with respect to Germany. Each series is broken into four segments corresponding to separate international exchange rate policy regimes:

- The classical gold standard period, 1880–1913 (base 1890-99 = 100).
- The interwar period, 1926–1938 (base 1927-29 = 100).
- The Bretton-Woods period, 1950–1970 (base 1963-66 = 100).
- The Post-Bretton-Woods period, 1974–2007 (base 1963-66 = 100).

The first and third of these periods were characterized by fixed exchange rates and the fourth period by flexible rates. The interwar period was characterized by an unstable mixture of fixed and managed flexible rates. The years of transition between these distinctive regimes are omitted.

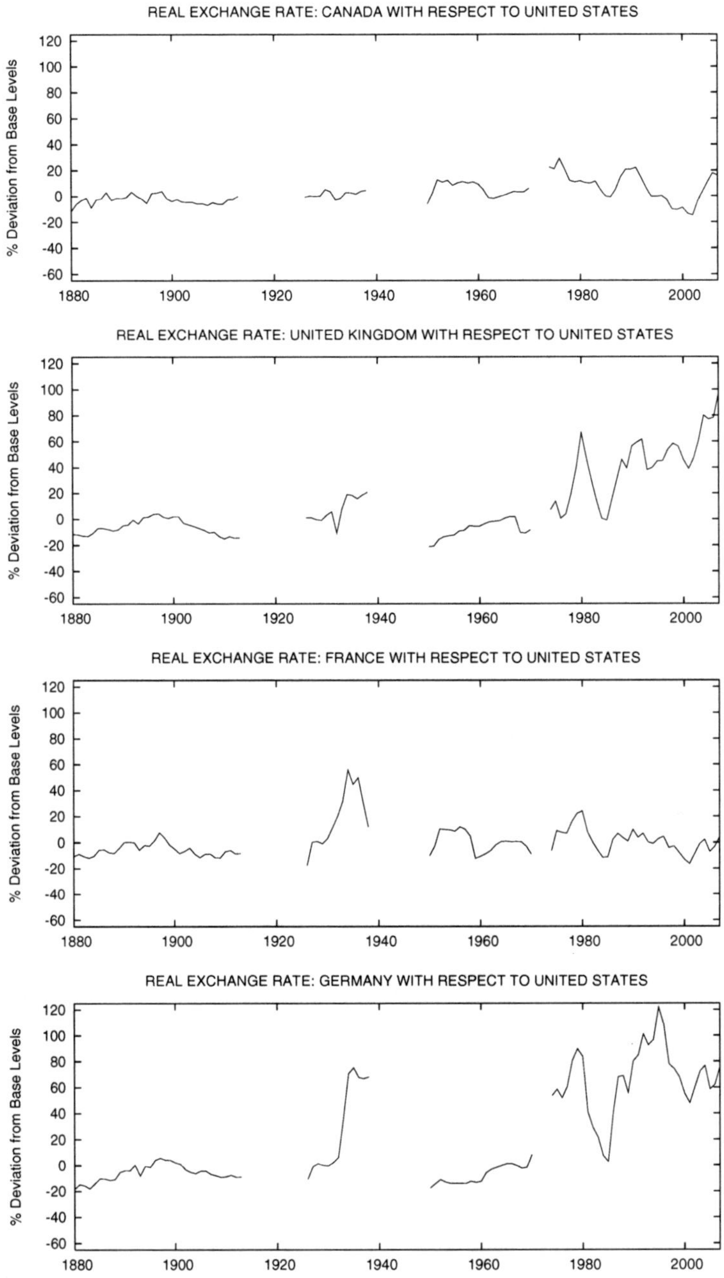

Fig. 15.1a. Percentage deviations of real exchange rates from base levels: 1880–1913 (1890–99 base), 1926–1938 (1927–29 base), 1950–1970 and 1974–2007 (1963–66 base)

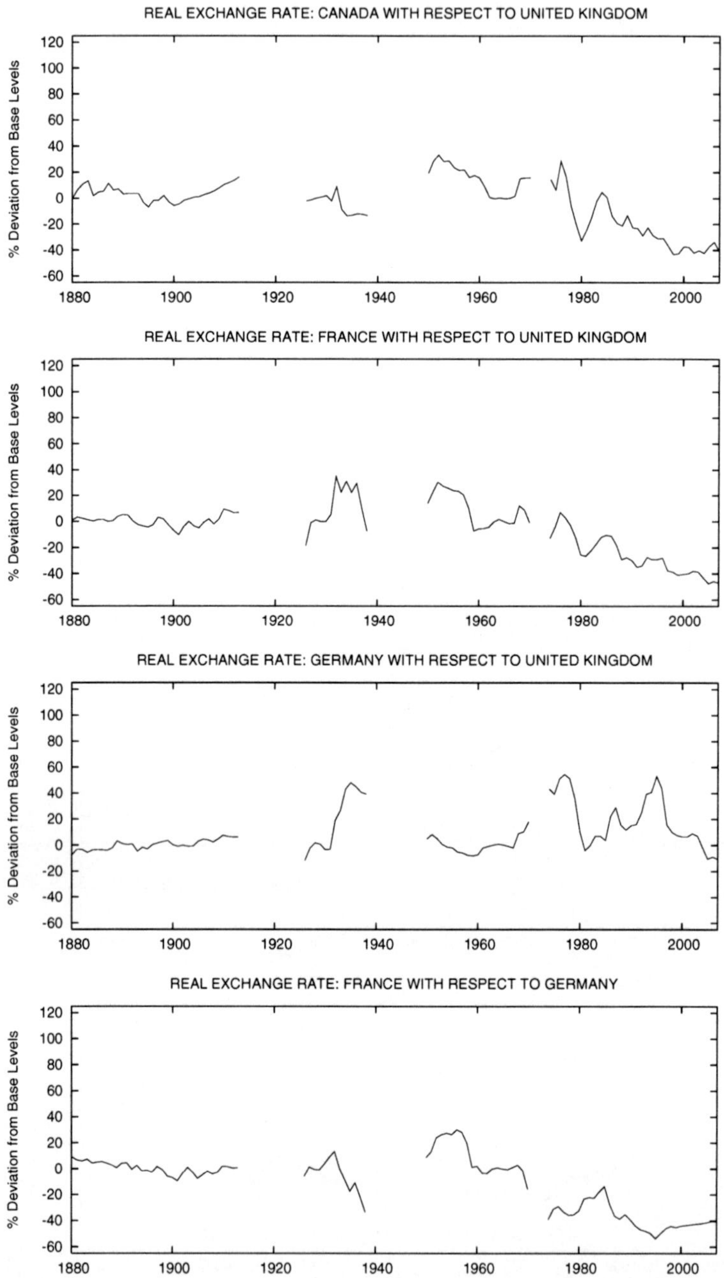

Fig. 15.1b. Percentage deviations of real exchange rates from base levels: 1880–1913 (1890–99 base), 1926–1938 (1927–29 base), 1950–1970 and 1974–2007 (1963–66 base)

Table 15.1. Statistics of historical percentage deviations of real exchange rates from base levels

		1880-1913	1926–1938	1950–1970	1974–2007
Canada	Mean	-2.90	1.44	5.39	7.47
viz.	Standard Deviation	3.50	2.56	5.47	11.63
U. S.	– Detrended	3.55	2.36	5.34	9.99
	Slope – % per year	-0.01	0.31	-0.27	-0.62
	Maximum	3.82	5.16	12.72	29.32
	Minimum	-11.79	-2.88	-6.03	-14.81
	Range	15.61	8.04	18.75	44.13
Canada	Mean	3.85	-5.13	14.89	-21.24
viz.	Standard Deviation	5.91	7.50	10.95	19.17
U. K.	– Detrended	5.98	5.36	7.90	10.67
	Slope – % per year	0.05	-1.40	-1.25	-1.61
	Maximum	16.51	8.99	33.29	28.60
	Minimum	-7.12	-13.69	-0.28	-43.32
	Range	23.63	22.68	33.57	71.92
U. K.	Mean	-6.30	7.62	-7.74	41.51
viz.	Standard Deviation	5.96	9.96	6.76	25.03
U. S.	– Detrended	6.03	6.59	5.00	16.47
	Slope – % per year	-0.05	1.98	0.76	1.91
	Maximum	4.24	20.73	2.00	96.71
	Minimum	-15.08	-10.90	-21.21	-0.93
	Range	19.32	31.63	22.21	97.64
France	Mean	-5.90	19.01	0.16	1.17
viz.	Standard Deviation	4.77	22.45	7.83	9.24
U. S.	– Detrended	4.83	15.70	7.57	8.28
	Slope – % per year	-0.03	4.28	-0.42	-0.44
	Maximum	7.60	55.93	11.93	23.99
	Minimum	-12.00	-16.04	-12.27	-16.60
	Range	19.60	71.97	24.20	40.59
Germany	Mean	-6.17	29.36	-7.38	65.53
viz.	Standard Deviation	6.41	38.88	7.28	26.41
U. S.	– Detrended	6.05	15.19	3.22	25.76
	Slope – % per year	0.24	8.14	1.06	0.74
	Maximum	5.71	75.23	8.26	122.00
	Minimum	-18.37	-10.77	-17.50	2.79
	Range	24.08	86.00	25.76	119.21

Table 15.1 Continued from previous page

		1880-1913	1926–1938	1950–1970	1974–2007
France	Mean	0.53	10.36	9.21	-26.30
viz.	Standard Deviation	4.30	16.60	12.68	14.70
U. K.	– Detrended	4.36	15.19	9.51	6.44
	Slope – % per year	0.03	2.05	-1.39	-1.33
	Maximum	9.44	34.89	30.37	7.00
	Minimum	-10.34	-16.99	-7.21	-47.60
	Range	19.78	41.88	37.58	54.60
Germany	Mean	0.19	18.69	0.56	18.78
viz.	Standard Deviation	3.85	22.52	6.65	19.67
U. K.	– Detrended	2.14	9.63	6.53	16.85
	Slope – % per year	0.32	5.27	0.31	-1.06
	Maximum	7.40	48.03	18.02	54.47
	Minimum	-7.64	-11.76	-8.27	-10.69
	Range	15.04	59.79	26.29	65.16
France	Mean	0.40	-5.56	8.93	-37.62
viz.	Standard Deviation	4.58	12.94	13.60	9.61
Germany	– Detrended	3.47	9.99	9.08	7.80
	Slope – % per year	-0.30	-2.23	-1.66	-0.58
	Maximum	9.32	13.28	30.15	-13.72
	Minimum	-9.49	-33.56	-16.01	-53.69
	Range	18.81	46.84	46.16	39.97

Table 15.1 gives relevant statistics for each series for each of the four periods.[2] Compare first the post-Bretton-Woods period with the gold standard years between 1880 and 1913. It is obvious from the numbers in the left-most and right-most columns of the Table 15.1 and the corresponding segments of the charts in Figs. 15.1a and 15.1b that the real exchange rate was much more variable in the years after 1974 than in the 1880-1913 period. Since the empirical evidence in Part II clearly indicated very minimal effects of monetary shocks on real exchange rates in the flexible exchange rate period, there is no possibility that

[2] Implicit GDP or GNP deflators were used to calculate the price level ratios. To obtain real exchange rates, the price level ratios were adjusted by the market exchange rate between the two currencies. The data are in the Gretl and Excel files **`jfdataan.gdt`** and **`jfdataan.xls`**, respectively, and are described in the text file **`jfdataan.cat`**. The preparation of the data for Figs. 15.1a and 15.1b and the calculation of the statistics presented in Table 15.1 are performed in Gretl using the script file **`histrex.inp`** with the output in **`histrex.got`**. The data sources are outlined in Appendix F.

the greater variability in this period was the result of the adoption of floating exchange rates – real forces of technological change and capital accumulation affecting real exchange rates cannot be created by merely eliminating nominal exchange rate parities. But can one conclude from this that the pre-1914 gold standard was chosen over a flexible exchange rate system because of the low variability of real exchange rates during the period? The answer has to be no!

The viability of the gold standard in the 19th century and earlier hinged on the restrictions it placed on government printing of money to finance public expenditures. There had been little experience with 'responsible' government management of fiduciary monetary systems up to that time. So one cannot rule out the possibility that flexible exchange rates would still have been adopted during the past three decades even if real exchange rate variability was as low in that period as it was during the period before 1914.

Except for Canada with respect to the United States, there is clear evidence of greater real exchange rate variability during the interwar period than before 1914. A gold standard was re-established by the mid-1920s in the face of considerable uncertainty about the appropriate gold-parities for the various currencies, and was maintained with difficulty until late 1931 when Germany adopted foreign exchange control and Great Britain went off gold.[3] Canada effectively left the gold standard in 1929 when the authorities suspended convertibility of government produced Dominion Notes although the exchange rate remained close to the gold parity until 1931 when restrictions were placed on the export of gold and substantial depreciation occurred.[4] France maintained the gold standard parity until 1937, and Germany did so beyond that year, although its exchange rate level was meaningless because of the presence of restrictions on capital flows, first adopted in 1931. The United States devalued in 1933.[5] More generally, the period was one of competitive devaluations and beggar-thy-neighbor impositions of tariffs and other trade restrictions as the world economy went through the Great Depression.

While it cannot be concluded that the United States was alone responsible for the world depression, the bank failures in that country and the Federal Reserve System's failure to expand base money to counter the effects on the money supply of the public's conversion of deposits to cash and the banks' scramble for reserves was an important fac-

---

[3] See Eichengreen [31], pp. 218-223.

[4] See Helleiner [51], pp. 45–57, and Bordo and Redish [9], pp. 357–363.

[5] See Eichengreen [31].

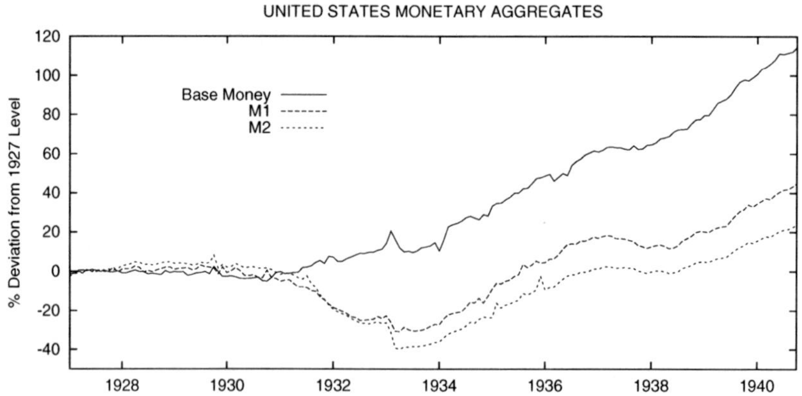

Fig. 15.2. United States monetary aggregates during the Great Depression

tor increasing its magnitude. As shown in Fig. 15.2, the U. S. money supply had fallen by more than one-third by late-1934.[6] Many years ago Daniel Racette [90] observed that, though Canada experienced no bank failures and resultant money-multiplier declines, that country's authorities reduced base money sufficiently to finance a reduction in the domestic money supply comparable to that in the United States, a result that would be predicted by the theory developed here.[7] There is little doubt that the money supplies of other countries also declined – otherwise it would be difficult to explain the general declines in price levels.

The data provide little support for an assertion that money shocks were unimportant during the interwar period, as can be seen from Figs. 15.3a and 15.3b.[8] A policy induced devaluation of a country's exchange rate is equivalent to a positive monetary shock – the domestic money stock must increase to finance the lower nominal value of the currency independently of whether the authorities operate on the exchange rate itself or on the domestic money supply. In Canada and the United Kingdom, the co-movements of the nominal and real exchange rates with respect to the U.S. associated with the British devaluation in 1931 and the U.S. devaluation in 1933 are clearly evident in the first and third charts in Fig. 15.3a accompanied by some temporary

[6] These data are in the Gretl and Excel files **usgdmon.gdt** and **usgdmon.xls** and are described in the file **usgdmon.cat**.

[7] For a graphical demonstration, see Fig. 3 on page 359 of Bordo and Redish [9].

[8] The data in these figures are generated from already-mentioned Gretl data file **jfdataan.gdt** using the script file **histrex.inp**.

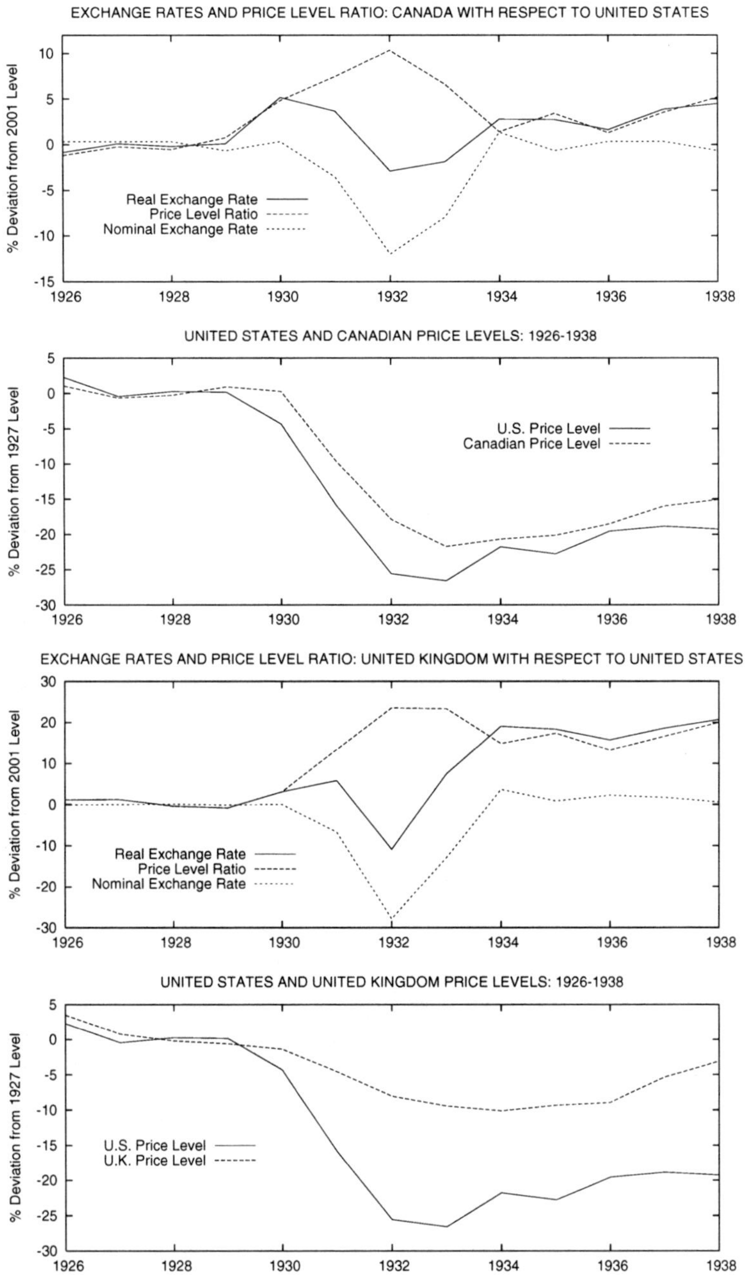

Fig. 15.3a. Percentage deviations of exchange rates, price level ratios and price levels from 1927–29 levels during the Great Depression

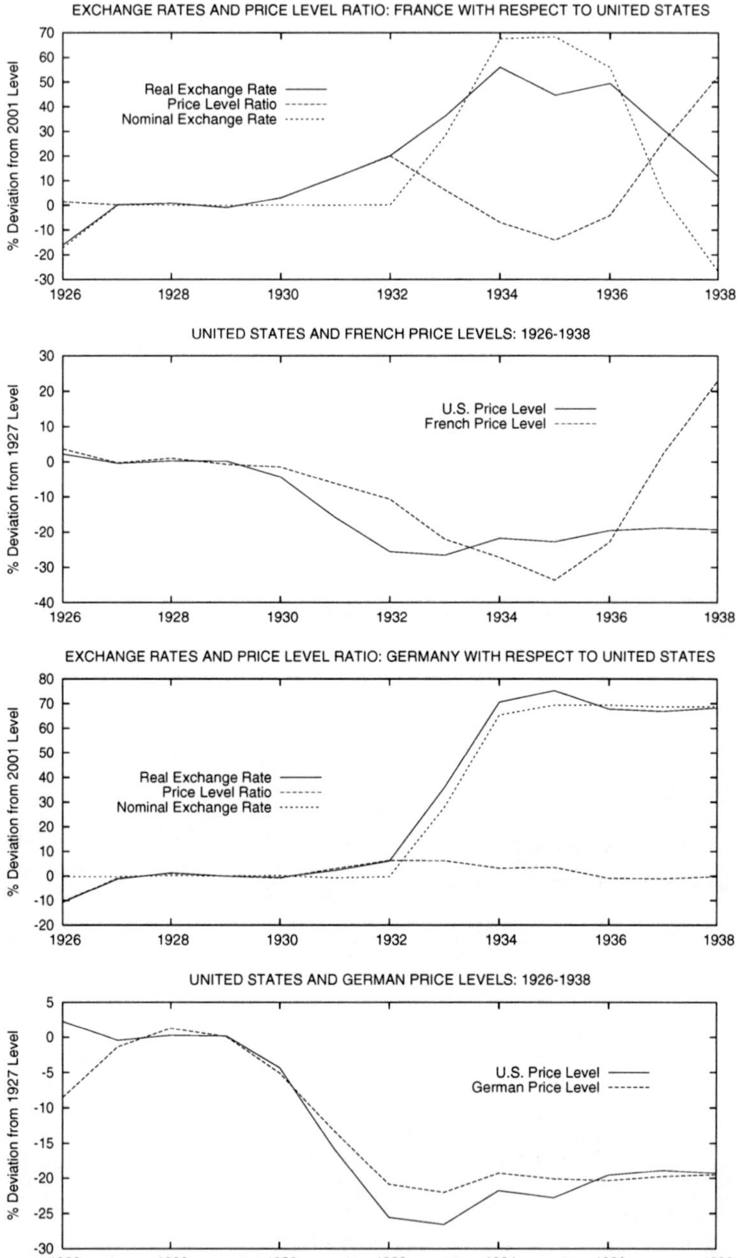

Fig. 15.3b. Percentage deviations of exchange rates, price level ratios and price levels from 1927–29 levels during the great depression

upward movement of the domestic relative to U.S. price levels. The real and nominal exchange rate co-movements in Germany in the third chart in Fig. 15.3b associated with the U.S. devaluation are even more pronounced, with little movement of the German relative to U.S. price level. The stability of the ratio of German to U.S. prices is undoubtedly the consequence of the heavy use of exchange controls and other trade restrictions.[9] In the case of France, the real and nominal exchange rates with respect to the U.S. also moved together in response to the U.S. devaluation in 1933 and the French devaluation after 1936, with the French price level falling and then rising relative to the U.S. price level.

It is also clear from the second and fourth panels of Figs. 15.3a and 15.3b that the other four countries' price levels moved in the same direction as the U.S. price level although the Canadian price level fell slightly less, and the British price level much less, than the price level in the United States. The lesser decline in the British price level cannot be explained by greater price level rigidity in that country because, as shown in Fig. 15.4, real income also declined by much less in the U.K.[10] There is reason to believe that British income and prices were already below their full-employment levels before the onset of the Great Depression,[11] so the process of reestablishing long-run equilibrium could well have been underway in that country when the declines in the U.S. occurred. It is also possible, though no corroborating evidence is apparent, that real forces associated with the decline in world income acted differentially on the demand for British as opposed to U.S. output. Another set of real forces that may well have been responsible are trade restrictions, capital and exchange controls which had the effect of inducing a shift of world demand toward U.K. output and thereby keeping domestic prices above the level they would have otherwise have been at.

The resort to tariffs and restrictions on trade and capital mobility during these years is fully consistent with the theory here developed. When the rest of the world is unstable, the only way a country can protect itself from shocks emanating abroad is to 'circle the wagons' and try to insulate itself from those shocks so that domestic policies can be applied without regard to what is happening in the rest of the world. The effects of such 'beggar-thy-neighbor' policies is to reduce world real

[9] See Feinstien et. al. [38], pp. 160-165.

[10] The raw data for this figure are present in the respective Gretl and Excel files `jfdataan.gdt` and `jfdataan.xls` and the series for the plots are generated in the latter file.

[11] See Cairncross and Eichengreen [11], Chapter 3.

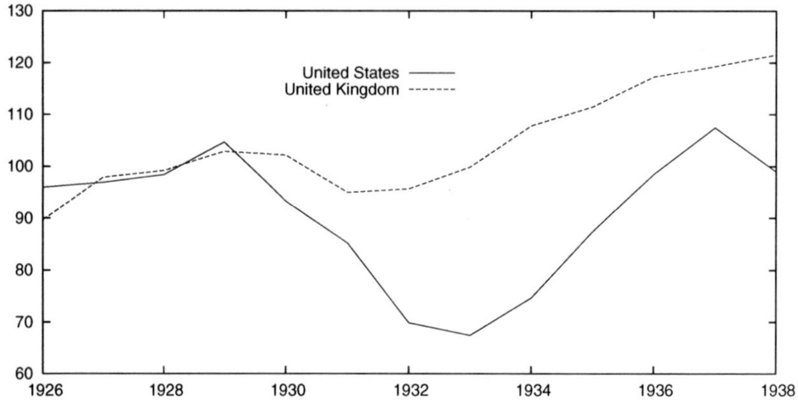

Fig. 15.4. Real income as a percentage of 1927 levels: United States and United Kingdom

income. Contrary to what is sometimes thought, however, competitive exchange rate devaluations are not 'beggar-thy-neighbor' policies in the aggregate because they require that the devaluing country increase its own, and hence the world, money supply.

It is clear from Table 15.1 and Figs. 15.1a and 15.1b that the real exchange rates of the countries being studied were less variable during the Bretton-Woods period than in the years that followed. The interpretation here agrees with that of Barry Eichengreen who argues that the smaller variability in during Bretton-Woods than afterward was a consequence of the restrictions imposed on international capital movements during those years.[12]

Following the debacle of the 1930s, it became apparent that an international monetary regime had to be established that would maintain orderly exchange rate movements and make it unnecessary and undesirable for countries to engage in the competitive imposition of restrictions on international trade. While the agreement concluded at Bretton Woods envisaged a gold standard similar to the one that had been successful prior to 1914, the result was really a key-currency system using the U.S. dollar as the key-currency with international reserves consisting of gold and U.S. dollars redeemable in gold at $35 per oz. Restrictions on international trade were to be eliminated as soon as possible and exchange rates were to be adjusted only in response to 'funda-

[12] Eichengreen's book [32] is an excellent source from which to acquire the institutional background and historical facts necessary to understand and apply the arguments developed here.

mental disequilibria' in consultation with the International Monetary Fund, the international agency created to coordinate management of the system. International capital movements could be restricted if required to prevent speculative deviations of exchange rates from their fundamental equilibrium levels. While the removal of trade restrictions was accomplished by 1958, widespread efforts to control international capital movements were common throughout the Bretton-Woods period, although as capital markets improved with the passage of time it became increasingly difficult to successfully control unwanted capital transfers.

As Eichengreen recounts,[13] maintaining the system became an increasing struggle as the years passed. The problem was that indications of a willingness to devalue under appropriate circumstances raised the possibility of near-certain profits from currency speculation when such circumstances began to appear, while an unequivocal commitment to the existing exchange rate level required either the use of direct controls and other restrictions to force the real exchange rate into line with the nominal parity value, or increases and declines in domestic employment and prices as the equilibrium real exchange rate varied through time, an inevitable occurrence given its near-random-walk nature.

Figure 15.5 plots the real and nominal exchange rates and the ratios of the domestic to the U.S. price level for the United Kingdom, France, Germany and Japan for the period 1957 through 1971.[14] The British real exchange rate with respect to the United States rose by slightly more than ten percent from the beginning of 1961 to the devaluation in November of 1967. The government was facing severe balance of payments pressure throughout these years as it continually tried to expand aggregate demand in excess of what would be consistent with the fixed level of the pound/dollar exchange rate.[15] It is therefore reasonable to conclude that at least some of this real exchange rate trend was the result of policies designed to shift world demand towards U.K. output, although the possibility that there was an underlying shift of world demand in this direction as a result of the world capital accumulation and technology growth cannot be ruled out. Indeed, as can be seen from the second panel from the top in Fig. 15.1a, the observed real

---

[13] See [32], Chapter 4.

[14] The data in this figure are generated from series in the respective Gretl, Excel and XLispStat data files `jfdatamo.gdt`, `jfdatamo.xls` and `jfdatamo.lsp` using the XLispStat batch file `bwnex.lsp` which simply changes the base of the relevant series to the first six months of 1957.

[15] For a detailed discussion of the situation faced by the United Kingdom and the government response see Cairncross and Eichengreen [11], Chapter 5.

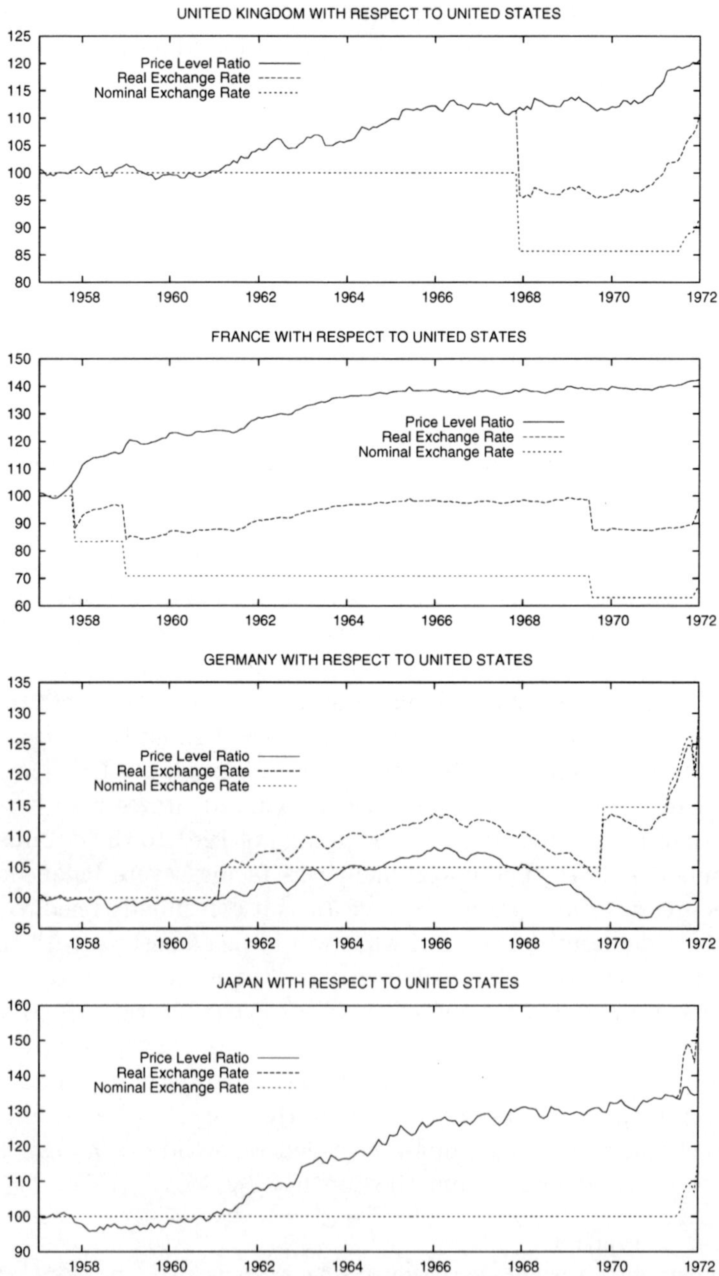

Fig. 15.5. Exchange rates and price level ratios of the United Kingdom, France Germany and Japan with respect to the United States during the Bretton-Woods period

exchange rate trend movements have been part of a more general trend that occurred through the whole period from 1950 through 2007. The real exchange rate dropped in unison with the decline in the nominal U.S. dollar value of the pound in late-1967 and the British price level showed no tendency to rise permanently relative to the U.S. price level before early 1971. This is consistent with a conclusion that the devaluation was not ultimately a monetary shock and was accompanied by a relaxation of controls that had been holding the real exchange rate above its true equilibrium level. The subsequent rise in both the real exchange rate and the ratio of the U.K. to the U.S. price level would seem to have resulted from a non-engineered relative increase in demand for British goods, because the nominal and real exchange rates both increased faster than the price level ratio when the pound was set free in late-1971.

The French real exchange rate with respect to the United States declined very little over the whole period from the beginning of 1957 to the beginning of 1972 while the price level ratio rose by roughly forty percent. This, together with the decline in the nominal exchange rate of similar magnitude, suggests that the rise in the French relative to the U.S. price level was likely the result of greater French monetary expansion. Almost all of the relative price level movement occurred before the beginning of 1965 and was presumably the result of monetary expansion that financed the devaluations of late-1957 and late-1959. It is no secret that the French government was under enormous pressure to expand aggregate demand during this period.[16] The devaluation in 1969, however, was not associated with any significant increase in the French relative to the U.S. price level before 1972, suggesting that any effects of this exchange rate adjustment on aggregate demand were offset by the relaxation of direct controls.

The German situation was the opposite of that of Britain and France – the authorities were under substantial public pressure to control inflation. The Deutschmark was revalued by about 6 percent in 1961 with the real exchange rate rising by the same amount with no decline in the German relative to the U.S. price level. This, of course, is what one would expect to occur under conditions in which downward adjustments in prices are slow to occur. By 1966, the real exchange rate had risen by roughly 12.5 percent and the German price level had risen by roughly 7.5 percent relative to the U.S. price level. Beyond that year both the real exchange rate and the price level ratio began to decline.

[16] For background to the discussion here of the French, German and Japanese cases, see Eichengreen [32], Chapter 4.

One cannot rule out the possibility that, because of the revaluation, the German price level was 5 percent lower relative to the U.S. price level in 1966 than it otherwise would have been. A further revaluation of the Deutschmark was made in 1969 and the exchange rate was freed in 1971. In this case, the real exchange rate again rose by roughly the amount of the revaluation and with the price level ratio continuing to fall for about a year and then remaining steady. As can be seen from the bottom panel of Fig. 15.1a the freeing of the exchange rate was associated with a pronounced rise in the real exchange rate during the 1970s.

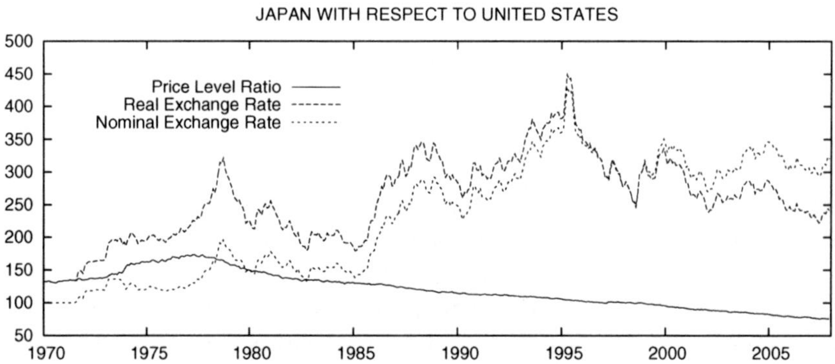

Fig. 15.6. Japanese exchange rates and price level ratio with respect to the United States

The Japanese maintained the nominal exchange rate fixed at 360 yen per U.S. dollar throughout the Bretton-Woods period until its end in 1971. Although the domestic price level fell somewhat relative to the U.S. price level in late 1957, and the real exchange rate declined accordingly, the Japanese real exchange rate and price level ratio with respect to the U.S. began to increase thereafter. As shown in Fig. 15.6, the price level ratio continued to increase past the mid-1970s, declining rather steadily thereafter through 2007.[17] Since the Japanese were unhappy about the aforementioned inflation during the Bretton-Woods period, and would have liked to control it, one must conclude that the real exchange rate increase was driven by real forces of technology and capital accumulation and not by trade and capital flow restrictions.

[17] The data for Fig. 15.6 are continuations of the series set up using the XLispStat batch file `bwnex.lsp` that were shown in the bottom panel of Fig. 15.5.

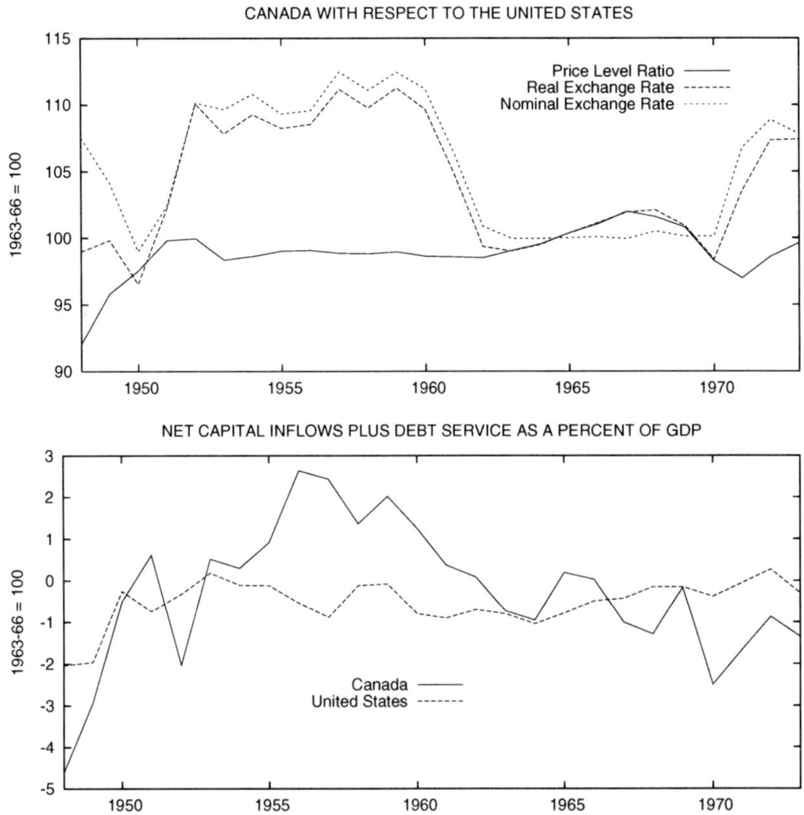

Fig. 15.7. Annual average net capital inflows plus debt service relative to GDP and real and nominal exchange rates and price level ratios of Canada with respect to the United States

The Canadian case is special because the country broke with the rules and adopted a floating exchange rate in 1950, fixing it again in 1962, and then abandoning that fixed rate in 1970. The exchange rates and price level ratio of Canada with respect to the United States are plotted in the top panel of Fig. 15.7.[18] The average annual U.S. dollar price of the Canadian dollar fell in 1949 with the September devaluation that accompanied the British devaluation of that year, and again in 1950 as a result of the fact that the previous year's devaluation, which applied to only three months of that year, applied to all twelve

[18] The data for this figure are in the Gretl and Excel files **jfdataan.gdt** and **jfdataan.xls** and were prepared for presentation using the Gretl input file **rexnci.inp**.

months of 1950. The magnitude of the average decline in 1950 may well have been moderated by an appreciation following the establishment of a floating rate in September of that year. The Canadian authorities decided to let the rate float because their attempts to reduce domestic inflation were resulting in massive inflows of foreign exchange.[19] The country's annual average real exchange rate rose by more than 10 percent by 1952 as compared to 1950, and stayed at that higher level throughout the 1950s. As can be seen from the bottom panel of Fig. 15.7 the net real capital inflow plus the debt service balance, measured as the negative of the balance of trade in goods and services divided by GDP, rose dramatically between 1948 and 1955. The strong positive relationship between Canada's real net capital inflow and the real exchange rate found in Part II seems also to have been at work here. Although the depreciation of the Canadian dollar in 1961 and 1962 and the associated currency crises that culminated in a fixing of its value at 92.5 U.S. cents occurred in the midst of a dispute between the Government in power and the Governor of the Bank of Canada, James Coyne, over the latter's commitment to tight monetary policy in the midst of recessionary conditions, it is interesting to note from Fig. 15.7 that the real net capital inflow into the country as a percent of GDP was declining and the real exchange rate, which declined in step with the nominal rate, remained far short of its 1960 level until after 1970. During the fixed exchange rate period, which lasted until 1970, the Canadian real exchange rate and price level ratio with respect to the United States rose about 8 percent, and further more substantial increases in the real exchange rate occurred after re-establishment of a floating exchange rate. The return to a floating exchange rate was prompted by the upward pressure on the price level imposed by a rising real exchange rate, although it is clear from the bottom panel of Fig. 15.7 that this could not have been the result of real net capital inflows which were on a downward trend after 1960.[20] As can be seen from the top panel of Fig. 15.1a the Canadian real exchange rate with respect to the U.S. continued to rise until after the mid-1970s.

The Canadian experience differed from those of the other countries examined because of the close proximity and interrelationship between the Canadian and U.S. economies which made it difficult for the Canadians to control real exchange rate movements by direct controls over international capital transfers – among other things, the Federal Gov-

---

[19] For background on the Canada's Bretton-Woods experience see Helleiner [51], Chapters 3 and 4.

[20] For a discussion of the politics involved, see Helleiner [51].

ernment could not impose restrictions on borrowing in the U.S. by the provincial governments. Under these circumstances it was virtually impossible to prevent real exchange rate movements from feeding through onto the domestic price level and employment.[21]

Reflecting the underlying problems with the Bretton-Woods system, three factors were instrumental in its collapse. First, as capital markets developed, it became increasingly difficult for countries to implement sufficient controls over international capital movements to offset underlying movements in real exchange rates that would otherwise be reflected in domestic employment and prices. Second, as world output grew and the need for foreign exchange reserves grew accordingly, the world stock of gold reserves became an increasingly small proportion of total reserves of gold and U.S. dollars. It became plausible to speculators that the U.S. dollar price of gold would eventually have to be increased and, as a result, private conversions of dollars into gold had to be stopped in 1968 – thereafter, gold reserves could only be exchanged among central banks at $35 per oz. and a two-tier system resulted with a private market price of gold above the official price. The problem of preventing central-bank hoarding of gold remained amid assertions that the United States should do something to cure its balance of payments deficit. These assertions were beside the point because in a key-currency system it is the peripheral countries that choose whether or not to have balance of payments surpluses, and thereby accumulate reserves, with the key-country's consequent payments deficit or surplus being a mere technicality. Third, the U.S. was entering into a period of increasing inflation associated with the financing of the Viet-Nam War and other countries, particularly Germany, objected to the pass-through of this inflation to the rest of the world via the fixity of exchange rates.

In 1971, under the pressure of foreign central banks on U.S. gold reserve holdings, President Nixon announced that the United States would no longer buy or sell gold at $35 per oz. or any other price. Under the Smithsonian Agreement in December of that year the price at which the U.S. would not buy or sell gold was increased, a number of countries' currencies were revalued in terms of the dollar and the permissible fluctuation bands of exchange rates from their parity values was increased from 1% to 2.25%. But U.S. policy remained too expansionary to be compatible with pegging foreign currencies to the dollar,[22] and by 1973 most countries had adopted flexible exchange rates. As will be shown in the next section, however, allowing exchange rates to float

[21] See Helleiner [51], page 119.
[22] See Eichengreen [32], p. 133.

did not insulate other countries from the increasing U.S. inflation rates of the 1970s and the subsequent inflation rate declines after 1980 – the other countries examined here ended up financing a similar pattern of inflation rates themselves.

The empirical evidence presented in this section suggests that the theoretical conclusions outlined in the previous chapter need to be moderated somewhat. There it was there argued that if the shocks to the real exchange rate are sufficiently small so that it moves only very gradually through time it would make sense for a country to forego the problems of managing a float by simply fixing its exchange rate with respect to the relevant trading partner. The Bretton-Woods experience clearly suggests that countries do not want to let even small pressures, especially downward ones, on the real exchange rate feed through onto domestic employment and prices. And in a world of international capital mobility, it is difficult to neutralize these pressures by direct controls. Moreover, given the near-random-walk nature of real exchange rate movements it is inevitable that downward trends of some magnitude will eventually occur. Accordingly, it would seem that situations in which it would be in a country's interest to adopt a fixed exchange rate that could be adjusted on occasion will rarely occur. To go the fixed exchange rate route, a country needs to join a currency union. This will necessitate free mobility of labour between itself and other members of that union and, hence, a degree of political integration.

The frequently heard argument that fixed exchange rate regimes lead to real exchange rate stability makes sense only to the extent that the fixed parities are supported by the massive imposition of direct controls over trade and capital movements – such controls are costly to implement and they reduce wealth by wiping out gains from trade. The opposite argument that real exchange rate stability leads to fixed exchange rates is also suspect because periods of sufficient real exchange rate stability are likely to be short and infrequent. Judging from the evidence presented here, it is difficult to imagine that a future period in which the underlying free-market real shocks to countries' real exchange rates are of a magnitude similar to those observed in the Bretton-Woods years, or in the gold standard years prior to World War II, would usher in a near-world-wide re-establishment of fixed exchange rates.

15.2 International Transmission of Business Cycles and Inflation Episodes

An obvious testable implication of the theory developed in the previous two chapters is that countries operating in an integrated world capital market under either fixed or flexible exchange rates will have approximately the same business cycles to the extent that the latter are monetary in origin, and the deviations of their inflation rates from their (perhaps different) underlying core inflation rates will be correlated. This will result from the fact that their monetary policies will be stochastically interdependent.

There is well-substantiated evidence that the business cycle is international in scope. Backus, Kehoe and Kydland [1] calculate the contemporaneous correlations of the logarithms of outputs of a number of countries with the logarithm of U.S. output after detrending the output variables using the Hodrick-Prescott technique.[23] The cross-correlations for the group of countries being examined here are as follows:

Canada	.77
France	.22
Germany	.42
Japan	.39
United Kingdom	.48

Contemporaneous correlations are not the best indication of the international scope of business cycle activity because they do not take account of differences in timing across countries and regions. In a spectral analysis of the GNP series of the U.S., U.K., Germany and Japan, Harris Dellas [17] found the following pairwise coherence coefficients:[24]

U.S.-Germany	0.9 at 2.5 years
U.S.-U.K.	0.7 at 9 quarters
U.S.-Japan	0.55 at 4 years
U.K.-Germany	0.6 at 2.5 to 4 years
U.K.-Japan	0.5 at 5 years
Germany-Japan	0.7 at 3.5 years

[23] The Hodrick-Prescott filter removes low-frequency variations from the data, acting as a flexible detrending procedure. For discussions of the technique see the paper by Hodrick and Prescott [55] .

[24] The coherence coefficient indicates the proportion of the variance of one economic series that is accounted for by variation in another series at some frequency.

Stefan Gerlach [46] also finds that the output movements of a group of countries – in particular, Belgium, Canada, France, Germany, Italy, the Netherlands, Norway, and Sweden – are correlated in the business cycle frequency band.

Table 15.2 presents the correlations between year-over-year GDP growth rates of the United States and Canada, United Kingdom, Japan, France and Germany over the post-Bretton-Woods period. The time-period for France and Germany is truncated to 1998, when these countries adopted the Euro and then further shortened for Germany to 1988 to forego the unification years.[25] Significant positive correlations of domestic and U.S. GDP growth rates are found in all cases. The growth rates are plotted in Figs. 15.8a and 15.8b.[26]

It is quite possible that the observed business cycles may have resulted, as the research just cited claims, from the interaction of real forces across countries, with monetary shocks playing no role at all. The theory developed here argues that monetary conditions should be similar across countries because monetary authorities will continually adjust domestic monetary conditions to prevent asymmetric monetary shocks from having portfolio effects on exchange rates. This will imply that the deviations of countries inflation rates from their respective core rates should be correlated. Because of the likelihood of real business cycle movements, conformity of inflation rates across countries should be a better test of the the theory advanced here than cyclical conformity of their output growth rates. The correlations of the domestic and U.S. inflation rates are also presented in Table 15.2 and are positive, all in excess of 0.7, and statistically significant. The countries' inflation rates are plotted in Figs. 15.9a and 15.9b – it is quite clear that inflationary peaks in the mid-1970s and early 1980s occurred in all the countries here examined.

Conformity of these major inflation episodes provides a strong degree of validation of the theory here developed. Year-to-year differences in inflation rates can be explained by differences in the growth rates of prices of the particular types of goods that are important in the respective countries and will be automatically financed by domestic governments that accommodate domestic demand for money changes to prevent portfolio shocks to nominal exchange rates. But major changes

[25] Correlations of real GDP growth rates and inflation rates were calculated in Gretl using the input file `coryinf.inp` and the results are in the output file `coryinf.got`.

[26] The relevant data for these figures as well as the inflation figures that follow can be found in the Gretl data file `jfdataqt.gdt` and the Excel worksheet file `jfdataqt.xls`.

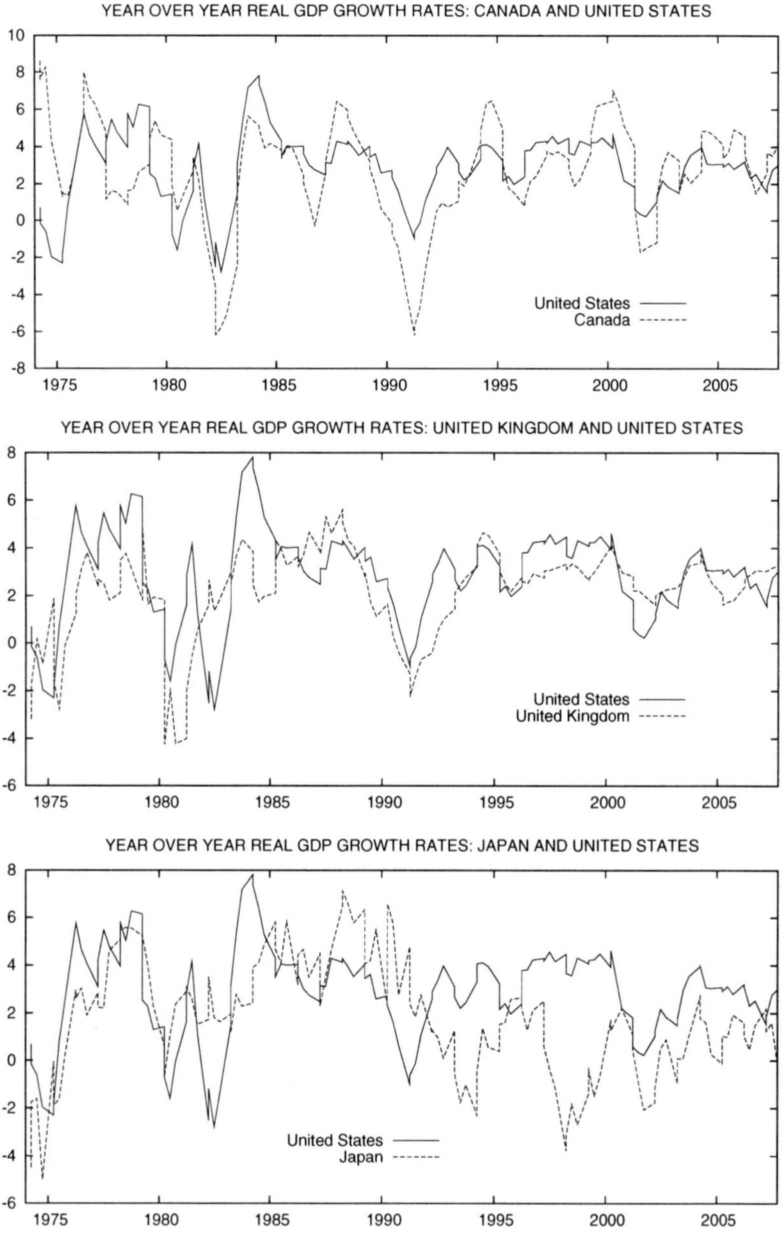

Fig. 15.8a. Year over year real GDP growth rates compared to that of United States

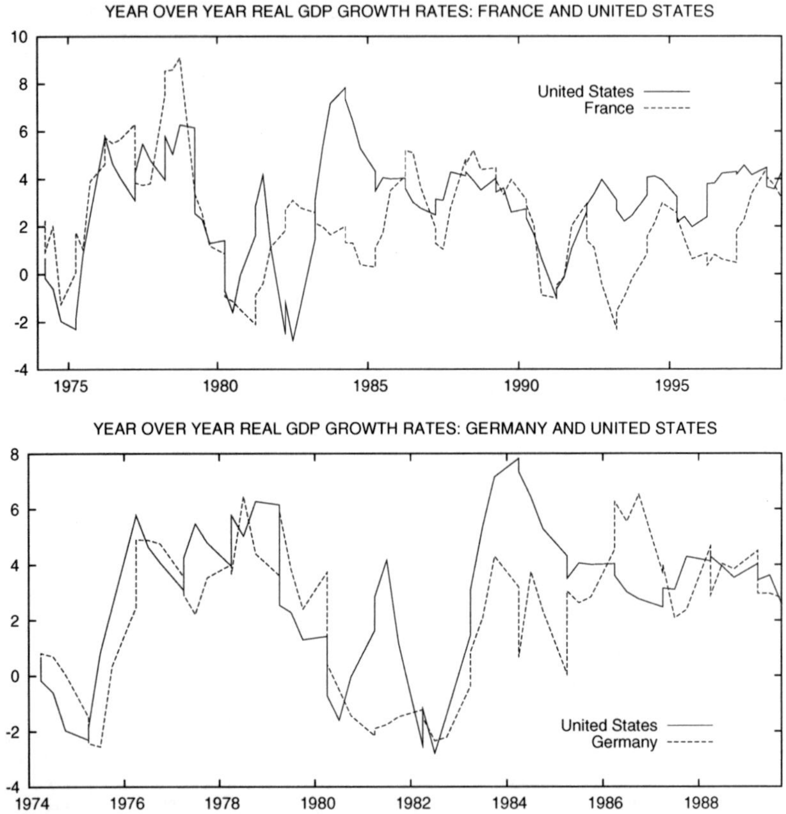

Fig. 15.8b. Year over year real GDP growth rates compared to that of United States

Table 15.2. Correlations betweeen domestic and U.S. real GDP growth and inflation rates, 1974–2007 for Canada, U.K. and Japan, 1974-98 for France and 1974-88 for Germany

	Real GDP Growth		Inflation Rate	
	Correlation	P-Value	Correlation	P-Value
Canada	0.528	0.000	0.874	0.000
United Kingdom	0.544	0.000	0.830	0.000
Japan	0.320	0.000	0.717	0.000
France	0.376	0.000	0.853	0.000
Germany	0.639	0.000	0.779	0.000

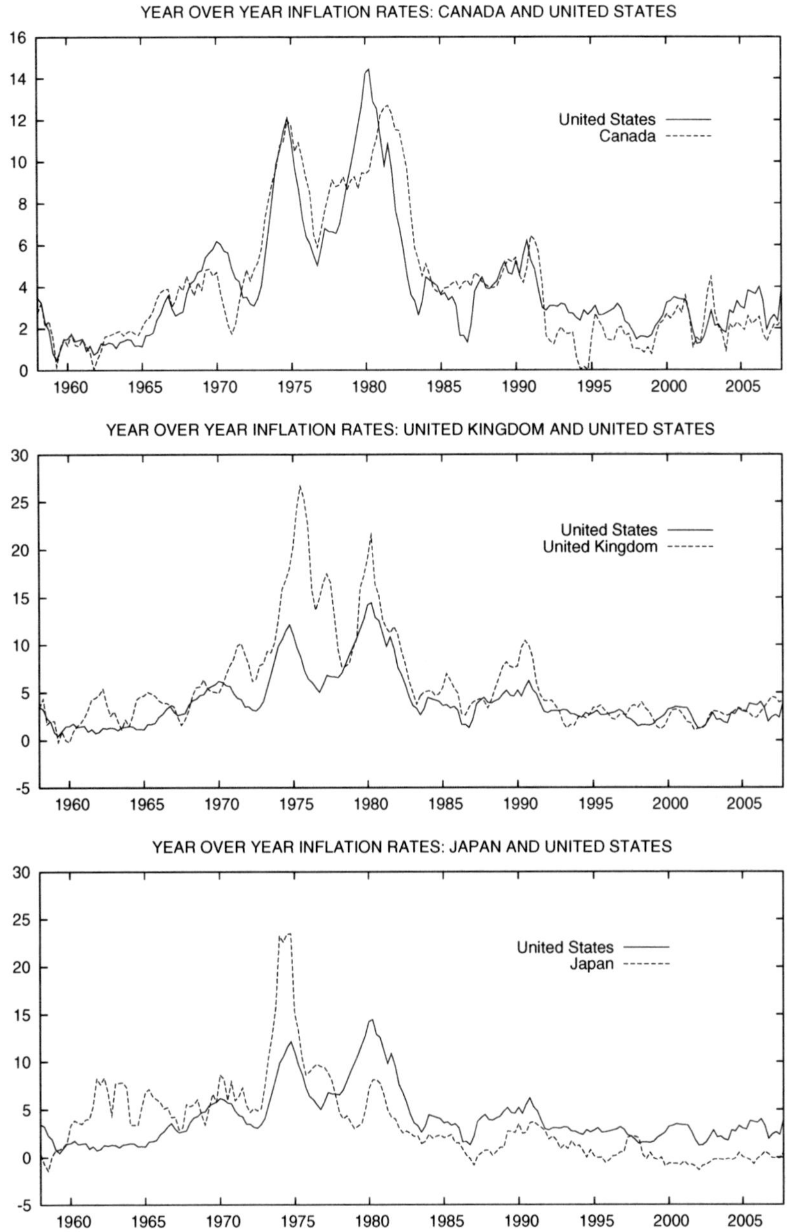

Fig. 15.9a. Year over year inflation rates compared to that of United States

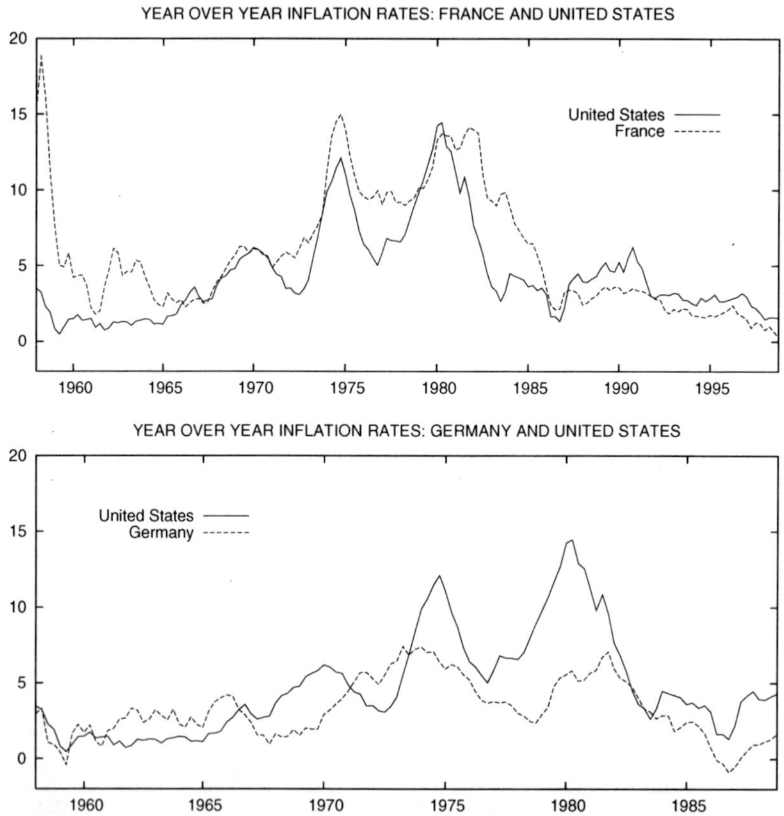

Fig. 15.9b. Year over year inflation rates compared to that of United States

in the supply or demand for money in the U.S. relative to what would be predicted by historic inflation and output growth rates should not only affect that country's output and prices, but should feed through as well onto price levels in foreign countries that pay attention to the stability of their U.S. dollar exchange rates.

Figure 15.10a plots the deviations of the logarithms of base money, M1, M2 and the consumer price index from standard linear trends for the United States for the period 1960 through 2007.[27] The base money aggregate has been adjusted so that increases (reductions) in reserve requirements result in corresponding reductions (increases) in the ad-

[27] The data on which this figure and Figs. 15.10b and 15.10c are based can be found in the Gretl and XLispStat data files `jfdataqt.gdt` and `jfdataqt.lsp` and in the Excel worksheet file `jfdataqt.xls`. The data in the figures are organized using the XLispStat batch file `monpol.lsp`.

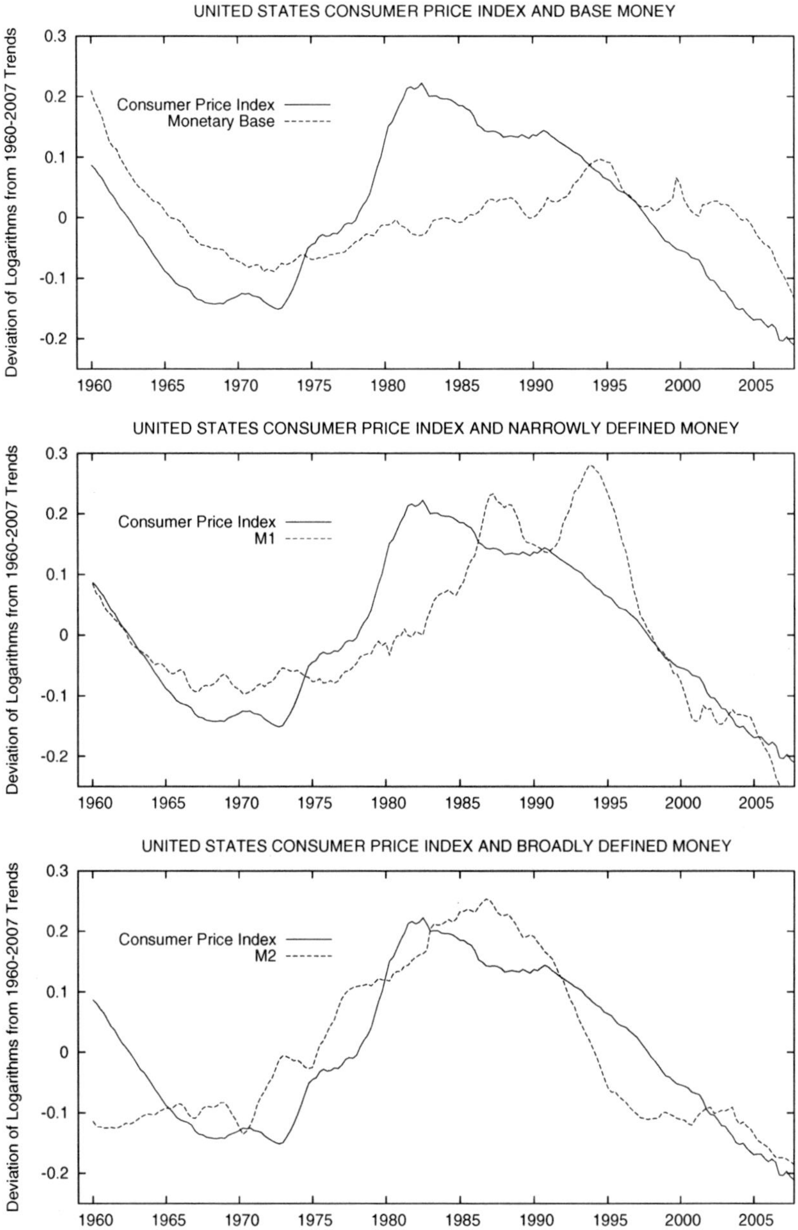

Fig. 15.10a. Deviations of the logarithms of monetary aggregates and price levels from their trends

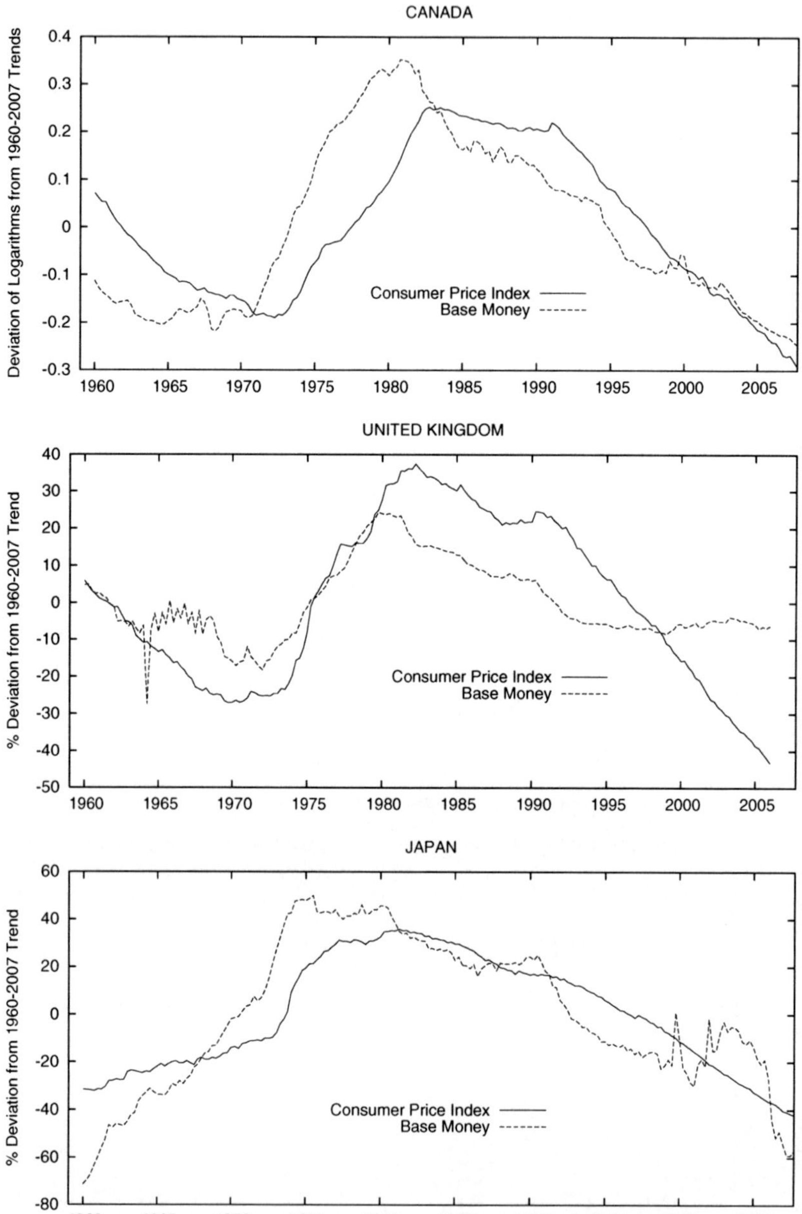

Fig. 15.10b. Deviations of the logarithms of monetary aggregates and price levels from their trends

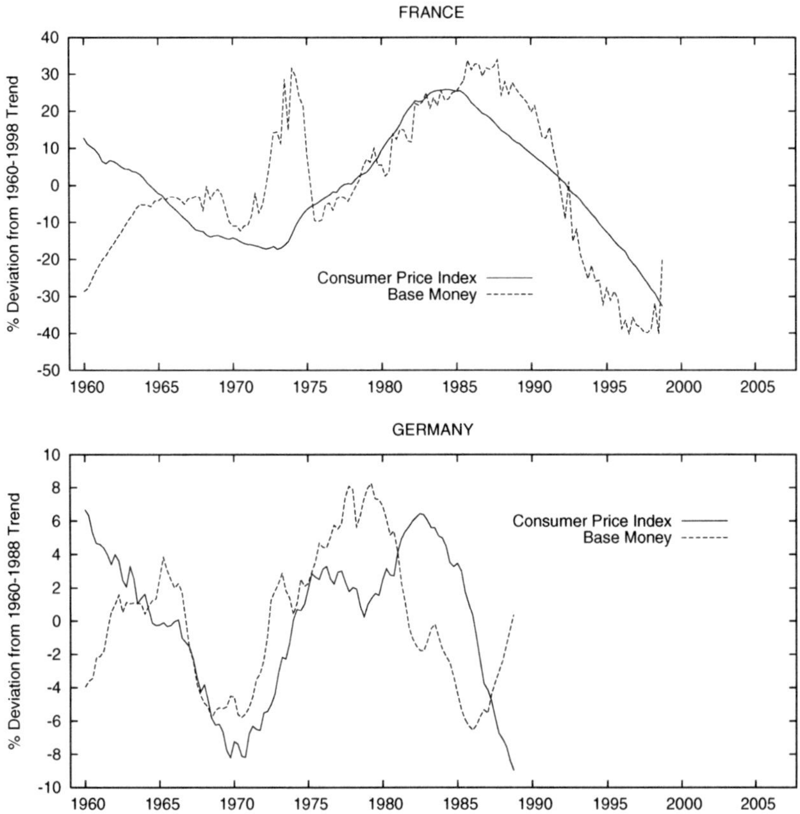

Fig. 15.10c. Deviations of the logarithms of monetary aggregates and price levels from their trends

justed series relative to the actual. Making these appropriate adjustments results in no fundamental difference in the conclusions reached. Note the increase in the logarithm of the consumer price index relative to trend between the early 1970s and the early 1980s and the decline relative to trend thereafter. This pattern bears no relationship to the time path of the logarithm of U.S. base money which showed relatively small, rather uniform and slightly increasing deviations around trend over the period. By contrast the patterns of deviations of the logarithms of M1 and M2 conform roughly with the deviations of the logarithm of the consumer price index, with M2 leading the peak in the CPI and M1 lagging it. Since these monetary aggregates together measure the time path of liquidity in the economy it is reasonable to conclude that they, and certainly not base money, explain the observed movements of the time path of the logarithm of the consumer price index. The inflation of the late 1970s and early 1980s and its demise thereafter appears to be the result of rises and subsequent falls in the money multipliers, not base money. As in the case of the Great Depression of the nineteen-thirties, the U.S. authorities appear to have failed to produce a time path base money that would offset changes in the money multipliers to stabilize M1 and M2 growth and thereby the domestic inflation rate.

The panels of Figs. 15.10b and 15.10c clearly indicate variations in the logarithms of other countries' base money aggregates relative to trend that can explain deviations in the logarithms of their CPI levels relative to trend that were very similar to the U.S. CPI movements.

This is exactly what the theory developed here predicts – the other countries' monetary authorities made adjustments in their base money aggregates sufficient, in the absence of domestic money multiplier changes, to finance roughly the same increases and declines of domestic prices relative to trend as occurred in the United States. And this result is fully consistent with the finding in Part II that money supply shocks had no significant effects on real exchange rate movements.

Although a complete analysis of the operation of U.S. monetary policy over this period is beyond the scope of this monograph, it is worthwhile to look briefly at what might have caused the money multiplier movements that seem to have driven that country's price level. Figure 15.11 plots the deviations of the logarithms of the monetary base, M2 and the implicit GDP deflator in the U.S. over a long historical period with respect to trends calculated for that whole period.[28] It is clear that there was a substantial upward shift in the trend of base money growth after the mid-1960s and that this new trend continued at least to the mid-1990s. This shift in base-money trend is a reasonable basic cause of the increase in inflation, quite apart from the resulting increases in M1 and M2. A plausible explanation of this shift in trend is the financing of the Viet-Nam War. The even greater upward shift of the trend of the logarithm of M2 after 1970 can probably be explained by the effect of the resulting inflation on interest rates and the associated opportunity cost of holding cash relative to time and savings deposits. While interest rates on those deposits were regulated,

[28] These data are contained in the Gretl file `jfdataan.gdt` and in the Excel worksheet file `jfdataan.xls`.

the ceilings were increased and deposits in denominations of $100,000 or more were exempt from the ceilings.[29]

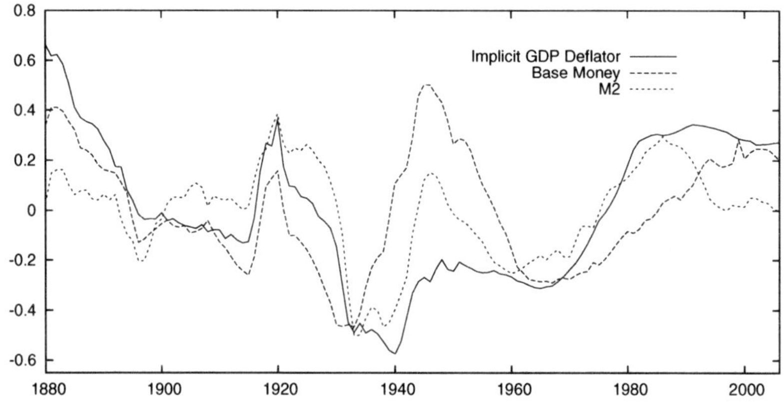

Fig. 15.11. Historical annual deviations of the logarithms of base money, M2 and the GDP deflator in the United States from their 1880-2006 trends.

Since the growth of U.S. base money continued at roughly the same rate well past 1990, the downward adjustment of the logarithm of the price level relative to trend after 1980 is clearly associated with the decline M2 growth and corresponding decline in the money multiplier. This would appear to be a consequence of deregulation associated with the elimination of regulation-Q. The gradual relaxation of constraints on interest paid for savings and time deposits between 1980 and 1986 would have the effect of reducing the cost of holding money and thereby increasing the demand for it and reducing aggregate demand for output. It is evident from Fig. 15.8a that output growth in the U.S. was lower in the early 1980s than previously, and it can be seen from Fig. 15.9a that the U.S. inflation rate also declined. Then, as the years passed, the reduction in nominal interest rates associated with the decline in inflation should have reduced the costs of holding cash rather than time and savings deposits, leading to the decline in the M2 multiplier. The effect on the ratio of currency to total deposits is evident in the middle panel of Fig. 15.12. The effects on the ratio of currency to demand deposits and the corresponding reserve/deposit ratio are shown in the top panel of that figure. The effect on the M1 multiplier is more

[29] Gilbert [47] provides an excellent discussion of regulation-Q and its demise in the 1980s. The average interest rate on time and savings deposits is plotted there in Chart 3 on page 20.

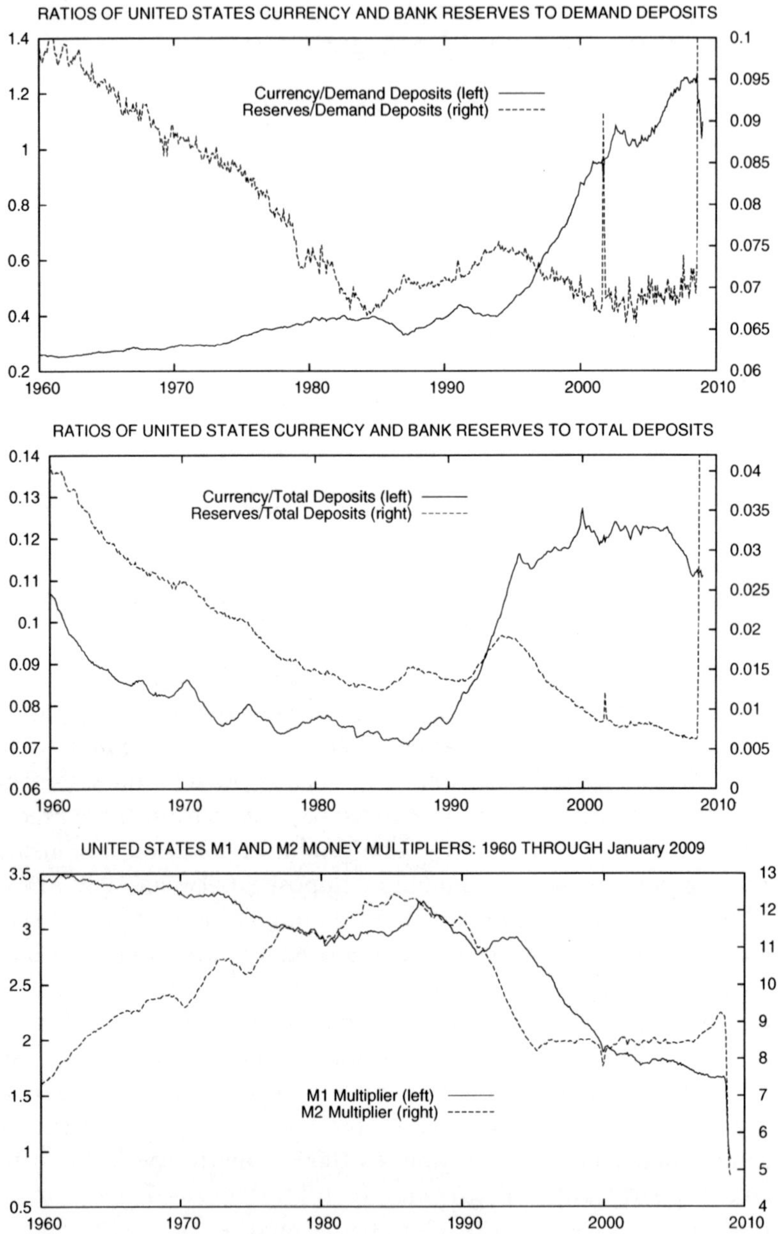

Fig. 15.12. Ratios of currency and reserves to deposits in the United States and resulting money multipliers

complicated in that both during and after regulation-Q no interest was allowed on demand deposits. Taking into account the changes in the ratios of both currency and reserves to deposits, the effects on the money multipliers during the period 1985 through 1995 are shown in the bottom panel of Fig. 15.12.[30]

While it may be an exaggeration to claim that the U.S. Federal Reserve under Chairman Paul Volker 'took the bull by the horns' and wrestled U.S. inflation to the ground, it is nevertheless the case that a correct policy was followed – the monetary aggregates were allowed to decline relative to trend by not increasing base money to compensate for increases in the demand for money and declines in the money multipliers. Of course, the Federal Reserve should have began reducing the rate of growth of base money much earlier and, indeed, should not have mistakenly financed the Viet-Nam War with its expansion of that aggregate from the mid-1960s onward. In any case, it is easier to criticize monetary policy on the basis of hindsight than to conduct it using information available at the time.

Although the data series analyzed throughout this monograph end with the year 2007, the temptation to extend the series in Fig. 15.12 as far as possible was overwhelming, given the world-wide financial crisis and recession at the time of this writing in early 2009. As the three panels clearly show, although the ratio of currency to demand deposits in the United States fell during the crisis the reserve/deposit ratios jumped upward off the charts! And the U.S. M1 and M2 multipliers declined very substantially, reminding one of the Great Depression! Accordingly, the logarithms of the U.S. M1 and M2 aggregates are plotted in the top panel of Fig. 15.13. The Federal Reserve has expanded base money sufficiently to more than offset the effects of these money multiplier changes on the two monetary aggregates. And, even though it is not clear from the top panel, the upward shift of the percentage deviation of M2 from the January 1999 through January 2009 trend, shown in the bottom panel, is very substantial. Ben Bernanke, who made distinguished research contributions as a university economist before his appointment as Federal Reserve Chairman, is not allowing

[30] Letting, for present purposes only, M denote the money aggregate, H the stock of base or high-powered money, C the stock of currency, R the stock of reserves and D the stock of deposits, and c and r the respective ratios of currency and reserves to deposits, the money multiplier can be expressed as

$$\frac{M}{H} = \frac{C+D}{R+D} = \frac{c+1}{c+r}.$$

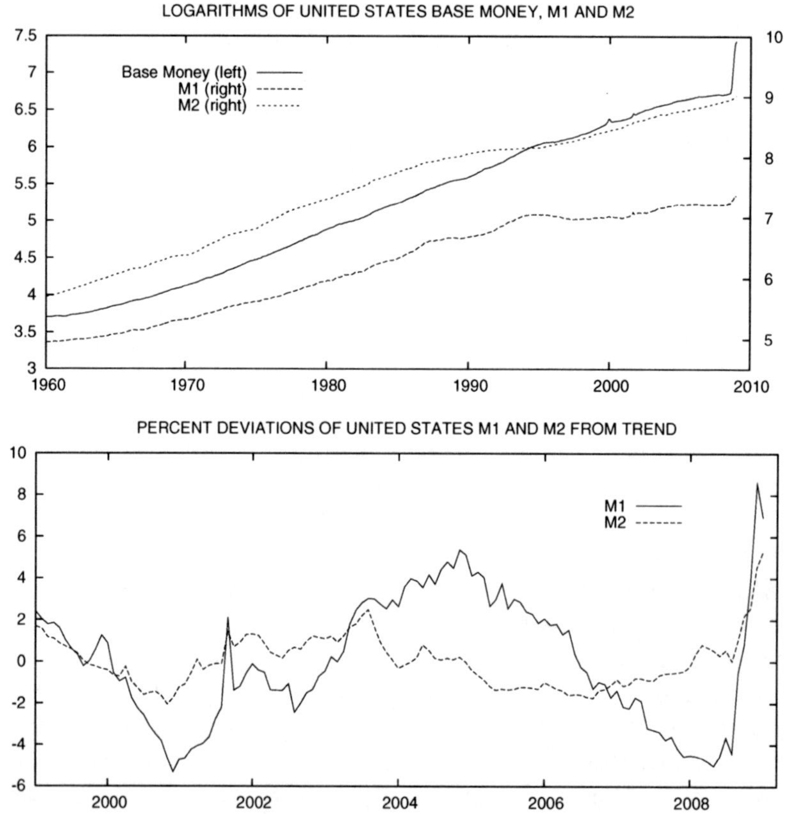

Fig. 15.13. United States base money and M1 and M2 aggregates from January 1960 through January 2009, expressed as logarithms of nominal levels and percentage deviations of M1 and M2 from their January 1999 through January 2009 trends

past mistakes to be repeated. Whether the observed monetary expansion is too little or too much is very difficult determine because the demand for money may have increased to a degree that is impossible to measure and the extent to which the distress in the financial system may be having negative effects on investment and output and employment independently of the magnitudes of the monetary aggregates is also impossible to quantify.

15.3 The European Monetary Union

The final section of this chapter examines the monetary union in Europe from the perspective of the analytical framework and evidence presented above.[31] As a basis for comparison, the real exchange rate behaviour of members of a successful monetary union, Canada, is presented in Fig. 15.14. Table 15.3 presents some relevant statistics regarding these real exchange rate movements. The real exchange rates are approximated by taking the ratio of each provincial consumer price index to the national consumer price index. These indices span the period from January 1979 through April 2007. The right-most column in the Table redoes the statistical calculations for period from January 2000 through April 2007 during which the euro has been fully in place.[32] The provinces differ widely in their resource bases and the types of technology being applied and Quebec differs significantly from the other provinces in language and culture.

As can be seen in Fig. 15.14, in no case does a provincial real exchange rate rise above 9% or fall below 4% of its 1992 level. Very few major real exchange rate movements have occurred and in only three instances, one in Newfoundland, one in Alberta and one in British Columbia, were there movements in excess of 1% per year, all over short time intervals. The real exchange rate of Newfoundland with respect to Canada as a whole rose by about 3% of its 1992 level between 1979 and 1982 and then declined about 6% between 1986 and 1990. General, but much more shallow, declines occurred in the other Maritime Provinces between 1979 and 1990. Very shallow declines occurred in Saskatchewan and Manitoba between the beginning of 1979 and the mid-1990s and then reversed themselves by the late-1990s. The real exchange rates of Alberta and British Columbia declined by about 6% of their 1992 levels between the early- and late-1980s. Thereafter, Alberta's real exchange rate increased rather steadily by over 10%, to about 9% above its 1992 level by early 2007. British Columbia's real exchange rate rose by about 6% of its 1992 level between the early-

[31] For a review of the history and development of European monetary integration, see Jay Levin's book [69].

[32] The data are provided in the Gretl file `jfdataeu.gdt` and the Excel worksheet file `jfdataeu.xls` and are described in the text file `jfdataeu.cat`. The basic data are also in the file `jfdataeu.lsp` and the calculations of the remaining series in `jfdataeu.gdt` and `jfdataeu.xls` are checked in XLispStat using the batch file `eucaprex.lsp`. The calculations for the table are also performed in the Gretl script file `eucaprex.inp` and are in the output file `eucaprex.got`.

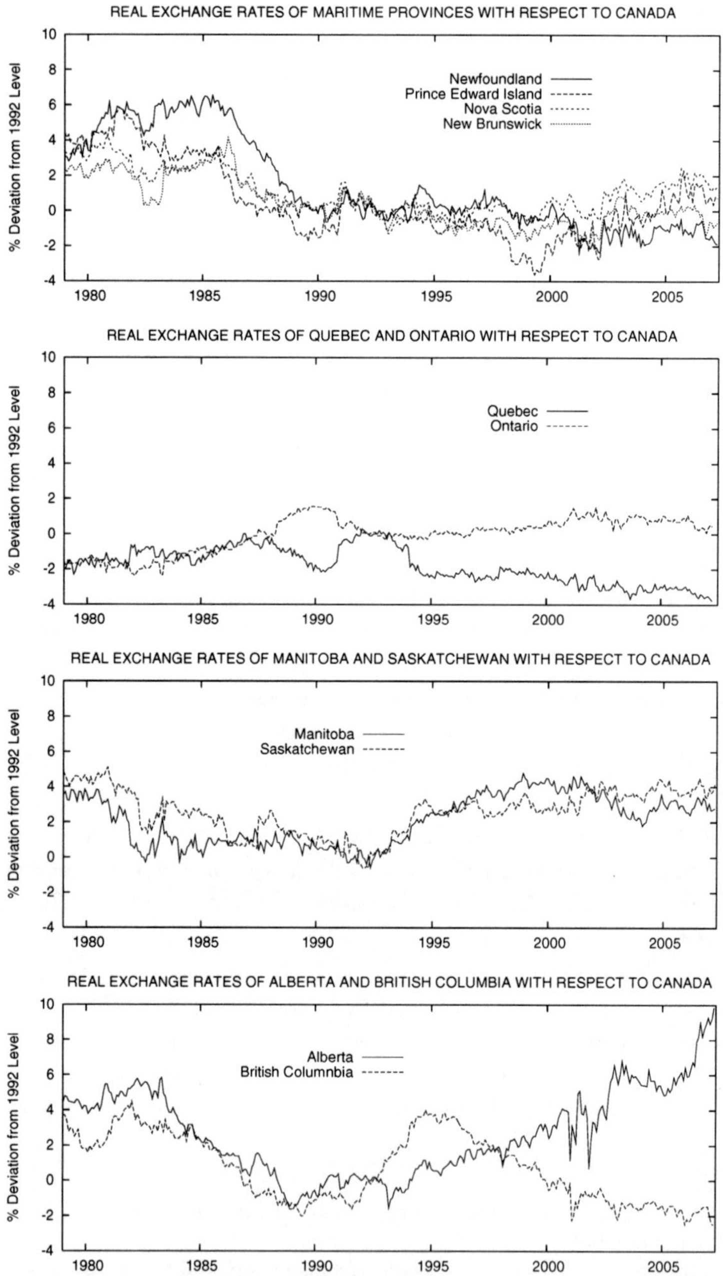

Fig. 15.14. Real exchange rates of the Canadian provinces with respect to Canada

Table 15.3. Statistics of real exchange rate movements of Canadian Provinces relative to Canada as a whole and of Canada relative to the United States and original Eurozone countries less Ireland.

		1979:1–2007:4 % of 2005 base	2000:1–2007:4 % of 2005 base
Newfoundland	Mean	1.40	-1.18
	Standard Deviation	2.65	0.61
	Maximum	6.53	0.45
	Minimum	-2.40	-2.40
	Range	8.94	2.85
Prince Edward Island	Mean	0.56	-0.34
	Standard Deviation	2.19	1.19
	Maximum	5.86	2.18
	Minimum	-3.62	-2.74
	Range	9.48	4.92
Nova Scotia	Mean	1.11	1.03
	Standard Deviation	1.27	0.75
	Maximum	4.20	2.48
	Minimum	-1.28	-0.51
	Range	5.48	2.99
New Brunswick	Mean	0.43	-0.39
	Standard Deviation	1.35	0.66
	Maximum	4.16	0.90
	Minimum	-1.74	-1.71
	Range	5.90	2.61
Quebec	Mean	-1.79	-3.00
	Standard Deviation	1.00	0.36
	Maximum	0.30	-2.14
	Minimum	-3.76	-3.76
	Range	4.07	1.62
Ontario	Mean	-0.05	0.79
	Standard Deviation	1.01	0.29
	Maximum	1.55	1.53
	Minimum	-2.38	0.08
	Range	3.93	1.45

Continued on Next Page

Table 15.3. Continued from previous page

		1979:1–2007:4 % of 1992 base	2000:1–2007:4 % of 2005 base
Manitoba	Mean	2.12	3.19
	Standard Deviation	1.42	0.68
	Maximum	4.78	4.60
	Minimum	-0.60	1.79
	Range	5.38	2.81
Saskatchewan	Mean	2.59	3.59
	Standard Deviation	1.27	0.51
	Maximum	5.09	4.51
	Minimum	-0.60	2.40
	Range	5.70	2.11
Alberta	Mean	2.69	5.23
	Standard Deviation	2.46	1.84
	Maximum	9.86	9.86
	Minimum	-1.63	0.69
	Range	11.49	9.17
British Columbia	Mean	0.73	-1.28
	Standard Deviation	1.94	0.63
	Maximum	4.51	0.17
	Minimum	-2.48	-2.48
	Range	6.99	2.66
Canada vs. U.S.	Mean	-2.53	-9.70
	Standard Deviation	10.42	10.38
	Maximum	18.33	7.90
	Minimum	-23.91	-23.91
	Range	42.24	31.81
Canada vs. Eurozone	Mean	4.86	1.51
	Standard Deviation	16.67	6.77
	Maximum	58.63	16.06
	Minimum	-19.12	-10.46
	Range	77.76	26.52

and mid-1990s and declined rather continuously by about the same percentage by early 2007.

It is important to note that the Canadian Federal Government has traditionally made 'equalization payments' to those provinces having the lowest per capita incomes. It is reasonable to expect that these payments would be eventually adjusted to offset the wealth effects of any major inter-provincial real exchange rate movements that are not eliminated by inter-provincial migration. Over the years such migration has been substantial.

The Canadian inter-provincial real exchange rate movements pale to insignificance when compared to the movements of the real exchange rates of Canada and the original eleven Eurozone countries minus Ireland with respect to the United States, presented for the period from 1957 through mid-2008 in Fig. 15.15 and Table 15.4. Relevant statistics for the real exchange rates of Canada with respect to the United States and the Eurozone as defined above are also presented in the bottom two sections of Table 15.3. Because of data limitations, Ireland could not be included in calculating real exchange rates with respect to the Eurozone.[33] The ranges of variation and the standard deviations of the real exchange rates of Canada with respect to the United States and the eleven original Eurozone countries minus Ireland are many times the magnitudes of those statistics for the real exchange rates of the individual provinces with respect to Canada.[34]

The real and nominal exchange rates and price level ratios of the individual eleven Eurozone countries with respect to the Eurozone, defined as the eleven countries less Ireland, are plotted in Figs. 15.16a, 15.16b, 15.16c and 15.16d. And Figs. 15.17a and 15.17b present these same variables for Sweden, Denmark and the United Kingdom, which are in the European Union but not the Eurozone, and Norway and Switzerland, which are not even in the European Union. Relevant statistics regarding the movements in all these real exchange rates are presented in Table 15.5. As in the case of the real exchange rates of the Canadian provinces with respect to Canada, the calculations for the individual Eurozone countries are with respect to the original eleven-country Eurozone as a whole minus Ireland, not the Eurozone so de-

[33] The GDP weights used in calculating the real exchange rate of the Eurozone can be found on page 4 of Levin [69].

[34] These calculations and all others pertaining to the Eurozone are performed in the XLispStat batch file `eucaprex.lsp` and and the statistical results are also calculated in Gretl using the input file `eucaprex.inp` and are contained in the output file `eucaprex.got`. The data are contained in `jfdataeu.lsp`, `jfdataeu.gdt` and `jfdataeu.xls` and are described in the text file `jfdataeu.cat`.

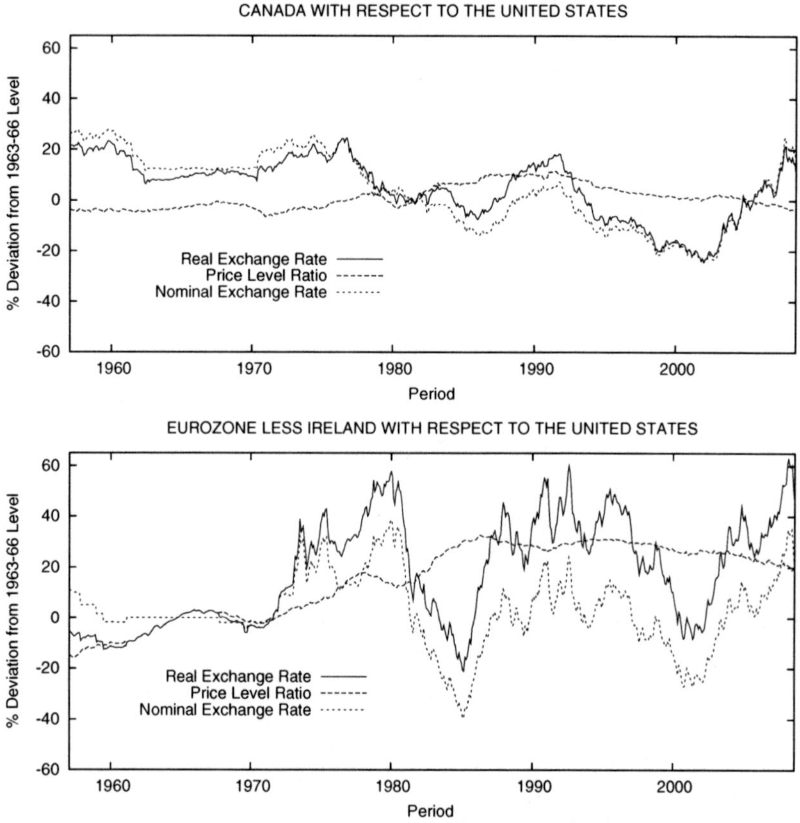

Fig. 15.15. Real and nominal exchange rates and price level ratios of Canada and the Eurozone minus Ireland with respect to the the United States

Table 15.4. Statistics of real exchange rate movements of Canada and the eleven original Euro Area countries less Ireland with respect to the United States from January 1957 through August 2008 for Canada and through September 2008 for the Euro countries, in percentages of 1963–66 Levels

	Canada	Eurozone
Mean	-3.61	17.68
Standard Deviation	10.90	20.75
Slope – % per year	-0.48	0.77
Maximum	14.23	62.84
Minimum	-30.21	-21.15
Range	44.44	84.00

fined minus both Ireland and the individual country in question. This approximation avoids complexities of calculation while making no difference with regard to the conclusions reached.

The average range of variation of the Eurozone countries' real exchange rates with respect to the Eurozone as a whole over the period from January 2000 through December 2008, calculated from Table 15.5, is about 5.7 percent of 2005 levels as compared to the average range of variation of Canadian provinces' real exchange rate with respect to Canada as a whole, which is about 3.4 percent of 2005 levels. But this masks the fact that, as evident from Figs. 15.16a through 15.16d, the Eurozone countries' real exchange rates each tended to move rather uniformly in one direction. In particular, the real exchange rates of Italy, Ireland, Spain, Portugal and Greece tended to rise throughout the period while those of France, Germany and Austria tended to fall. The movements of the countries' price level ratios with respect to the Eurozone group for the period prior to 1999 indicates clearly that for Italy, Spain, Portugal and Greece the adoption of the euro required the elimination of monetary finance of government expenditures and the end to chronic inflation. It is reasonable to expect that this greater stability will have resulted in movements of resources to these countries from Germany, France and Austria in response, accounting for the observed trends in real exchange rates. The real exchange rates of Belgium and Luxembourg with respect to the Eurozone less Ireland tended to trend upward very slightly while that of the Netherlands tended to move slightly upward to mid-2003 and then slightly downward thereafter. Some of the upward trends in those countries experiencing them were in excess of 1% of 2005 levels per year. And the declines in France and Germany with respect to the rest of the Eurozone might well have been as great as 1% of 2005 levels because these countries together account for more that 50 percent of the GDP of the Eurozone as here measured.

Examination of Figs. 15.16a and 15.16b indicates very similar movements of the real exchange rates in Belgium, the Netherlands, Luxembourg, Germany, Austria and France between 1992 and 1999. And the top two panels of Figs. 15.16c and 15.16d indicate sharp opposite movements in Italy, Finland, Spain and Portugal. These real exchange rate adjustments are likely a consequence of the aftermath of German unification – resources were drawn from the latter countries to Germany and its neighbors to produce goods and capital for the revitalization of East Germany.

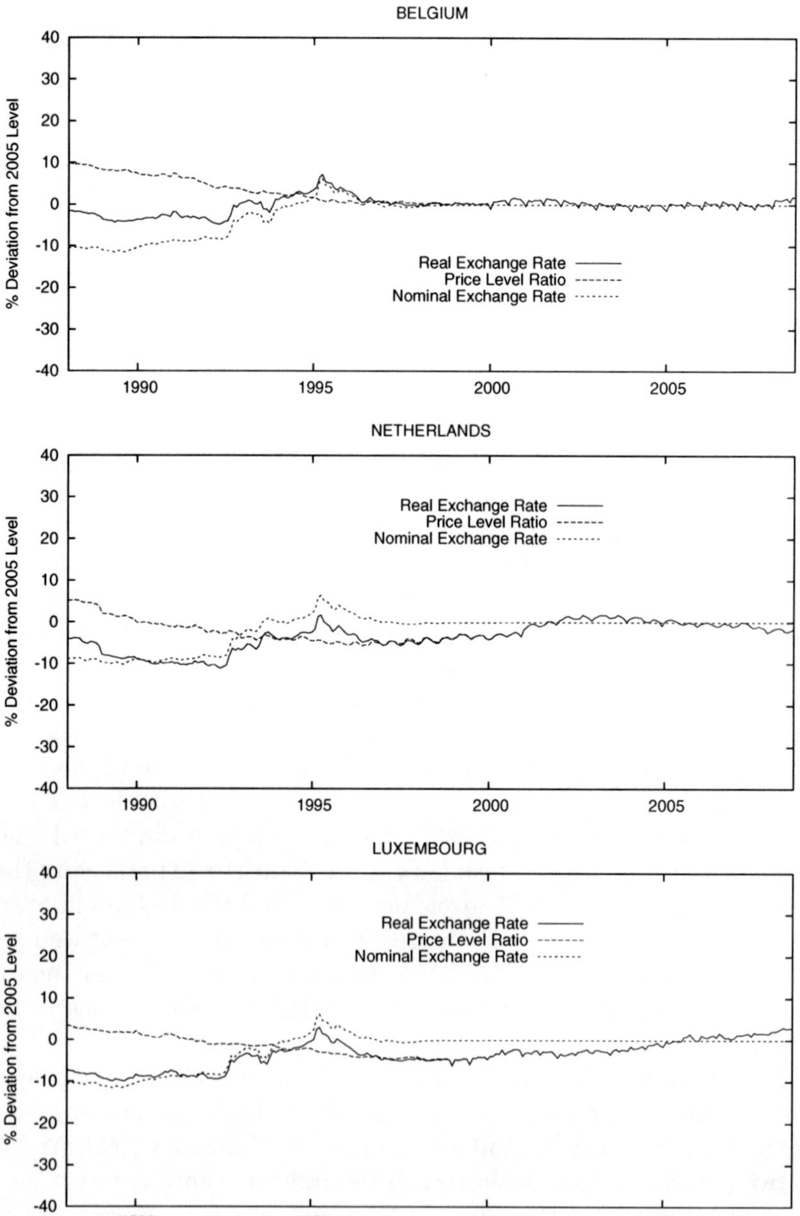

Fig. 15.16a. Real and nominal exchange rates and price level ratios of Eurozone countries with respect to the Eurozone exclusive of Ireland

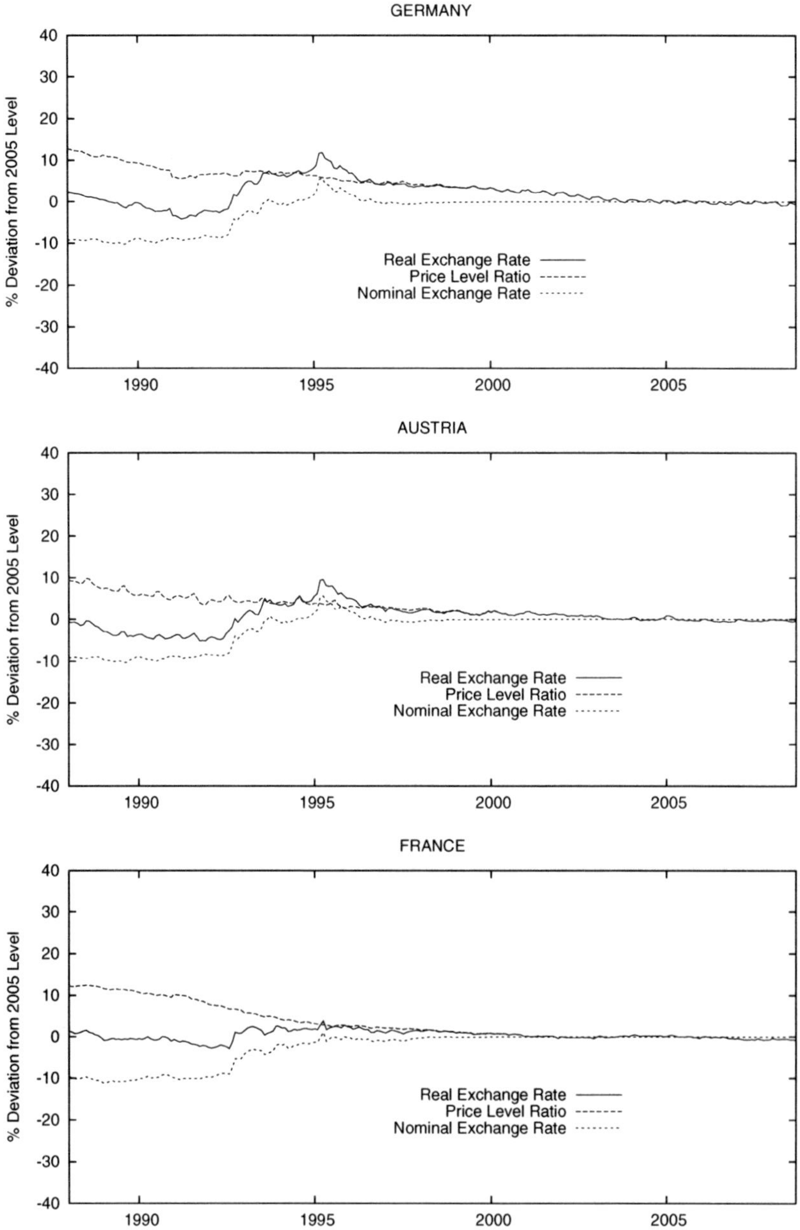

Fig. 15.16b. Real and nominal exchange rates and price level ratios of Eurozone countries with respect to the Eurozone exclusive of Ireland

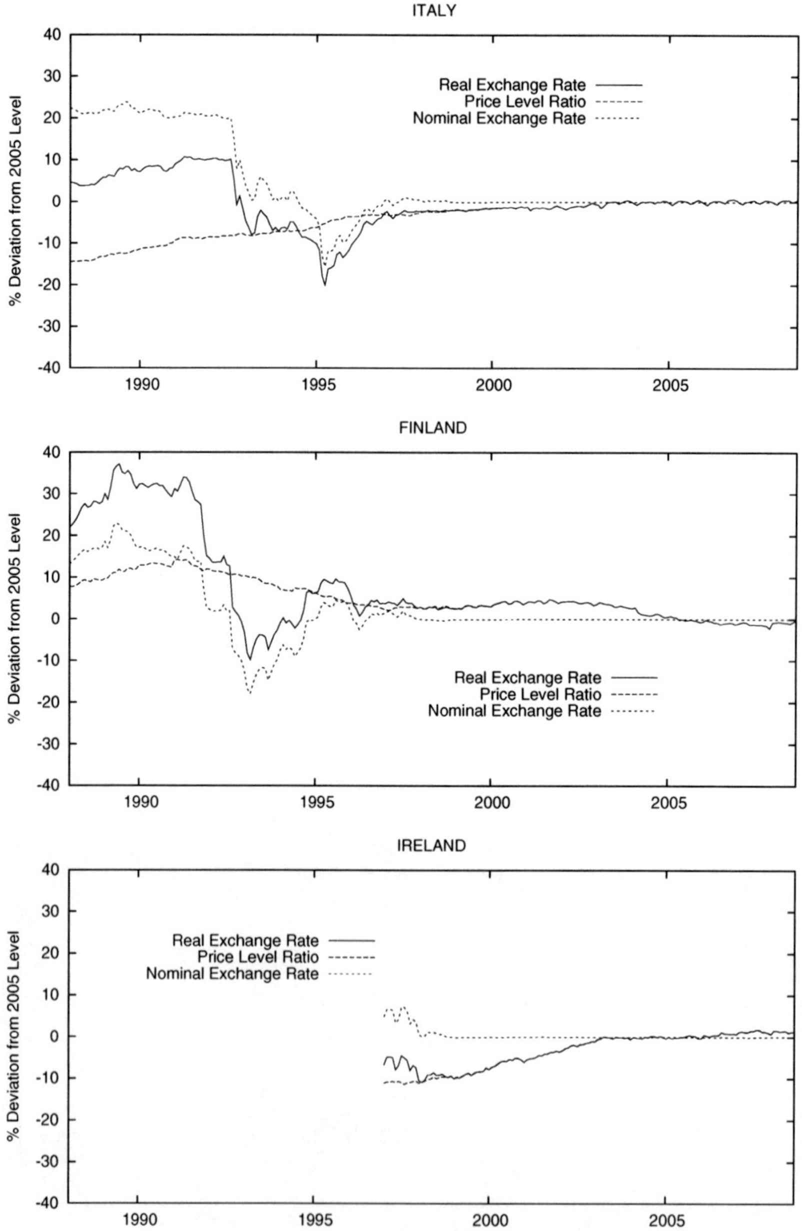

Fig. 15.16c. Real and nominal exchange rates and price level ratios of Eurozone countries with respect to the Eurozone exclusive of Ireland

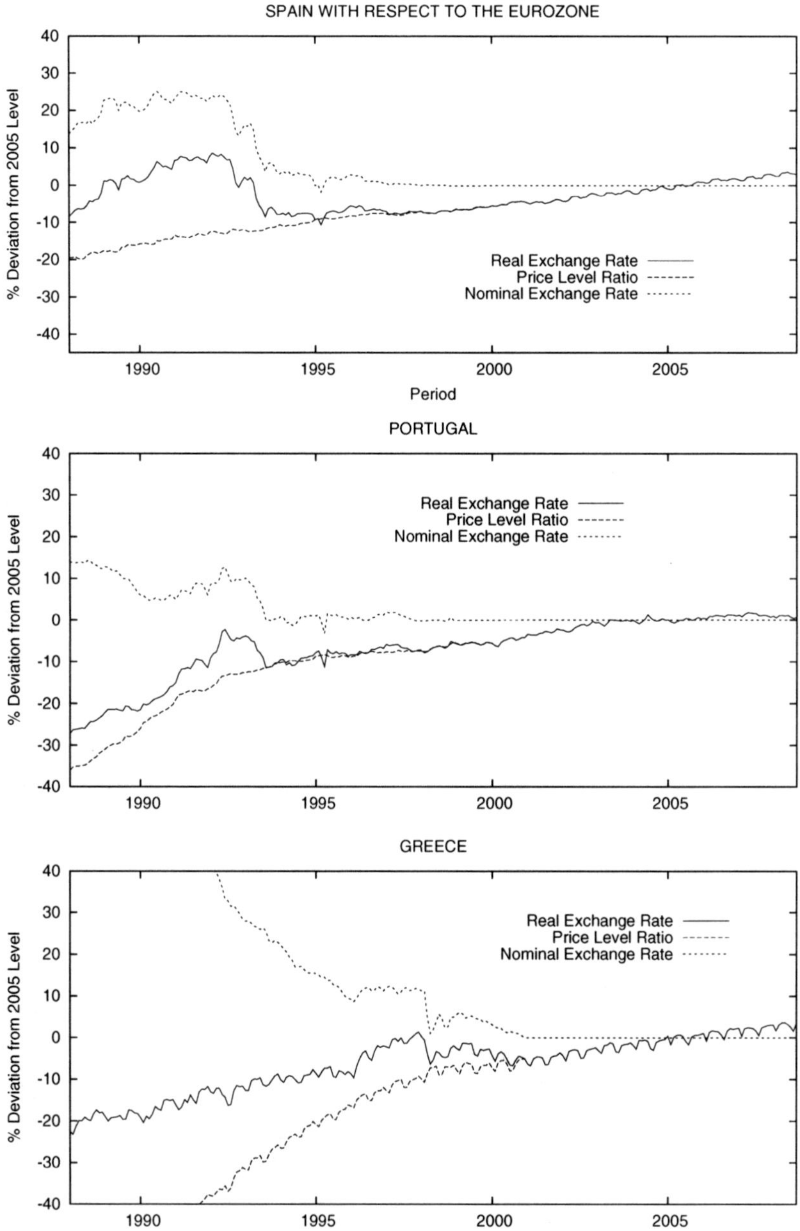

Fig. 15.16d. Real and nominal exchange rates and price level ratios of Eurozone countries with respect to the Eurozone exclusive of Ireland

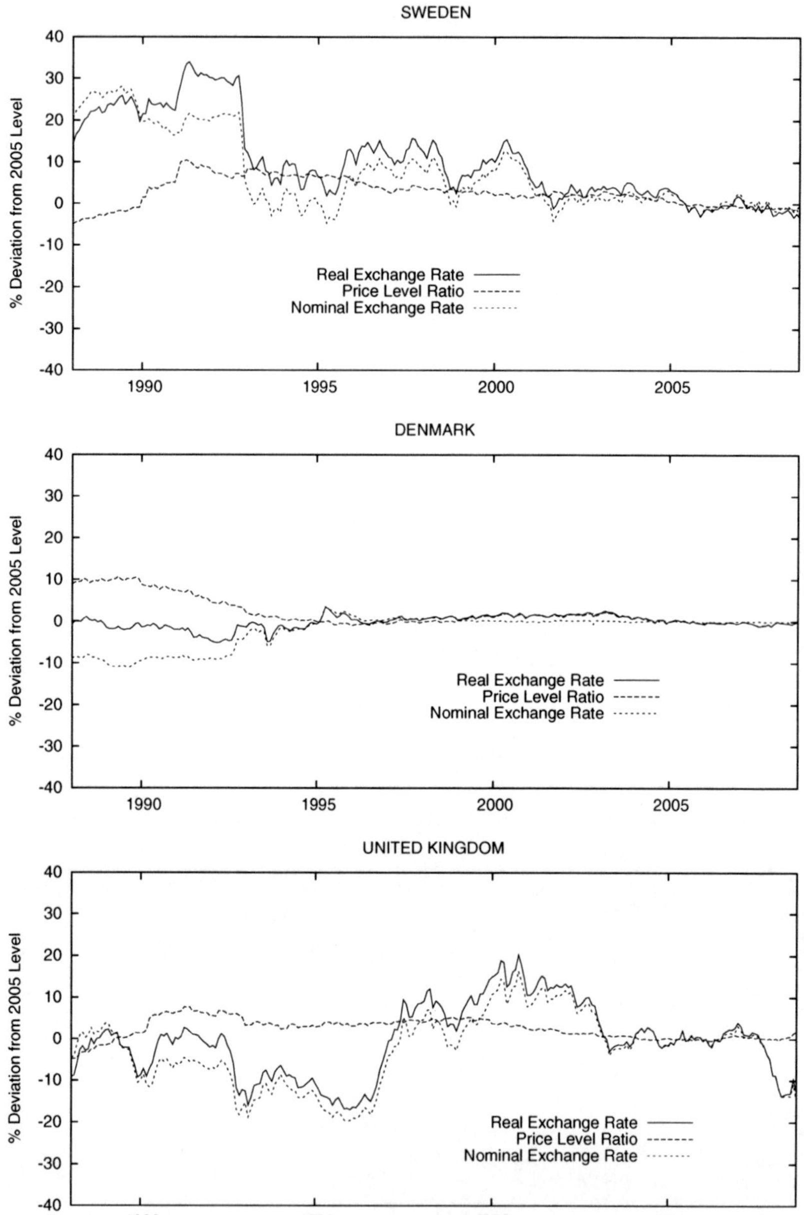

Fig. 15.17a. Real and nominal exchange rates and price level ratios of other European countries with respect to the Eurozone

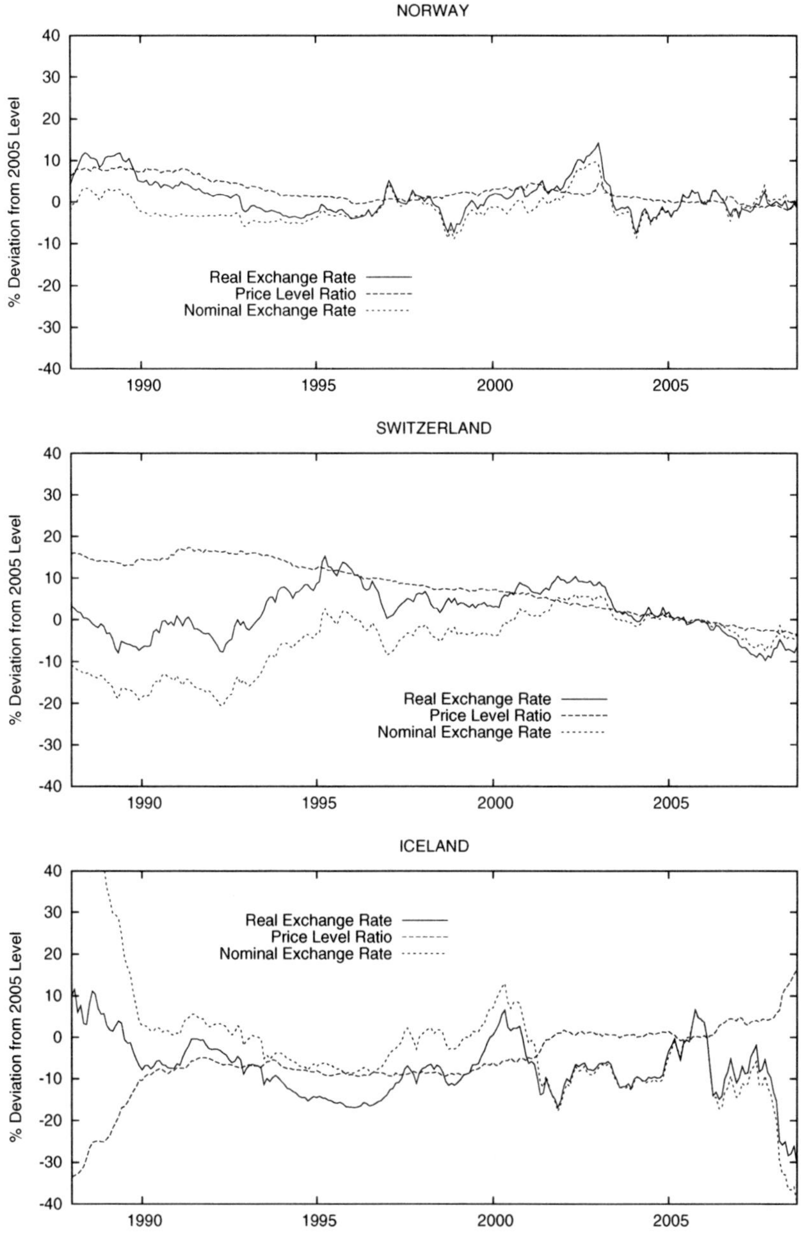

Fig. 15.17b. Real and nominal exchange rates and price level ratios of other European countries with respect to the the Eurozone

Table 15.5. Statistics of real exchange rate movements relative to the eleven original Eurozone countries less Ireland in percentages of 2005 levels, January 1974 through September 2008

		1974–87	1988–93	1994–99	2000–08
Belgium	Mean	5.33	-2.56	1.47	0.29
	Standard Deviation	7.51	1.57	1.78	0.76
	Slope – % per year	0.18	-0.07	0.04	0.01
	Maximum	21.26	1.28	7.21	1.97
	Minimum	-4.99	-4.84	-0.39	-1.48
	Range	26.25	6.13	7.60	3.45
Netherlands	Mean	0.13	-7.80	-3.55	-0.39
	Standard Deviation	3.84	2.46	1.50	1.45
	Slope – % per year	-0.01	-0.24	-0.09	0.01
	Maximum	9.77	-2.46	1.71	1.80
	Minimum	-5.69	-11.11	-5.62	-4.19
	Range	15.46	8.65	7.34	5.99
Luxembourg	Mean	1.66	-7.74	-3.16	-1.88
	Standard Deviation	7.47	1.93	2.09	2.10
	Slope – % per year	0.02	-0.22	-0.08	-0.02
	Maximum	16.14	-2.61	3.03	3.07
	Minimum	-8.90	-9.92	-6.19	-4.66
	Range	25.04	7.31	9.22	7.73
Germany	Mean	5.53	0.08	5.42	0.72
	Standard Deviation	3.77	3.04	2.20	1.17
	Slope – % per year	0.20	0.00	0.13	0.01
	Maximum	15.06	7.42	11.85	3.36
	Minimum	0.37	-4.22	3.10	-0.94
	Range	14.69	11.64	8.75	4.30
Austria	Mean	-6.27	-2.23	3.36	0.33
	Standard Deviation	3.16	2.67	2.08	0.72
	Slope – % per year	-0.24	-0.06	0.08	0.01
	Maximum	0.10	4.75	9.55	2.07
	Minimum	-13.58	-5.17	0.93	-0.64
	Range	13.68	9.92	8.62	2.71

Continued on Next Page

Table 15.5. Continued from previous page

		1974–87	1988–93	1994–99	2000–08
France	Mean	3.90	-0.28	1.55	-0.07
	Standard Deviation	2.88	1.41	0.62	0.39
	Slope – % per year	0.14	-0.01	0.04	0.00
	Maximum	10.91	2.60	3.94	0.78
	Minimum	-3.36	-2.89	0.54	-0.84
	Range	14.27	5.49	3.40	1.62
Italy	Mean	-5.06	5.23	-5.72	-0.45
	Standard Deviation	7.05	5.47	4.59	0.73
	Slope – % per year	-0.17	-0.15	-0.14	-0.01
	Maximum	5.94	10.72	-1.64	0.66
	Minimum	-19.16	-7.97	-20.11	-2.08
	Range	25.10	18.69	18.47	2.74
Finland	Mean	16.17	20.68	3.74	1.62
	Standard Deviation	8.00	14.63	2.71	2.23
	Slope – % per year	0.68	0.59	0.09	0.03
	Maximum	29.14	37.17	9.65	4.75
	Minimum	1.80	-9.87	-2.25	-2.27
	Range	27.34	47.04	11.90	7.02
Ireland	Mean				-1.18
	Standard Deviation				2.55
	Slope – % per year				0.02
	Maximum				1.82
	Minimum				-7.79
	Range				9.61
Spain	Mean	-11.40	1.40	-7.12	-1.15
	Standard Deviation	5.07	5.23	0.88	2.75
	Slope – % per year	-0.45	0.04	0.18	-0.02
	Maximum	-0.68	8.61	-5.50	3.62
	Minimum	-21.50	-8.53	-10.67	-5.64
	Range	20.82	17.14	5.17	9.26

Continued on Next Page

Table 15.5. Continued from previous page

		1974–87	1988–93	1994–99	2000–08
Portugal	Mean	-20.18	-14.98	-7.39	-0.82
	Standard Deviation	6.80	7.53	1.51	2.04
	Slope – % per year	-0.84	-0.43	-0.18	-0.01
	Maximum	-2.59	-2.31	-5.09	1.77
	Minimum	-30.58	-27.22	-11.27	-6.38
	Range	27.99	24.91	6.18	8.15
Greece	Mean	-13.06	-15.70	-4.88	-1.35
	Standard Deviation	5.82	3.59	3.51	2.92
	Slope – % per year	-0.55	-0.45	-0.12	-0.02
	Maximum	2.84	-8.70	1.34	3.70
	Minimum	-25.24	-23.21	-10.88	-6.76
	Range	28.08	14.51	12.22	10.46
Sweden	Mean	27.04	22.37	9.44	2.48
	Standard Deviation	8.71	7.76	3.76	4.23
	Slope – % per year	1.04	0.65	0.24	0.05
	Maximum	44.84	34.00	15.72	15.47
	Minimum	9.36	4.38	1.88	-3.27
	Range	35.48	29.62	13.84	18.74
Denmark	Mean	-3.84	-1.88	0.43	0.67
	Standard Deviation	2.94	1.60	1.15	1.03
	Slope – % per year	-0.16	-0.06	0.01	0.01
	Maximum	2.46	1.08	3.43	2.63
	Minimum	-9.50	-5.15	-2.31	-1.17
	Range	11.96	6.23	5.74	3.80
United Kingdom	Mean	-5.43	-3.65	-2.80	3.63
	Standard Deviation	12.13	4.91	10.36	7.96
	Slope – % per year	-0.18	-0.11	-0.06	0.07
	Maximum	20.40	2.76	14.22	20.29
	Minimum	-26.09	-16.02	-17.04	-13.81
	Range	46.49	18.78	31.26	34.10

Continued on Next Page

Table 15.5. Continued from previous page

		1974–87	1988–93	1994–99	2000–08
Norway	Mean	6.16	4.40	-1.71	1.30
	Standard Deviation	5.97	4.39	2.44	4.19
	Slope – % per year	0.26	0.12	-0.04	0.02
	Maximum	17.20	11.92	5.25	14.25
	Minimum	-8.77	-2.49	-7.36	-7.54
	Range	25.97	14.41	12.61	21.79
Switzerland	Mean	-6.14	-2.05	6.46	1.41
	Standard Deviation	6.57	3.44	3.58	5.94
	Slope – % per year	-0.21	-0.06	0.16	0.02
	Maximum	9.19	7.03	15.27	10.49
	Minimum	-21.17	-7.94	0.28	-9.75
	Range	30.36	14.97	14.99	20.24
Iceland	Mean		-2.57	-11.67	-7.98
	Standard Deviation		5.77	4.08	7.46
	Slope – % per year		-0.08	-0.29	-0.17
	Maximum		11.64	0.02	6.79
	Minimum		-11.42	-16.93	-30.30
	Range		23.06	16.95	37.09

The Eurozone examined here seems to be functioning quite well as a currency union in comparison with a union like Canada, although a number of possibilities remain that could eventually signify a contrary result.

The real exchange rates of Sweden and the United Kingdom with respect to the Eurozone, plotted in Fig. 15.17a, were substantially more variable than those of the eleven Eurozone countries with respect to the Eurozone less Ireland. And these real exchange rate movements were matched by similar nominal exchange rate movements in the face of stable price level ratios with respect to the Eurozone. On the one hand, this suggests that these two countries were wise not to join the Eurozone – in contrast to Denmark, whose real exchange rate with respect to the Eurozone, shown in the bottom panel of Fig. 15.17a, indicates that it might as well have been a member. On the other hand, there appear to have been no greater restrictions on labour mobility between the rest of the European Union and Britain and Sweden than among the Eurozone countries. Why, then, are the real exchange rates of these countries so variable? One possibility is that the asymmetric shocks between Britain and Sweden and the eleven Eurozone countries are not of a sort that can be neutralized by labour mobility – the observed real exchange rate movements would thus be reflected in rents to specific types of technological capital whose supply can only be adjusted in the long run. Another possibility is that, because of institutional wage rigidity, equilibrium real exchange rate movements that cannot feed through onto nominal exchange rates result in variations in output and employment rather than price levels with the result that the observed real exchange rate movements among the Eurozone countries are much less than they would be if nominal exchange rates were flexible.

As can be seen from Fig. 15.17b, the real exchange rates with respect to the Eurozone less Ireland of Norway and Switzerland, which were not even in the European Union, were less variable than those of Sweden and the United Kingdom but clearly more variable than those of the individual Eurozone countries after 1999. And the Swiss real exchange rate with respect to the Eurozone, like those of its Eurozone neighbors, tended also to decline after 2002.

It remains to be seen whether the currency union in Europe will succeed without problems over the long term. One can only speculate on what might happen if there is a major downward shock to a member country's real exchange rate with respect to the rest of the union – there is no history on which to base an opinion. Much will depend on the ability of the Union to provide assistance to member countries that are falling behind. This is a subject for further study – all that this monograph can provide is an analytical framework in which to pose the questions that need to be answered.

16

Conclusions and Suggestions for Future Work

The research presented in this monograph has produced some important new conclusions about how how nominal and real exchange rates are determined and about the conduct of monetary policy in countries other than the United States. But much remains to be done. This concluding chapter briefly reviews the basic conclusions and suggests some directions for future work.

16.1 Conclusions

The fundamental conclusion of this work is that the real exchange rates with respect to the United States of the five major industrial countries examined were determined almost entirely by underlying real forces related to economic growth, technological change and capital accumulation and, more specifically, their roles in determining oil and commodity prices, the terms of trade, and changes through time in the allocation of world investment across countries. This is consistent with the conclusion that real exchange rates are the relative prices of domestic in terms of foreign output and, although related to asset values, exchange rates cannot be viewed primarily as asset prices. Monetary shocks to real exchange rates turn out to have been of trivial importance with respect to all countries examined except for Germany although even in that case real shocks were predominant. Unanticipated money supply shocks nowhere had effects of any importance.

These conclusions concerning real exchange rate determination combine with two important theoretical results developed here concerning monetary equilibrium to yield important implications for the process by which monetary policy is and should be conducted. The first theoretical result, which is by no means new to the literature, is that it is impossible to reject the notion that exogenous monetary shocks will have major overshooting effects on nominal and real exchange rates in the short run. The main avenue through which portfolio disequilibria are eliminated is the purchase and sale of assets abroad, leading to adjustments of real and nominal exchange rates and resulting changes in the trade account balance leading to changes in domestic income and employment that bring about adjustment of the quantity of money demanded to equal the supply. The response of the current account balance to changes in the real exchange rate will certainly not be immediate and considerable time will surely pass before adjustment is complete. While that adjustment is taking place, nominal and real exchange rates will shoot far beyond their ultimate equilibrium levels. Any argument to the contrary has to be based on an assumption that asset markets are as slow to adjust as real output markets.

The fact that no short-term effects of monetary shocks on real exchange rates can be found suggests that such excess demand and supply shocks are largely non-existent. But nobody would argue that substantial shocks to the demand for money are unlikely to occur from time to time, given the fact that the standard deviations of quarter-to-quarter percentage changes in all conventional monetary aggregates are substantial. The absence of the effects of unanticipated monetary shocks on real exchange rates combined with no observed exchange rate overshooting can best be explained as the consequence of a response of money supply creation by the authorities to changes in the demand for money – the last thing the authorities want is overshooting exchange rate movements.

The second theoretical conclusion, undoubtedly understood by many academic economists though not recognized in the popular press, is that there is no basis for the belief that monetary policy in a small open economy can operate by changing those real interest rates relevant for domestic investment. This means that monetary policy in a small open economy has to operate by pressure on that country's real and nominal exchange rates that does not lead to overshooting movements of those exchange rates.

Given the desire of the authorities to prevent exchange rate overshooting, together with the fact that manipulation of exchange rates makes their underlying equilibrium values no longer observable, the process of keeping the exchange rate within normal trading ranges will automatically finance on-going changes in the domestic demand for liquidity. This will tend to make changes in domestic inflation expectations self-fulfilling. Accordingly, it becomes important for the authorities to make their policy intentions as clear as possible to the financial community. It is thus reasonable for the authorities to set inflation targets and to promote the interest rate at which they will provide reserves to the banking system as an indicator of their policy stance, even if they have no control over those real interest rates relevant for ongoing domestic investment. A Taylor rule may well make sense for an economy like the United States that can influence world interest rates both because it it is a large country and because other countries, who care about their exchange rates, will make similar domestic money supply changes to avoid overshooting.[1] But a Taylor rule is of no use whatsoever in conducting or analyzing monetary policy in small open economies.

There is substantial evidence that inflation episodes in the post-Bretton-Woods period have been similar in the countries here examined. While individual countries have followed different policies with regard to the underlying core rates of inflation and have made changes in those core rates, the major deviations of the inflation rates form core have everywhere been quite similar. Business cycles have also been roughly the same across countries, although one cannot rule out the possibility that real rather than monetary factors have been primarily responsible for this.

There is evidence that Canada's real exchange rate with respect to the United States is positively correlated with the excess of Canadian over U.S. nominal interest rates. In the past this has been interpreted as an effect on the real exchange rate of capital movements resulting from monetary policy induced changes in Canadian interest rates. The interpretation here, which takes into account the lack of any theoretical basis for arguing that monetary policy in small open economies works through changes in domestic relative to foreign interest rates, is that the real exchange rate is positively related to the expected inflation rate in Canada relative to the United States. Effects on the risk premium for holding domestic assets are ruled out by the fact that it makes no sense to argue that the default risk on government securities would be affected by the observed real exchange rate movements and other factors related to them. In fact, it is possible to explain Canada minus U.S. interest rate differentials by real factors determining the domestic real exchange rate as well as the real exchange rate itself or by the excess of the Canadian over the U.S. inflation rate in previous periods. Past inflation rates, however, become statistically insignificant when the real exchange rate and other real factors related to it are added to the re-

[1] See the paper by John Taylor [102].

gression as explanatory variables. For the other countries, there is not always a statistically significant positive relationship between domestic minus U.S. nominal interest rates and the real exchange rate, while past excesses of domestic over U.S. inflation are always significantly and positively related to the interest rate differential. For these countries, and also for Canada to a lesser extent, any attempt to explain the observed signs of various real factors in regressions purporting to explain the domestic minus U.S. interest rate differentials turns into an exercise in ad-hoc theorizing. Significant relationships appear but it is not clear how to interpret the signs of the variables. In some cases, unanticipated domestic money supply shocks are significantly related to the observed domestic minus U.S. interest rate differentials but that relationship can be interpreted as the authorities' money supply response to the demand-for-liquidity effect of the interest rate changes, particularly when no significant effects of unanticipated money supply shocks on the real exchange rate are observed.

As in previous work it is clear that the null hypothesis that real exchange rates are random walks cannot be rejected for short sample periods but can clearly be rejected for long ones and there is no basis for concluding that real exchange rates are non-stationary. The rates of mean reversion, however, are very small. As a consequence, the best predictor of next period's real exchange rate level is its current level although forecasts based on current forward rates are virtually equivalent for the countries examined and would be expected to do better when there are substantial differences between the domestic and foreign inflation rates.

The empirical analysis in this book also concludes that there is no reason to be puzzled about the fact that linear regressions of the relative change in the spot exchange from the current to next period on the current-period forward premium do not yield unitary coefficients. Given the very low rates of mean reversion of real exchange rates in response to current shocks, the expected value of that slope coefficient should be virtually zero and actual estimated values should be negative almost half the time. A puzzle remains, however, as to why for the country combinations examined here the signs were predominantly though not always negative, and statistically significantly negative in a number of cases. At the same time, the coefficients of regressions of next-period's spot rate on the relevant current forward rate were typically close to but less than unity as would be expected from the fact that forward premiums are very small relative to the changes in spot rates and forward rates follow spot rates with a one-period lag. None of the results here provide any basis for an argument that foreign exchange markets are inefficient in the sense that market participants fail to use, as best they can, all available current information.

16.2 Suggestions for Future Work

Perhaps the most important implication of the above conclusions for the direction of future work is the importance of embedding forecasts of rest-of-world conditions in domestic forecasts of output, employment, prices, and interest rates in small open economies, together with the relative unimportance of differences between domestic and rest-of-world monetary conditions. The most important part of any forecast of Canadian economic activity, for example, is the forecast of economic activity in the United States. The second most important part is the forecast of future movements in the Canadian real exchange rate with respect to the U.S. The real exchange rate will capture both the effects of shifts of world real investment toward or away from the Canadian economy as well as shifts in world demand for Canadian exports relative to imports. The use of the current account balance alone as a measure of the international demand for Canadian goods is flawed by the fact that the current account may be 'improving' because world investment is shifting out of the Canadian economy. The real exchange rate will adjust to equate the current account balance with the real net capital inflow. If the real exchange rate is increasing then either the demand for domestic exports is increasing or world investment is shifting into the Canadian economy or the world relative prices of the traded components of domestic output are increasing. This importance of real exchange rate changes suggests potential benefits from the daunting task of developing a rigorous general equilibrium model of the real sector of the economy that incorporates the resource base and the technology of production of the important domestic goods and extending that model to incorporate real forces operating in the rest of the world. The problem, of course, is to develop a model that sufficiently incorporates the relevant underlying forces and at the same time can be solved with sufficient ease.

Though the results here suggest that real factors rather than domestic monetary ones are of primary concern in forecasting and analyzing conditions in small open economies like Canada, the possibility of monetary shocks, particularly those that involve persistent pressure on exchange rates and lead to changes in the underlying core inflation rate, should not be ignored. Any realized importance of such monetary forces and the nature of their effects would be an important empirical test of conclusions presented in this book.

For countries like France and Germany, the appropriate forecasting model suggested by the work here is in one sense simpler because these countries are embedded in a monetary union with other European countries, with conditions in the European Union being of even more importance than is the United States with respect to Canada. Yet it is complicated by the fact that conditions in the United States are still of great importance. The empirical results presented here suggest that understanding the effects of terms of trade changes compared to those of the U.S. and, indeed, terms of trade changes with respect to the United States, is a crucial task. More generally, since the Euro Area is large compared to most countries both outside and inside it, the question arises as to whether the actions of its central bank affect world, and hence local, real interest rates or whether its authorities avoid overshooting by creating internal monetary conditions similar to those in the United States. Another question that emerges from the analysis of real exchange rates within the Euro Area is whether the observed stability of countries' real exchange rates with respect to the rest of the Euro Area is arising because of stabilizing effects of adjustments to individual members' unemployment rates rather than stability of the underlying equilibrium real exchange rates due to cross-country labor mobility.

The problem of developing forecasting models for the United Kingdom is more complicated than for Canada, France and Germany because the Euro Area and the United States are equally important sources of external shocks as well as are many other countries with which Britain has long had economic involvement. And the problem is even greater for Japan which is closely involved with other Asian countries that do not figure at all in the analysis here.

Finally, the conclusion that there is no forward premium puzzle as typically thought and that the coefficient of the forward premium in regressions explaining relative changes in spot exchange rates to next period can be negative almost half the time, and never both positive and close to unity, still leaves unexplained the fact that these coefficients are negative for most of the country combinations here examined. The analysis here suggests further work taking the form of comparisons the real exchange rate trends with simultaneous but unrelated changes in domestic relative to foreign inflation rates. This will require the development of more sophisticated models of real exchange rate determination and expectations formation than were used here.

A

Optimal Allocation of the Capital Stock Among its Alternative Forms

Divide the economy's capital stock into two parts consisting of the stock of a particular type of capital and the remaining stock where the aggregate production function takes the simple form

$$Y = \mu K_1^{\varepsilon} K_2^{1-\varepsilon} \tag{A.1}$$

The total differential of this function is

$$\begin{aligned} dY &= \mu\,\varepsilon K_1^{\varepsilon-1} K_2^{1-\varepsilon}\, dK_1 + \mu K_1^{\varepsilon}\,(1-\varepsilon)\, K_2^{-\varepsilon}\, dK_2 \\ &= \mu\,\varepsilon \left(\frac{K_2}{K_1}\right)^{1-\varepsilon} dK_1 + \mu\,(1-\varepsilon) \left(\frac{K_1}{K_2}\right)^{\varepsilon} dK_2 \end{aligned} \tag{A.2}$$

with the coefficients of dK_1 and dK_2 representing the marginal products of the two types of capital

$$m1 = \mu\,\varepsilon \left(\frac{K_2}{K_1}\right)^{1-\varepsilon} \quad \text{and} \quad m2 = \mu\,(1-\varepsilon) \left(\frac{K_1}{K_2}\right)^{\varepsilon}.$$

An optimum requires that $dY = 0$ when $dK_1 = -dK_2$, which implies

$$0 = \mu \left[\varepsilon \left(\frac{K_2}{K_1}\right)^{1-\varepsilon} - (1-\varepsilon) \left(\frac{K_1}{K_2}\right)^{\varepsilon}\right] dK_1 \tag{A.3}$$

and hence

$$\varepsilon \left(\frac{K_2}{K_1}\right)^{1-\varepsilon} = (1-\varepsilon) \left(\frac{K_1}{K_2}\right)^{\varepsilon} \tag{A.4}$$

which reduces to

$$\varepsilon\,\frac{K_2^{1-\varepsilon}}{K_1^{1-\varepsilon}} = (1-\varepsilon)\,\frac{K_1^{\varepsilon}}{K_2^{\varepsilon}} \tag{A.5}$$

or

$$\varepsilon K_2 = (1 - \varepsilon) K_1 \tag{A.6}$$

so that the condition of optimization becomes

$$K_1 = \frac{\varepsilon}{1 - \varepsilon} K_2 \tag{A.7}$$

with the result that the optimum fractions of the capital stock composed of K_1 and K_2 are[1]

$$\frac{K_1}{K} = \varepsilon \qquad \text{and} \qquad \frac{K_2}{K} = 1 - \varepsilon. \tag{A.8}$$

The maximum return to capital in Fig. 3.1 is therefore at $K_1 = .3\,K$, given that $\varepsilon = .3$.

In constructing the data plotted in Fig. 3.1 the scale parameter μ is chosen to normalize the output flow at .05 times the capital stock when that stock is optimally allocated among the alternative forms that comprise it. Under the optimal allocation

$$\begin{aligned} Y &= \mu\,(\varepsilon\,K)^{\varepsilon}[(1 - \varepsilon)\,K]^{(1-\varepsilon)} \\ &= \mu\,\varepsilon^{\varepsilon}(1 - \varepsilon)^{1-\varepsilon}\,K \end{aligned} \tag{A.9}$$

so that

$$\begin{aligned} \mu &= \frac{1}{\varepsilon^{\varepsilon}(1 - \varepsilon)^{1-\varepsilon}} \frac{Y}{K} \\ &= \frac{.05}{\varepsilon^{\varepsilon}(1 - \varepsilon)^{1-\varepsilon}} \end{aligned} \tag{A.10}$$

The values of the marginal products plotted in Fig. 3.1 are calculated using the XLispStat batch file `allocap.lsp` and, alternatively, using the R script file `allocap.R`. The results are contained in the respective output files `allocap.lou` and `allocap.Rot`.

[1] To verify this, simply substitute $K_1 = \varepsilon K$ and $K_2 = (1 - \varepsilon)K$ into equation A.6.

B

Derivation of the Real Exchange Rate

The first step in deriving the real exchange rate is to take the partial derivatives of equations (3.33) through (3.36) with respect to their arguments. The derivatives of (3.33) with respect to C_{Dt} and $\tilde{C_{Dt}}$ are

$$\frac{\partial C_t}{\partial C_{Dt}} = \frac{\sigma}{\sigma-1}\left[\xi^{\frac{1}{\sigma}}\left(C_{Dt}\right)^{\frac{\sigma-1}{\sigma}} + (1-\xi)^{\frac{1}{\sigma}}\left(\tilde{C_{Dt}}\right)^{\frac{\sigma-1}{\sigma}}\right]^{\frac{\sigma}{\sigma-1}-1} \xi^{\frac{1}{\sigma}}\frac{\sigma-1}{\sigma}\left(C_{Dt}\right)^{\frac{\sigma-1}{\sigma}-1}$$

$$= \left[\xi^{\frac{1}{\sigma}}\left(C_{Dt}\right)^{\frac{\sigma-1}{\sigma}} + (1-\xi)^{\frac{1}{\sigma}}\left(\tilde{C}_{Dt}\right)^{\frac{\sigma-1}{\sigma}}\right]^{\frac{\sigma}{\sigma-1}-1} \xi^{\frac{1}{\sigma}}\left(C_{Dt}\right)^{-\frac{1}{\sigma}}. \tag{B.1}$$

and

$$\frac{\partial C_t}{\partial \tilde{C_{Dt}}} = \frac{\sigma}{\sigma-1}\left[\xi^{\frac{1}{\sigma}}\left(C_{Dt}\right)^{\frac{\sigma-1}{\sigma}} + (1-\xi)^{\frac{1}{\sigma}}\left(\tilde{C_{Dt}}\right)^{\frac{\sigma-1}{\sigma}}\right]^{\frac{\sigma}{\sigma-1}-1} (1-\xi)^{\frac{1}{\sigma}}\frac{\sigma-1}{\sigma}\left(\tilde{C_{Dt}}\right)^{\frac{\sigma-1}{\sigma}-1}$$

$$= \left[\xi^{\frac{1}{\sigma}}\left(C_{Dt}\right)^{\frac{\sigma-1}{\sigma}} + (1-\xi)^{\frac{1}{\sigma}}\left(\tilde{C}_{Dt}\right)^{\frac{\sigma-1}{\sigma}}\right]^{\frac{\sigma}{\sigma-1}-1} (1-\xi)^{\frac{1}{\sigma}}\left(\tilde{C_{Dt}}\right)^{-\frac{1}{\sigma}}. \tag{B.2}$$

Since in equilibrium the prices of the two countries' outputs must equal their value marginal products in producing consumption and investment, the relative price of domestic output in terms of foreign output will equal the ratios of the marginal products. The real exchange rate – that is, the price of domestic output in units of foreign output – must therefore equal (B.1) divided by (B.2)

$$Q = \frac{\partial C_t}{\partial C_{Dt}} \Big/ \frac{\partial C_t}{\partial \tilde{C}_{Dt}}$$

$$= \left(\xi^{\frac{1}{\sigma}} C_{Dt}^{-\frac{1}{\sigma}}\right) \Big/ \left((1-\xi)^{\frac{1}{\sigma}} \tilde{C}_{Dt}^{-\frac{1}{\sigma}}\right)$$

$$= \left(\frac{\xi}{1-\xi} \frac{\tilde{C}_{Dt}}{C_{Dt}} \right)^{\frac{1}{\sigma}} . \tag{B.3}$$

These ratios must be the same in both countries for the production of consumer goods and new additions to the stocks of capital. Repeated application of the above operations thus yields all the equalities in (3.37).

The elasticities of Q with respect to C_{Dt} and $\tilde{C}_{Dt}$ can be easily obtained by taking the logarithm of the above expression.

$$log(Q) = \frac{1}{\sigma} \left[log\left(\frac{\xi}{1-\xi} \right) + log(\tilde{C}_{Dt}) - log(C_{Dt}) \right]$$

The elasticities of Q with respect to C_{Dt} and $\tilde{C}_{Dt}$ are

$$\frac{\partial log(Q)}{\partial log(C_{Dt})} = -\frac{1}{\sigma}$$

and

$$\frac{\partial log(Q)}{\partial log(\tilde{C}_{Dt})} = \frac{1}{\sigma} .$$

Accordingly, the elasticities of C_{Dt} and $\tilde{C}_{Dt}$ with respect to Q are simply $-\sigma$ and σ. The elasticities of I_{Dt}, $\tilde{I}_{Dt}$, C_{Ft} , $\tilde{C}_{Ft}$, I_{Ft} and $\tilde{I}_{Ft}$ with respect to Q are identical and obtained in the same way.

C

Analysis of the GG and AA Curves

The GG and AA curves are plotted, for reasonable values of the parameters in Figs. C.1, C.2 and C.3. Monetary shocks are incorporated in the first of these and real shocks in the other two. In constructing these plots, K was normalized at unity and o at zero and equation (4.1) was substituted into (4.2) and (4.3) to produce

$$r = \frac{\hat{m}(1-\gamma)-\delta}{1+2\alpha\left[g+(K_U-1)\,Y_f\right]}\left[1-\frac{1}{3\lambda}\left(\varphi-\lambda\frac{L}{K_U}\right)^3\right] \tag{C.1}$$

and

$$r+o = \left[\hat{m}(1-\gamma)-\delta\right]\left[\varphi-\lambda\frac{L}{K_U}\right]^2 \tag{C.2}$$

where K_U is the fraction of the capital stock utilized and, alternatively, the ratio of actual output to its full-employment level. These two equations determine r and K_U at given levels of g, o and L. When K is normalized at unity, L is the ratio of the stock of liquidity to the the level of the capital stock. In situations where there are exogenous changes in $\hat{m}$, γ, o or τ, the steady-state growth rate and full-employment levels of income and r will change. To incorporate this possibility, it is necessary to add equation (3.14),

$$r = \frac{1+\varpi}{1-\tau}(1+g)-1 \tag{C.3}$$

which combines with equations (C.1) and (C.2) under conditions where $K_U = 1$ to produce the steady-state growth rate, the full-employment interest rate and the equilibrium full-employment level of L. The latter is achieved through a behind-the-scene adjustment of the nominal price level.

The calculations are programmed in XLispStat in the code file `GGAA.lsp` using results obtained from running the code file `GGAAssg.lsp`. The same calculations are also programmed in corresponding R script files `GGAA.R` and `GGAAssg.R`. Some consolidated terms from the three equations above are used in these code files. These are

$$\text{mterm} = \hat{m}(1-\gamma) - \delta \tag{C.4}$$

$$\text{acterm} = 1 + 2\alpha\left[g + (K_U - 1)\,Y_f\right] \tag{C.5}$$

$$\text{tterm} = 1 - \frac{1}{3\lambda}\left(\varphi - \lambda\frac{L}{K_U}\right)^3 \tag{C.6}$$

$$\text{dmterm} = \left(\varphi - \lambda\frac{L}{K_U}\right)^2 \tag{C.7}$$

$$\text{ssgterm} = \frac{1+\varpi}{1-\tau}(1+g) - 1 \tag{C.8}$$

The values of the underlying parameters chosen are as follows:

$\hat{m}$	maximum marginal product of capital	0.14
δ	depreciation rate	0.05
ϖ	rate of time preference	0.015
α	adjustment cost parameter	20 & 100
γ	misallocation of capital parameter	0.20
τ	implicit tax on saving	0.01
ϕ/λ	optimum ratio of liquidity to capital	.03
Υ	fraction of output remaining under zero liquidity	0.2

On the grounds that it is much more costly to adapt new capital to existing capital inputs in the short run than in the long run a short-run value of α equal to 100 was chosen for those situations, making the marginal cost of adjustment correspondingly higher for deviations of investment from full-employment levels.

Before the *GG* and *AA* curves can be calculated, the full-employment equilibrium levels of r and g must be obtained where $K_U = 1$. This is done by solving the three equations for the equilibrium levels of r, g and L. If the level of liquidity is to be at its optimum level, the optimum liquidity/capital ratio can be imposed, in which case o becomes a dependent variable whose equilibrium value will turn out to be the negative of r. More realistically, a value of zero for o can be imposed and the system solved for the equilibrium level of L, which will necessarily be below the level of the previously-imposed optimum liquidity/capital ratio.

When the optimum level of liquidity per unit of capital is imposed, dmterm $= 0$ and $o = -r$ and equations (C.1) and (C.3) can be solved for r and g. Eliminating r by substitution yields

$$\text{ssgterm} = (\text{mterm}/\text{acterm})\ \text{tterm} \ = \text{mterm}/\text{acterm}$$

where the assumption of optimal liquidity raises tterm to unity. After solving this equation numerically for g, the full-employment real interest rate will equal the resulting value of ssgterm. When a value of zero for o is to be imposed the three-equation system must be solved by numerical approximation. All these calculations are done in `GGAAssg.lsp` and `GGAAssg.R`. The optimum value of L is first imposed and the system solved iteratively for the magnitudes of g, and r and o, with the latter equaling the negative of r. Then L is reduced by a tiny amount and the system solved again for g, r and o – the resulting negative value of o will be closer to zero than in the optimal case. The procedure is then to continually reduce L and solve for g, r and o until o becomes ever-so-slightly positive. The resulting value of L is the equilibrium value along with the values of g and r obtained on the final iteration. One could repeat the solution imposing any non-zero value of o to incorporate the possibility of the marginal cost of holding liquidity different from r.

Once the steady-state levels of g, r and o are thereby established, these values can be used in the code files `GGAA.lsp` and `GGAA.R` to derive the GG and AA curves. Values of K_U ranging from 0.96 through 1.06 are successively imposed and the resulting values of r calculated in equations (C.1) and (C.2) trace out, respectively, the GG and AA curves. GG will be negatively sloped, and AA positively sloped, with the two curves crossing where $K_U = 1$ at the full-employment interest rate.

A monetary shock can be imposed by making the initial level of L fractionally higher. A new level of the AA curve can be traced out using the original set of commands. The imposition of real productivity shocks turns out to be somewhat more difficult. First, γ has to be adjusted to a new level – in this case, from .2 to .1822857 – and the new full-employment values of g, r, and L obtained at the previous assumption about the level of o. This new level of γ was chosen to increase full-employment income by approximately 4 %. The new level of the GG curve can then be calculated by taking the ratio of the new full-employment interest rate to the previous interest rate at the level of income approximately 4% above the old full-employment level and then multiplying all levels of r on the old GG curve by that proportion. The imposition of a different tax on saving – 1.5% as opposed to 1.0% – can be handled in a similar fashion, by changing τ to its new level, calculating the new levels of g, r and L, and then taking the ratio of the new full-employment level of r and to its old level and multiplying every level of r on the old GG curve by that proportion. This will give only an approximate result because the full-employment level of income will have declined slightly. The result is also only approximate in the case of the improved efficiency resulting from the decline in γ because full-employment output will end up increasing by 4.003% rather than 4%.

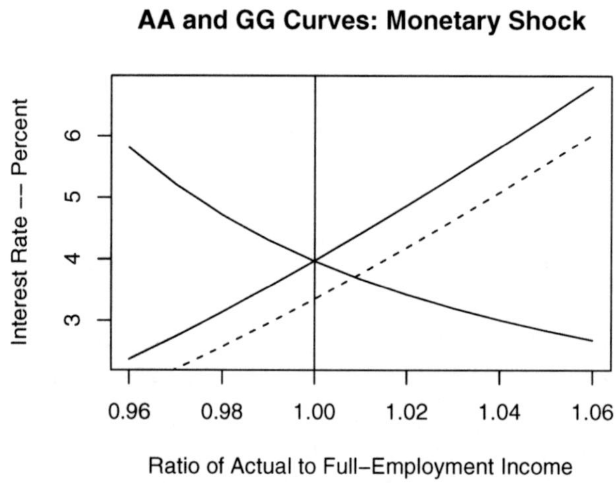

Fig. C.1. Effect of monetary shocks on mathematically derived AA and GG curves for closed or dominant open economy where the expected rate of inflation is zero.

The effects of these shocks are plotted in Figs. C.1, C.2 and C.3. Figure C.1 gives the effect of a 1.5% increase in the level of nominal and real liquidity, holding the price level constant. The attempt of the public to reestablish portfolio equilibrium by purchasing non-monetary assets with their excess liquidity leads to a rightward shift of AA and a fall in the rate of interest which increases income relative to its full-employment level. In the long-run, of course, when the price level can adjust, it will rise to reduce real liquidity to its old level, shifting AA back to its original level and removing the deviation of output from full-employment.

The effects of a reduction in resource misallocation that increases real productivity of the capital stock are shown in Fig. C.2. The full-employment level of output rises to 1.04 times its previous level and the real interest rate at that new full-employment level of output increases by a small absolute amount equal to roughly 1.04 times its original level. The new full-employment level of output will be at point c, which will be achieved when the price level has fallen sufficiently to increase the level of real liquidity to the point where AA has shifted to the right to cross the new GG curve at the new full-employment income level. In the short-run, when the price level is rigid, a new equilibrium will be established at point b with income, though higher than before, now substantially below its full-employment level.

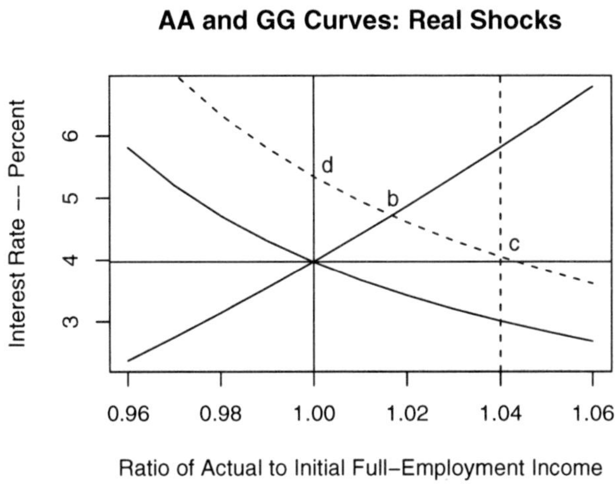

Fig. C.2. Effects of real productivity shocks on mathematically derived AA and GG curves for closed or dominant open economy where the expected rate of inflation is zero.

The above result describes a situation where the level of output is expected to be higher and is in fact higher than originally. Figure C.2 can also illustrate two alternative related situations. One arises where $\hat{m}(1-\gamma)-\delta$ is expected to permanently increase as a result of a fall in γ, or perhaps an increase in $\hat{m}$, that never in fact occurs. The expected permanent full-employment income level has risen by 4%, an expectation that will be discovered later to be unfounded. The increase in $\hat{m}(1-\gamma)-\delta$ represents an increase in the present value of capital which, in the presence of price flexibility and no resultant increase in either investment or output, will cause the real interest rate to rise to the point d. Under price-level rigidity, investment and output will increase, with increased adjustment costs moderating the rise in the interest rate until a new equilibrium is achieved at point b. This is the same point of short-run equilibrium as in the case where the full-employment level of output actually does increase. The only difference is the long-run result which will be a return to the old level of output and real interest rates as opposed to a movement to point c. The other situation occurs when, through an improvement of weather or some other chance event, output increases by 4% in the current period with no expectation that this higher level will be retained in the future. In this situation $\hat{m}(1-\gamma)-\delta$ will be unaffected even though the current-period full-employment output actually increases. It is as though there were a temporary one-period upward spike in $\hat{m}$ of roughly 4%. The *GG* curve will thus remain unchanged, as will the current level of income. Given the constant level of real liquidity, the upward shock to full-employment income will be completely offset by an equivalent rise in unemployment.

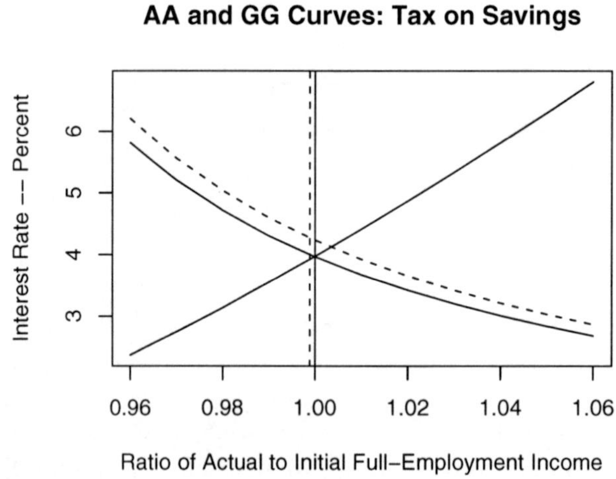

Fig. C.3. Effects of savings taxes on mathematically derived AA and GG curves for closed or dominant open economy where the expected rate of inflation is zero.

The effect of increasing the tax on savings from .01 to .015 is shown in Fig. C.3. Perhaps surprisingly, the tax increase causes the *GG* curve to shift upward. This occurs because the resulting reduction in investment causes the marginal adjustment costs of investment to decline, reducing the term $1+2\alpha\,[g+(K_U-1)Y_f]$, otherwise defined as acterm, in equation (C.1) and thereby raising the level of r associated with each level of K_U. The short-term effect on the level of income and employment is thus positive. The long-term effect will simply be an increase in the full-employment level of r. The level of full-employment income, which equals

$$(\hat{m}(1-\gamma)-\delta)\left[1-\frac{1}{3\lambda}\left(\varphi-\lambda\frac{L}{K_U}\right)^3\right]K$$

– that is, the product of mterm, tterm and K – falls slightly because the equilibrium stock of liquidity declines on account of the increase in r. Also, the capital stock itself, which is normalized to equal unity, will be lower in all future periods because capital is being accumulated at a slower rate.

D

The Determination of Risk Premiums

Imagine an individual who has an horizon of T periods and in each period maximizes the expected discounted value of the utility levels achieved in the current and subsequent $(T-1)$ periods:[1]

$$E\left\{\sum_{t=0}^{T-1}(1+\varpi)^{-1}U(c_t)\right\} \tag{D.1}$$

where $U(c_t)$ is the utility of consumption c_t in the t-th period and ϖ is the subjective discount rate. Suppose that at each point in time t this individual can hold her wealth in any of n risky assets having net stochastic rates of return z_{it}, $i = 1 \ldots n$, and in a riskless asset, with a rate of return $\bar{r}_t$. If the individual has chosen an anticipated consumption path for which her expected utility is maximized, she will not be able to increase her expected utility by shifting a unit of consumption from any period to any other period through the purchase of additional units of any of the assets in her portfolio. This means that for every risky asset,

$$U'(c_t) = (1+\varpi)^{-1}E\{U'(c_{t+1})(1+z_{it})\} \tag{D.2}$$

and for the riskless asset

$$\begin{aligned} U'(c_t) &= (1+\varpi)^{-1}E\{U'(c_{t+1})(1+\bar{r}_t)\} \\ &= (1+\varpi)^{-1}(1+\bar{r}_t)E\{U'(c_{t+1})\} \end{aligned} \tag{D.3}$$

where $U'(c_t)$ is the marginal utility of consumption in the t-th period. By shifting a unit of consumption from period t to period $t+1$, for example, the individual would give up $U'(c_t)$ units of utility in period t

[1] The analysis here follows that in Blanchard and Fischer [7].

in order to obtain $(1+z_{it})$ units of output in period $t+1$. These units of output would yield an expected utility of $E\{U'(c_{t+1})(1+z_{it})\}$ in period $t+1$. The discounted value of this expected $t+1$ utility in period t is obtained by multiplying by $(1+\varpi)^{-1}$. Since the individual will adjust her consumption path until it does not pay to shift consumption in this fashion, the equalities in (D.2) and (D.3) must hold in equilibrium. Substitution of (D.3) into (D.2) to eliminate $U'(c_t)$ and multiplication of both sides by $(1+\varpi)$ yields

$$\begin{aligned} E\{U'(c_{t+1})(1+z_{it})\} &= (1+\bar{r}_t)E\{U'(c_{t+1})\} \\ E\{U'(c_{t+1})\} + E\{U'(c_{t+1})(z_{it})\} &= E\{U'(c_{t+1})\} + E\{U'(c_{t+1})(\bar{r}_t)\} \\ E\{U'(c_{t+1})(z_{it} - \bar{r}_t)\} &= 0. \end{aligned} \tag{D.4}$$

Next, note from the constancy of $\bar{r}_t$ in the above equation and the definition of covariance that[2]

$$\begin{aligned} Cov\{U'(c_{t+1})\, z_{it}\} &= Cov\{U'(c_{t+1})\,(z_{it} - \bar{r}_t)\} \\ &= E\{U'(c_{t+1})(z_{it} - \bar{r}_t)\} - E\{U'(c_{t+1})\}E\{z_{it} - \bar{r}_t\} \\ &= -E\{U'(c_{t+1})\}E\{z_{it} - \bar{r}_t\} \\ &= -E\{U'(c_{t+1})\}E\{z_{it}\} + E\{U'(c_{t+1})\}E\{\bar{r}_t\} \end{aligned} \tag{D.5}$$

which, noting that $E\{\bar{r}_t\} = \bar{r}_t$, can be manipulated to yield

---

[2] The derivation here also uses the facts that, given two random variables x and y and a constant a,

$$\begin{aligned} Cov\{x,y\} &= E\{(x - E\{x\})(y - E\{y\})\} \\ &= E\{xy - E\{x\}y - E\{y\}x + E\{x\}E\{y\}\} \\ &= E\{xy\} - E\{x\}E\{y\} - E\{x\}E\{y\} + E\{x\}E\{y\} \\ &= E\{xy\} - E\{x\}E\{y\} \end{aligned}$$

and

$$\begin{aligned} Cov\{x,y+a\} &= E\{(x - E\{x\})((y+a) - E\{y+a\})\} \\ &= E\{(x - E\{x\})((y - E\{y\}) + (a - E\{a\}))\} \\ &= E\{(x - E\{x\})((y - E\{y\})\} \\ &= Cov\{x,y\}. \end{aligned}$$

$$E\{z_{it}\} = \bar{r}_t - \frac{Cov\{U'(c_{t+1}),\, z_{it}\}}{E\{U'(c_{t+1})\}} \tag{D.6}$$

The risk premium on the i-th risky asset is therefore

$$-\frac{Cov\{U'(c_{t+1}),\, z_{it}\}}{E\{U'(c_{t+1})\}} \tag{D.7}$$

The risk premium on each risky asset is inversely related to the covariance of the return on that asset with the marginal utility of consumption.

Imagine now a composite asset, s, whose return is perfectly positively correlated with consumption and hence perfectly negatively correlated with the marginal utility of consumption. This asset can be thought of as a market portfolio consisting of every asset in the economy weighted in proportion to its share of the country's wealth – its return is the return to capital in the economy as a whole. Letting z_{st} be the return to the market portfolio, we have

$$U'(c_{t+1}) = -\upsilon\, z_{st}. \tag{D.8}$$

where υ is the constant of proportionality. It follows that for any risky asset z_{it}[3]

$$Cov\{U'(c_{t+1}),\, z_{it}\} = Cov\{-\upsilon z_{st}, z_{it}\} \;=\; -\upsilon\, Cov\{z_{st}, z_{it}\} \tag{D.9}$$

Using equation (D.6) to characterise the expected return from holding the market portfolio $E\{z_{st}\}$ and then substituting (D.9), the difference between the expected return on the market portfolio and the return on the risk-free asset as can be expressed as[4]

$$\begin{aligned} E\{z_{st}\} &= \bar{r}_t + \upsilon \frac{Cov\{z_{st}, z_{st}\}}{E\{U'(c_{t+1})\}} \\ E\{z_{st}\} - \bar{r}_t &= \upsilon \frac{Var\{z_{st}\}}{E\{U'(c_{t+1})\}}. \end{aligned} \tag{D.10}$$

[3] The argument here uses the fact that

$$\begin{aligned} Cov\{ax, y\} &= E\{(a\,x - E\{a\,x\})(y - E\{y\})\} \\ &= E\{(a\,x - a\,E\{x\})(y - E\{y\})\} \\ &= a\,E\{(x - E\{x\})(y - E\{y\})\} \\ &= a\,Cov\{x, y\}. \end{aligned}$$

[4] This uses the fact that $Cov\{z_{st}, z_{st}\} = Var\{z_{st}\}$.

This equation can be rearranged to obtain an expression for υ:

$$\upsilon = [E\{z_{st}\} - \bar{r}_t]\frac{E\{U'(c_{t+1})\}}{Var\{z_{st}\}} \tag{D.11}$$

Now, substitute (D.9) into (D.6) and using (D.11) to eliminate υ to obtain

$$E\{z_{it}\} - \bar{r}_t = \frac{Cov\{z_{it}, z_{st}\}}{Var\{z_{st}\}}[E\{z_{st}\} - \bar{r}_t]. \tag{D.12}$$

The i-th asset will be more risky than the market portfolio when its return is positively correlated with the return to the market portfolio and its covariance with the return to the market portfolio exceeds the variance of the return to that portfolio – that is, when its return varies directly with and more widely than the return to capital in the economy as a whole.

E

Analysis of the Forward Rate Equation

Under conditions where there are slight random differences between the forward and current spot exchange rates the estimation of equation (9.3) involves fitting

$$s_{t+1} = a + b f_t + e_t \quad = \quad a + b\,(s_t + u_t) + e_t \tag{E.1}$$

where u_t is the zero-mean random deviation of the current forward exchange rate from the current spot rate. The estimated coefficient b will equal the covariance of $s_t + u_t$ and s_{t+1} divided by the variance of $s_t + u_t$ and can be expressed

$$b = \frac{\sum_{t=1}^{T}[(s_t + u_t - \bar{s})(s_{t+1} - \bar{s})]}{\sum_{t=1}^{T}[(s_t + u_t - \bar{s}]^2} \tag{E.2}$$

where $\bar{s}$ is approximately equal to the means of s_t, and s_{t+1} which, over any sample period, have all but one observation in common. Expansion of the numerator and denominator of the above expression yields

$$\begin{aligned} b &= \frac{\sum_{t=1}^{T}[s_t s_{t+1} - s_t \bar{s} + u_t s_{t+1} - u_t \bar{s} - \bar{s} s_{t+1} + \bar{s}^2]}{\sum_{t=1}^{T}[s_t^2 + s_t u_t - s_t \bar{s} + s_t u_t + u_t^2 - u_t \bar{s} - s_t \bar{s} - u_t \bar{s} + \bar{s}^2]} \\ &= \frac{\sum_{t=1}^{T}[s_t s_{t+1} - s_t \bar{s} + u_t s_{t+1} - u_t \bar{s} - \bar{s} s_{t+1} + \bar{s}^2]}{\sum_{t=1}^{T}[s_t^2 + 2 s_t u_t - 2 s_t \bar{s} + u_t^2 - 2 u_t \bar{s} + \bar{s}^2]} \end{aligned} \tag{E.3}$$

Taking into account the fact that

$$\sum_{t=1}^{T} s_t\,\bar{s} = T\,\bar{s}^2, \quad \sum_{t=1}^{T} s_{t+1}\,\bar{s} \approx T\,\bar{s}^2 \quad \text{and} \quad \sum_{t=1}^{T} u_t \approx 0$$

the above expression can be reduced to

$$b \approx \frac{\sum_{t=1}^{T}(s_t\, s_{t+1}) + \sum_{t=1}^{T}(u_t\, s_{t+1}) - T\,\bar{s}^{\,2}}{\sum_{t=1}^{T} s_t^2 + \sum_{t=1}^{T}(s_t\, u_t) - T\,\bar{s}^{\,2} + \sum_{t=1}^{T}(s_t\, u_t) + \sum_{t=1}^{T} u_t^2}. \tag{E.4}$$

Taking into account that

$$\sum_{t=1}^{T}(s_t\, s_{t+1}) \approx \sum_{t=1}^{T} s_t^2 \qquad \text{and} \qquad \sum_{t=1}^{T}(u_t\, s_{t+1}) \approx \sum_{t=1}^{T}(s_t\, u_t)$$

the denominator in the above expression is approximately equal to the numerator plus the terms

$$\sum_{t=1}^{T}(s_t\, u_t) + \sum_{t=1}^{T} u_t^2$$

which will likely, but not necessarily, sum to a positive number. Since u_t is uncorrelated with s_t, its negative values are no more likely to occur in periods when s_t is above rather than below its mean. Accordingly the sum of $s_t \times u_t$ should not differ much from zero. And the sum of the u_t^2 will necessarily be positive, making it likely that b will typically be less than unity, though if the u_t have very small variance the difference from unity will be very small. Indeed, the possibility of an estimated value of b above unity cannot be ruled out.

The estimated level of α will equal

$$a = \bar{s}_{t+1} - b\,\bar{s}_t \approx (1-b)\bar{s} \tag{E.5}$$

which will tend to be positive when $b < 1$ and negative if $b > 1$.

The above results will be independent of the levels of domestic and foreign inflation, whether the latter are unanticipated by market participants or fully anticipated, as long as the inflation differences are insufficient to substantially change the relative magnitudes of $\bar{s}_t$ and $\bar{s}_{t+1}$.

F

Data Sources

F.1 Annual Data

The exchange rate of the U.K. pound with respect to the U.S. dollar is available back to 1803 from L.H. Officer [85]. For the years 1834 to 1868 it was obtained from B.R. Mitchell, *European Historical Statistics* [77], and for the period 1869 to 1975 from Milton Friedman and Anna J. Schwartz [45]. For the years since 1975 the data were obtained from the International Monetary Fund's *International Financial Statistics* [57], series 112/RF. Annual Canadian nominal exchange rate data were obtained back to 1871 from M.C. Urquhart, K.A.H. Buckley, and F.H. Leacy, *Historical Statistics of Canada* [105]. The German exchange rate series prior to 1939 is from S.B. Carter et. al., *Historical Statistics of the United States, Millennial Edition* [13] and the French exchange rate series is from Saint Marc [94] and S.B. Carter et. al.[13]. Exchange rate series for the years 1950 onward were obtained from *International Financial Statistics* [57] for Canada (series 156/RF), France (series 132/RF) and Germany (series 134/RF).

A series for the United States GDP deflator back to 1803 was available from Thomas Senior Berry [5]. For the years 1869-1975 the series was obtained from Friedman and Schwartz [44][45] and from 1975 onward, series 111/99A.R from *International Financial Statistics* [57] was used. Price level series for the United States for the years 1880 through 1913 are also available from Christie Romer [92]. The consumer price index for the United States was obtained from S.B. Carter et. al. [13] and from *International Financial Statistics* [57], series 112/64. For the United Kingdom, a GDP deflator series back to 1803 was obtained from Simon Kuznets [66] and for 1926 through 1938 and for the period after World War II from Friedman and Schwartz [45]. From 1975 to the present, the *International Financial Statistics* [57] series 112/99A.R was used. United Kingdom price series for 1880 through 1913 are also available from Deane [16]. The Canadian price series are from Green and Urquhart [49] for the years 1880 through 1913 and from *CANSIM* [96] for the interwar years. The price series for France for the years prior to 1936 was obtained from Toutain [104] and for the years 1936 through 1938 was calculated from B.R. Mitchell, *International Historical Statistics: Europe* [78]. The German price series for these years is from B.R. Mitchell, *European Historical Statistics* [77]. From 1950 onward CPI series from *International Financial Statistics* [57] are used for the U.S. (series 111/64), the U.K. (series 112/64), Canada (series 156/64), France (series 132/64) and Germany (series 134/64). All of the early historical data was collected by the present author's late colleague Trevor Dick.

Nominal GDP, exports of goods and services and imports of goods and services for Canada were obtained from *International Financial Statistics* [57] for the period 1948 through 2007 (series 156/99BC, 156/90C.C and 156/98C.C respectively). The same series for the United States for the same period were also obtained from this source (the country code is 111 instead of 156). Base money and M2 series for the United States for the were obtained from Friedman and Schwartz [45] for the period 1880 through 1975 and from the IMF/IFS [57] (series 111/59MA and 111/59MB) thereafter. Real income data for the United States and the United Kingdom for the period 1926-38 were also obtained from Friedman and Schwartz [45].

These annual data are all contained in the Gretl file `jfdataan.gdt`, in the Excel worksheet file `jfdataan.xls`, and in the Lisp text file `jfdataan.lsp`. A short description of all series and additional ones derived from them is in the text file `jfdataan.cat`.

F.2 Quarterly Data

Almost all of the quarterly data used in this monograph were obtained from the International Monetary Fund's *International Financial Statistics* [57]. Exceptions are the interest rates on Canadian and U.S. corporate paper, the Canadian monetary aggregates and the Bank of Canada indexes of commodity and energy prices, which were obtained from CANSIM [96], the index of U.S. crude oil prices, which was obtained from the CITIBASE [28] data set and the U.S. monetary aggregates, which were obtained from Federal Reserve Bank of St. Louis web-site data facility FRED. The mnemonics of all series along with short descriptions are listed in the Gretl data file `jfdatamo.gdt` and somewhat expanded descriptions are in the text file `jfdatamo.cat`. The basic series from which others are derived by methods explained in the text can also be found in the lisp file `jfdataqt.lsp`. All of the series in the Gretl data file are also in the spreadsheet file `jfdataqt.xls`. The unanticipated shocks to the money supplies of the six countries under study are presented in the Gretl, XLispStat and Excel files `jfumdata.gtl`, `jfumdata.lsp` and `jfumdata.xls` and the calculation procedure for each series is explained in the text file `jfumdata.cat`.

F.3 Monthly Data

The monthly real exchange rate data used in the Dickey-fuller and Phillips-Perron tests in Chapter 8 were calculated from series obtained, with one exception from International Financial Statistics [57] – the exception is the Euro-Dollar exchange rate, which was obtained from the Federal Reserve Bank of St. Louis web-site data facility FRED.

The discussion of efficient markets and interest rate parity in Chapter 9 utilizes Canadian and U.S. commercial paper rate series obtained from CANSIM [96], Eurocurrency off-shore deposit rates and forward and spot exchange rates obtained from REUTERS and DATASTREAM at the Business Information Center, Rotman School of Management, University of Toronto. The mnemonics for the series are listed along with descriptions in the text file `jfdatamo.cat`. The above monthly data together with series produced by combining them are presented in the Gretl data file `jfdatamo.gdt` and the Excel spreadsheet file `jfdatamo.xls`. The basic series, from which the others are derived are also in the XLispStat data file `jfdatamo.lsp` and the real exchange rate data, together with the series required to calculate them, are in the text file `jfdatamo.tab` which is readable by the statistical program R.

Monthly series for United States base money, currency plus demand deposits and currency plus demand and time deposits for the period 1927 through 1940 were obtained from Friedman and Schwartz [44] and are in the Gretl, XLispStat and Excel files `usgdmon.gdt`, `usgdmon.lsp` and `usgdmon.xls`

Monthly data on consumer price indexes together with real exchange rates calculated therefrom were obtained for the ten provinces of Canada as well as for the country as a whole from CANSIM [96]. And consumer price indexes for the countries in the European Union were obtained from EUROSTAT [97]. The mnemonics for these series together with those for a whole range of consumer price index and nominal exchange rate data for the European countries obtained from *International Financial Statistics* [57] are presented in the text file `jfdataeu.cat`. All these data are in the Gretl and Excel files `jfdataeu.gdt` and `jfdataeu.xls` and the basic series from which the remaining ones are derived are also in the XLispStat data file `jfdataeu.lsp`.

References

1. Backus D, Kehoe PJ, and Kydland F (1992) International real business cycles, Journal of Political Economy 100:745–775
2. Balassa B (1964) The purchasing power parity doctrine: a reappraisal, Journal of Political Economy 72:584–596
3. Barro RJ (1974) Are government bonds net wealth? Journal of Political Economy 82:1095–1117
4. Barro RJ (1989) The Ricardian approach to budget deficits, Economic Perspectives 3:37–54
5. Berry TS (1988) Production and population since 1789: Revised GNP series in constant dollars, Bostwick Paper No. 6, The Bostwick Press, Richmond Virginia
6. Betts C and Devereux MB (2000) Exchange rate dynamics in a model of pricing-to-market, Journal of International Economics 50:1 215–44
7. Blanchard OJ and Fischer S (1989) Lectures on macroeconomics. MIT Press
8. Blanchard OJ and Quah D (1989) The dynamic effects of aggregate demand and supply disturbances, American Economics Review 79:655–673
9. Bordo MD, and Redish A (1990) Credible commitment and exchange rate stability: Canada's interwar experience, Canadian Journal of Economics 23:357–389
10. Breusch TS (1978) Testing for autocorrelation in dynamic linear models, Australian Economic Papers 17:31 334-355
11. Cairncross A, and Eichengreen B (1983) Sterling in decline: The devaluations of 1931, 1949 and 1967. Basil Blackwell
12. Carr JL, and Floyd JE (2001) Real and monetary shocks to the Canadian dollar: Do Canada and the United States form an optimal currency Area?, North American Journal of Economics and Finance 13:1 21-39
13. Carter SB, Gartner SS, Haines MR, Olmstead AL, Such R, and Write G (2006) Historical statistics of the United States, millenial edition, vol. 5, part E. Cambridge University Press

14. Chari VV, Kehoe P and McGrattan ER (2002) Can sticky price models generate volatile and persistent exchange rates, Review of Economic Studies 69:3 533–563
15. De La Torre A, Levy Yeyati E, and Schmukler SL (2003) Living and dying with hard pegs: The rise and fall of Argentina's currency board, Economia 1:43–105
16. Deane P (1968) New estimates of gross national product for the United Kingdom, 1838-1914, Review of Income and Wealth 14:95–112
17. Dellas H (1986) A real model of the world business cycle, Journal of International Money and Finance 5:381–394
18. Devereux MB (1997) Real exchange rates and macroeconomics: Evidence and theory, Canadian Journal of Economics 30:4 773–808
19. Devereux MB and Engel C (2002) Exchange rate volatility, exchange rate pass-through and exchange rate disconnect, Journal of Monetary Economics 49:5 913–40
20. Dick TJO and Floyd JE (1991) Balance of payments adjustment under the international gold standard: Canada 1871-1913, Explorations in Economic History 28:2 209–238
21. Dick TJO and Floyd JE (1992) Canada and the gold standard: Balance of payments adjustments under fixed exchange rates, 1871-1913. Cambridge University Press
22. Dick TJO, Floyd JE and Pope D (1996) Balance of payments adjustment under gold standard policies: Canada and Australia compared. In: Bayoumi T, Eichengreen B and Taylor M, (eds) Modern perspectives on the gold standard. Cambridge University Press 218–259
23. Dick TJO and Floyd JE (1997) A portfolio balance model of the gold standard. In: Eichengreen B and Flandreau M, (eds) The gold standard in theory and history, 2nd ed. Metheun, New York 76–98, (Abridged reprint of the 1991 paper published in Explorations in Economic History)
24. Dick TJO and Floyd JE (2001) Capital imports and the Jacksonian economy: A new view of the balance of payments. Working paper UT-ECIPA-Floyd-01-01, University of Toronto
25. Dickey D and Fuller WA (1979) Distribution of the estimates for autoregressive time series with a unit root, Journal of the American Statistical Association 74:366 427–431
26. Dickey D and Fuller WA (1981) Likelihood ratio statistics for autoregressive time series with a unit root, Econometrica 49:5 1062–1063
27. Dornbusch R (1976) Expectations and exchange rate dynamics, Journal of Political Economy 84:6 1161-1176
28. DRI BASIC Economics, CITIBASE, DRI/McGraw-Hill
29. Duarte M (2003) Why don't macroeconomic quantities respond to exchange rate variability, Journal of Monetary Economics 50:4 889–913
30. Edwards S (1989) Real exchange rates, devaluation and adjustment. MIT Press

31. Eichengreen B (1990) Elusive stability: Essays in the history of international finance, 1919–1939. Cambridge University Press
32. Eichengreen B (1996) Globalizing capital: A history of the international monetary system. Princeton University Press
33. Enders W (1995) Applied econometric time series. John Wiley and Sons.
34. Engel C (1993) Real exchange rates and relative prices: An empirical investigation, Journal of Monetary Economics 32:1 35–50
35. Engel C (2001) Optimal exchange rate policy: The influence of price setting and asset markets, Journal of Money, Credit and Banking 33:2 Part 2 518–541
36. Engel C and Rogers JH (1996) How wide is the border, American Economic Review 86:5 1112–1125
37. Engle RF and Yoo B (1987) Forecasting and testing in co-integrated systems, Journal of Econometrics 35:1 143–159
38. Feinstien CH, Temin P, and Toniolo G (1997) The European economy between the wars. Oxford University Press
39. Fleming JM (1962) Domestic fiscal policies under fixed and flexible exchange rates, International Monetary Fund Staff Papers 9:369–379
40. Friedman M (1969) The optimum quantity of money and other essays. Aldine Publishing
41. Floyd JE (1969a) International capital movements and monetary equilibrium. American Economic Review 49:4 472–492
42. Floyd JE (1969b) Monetary and fiscal policy in a world of capital mobility. Review of Economic Studies 36:4 503–517
43. Floyd JE (1985) World monetary equilibrium. University of Pennsylvania Press
44. Friedman M, and Schwartz A (1963) A monetary history of the United States, 1876-1960. NBER, Princeton University Press
45. Friedman M, and Schwartz A (1982) Monetary trends in the United States and the United Kingdom: their relation to income prices and interest rates, 1867-1975. NBER, University of Chicago Press
46. Gerlach S (1988) World business cycles under fixed and flexible exchange rates, Journal of Money, Credit and Banking 21:620–630
47. Gilbert RA (1986) Requiem for Regulation Q: What it did and why it passed away, Federal Reserve Bank of St. Louis Review, February, 22–37
48. Godfrey LG (1978) Testing for higher order serial correlation in regression equations when the regressors include lagged dependent variables, Econometrica 46:6 1303–1310
49. Green A, and Urquhart MC (1994) New estimates of output growth in Canada: measurement and interpretation. In: McCalla D and Huberman M (eds) Perspectives on Canadian economic history, 2nd ed. Copp Clark Longman, Toronto 182-89
50. Hamilton JD (1994) Time series analysis. Princeton University Press

51. Helleiner E (2006) Towards North American monetary union? The politics and history of Canada's exchange rate regime. McGill-Queens, Montreal-Kingston London Ithaca
52. Helpman E (1981) An exploration in the theory of exchange rate regimes, Journal of Political Economy 89:5 865–890
53. Helpman E and Razin A (1982) Dynamics of a floating rate regime, Journal of Political Economy 90:4 728–754
54. Hoderick R (1987) The empirical evidence on the efficiency of forward and futures foreign fxchange markets. Harwood Academic Publishers, New York
55. Hoderick R, and Prescott EC (1997) Post-war U.S. business cycles: An empirical investigation, Journal of Money Credit and Banking 29:1–16
56. Hume D (1898) Of the balance of trade. In: Essays, moral, political and literary. Longmans Green, London, 330–345,(originally published in 1752).
57. International Monetary Fund, International Financial Statistics. Washington
58. Johansen S (1988) Statistical analysis of cointegration vectors, Journal of Economic Dynamics and Control 12:2 231–254
59. Johansen S (1991) Estimation and hypthesis testing of contegrating vectors in Gaussian vector autoregressive models, Econometrica 59:6 1551–1580
60. Johansen S and Juselius K (1990) Maximum likelihood estimation and inference on cointegration with application to the demand for money, Oxford Bulletin of Economics and Statistics 52, 169–209
61. Johansen S and Juselius K (1992) Testing structural hypotheses in a multivariate cointegration analysis of PPP and UIP for UK, Journal of Econometrics 53:2 211-244
62. Johnston JW (1993) Real and nominal exchange rate determination in a small open economy: An empirical investigation of the Canadian case. PhD Thesis, University of Toronto, Toronto
63. Korteweg P (1980) Exchange rate policy, monetary policy, and real exchange rate variability. Princeton Essays in International Finance 140, Princeton University Press
64. Kravis I and Lipsey R (1983) Toward and explanation of national price levels. Princeton Studies in International Finance 52, Princeton University Press
65. Krugman P (1991) Target zones and exchange rate dynamics, Quarterly Journal of Economics 106:3 669–682
66. Kuznets S (1930) Secular movements in production and prices. Houghton Mifflin, New York
67. Laidler DEW (1977) The demand for money, 2nd. edition. Dun-Donnelly, New York
68. Levich RM (1985) Empirical studies of exchange rates: Price behavior, rate determination and market efficiency, In: Jones RW and Kenen PB

(eds) Handbook of international economics, Vol. II, North Holland, Amsterdam
69. Levin JH (2002) A guide to the euro. Houghton Mifflin Company, Boston and New York
70. Liesner T (1989) One hundred years of economic statistics. The Economist Publications Ltd., London
71. Lucas RE (1978) Asset prices in an exchange economy, Econometrica 46:4 1426–1445
72. Lütkephol H (1991) Introduction to multiple time series analysis. Springer-Verlag, Heidelberg
73. Maynard A and Phillips PCB (2001) Rethinking an old empirical puzzle: Econometric evidence on the forward discount anomaly. Journal of Applied Econometrics 16:6 677–680
74. McCallum J (1998) Drivers of the Canadian dollar and policy implications. Royal Bank of Canada Current Analysis 2:9 1–5
75. McGrattan ER (1988) A defence of AK growth models, Federal Reserve Bank of Minneapolis Quarterly Review 22:4 13–27
76. Meese R and Rogoff K (1983) Empirical exchange rate models of the seventies: Do they fit out-of sample? Journal of International Economics 14:1-2 3-24
77. Mitchell BR (1975) European historical statistics, 1750-1970. MacMillan
78. Mitchell BR (2003) International historical statistics: Europe, 1750-2000. Palgrave MacMillan
79. Mundell RA (1963) Capital mobility and stabilization under fixed and flexible exchange rates, Canadian Journal of Economics and Political Science 29:475–485
80. Mussa M (1979) Empirical regularities in the behavior of exchange rates and theories of the foreign exchange market. In: Brunner K and Meltzer A (eds) Carnegie-Rochester Conference Series on Public Policy 11:9–57
81. Obstfeld M and Rogoff K (1995) Exchange rate dynamic redux, Journal of Political economy 103:3 624–660
82. Obstfeld M and Rogoff K (1996) Foundations of international macroeconomics. MIT Press, Cambridge Massachusetts, London England
83. Obstfeld M and Rogoff K (2000) The six major puzzles in international macroeconomics: Is there a common cause. National Bureau of Economic Research Macroeconomics Annual 15 403–411
84. Officer LH (1982) Purchasing power parity and exchange rates: Theory, evidence and relevance. JAI Press, Greenwich Connecticut, London England
85. Officer LH (1983) Dollar-sterling mint parity and exchange rates, 1791-1834, Journal of Economic History 43:3 579–616
86. Pasula KP (1996) Monetary independence under Bretton Woods: Perspectives from a stochastic maximizing model, Canadian Journal of Economics 30:3 643–664

87. Pasula, Kit P. M. (1993) Capital controls, imperfect asset substitutability, and the independence of monetary policy under fixed exchange rates: The British experience, Unpublished manuscript, University of Western Ontario
88. Phillips CB and Ouliaris S (1990) Asymptotic properties of residual based tests for cointegration, Econometrica 58:1 165–93,
89. Phillips CB and Perron P (1986) Testing for a unit root in time series regression, Biometrika 75:2 355–346
90. Racette D (1980) Monetary aspects of the interwar period in Canada and the United States: an econometric model. PhD Thesis, University of Toronto, Toronto
91. Rogoff K (1996) The purchasing power parity puzzle, The Journal of Economic Literature 34:2 647–668
92. Romer C (1989) The pre-war busines cycle reconsidered: New estimates of gross national product, 1869-1908, Journal of Political Economy 97:1–37
93. Said S and Dickey D (1984) Testing for unit roots in autoregressive-moving-average models with unknown order, Biometrika 71:3 599–607
94. Saint Marc M (1983) Histoire monetaire de la France. Presses Universitaires de France
95. Samuelson PA (1964) Theoretical notes on trade problems, Review of Economics and Statistics 46:145–154
96. Statistics Canada, CANSIM. Ottawa
97. Statistical Office of the European Communities, EUROSTAT. Luxembourg
98. Stock JH and Watson MW (2003) Introduction to econometrics. Addison Wesley
99. Stockman AC (1980) A theory of exchange rate determination, Journal of Political Economy 88:4 673–698
100. Stockman AC (1983) Real exchange rates under alternative exchange rate regimes, Journal of International Money and Finance 2:2 147–166
101. Stockman AC and Svensson LEO (1987) Capital flows, investment and exchange rates, Journal of International Money and Finance 19:2 171–202
102. Taylor JB (1993) Discretionary versus policy rules in practice. In RG King and CI Plosser (eds) Carnegie-Rochester Conference Series on Public Policy 39:1 195-214
103. Tobin J (1969) A general-equilibrium approach to monetary theory, Journal of Money, Credit and Banking 1:15–29
104. Toutain JC (1987) Le produit interieur brut de la France de 1789 à 1982. In: Perroux F (ed) Economies et Societies, Cahiers de l' I.S.M.E.A., Serie Historic Quantitative de l'Economie Francaise. Paris
105. Urquhart MC, Buckley KAH and Leacy FH (1983) Historical statistics of Canada. Statistics Canada and Social Science Federation of Canada, 2nd. Edition
106. Viner J (1937) Studies in the theory of international trade. Harper, New York

Index

Lightning Source UK Ltd.
Milton Keynes UK
23 December 2009

147861UK00001B/52/P

9 783642 102790